I AM SUPER PLACEBO

Ed Rychkun

www.edrychkun.com

ISBN 978-1-927066-14-0

There is no copyright to this book. If it helps you to understand life and choose the better one that is now before you, go ahead and copy whatever you need. Please pass it on and credit my site.

CONTENTS

	INTRODUCTION	6
1	WE ALL HAVE PLACEBO POWER	12
	The consciousness boxes	14
	Who really has the power?	18
2	WHY SUCH A CRAPPY LIFE?	26
	Understanding us	28
	The law of karma	33
	The law of Cause & Effect	34
	The Law of Attraction	36
	Who carries the load?	37
3	DO WE ALREADY CREATE REALITY?	40
	Creating reality is ongoing	40
	What is your energy balance?	42
	Let us test your mind power	46
4	HOW DO YOU MANAGE THESE CRAPPY ENERGIES?	53
	The energy portfolios	53
5	THE STAGES OF HUMAN EVOLUTION	59
	Brainwave patterns	61
	The brains evolution	63
	Subtle energies not so subtle	71
6	THE CHIEF IN THE ATTIC	76
	So who is in charge?	76
	How does the brain program?	80
	The placebo and brain in action	83
	Changing your mind	85
7	THE HOME OF SUPERNOCEBO	88
	Where Supernocebo gets carried away	89
	Implicit and explicit memory	94
	Mind and matter are not separate	96
8	THE HOME OF SUPERPLACEBO	98
	The energetic body anatomy	99
	The energy body higher planes	100

9 AN ASTRAL CONNECTION 109
    A word about chakras 109

10 THE ROLE OF THE HEART BRAIN 122
    Your heart energetic system 122
    The energy vortexes 124
    Heart brain emotions 129
    Get into alpha permanently! 132
    Being in the heart brain 134
    Being in the love center 135

11 CAN WE CREATE HEALTH MIRACLES? 138
    Miracles happen out of the box 140

12 CAN WE CREATE MIRACLES OF EXTERNAL REALITY? 148
    So who's creating new reality? 150
    Setting the wealth environment 154

13 THE PROGRAMMING PORTALS 159
    Back to that brain again 160
    The power of meditation 162
    Hypnosis is a program portal 166
    The altered state is key 166
    A self-hypnosis process 169

14 WHEN YOU NEARLY DIE 176
    Where am I if not dead? 176
    The stages of nearly dying 178

15 YOUR IMMERSION MOVIE OF LIFE 183
    The review appearance 184
    Under free will I created this life? 187
    The prebirth planning process 190

16 THE ASTRAL PLANE 197
    The Astral Interface 197
    The light body 199
    Opening astral abilities 202
    Where are you really? 206
    An astral projection process 210
    Step 1: setting the objectives 213
    Step 2: creating the environment 215
    Step 3: Inducing the trance 216
    Step 4: Physical disengagement 218
    Step 5: Ascent into the void 219

	Step 6: destination	220
17	**WHAT DID I DO WRONG?**	222
	Past life regression	223
	How regression heals	226
	Past life process	227
18	**I DON'T LIKE THIS MOVIE ANYMORE**	233
	Future life progression	233
	A Future life progression process	239
	Your soul purpose review	241
19	**THE MYSTERY OF THE MIDBRAIN**	243
	The secret of the midbrain	245
	Where I live in the brain	249
	No time no place no thing	252
	The issue with Mr Smarty Brain	253
	On The junk DNA	258
	The God code in DNA – really?	264
	The power of prayer	269
20	**THE IMPORTANCE OF THE WORD**	272
	Importance of sound waves	272
	The bible code life plan – really?	275
	Words describe reality	278
	The midbrain miracle method	280
	A Science behind miracles?	281
	Sounds control consciousness and matter	285
	The Pillai miracle method	287
	The Pillai money mantra	291
	Master Sha miracles	293
	Sha miracle healing process	295
	The karmic conundrum	298
21	**IS THERE A SCIENCE TO THE ILLUSION?**	302
	What is this quantum reality?	304
	The brain is a holographic processor	308
	Morphogenesis is a greater intelligence	310
	The electromagnetic quantum processor	314
	A holographic universe – really?	316
	What the science box is saying	318
	The world is flat – again!	321
	So who is in charge of reality?	323
	The myth of free will	324

22 IN THE VOID OF INFINITE MIND   333
       Changing the way of being   333
       why placebos work   335
       What is divine intervention?   337
       Where do we go now?   339
       On miracle processes   341

23 HOW DOES IT ALL WORK?   347
       Why are you here Ed?   347

24 GENESIS – WHICH ONE?   358
       Is there some Divine plan?   359
       The new earth genesis II   362
       Theme of prevailing consciousness   365
       New Rapture Revelation and Resurrection   367
       New end time of revelation   368
       Carbon to silicon light body   371
       A place called new earth   378
       Playing in Agartha   382

25 THE GOOD THE BAD AND THE EVIL   386

INTRODUCTION

First and foremost, I want you to meet **Superplacebo**.

Before you classify me as a nutcase, I will tell you that **Superplacebo** is in my subconscious imagination. As a kid I had superheroes like Superman, Wonder Woman and others that had all these special powers. They were always out there saving people and making them happy. Later when I got into the world of business, there were many wealthy icons of success that became my superheroes but these all faded as they were seldom there to help others. When I got older, Superplacebo became my hero. This book is about him, how I met him and what I learned from him.

Of course my old superheroes were just comic book types so they eventually faded. Later, I had my business heroes who lost their luster when I learned how cutthroat they were. Now in my later years, I found this dude I call Superplacebo. He is an imaginary hero that became a different version of me, helping to save me. He is the one I strive to be in my dreams. We all have one of these heroes in our imagination waiting to be brought into reality. I also refer to him as my Higher Self because he is much higher in his thinking than I have ever been. Better described as a Soul, it seems that he came here on a mission to enjoy life to the fullest but he needed a partner as a physical body so the silly dude chose me!

He's a pretty happy guy because nothing phases him. He is funny and always smiling. It is always thumbs up for him because there is really nothing that can go wrong for him. Nothing ruffles this guy. And he is holding a red placebo pill in his hand because it is a pill that he offers unconditionally to give you placebo power of mind over matter.

Incidentally, my hero is obviously in my mind a male. But there is a female version that is Superplacebo's sister. And of course there is his dear brother Supernocebo who is a bit of a villain.

I will be talking more about this Super family of mine as we talk about my conversations with Superplacebo. As I said, he has a higher perspective of things. Oh, they are holding a placebo pill that is blue or red. These represent the pills like in the movie **The Matrix** where Neo could make a choice of the red or blue pill. Remember when Morpheus said to Neo:

"You take the blue pill, the story ends. You wake up in your bed and believe whatever you want to believe. You take the red pill, you stay in wonderland, and I show you how deep the rabbit hole goes."

My conversations with Superplacebo gave me the red pill to attain a new awareness of life and how things work much differently than the story I had learned to believe. Why placebo? Because the placebo or nocebo represents the magic of mind over matter. If it is blue, matter controls mind. If it is red it is mind that controls matter. If you want to understand the practical implications it is the red pill that leads the mind to control reality. If it is the blue pill then reality controls the mind. The placebo is exactly that. A placebo effect as one of the most powerful process of healing on the planet is simply the mind doing the healing – one of the more common unexplained mysteries of our time.

When he came into my awareness, my life was full of a lot of things happening and most of the time these were very unpleasant, dramatic and emotionally difficult to deal with. It made me wonder what the hell I had done to deserve this terrible drama of ups and downs in life and why it would not go away. I had heard about karma but I did not understand it as it was just meta-nonsense to a scientifically trained dude like myself. My questions and research of why this was happening to me just led to more questions about life, its purpose and why was I even here. Who the hell asked me to even be in existence? I wondered why there were so many people very rich, famous, and healthy having such a wonderful time when I seemed to be in these boom bust cycles – especially in the financial area. These others just seemed to have a lot more luck than brains so their seemed to be no logic as to why I could not succeed like those big business superheroes. Because I had learned about all these business success icons, I had chosen a business career. Boy it had its ups and downs, each down taking its toll on my mind and body. So I made a lot of money but I lost a lot of money. My relationship with my first wife was just as horrible. I could only think *"what the bleep is going on? This is not fair!"*

You can imagine the stress levels! Well, on another upswing, I met my second wife; an angel in disguise so I must have done something right, even though a lot of business stuff still sucked. At some point because I heard meditation was a good way to get some peace from my torments of business and relationships, I decided to start doing it - even took a course. I had to find some peace and quiet away from the incessant chattering of my conscious brain that told me it was just nonsense. I had to deal with the conscious mind that generates some 70,000 to 90,000 thoughts a day. That's a lot of chatter to shut up!

For 30 minutes I could get away from the drama around me. I didn't know it at the time but this incessant mind chatter was coming from Superplacebo's dear brother that was giving me all these ideas and influencing the way I was perceiving and dealing with the world around me. Well, I have to tell you that his way of thinking was creating a lot of harm. It seemed that a lot of the things I was doing in my relationships and with business was coming back to haunt me big time. That's why I named this other guy living in my mind as Supernocebo. Unknowingly he was my old hero that I grew up with and stayed with me in business. It was his responsibility to help my ego, body and brain evolve and develop survival habits. He did a good job at first. Then he got carried away and that is why he got the name Supernocebo.

After a while, his nattering about business ceased and I entered a different place of silence – and the whisperings of Superplacebo. And these were hard to hear at first, the reason for which I will tell you later but he had a different way of thinking opposite to Supernocebo's. Superplacebo's whisperings were thoughts that came forward to please; not only me but everyone and everything. Well, if you want power, money and success in your life that can be a conundrum because you simply cannot please everyone all the time.

It took a while to get into this space of listening to Superplacebo. It was a practice that I learned where I had to get centered into the heart, slowly moving attention away from the outside to the inside, then silencing the chatter of the mind. I tried to get deeper and deeper doing it with my wife. But there never seemed to be time to concentrate. It wasn't until later in life after a new deluge of crap that I began again. So this one day I started to pick up these different thoughts. They were certainly not the usual because most of the time my thoughts were always filled with the crap of life, conflict, fear of future, health, work issues, blah, blah; the ones I wanted to subdue.

So I continued and these thoughts – good ones – became more and more pronounced the quieter I became. And these were not really coming from my mind. Then I began to sense an entity that sort of shocked me at first. It was a bit bizarre and I thought maybe I was going nuts. But I trusted it was ok and continued. It gave birth to listening better and better. Truthfully, I never really saw clear images or felt energies; I just had a knowing and feeling that this was right. Of course at that time I never knew whether it was just delusion or what; I just sensed it wasn't. What I did know was that this place of peace, silence and nothingness was good and after a while many new thoughts of positive inspiration were coming forward seemingly out of nowhere.

I had heard of channeling and a lot about spiritual stuff which I had pretty well relegated to the quack side of specialized religions and cults – none of which had any relevance in my life. But here I was quietly listening to these different thoughts. Needless to say I did not share this potential insanity with many!

Oh, by the way, the reason I used placebo is because before someone gave it a medical definition of an inactive substance the original Latin meaning was "***I please***". This is quite different than nocebo that in Latin means "***I shall harm***". Not that I give two poops about Latin but the original meaning meant something.

As this continued I learned the power of the placebo. In a world where we believe solely in matter, the mind and its power comes second. We live in a world of self defining scientific limits where anything "out of the ordinary" beliefs cannot be; and even though so many unexplainable things like miracles of health exist, in the cultural belief system they do not exist because they are simply not credible. The group consciousness simply does not accept anything out of its belief box. The placebo reminds us over and over that they really do exist; and astonishing, dramatic, unexplained healing miracles occur all the time, all over the world. And the thing that does the most astonishing healing is the placebo, a fake pill that is supposed to do nothing to the physical matter of the human, except "please".

This placebo demonstrates the stark reversal of thinking; *matter over mind* changes to *mind over matter*. It is simply the mind that creates the miraculous physical healing! That is why I have this super dude called Superplacebo that I strive to be. He is part of my consciousness, that part of the mind that has power over matter. All you have to do is take one of his Superplacebo pills called belief.

As I got better and better at meditating and listening to Superplacebo, I began to telepathically speak to him. I got answers to a whole list of questions that bothered me.

> **Did we create a plan here?**
> **What is consciousness?**
> **Why is my life so crappy?**
> **What are we here for?**
> **Can we change reality**?
> **What is my purpose?**
> **What are we?**
> **Are we eternal?**
> **Is our reality real?**
> **Is there a God – really?**
> **Can we create miracles?**
> **Do we really have free will?**

Some people can talk to God to get these answers. Some talk to gods, others talk to Angels. Some say they get channeling on wisdom from the Creator. Some just don't care and become wise about these matters. With me, I talked to Superplacebo who turned out to be me; at least a higher version of me that I had no clue of. It is really all in the mind; consciousness. I just talk to myself as I see myself now.

I did not realize this at first but what was transpiring was that my meditation was taking me to a place where I was "in the heart" so to speak, concentrating on finding peace, silence and a new "tolerance" for the crap outside my little world because I could feel its stress effect on mind and body. The heart, I was to learn was the center of love energy and was a good place to be. This is sort of like going over and choosing to hug someone who is pissed at you. The negative energy meltdown is a typical result dissolving the stress instantly– a nice place to be. It wasn't easy because my belief box of life was formed by a formal science education and business hard knocks school. So it wasn't until I got out of that dark pool of business energy and survival of the fittest that Superplacebo became my hero and Supernocebo was not.

This book is really about **"A Conversation With Myself"** before I came to a rather startling conclusion: **"I Am Superplacebo".** The purpose is to share with you what I learned. I am also going to share with you some clever little tidbits of information that came forward; and of course some of the dry humor of these super dudes in a "poetic license" mode!

Let's take a trip you and me
To know the power you can't see

1

WE ALL HAVE PLACEBO POWER

Your placebo power opens when you believe, accept and surrender to the power of mind over matter rather than defaulting to matter over mind.

It was early morning and my wife and I settled into our morning meditation. This was like a ritual for us because we awoke fresh to celebrate the day and start with that reverence for all in our environment. We had built a habit of entering the silence and peace by meditation practices so as to feel the quiet by first becoming present to our bodies, breathing, and then going inside as we called it to the heart-mind of well being.

This would take a few minutes to bring silence, then I would eventually come into a void of pure thought and consciousness of which I had learned was part of the whole. We already are connected to this sea consciousness through our minds because we can imagine infinite possibilities. The problem is that this simply remains in our imaginations and we do not tap into the true power of it by using the mind to effect matter – knowingly that is.

After settling into this space of nothing and everything, nowhere and everywhere, I would settle into the knowing and feeling that I was pure consciousness, no one, no place, no time, no space only pure thought outside the lower material world. This would take several minutes to feel the void, feel the peace and stillness and integrate my being into it. I was now out of all the boxes of "normal" reality.

Then I would simply be in this space of peace and stillness. Nothing in particular was coming into my awareness because I did not want it there – that was the whole idea. This morning there was something in my awareness. Silent voices and thoughts – sort of like intuition – were there.

I just let it go as I was the last guy to be intuitive. Sure I could instantly hate or like someone by just being in their presence but I really didn't analyze why.

After several sessions, the voice became clear and it just felt right. I didn't feel I was going nuts. It wasn't the usual thoughts of dealing with crisis and conflicts in the daily life. It was this day that I also sensed a presence. Not like a ghost or some freaky thing, but just a presence. I wasn't really good at visualizing things anyway but I was developing a sense of something being there. The strange part came when I realized there was a separation of thoughts. These telepathic type communications were exactly that. My thoughts and the thoughts coming back were separate and distinctly different.

This voice began to respond to my thoughts. So this day I fired out the thought: "Who or what are you?" You would not believe the surprise - nearly crapped my pants when I heard: "I am your Soul, or Higher Self, an energetic component of you."

So I asked: "What do you mean part of me?"

I noticed that I was still asking the question when the answer "popped" out.

"You and I are one. You have discovered my existence by entering the space of the heart mind that I am attuned to as a larger segment of consciousness that your consciousness is part of. It is here that we can communicate and answer your questions."

Well, after I deducted that this was not looney bin stuff, it started a whole new relationship. I was to learn that it was in this space where you take a proactive engagement in changing your past, present, future reality, launching higher abilities, and opening to a whole new state of living and being. It was here that you really did go out of your mind – your normal one that is.

It became a daily session and many times I would drop out a few questions before sleep to be answered in the morning. The process became one of having a session with questions, then sitting and writing these in a journal. Later I could simply recall these and type them into my computer.

But now that I introduced my Higher Self or Soul, I want to start with a simple session about consciousness and continue on why I named this Higher Dude Superplacebo.

THE CONSCIOUSNESS BOXES

In one session I asked: "What is consciousness?"

"Your scientific community will tell you there is no definition. It is just a void of space. It is the material world that we see and feel that is important and that world of matter behave according to the Newton Laws of physics. Your new science of quantum physics says it is everything else and matter is a product of consciousness. That it is consciousness that creates matter by you bringing a thought into awareness."

"Yes, I have read this. It is pretty confusing."

"Consciousness is live energy filled with information. What is your mind? Where and what is it? It is everything and nothing. Yet it is alive and evolving. It is that 99.9% of everything that you have been trained to believe is nothing – just space. It contains that other fraction of a percent that is your material world. Think about how you think to evolve consciousness."

"What do you mean?"

"You bring thoughts into your awareness which is your own personal consciousness. What you train yourself to do, what you believe in, comes from you bringing this into your awareness and then creating the abilities and programs that remember how to do this. Once physical processes are learned, or thoughts accepted as your truth, they are then programmed into your subconsciousness. This is all created by your own preference as you determine from your environment; how you think and act through your five senses."

What about the unconscious part?"

"Unconscious is still part of what you describe in generic terms as consciousness so there are three parts to make it simple. The unconscious is also holding programs that have to do with your biology and chemistry and physical/mental growth and evolution. At the top is your conscious mind, then subconscious mind, then unconscious mind. All of it is your own private compartment of consciousness and it is you that determines the rules, the beliefs, and the programs that are recorded within that compartment."

"It is like a private belief box, right?"

"Yes, in addition to the programs that are developed in the unconscious and subconscious that are your physical and physiological, chemical programs, you decide what it is that you want to place into your subconscious so it is indeed a private belief box."

"And there are many levels of this consciousness'?"

"There are levels yes but really it is your awareness that opens to that level."

"So where are you in this consciousness?"

"I am part of your subconsciousness. You just simply became aware of me and opened your belief to me. You see we are all part of one Greater Consciousness. What we or you bring into awareness and beliefs determines the extent of the consciousness and the rules that govern it."

"You mean I brought my awareness outside of my belief box, right?"

"Yes, and that was not easy for you, was it? You had been conditioned to not believe that there was more to your consciousness than just what you had in your daily mind. But to reduce your daily stress, you choose to meditate – which is not exactly a scientific process to reduce stress – and you chose to listen in a mode of peace, silence and love. That opened your consciousness to a place outside of your box."

"I take it that this can keep expanding by my choice, into greater and greater awareness and consciousness?"

"And becoming aware of new thoughts, ideas, abilities and awareness that are within that level of consciousness, yes."

"Are these the powers that go outside of the norm that says we cannot do things with our minds alone? Is that like miracles and placebo that seem to be mind power alone?"

"It is because these people chose to think and believe outside the consciousness box that limited them."

"I can understand the box. It is because we live in a consciousness that says mind over matter is a stupid idea. Science, right from when you are a kid, teaches us that it's matter over mind – matter rules according to Newtonians as you said. I know quantum science is the opposite – it is the mind – consciousness that rules but that has not hit the mainstream norm of acceptance. So it is not quite science."

"Humans and their mental abilities like to box their potential powers that come from outside the box. They accept that it is matter that has power over the mind. It is because your limits of what you can do govern you."

"I know. Getting out of the box is not simple of course because all your training and subconscious programming has been done by the world we live in. Whether it is a family consciousness, a society, a race, or a planet, it is the same process. Each comprises special beliefs that create rules of life and living. We accept these and allow ourselves to surrender to that fate."

"Understand that these consciousness boxes carry several important things about them. They reflect the beliefs that influence the type of programs of behavior that become encoded in the brain and the subconscious. So first, you may have to step outside beliefs of a family as it forms a unit of consciousness. And that family consciousness may be constrained by the culture that it belongs to. That then belongs to a national belief system, and then there is a global system that becomes the accepted norm of behavior of both mind and body. Each is a subset of the other forming constraints and limitations as set out by each consciousness as determined by the group of beliefs and behaviors. So to step outside may not be so easy because starting from when you were a kid, these external environment factors create hardwired neurological response systems that become more and more difficult to change, or add to as age evolves."

"So you have to step out of the box first?"

"The most dramatic exceptions come when people move their minds outside of that box, outside the norm and believe, accept and surrender to something outside from the realm of possibilities. The best examples of these are healing miracles where nothing but the mind taking a placebo pill makes totally unbelievable, incredible, unexplainable physiological, chemical and physical changes. These are totally outside of the belief boxes. That is true placebo power and everyone has it."

"So why can't I do it now?"

"How do you know you are not doing it now with your pills? You are now on the lower fringe of attaining such power and people are doing it all the time. Your question is going to take some time to answer properly, and we will, as your awareness of the rules in this place you have found open to you."

"But there are people doing these placebo things all the time, aren't they?"

"Yes, in these placebo situations there is nothing but the mind changing physical matter. What is particularly ironic about placebo power is that it is one of the best documented and observed phenomenon around the planet because it is the scientific community of medicine that has so many examples, yet they form the limits because of them influencing the consciousness box limits. That is the way these minds work."

"Ok, I am starting to understand."

"Yes and what is particularly perplexing about this is that humans are engaged in this process of creating reality all the time. But in the vast majority of cases it is within the rules and limits of the box that they as a collective call consciousness."

"I get that but that is not so easy and clearly many do not escape the norm."

"That is a primary consideration as it is self policing. There is an important variable in this process; being outside the norm. Without exception, the healing miracles were outside of the norm in that the consciousness of the individuals engaging had to believe that what they were doing, what they believed in, was outside of the limits of the medical system, science, and whatever norm said that it would not work. This belief placed no credibility on the limits as defined by the 'norm' of consciousness. And whether this was a norm of limits created by global consensus, cultural consensus, family or science, it was not relevant. The belief and the process went outside of it typically said to have been instigated by some 'Divine Intervention' or engagement of a Divine Force. Where the process did not work, is where the limits of the belief box remained in the norm and all those old norm programs that were placed there reflecting the norm took priority. When people went outside the norm of consciousness, the old programs were replaced or ignored."

"So one has to be mindful of what has been programmed through the norm and how difficult it may be to ignore them. But this brings another question into the process. How do we get out of the norm?"

"You or any group always has a choice to do so. You need to understand that consciousness can be a collective of like minds and can reflect anything. It can be yours, your family, your culture, your government, your race, your global consciousness, and so on. Each one is unique and like a game, has rules of engagement that the collective consciousness creates that police it. The consciousness is always evolving and can be changed but it is by the collective so engaged that allows it to be changed. This forms the rules of behavior, beliefs and perception and to attempt to step outside of this box is not without consequences. What you will understand later is that these limiting boxes have their more subtle controls on mind over matter. People are finding through science that the subconscious is like this – always evolving with new rules that get hard wired neuron circuits creating a predictable behavior. Your global consciousness is also like that, constantly creating new rules and programs that apply to all the little consciousnesses like us that make up the group."

"What you want to tell me is that the mind can and does affect matter. This is because the mind can and does affect physical reality to certain degrees. But just like there are different levels of consciousness that each has their limiting boxes, there are also different levels of mind that conform to those limiting rules – and the different degrees to which mind can affect the physical. At the lowest level, our physical reality based minds conform to a consciousness mindset that believes matter rules mind. In order to approach the state where the mind rules matter, it is necessary to be in a higher state of mind outside of the box like you are here. In order to move into a mind or consciousness outside the norm, one starts with engaging in a different state of being and belief that allows new things to happen."

WHO REALLY HAS THE POWER?

"I read an article recently that said in the USA, 50% of doctors admit to using placebo in clinical practice, and 97% of doctors in the UK have also prescribed placebo medication. This must be an indication that this stupid consciousness is changing!"

"It is so, but it is still not accepted. Indeed the consciousness is evolving slowly as more and more bring it into awareness. But I want to use an example of this placebo and introduce you to the other power that everyone has that is not mentioned – the nocebo."

"That is the opposite, right?"

"Yes, you go to visit your Doctor because you accept the idea you have some medical issue. He checks you out and because he is the *authority* you *believe* him when he writes the prescription. As you pick up the pills from the pharmacy, you *accept* this new *possibility* that it will work and *surrender* to the fate that he has prescribed – namely that you will feel better. Typically, when you take the pills without question or analysis, magically the body chemicals and physiology suddenly make it better. And you relate the cause of the pill with the effect of being better and this process becomes hardwired into your subconscious simply because it pleases you and helps you survive. But he could have given you a fake pill or something totally useless. Of course he is the respected authority on why it should work so most likely you have strong faith and trust in him. On the other hand, his prescription may have done absolutely nothing. If it did not work, then something else happened. In a nutshell, that is placebo power and even though the pill is the hero either way, it is the pill and the result that worked."

"And of course there is faith in the doctor who is the accepted authority on a cure."

"Yes, but the big question is: Who instigated the changes? Was it the Doc, the Pills, the Body or the Mind that actually made the body better? Was it only your faith and trust in the Doc and his credibility that convinced your subconscious, your brain, and your cells to do it?"

"Surely you are not saying that all medical issues can be healed with placebos?"

"Of course not now, but they could be if people opened their consciousness to that new possibility, believed it and over time as new awareness came into the group that became the norm. It is the rules of the consciousness box that must be advanced."

"Let me give you an example of the placebo and nocebo in action. There is a well documented story of a fellow named Wright who had been hospitalized with advanced lymph node cancer. Wright was bedridden needing an oxygen mask to survive. Diagnosed with a few days left to live, this man was filled with tumors of the lymph nodes the size of oranges. All hope of *any* recovery was exhausted. But Wright did not want to die. He heard about Krebiozen, a new drug that was available for trial. Of course this was a waste of time to the doctor but with Wright's persistence, he finally gave in and the drug was administered to Wright on a Friday."

"On Monday, when the Doc came in, he found Wright out of bed walking around. Inspections indicated his tumors had melted like snowballs on a hot stove. Ten days later, Wright left the hospital cancer free."

"But the drug could have done that."

"In this case no. Wright was active for about two months until he read some articles stating that Krebiozen actually had no affect on cancer of the lymph nodes."

"Then what happened?"

"Wright suffered a relapse and was readmitted to the hospital. The tumors were back, as were lung issues that required oxygen; it was all the same again."

"Ok, so it was pretty dramatic placebo and nocebo effects, I will admit."

"Indeed it is considering the incredible changes in the physical body. But that's not the end of it. Quite perplexed about this strange and dramatic shifting, the Doc decided to try something like a placebo. In this experiment he told Wright Krebiozen was actually effective and that the problem was that some of the initial supplies had deteriorated during shipping. He said he had a new concentrated version and did Wright want to try it. The Doc had a plan to inject Wright with a plain water placebo but with the usual ceremony."

"What? Not again?"

"Within days, the tumors melted, the chest fluid vanished and Wright was back on his feet feeling great. This went on for two months."

"Oh Oh, what happened?"

"Then Wright found out the American Medical Association announced that the nationwide study of Krebiozen had found the drug useless in treating cancer. So it is nocebo time again."

"What happened?"

"Wright's cancer instantly blossomed and he died two days later."

"How do you explain that?"

"On one hand, Wright refused to accept a fate which doomed him. He accepted, believed and surrendered to a different outcome and got super excited about it. So his mind, brain and body got together and got rid of the tumors. Wright suddenly accepted the old fate and believed that outcome so the brain instituted the old programs. He surrendered to a different fate. His body and mind lost their power and succumbed to the old reality to bring it all back, and died."

"Wow! Just consider the number of chemicals and physiological processes of healing and non-healing that are going on here with no real cure. What was it that instigated the cure and return of the disease? Who and what instigated these dramatic changes in physical reality? Most certainly what happened was totally outside the boxes of limitations as far as our society understand it!"

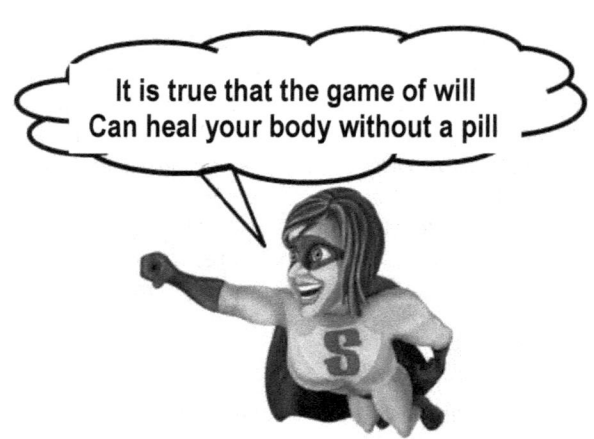

"This does make you think doesn't it? First, what does any pill really do? This placebo effect is not isolated as it is reported that 30% of medical treatments are due to placebo. And then there is the nocebo created in the mind by the power or unfettered authority of your doctor's statements that tell you negative news. What power does your mind actually have that you are not aware of? Is there any reason why anybody can't create an endless supply of placebo pills with placebo power simply BS'ing about some secret healing ingredient? Of course not. But you do not go there knowingly because it is outside the box."

"What about the surgeons that hack people and cut out tumors and stuff? Are you saying these can be healed too?"

"These placebos and nocebos are presented to people within the rules and scope of the box consciousness. If you made that statement now, you would be cast out of society even though it may be perfectly true. What is true, however, is governed by the rules of what is believed to be true. But to answer your question, let me give you another documented case that has to do with surgery. I know you as a pragmatic dude like real examples!"

"Yes, otherwise how can this mind rationalize it? This should be good!"

"A Baylor school of medicine published in 2002 in the **New England Journal of Medicine** an article which evaluated surgery for a patient with severe debilitating knee pain. Dr. Bruce Moseley knew that knee surgery helped his patients as he stated: '*good surgeons know there is no placebo effect in surgery*'. To figure out what part of the surgery was responsible for most of the pain, he set up three groups."

"He shaved the damaged cartilage in one group. He flushed out the knee joint removing inflammatory material in the second group and the third group got fake surgery. With the fake group the patient was sedated, got 3 incisions and the Doc talked and acted like in a real surgery. He even splashed salt water to simulate the sound of knee washing. After 40 minutes he sewed up the incisions as if it was real surgery. All three groups got the same postoperative care."

"The surprise came when the groups who received surgery improved but the placebo group improved equally. A TV provided for viewing graphically illustrated the results. They all got better functionality even though the placebo group did not find out for two years."

"Wow!"

"Your scientific evidence on the placebo effect shows that people are healed through thought alone. The belief that they were taking real medication when they were actually taking placebo caused changes in their brain to the degree that it looked like they were taking the real drug."

"So when the mind makes up its mind, the pill or the surgery is not relevant!"

"Not in these cases of which there are many. There is another study in 2001 that showed the powerful effects of placebo medication in treating Parkinson's disease. The placebo induced the brain to produce more dopamine, known treatment for Parkinson's, which was similar to that of real medication."

"It has been shown that in a trial of women with polycystic ovarian syndrome they found that 15% got pregnant while taking placebo compared to 22% who actually received the drug."

"When compared to morphine, placebos given to patients in place of morphine were almost equally effective at treating pain."

"The Institute of Noetic Sciences (IONS) compiled a database from the Spontaneous Remissions project, with 3500 case studies of miraculous healings with the placebo effect, showing *seemingly incurable conditions, being cured*. Diseases ranging from patients with stage 4 cancer were cured spontaneously, HIV positive patient that became HIV negative, thyroid disease that healed without treatment, aneurysms, cardiovascular disease, autoimmune conditions and many more."

"We need more and more of these publications."

"Yes, that is the way a group consciousness, and yours as well, expands and evolves. If you accept the rules within it, you are governed by it. This is indeed changing. In a fascinating study performed by Harvard professor of Medicine, Ted Kaptchuk, he conducted a placebo study whereby the patients were actually told they were receiving an inert substance, a placebo. They still got better! Of course, since he was still in his box and the consciousness of the medical profession prevailed as a self policing system, he had to conclude that the nurturing care and support of the healthcare practitioner was actually facilitating the self-healing process in placebo studies, not just the ritual of taking medication."

"That's funny!"

"So it will change. In the USA, 50% of doctors admit to using placebo in clinical practice, and 97% of doctors in the UK have also prescribed placebo medication."

"Wow. That's placebo power! But how do I get it?"

"Everyone has Superplacebo power. We will explore this in another session. All you have to do is learn to listen, expand your awareness outside the box and know me better."

"What is the secret?"

"Live, love and laugh in every moment within a mindset connected to your heart, allowing your brain to be the soul mind to see bliss and joy in all that is as one. Use the gifts of your energetic anatomy to think, see, speak, and act in a new mind, totally enfolding your completed desires in passion and gratitude to open fully your gifts in DNA and to walk in light, love, forgiveness and compassion."

"That is the secret to placebo power?"

"Indeed."

It sounded too simple. What was I missing? It was after this session that I thought about Placebo power being like the red and blue pill of the Matrix. Take a pill which is really nothing and you get out of the box formed by a community consciousness. That's why I named this Higher Self of Me as Superplacebo who in this story is holding a red pill. Take it and you free your mind to control matter. The placebo effect is one of the starkest examples of how a pill containing nothing can create miracles of healing by way of the mind alone.

But continue taking the blue pill and the belief and rules of the prevailing consciousness prevail – Supernocebo.

Take the red pill and open your life
Take the blue pill continue your strife

2

WHY SUCH A CRAPPY LIFE?

You receive exactly what you create through the Laws of Karma, Cause & Effect and Attraction.

After I met Superplacebo, and named him, my meditations would start with many questions about my life and why it was the way it was. I have already introduced him but now I am going to phase into our conversations that I wrote down after my sessions. It was not an easy realization but as time passed, I began to know that this was truly a separate and greater consciousness that I was part of but not aware of. Typically I would ask that I be able to write these down clearly after a session. And sometimes I would ask that answers come to me from anywhere. I did not care.

After the session on the belief boxes, I was beginning to understand how perhaps I was trapped in my own mind of beliefs. Certainly I was a scientific based pragmatic type. My hesitancy to believe this new buddy was because my belief box had been conditioned to not consider it as real. My university education in science and mathematics had certainly accounted for some of it. And certainly my engagement in business had to have rules. But being focused on getting to the top in business was another thing. Even at the top positions in my life as CEO, as Director, Founder, Board member, Partner and a whole lot of other titles that I thought were important, there were these horrible boom-bust cycles that happened along with stress that I seemed to acquire as well. I had to test this and find out what the bleep was I doing wrong?

So in the next session it was time to ask Superplacebo about this. I wanted answers about my life and why it was so full of issues, problems and what I called crap. Sure there were great moments, but past relationships and financial matters were anything but.

"Superplacebo," I said after calling him forward, "I am struggling with a lot of what I called health and wealth issues. First, I am getting worn out from the stress of business and second, every time I seem to get anywhere financially, the whole thing just collapses. It is like a stupid game of snakes and ladders except my body is getting pretty worn out from the falling and climbing. I cannot even begin to tell you how many things I have tried that just never get anywhere. So where is my placebo power you spoke of before? I am listening now. Why is my life so crappy?"

UNDERSTANDING US

"Dear Ed, before we get started I would like to tell you about me and my brother. We are of course in your mind as thoughts that you bring forward. But your mind is full of many, many thoughts that are very different in their energies. As a Higher Self, or let us say a representative of Soul, you have named me Superplacebo and I have a responsibility to guide you when you are able to listen. I as a Higher form of you do have form as an energy body but the mind and what you understand as consciousness is the means of communication. In using the term higher, I do not mean I am better, I mean the level of vibrational energy which we all are. Part of that higher energy is called spiritual. It is my responsibility to bring positive spiritual growth into your life because that is what I am all about and you are my partner in this process. As a counterpart in your mind there is a masculine and feminine part of this as we are a balanced unification of this energy. So you are seeing that as my 'sister' she is also a Superplacebo."

"Yes, I understand."

"But we have what you have called Supernocebo as a brother who is part of your mind as the Lower Self. You best understand him as ego which develops a self awareness and identity in your lower material world. He is definitely rooted in the masculine energies. It is his purpose to assist you in the development of behaviors and happiness or success or purpose in the material world. Although my sister and I have an obligation to assist in the self awareness and development from a spiritual or soft spoken balanced perspective, our brother does not and he speaks loudly. In the early development years a child is focused on learning skills and self awareness. And because this is important in these first six years, much of the conditioning, beliefs and behaviors are a result of Supernocebo's philosophy."

"Ok, and what are these philosophies?"

"Supernocebo specializes in *matter over mind*. His primary philosophy says you are on this earth to enjoy life to the fullest and take advantage of the body and mind you were given. He says that if you really want something you need emotional intensity because that is what gets you fired up and allows you to take control of your destiny. Intense emotion like anger is really good as is intense fear that gets you motivated."

"Well, that makes sense to me since that was what business is all about; intense anger would get the fear into non cooperative employees and they would perform better. It gets you off your butt!"

"Understand that this has its consequences of affecting your body through stress. Supernocebo has a role to explore the lower self of indulgence and selfishness, rooted in the body and mind. His leadership is to have his followers be totally focused on the self for personal desires, exploitation, and enjoyment of life. To do this wisely, he supports 12 Rules which I will place in your mind."

1. **The Law of Oneness says** we live in a world where you are the important one. Everything you do, say, think and believe affects others and the universe around us to respond to your needs.
2. **The Law of Vibration** says everything in the world of our reality vibrates as matter. Each sound, thing, and even thought has its own vibrational frequency, unique unto itself that must be focused to understand and manipulate the laws of matter.
3. **The Law of Action** must be applied in order for us to manifest things on earth. Therefore, we must engage in actions that materialize into our reality our thoughts, dreams, emotions and words. Without pain there is no gain.
4. **The Law of Correspondence** states that the principles or laws of physics that explain the physical world is all there is.

5. The Law of Cause and Effect states that everything we act on has a reaction or consequence and we "reap what we have sown". Acknowledge the power of your intellectual mind to cause something to happen and show no mercy in using it.
6. The Law of Compensation this law is that abundance can only be provided by hard work, perseverance, and passion. The real world is ruled by the fittest and the meek never rule or prosper. They are weak for you to use for your benefit.
7. The Law of Attraction demonstrates how we create the things, events, and people that come into our lives by continued attention to seek out our desires. It is strength of conviction that attracts winners and wins.
8. The Law of Perpetual Transmutation of Energy states that all persons have within them the power to change the conditions in their lives by understanding the Universal Laws of survival of the fittest and applying the principles in such a way as to effect change.
9. The Law of Relativity this law teaches us to compare our problems to others problems and put intellectual superiority into its proper perspective to profit from others failures or inadequacies. No matter how bad we perceive our situation to be, there is always someone who is in a worse position. It is all relative.
10. The Law of Polarity states that everything has an opposite. We can take advantage of others undesirable situations to transform them to benefit us.
11. The Law of Rhythm states that everything vibrates and moves to certain rhythms. Masters know how to take advantage of negative parts of a cycle by getting excited about the opportunities that will ensue as a result of other's failures.
12. The Law of Gender states that everything has its masculine and feminine principles, and that these define the rules of behavior. Either can be used to the one's advantage to ensure propagation of species and provide gratification of family and self

"You see the obvious is that the mind and body are to express fully the basic instinctual abilities of survival, even carnal and physical desires without mercy or reservation. Your history is this way; kings and queens, power and greed, conflict and dominion. Your societies are infatuated and obsessed with this. He is totally present in the self conscious brain, shouting at you through the thoughts that enter your head. He is best described as Super Ego and it is important to develop an ego simply to survive in this prevailing consciousness."

"Well, I have to say that in my history, I had many occasions to listen to this philosophy and after years I can't say it is a very nice philosophy. Most of these actions turn out to be so negative, never seeing any good in anything. And quite obviously, many have repercussions. I have dealt with much stuff in business and life where I get pissed off and scream, get mad, do things that seem to make me feel better about it and it has repercussions later. In business it is easy to say that if shit happens, then shit on what happens and if it means people then shit on them too. We seem to gravitate to the belief that if you are going to get anywhere or be happy you have to step on people who get in your way, and you have to build your ego to be strong and satisfied or you will die with a lack of satisfaction in your life."

"That is what historically humans believe so Supernocebo has done a great job. Are you now coming to a conclusion that these thoughts and ideas are harmful?"

"Well, I can see that much of this attitude just comes back to me in some way to haunt me. And then the stress is creating many physical issues that the doctors all say is a result of stress and anxiety. It's a terrible cycle."

"Then it is appropriate you have named him Supernocebo because his name means *I harm;* because you have to learn how to harm others who get in your way and use things to your benefit. In the end, you end up as a cutthroat businessman harming yourself."

"Yes, I can relate to these 12 rules. It is not foreign stuff to a businessman who wants to succeed to the top at the expense of others and other's resources. But I can also see all they did on many an occasion was get me into more crap. And all the thoughts and emotions frothing out were usually a result of the conflicts I somehow attracted. That's why I got deeper into meditation. What about you? Do you also have 12 Rules?"

"Indeed. We do have the same rules but from a different perspective. We are with the opposite philosophy always trying to please everyone and be in harmony with everything. We come from a place of peace, silently speaking in reverence and gratitude with everything. We have a more spiritual tendency so we always speak quietly and softly, love everything and everybody as we see ourselves as all One. We do not support fighting or conflict so one who follows the philosophy can never get stressed. Of course our dear brother simply talks louder, is more dramatic and railroads anything we may suggest. He knows we are not interested in engaging in cutthroat business and self gratification of ego. So because many choose to live in a world of stress and need to survive, he is the one that forms a belief box of subconscious programs that most listen to and abide by unconsciously."

"What are your 12 Rules?"

1. The Law of Divine Oneness says we live in a world where everything is connected to everything else. Everything we do, say, think and believe affects others and the universe around us.
2. The Law of Vibration says everything in the Universe moves, vibrates, and travels in circular patterns. The same principles of vibration in the physical world apply to our thoughts, words, feelings, desires, and wills in the Etheric world. Each sound, thing, and even thought has its own vibrational frequency, unique unto itself.
3. The Law of Action must be applied in order for us to manifest things on earth. Therefore, we must engage in actions that support our thoughts, dreams, emotions and words.
4. The Law of Correspondence states that the principles or laws of physics that explain the physical world - energy, light, vibration, and motion - have their corresponding principles in the etheric or universe. "As above, so below"
5. The Law of Cause and Effect states that nothing happens by chance or outside the Universal Laws. Every action has a reaction or consequence and we "reap what we have sown."
6. The Law of Compensation this law is the Law of Cause and Effect applied to blessings and abundance that are provided for us. The visible effects of our positive deeds are given to us in gifts, money, inheritances, friendships, and blessings.
7. The Law of Attraction demonstrates how we create the things, events, and people that come into our lives. Our thoughts, feelings, words, and actions produce energies which, in turn, attract like energies. Negative energies attract negative energies and positive energies attract positive energies.
8. The Law of Perpetual Transmutation of Energy states that all have within them the power to change the conditions in their lives. Higher vibrations consume and transform lower ones; thus, each of us can change the energies in our lives by understanding the Universal Laws and applying the principles in such a way as to effect change.
9. The Law of Relativity states that each person will receive a series of problems for the purpose of strengthening the Light within. We must consider each of these tests to be a challenge and remain connected to our hearts when proceeding to solve the problems. This law also teaches us to compare our problems to others' problems and put everything into its proper perspective. No matter how bad we perceive our situation to be, there is always someone who is in a worse position or there is something to be learned from it. It is all relative.
10. The Law of Polarity states that everything is on a continuum and has an opposite. We can suppress and transform undesirable thoughts by concentrating on the opposite pole. It is the law of mental vibrations.
11. The Law of Rhythm states that everything vibrates and moves to certain rhythms. These rhythms establish seasons, cycles, stages of development, and patterns. Each cycle reflects the regularity of the universe. Masters know how to rise above negative parts of a cycle by never getting too excited or allowing negative things to penetrate their consciousness.

> **12. The Law of Gender** states that everything has its masculine (yang) and feminine (yin) principles, and that these are the basis for all creation. The spiritual purpose is to balance the masculine and feminine energies within to become a Master and a true co-creator with a greater intelligence.

"Understand that we are all just your consciousness – your mind - and it is a choice as to whose thoughts you listen to and act on."

"I have learned to listen to Supernocebo and that was easy because he is very loud in his yelling into my conscious brain. As I said, it wasn't until I learned to shut that out that I could hear you speaking softly to me. Some people call it an altered state, meditation, or whatever. To me it was just being able to shut the door on him and get my mind silent and peaceful enough to be able to listen above his incessant clatter of emotional intensity to learn how to survive and be powerful."

"Understand that we are all here to assist in your purpose of life. Supernocebo was here to assist in the development of the human vessel for the purpose of survival focused on the world of matter; that physical and mental evolution in the material world. He was not designed to assist you in your evolution in the non-material spiritual world where the focus is mind over matter. It was your choice to follow his philosophy."

"Ok, I understand that this philosophy has its consequences but how does this actually work to create my reality of a crappy life?"

"You are now beginning to understand that your life is crappy because you don't pay attention to the way you create things. You can see now that you have been too busy listening to my brother who likes to tell you things that end up harming; and that includes you."

"I am beginning to understand, yes. But how?

"You understand that you create your reality, don't you? You don't seem to understand that you are receiving what you are asking for."

"I do not ever ask for this crap to happen!"

"Well, it's because you don't understand how you are asking. You have to think, feel and act differently. Do you understand the Laws of Karma, Cause & Effect and Attraction?"

"Yes, I heard a lot about them, especially the Law of Attraction. I think it is just more marketing crap to sell stuff. What should I know about them?"

"You should know that thoughts, visions, words and feelings are energies that have a unique frequency signature and you are creating these all the time without exception. Because they are vibrating within what I will explain later as one consciousness of your planet, they have a job to do once they are created. That job is to find a buddy for you through the Law of Attraction. That is just the way things work."

"You mean if I think about crap, I will get more crap?"

"Exactly! Look at your everyday life. Do you think that if you treat someone badly, they will not try to get you back in some way? Do you think that if you send out a nasty memo at work that it won't come back to you at some time in its own way? You clearly understand the energy of word and how it effects you or others. If you can understand that it carries energy of negativity with it, then you can understand that thoughts, images, words all work the same way. What about the words you speak to people at work as a cause? Do they have an effect? Let me explain this is terms of the Laws of Karma, Cause & Effect, and the Law of Attraction."

"Ok, I have heard a lot about the Law of Attraction and tried it but it is pure crap as it does not work for me. I can understand that if I piss someone off, they are going to retaliate, but just thinking stuff does the same? Come on!"

THE LAW OF KARMA

"That is because you don't understand some simple rules. What is Karma? Karma is the Sanskrit word for action. It is equivalent to Newton's law that every action must have a reaction. When we think, speak or act we initiate an energy force that will react or attract accordingly. I am responsible for our karma. I carry it until I evolve above it as it forms a limit to my growth and evolution. This is a returning force that you inherit. It may be modified, changed or suspended, but most people will not be able to eradicate it easily because my dear brother gets carried away. This law is not punishment, but is wholly for the sake of education or learning through you and me together. And that is for the greater purpose of spiritual growth, with a true evolution to turn negative to positive by engagement and experience using mental and emotional gifts."

"By react you mean the Law of Cause & Effect and by attract you mean the Law of Attraction? So these are experiences that have yet to be learned and they continue to come forward as an experience until a lesson is learned. It is to stand above it and see and feel a positive outcome as a result of it?"

"Exactly! The key here is to understand that the situation as recorded is what comes into the next life reality. It is designed into a life plan because it may well have been recorded as a trauma. Suppose for example if in a previous life, you had a plan that involved starvation that created drama and trauma. That situation ended up being recorded and a situation will most likely be planned in the next incarnation that would allow you to try dealing with it again."

"That life situation would be registered as a fear of starvation because of the terrible life that resulted. It would become the energetic emotional signature that would be recorded as incomplete karma. Nothing was learned that contributed to the greater purpose of spiritual growth."

"So you mean it would mean that it would need to be dealt with in another life?"

"Exactly."

"And you said life plan. You mean mine? I designed it? Whoaa! And a previous life?"

"Relax into the space you are in or you may fall out of it. We will have discussions on these later. Allow me to continue."

LAW OF CAUSE AND EFFECT

"Now, the **Law of Cause and Effect** states that nothing happens by chance or outside the Universal Laws. Every action has a reaction or consequence and you reap what you have sown."

"Now along comes the same old issue that is embedded in your consciousness as the trauma that created a bad situation of starvation. How will you deal with this issue? You can recognize that it is an issue held deep in your subconscious because it remembers and you can overcome the issue. Then if you do, your karma is balanced. But if you recall the trauma you fall into fear and further emotionalize it so to counter this, you may choose to eat to the point of excess."

"So the fear of starving becomes my center of attention as a renewed Cause and the Effect in this life? To become obese?"

"That is one consequence as you do not know exactly how it will come to you, nor what you will choose as a reaction. Nothing was learned from this because in this life the result of that cause was an overindulgence of food, then the karmic lesson would not be learned because it would be the fear of starvation that was the hangover to be over come in another life."

"So in the normal sense, then if I get over the fear and launch a new thought-emotion plan, it would be one which would override the old trauma in the subconscious. So if I came here to eliminate a fear I would have learned my lesson and from that point on dissolve the karma and at the same time institute a different outcome, the potential of which would then attract different realities? So where does the Law of Attraction come in?"

THE LAW OF ATTRACTION

"The Law of Attraction demonstrates how you attract the things, events, and people that come into your life. Once the potential effect, like the fear of starving becomes a strong energy, your thoughts, feelings, words, and actions produce energies which, in turn, attract like energies. Negative energies attract negative energies and positive energies attract positive energies."

"Well, I do notice that the more I concentrate on something that I need in business, it seems that sometimes it actually comes before me in some way. But that is because I am being more selective, not because I attracted some energy."

"Not necessarily, that is the way you have been taught."

"Ok, you are saying as a result of trauma creating the intense fear of starvation, the energy that is constantly being created to overcome it is a total mental preoccupation with food and I am attracting that?"

"Does that not follow? That preoccupation becomes the emotionally charged desire that creates the energy signature in the morphic field of infinite possibilities and it would be fed by opposite energies that would attract situations where one was always eating to respond to trauma of fear of starvation."

"What's this morphic field of infinite possibilities?"

"It is consciousness. There are infinite possibilities within your mind that you can imagine, aren't there? Have you ever noticed how you can 'feel' negative energies from someone in a room? It sends chills down your spine? It is like magnetism that suddenly you picked it up. Your mind, which is like a void of infinite thoughts and ideas, a morphic field. When you pull an idea or thought out, or imagine it, that idea vibrates with energy depending on the charge of passion you give it. As a result it will resonate in the field of your mind and attract other thoughts and ideas or situations that have a similar signature."

"Jeez, that's hard to understand. You are saying that my consciousness, as part of the larger field of consciousness that is a morphic field also works the same way? What I place in it as thoughts, words, and images vibrates and attracts other energies? Is that why I get these crappy things coming back?"

"Depending upon the emotional charge you give it and the clarity will affect the speed and accuracy of the attraction. Now you are beginning to understand, yes. But perhaps you can see the relationship between Karma, Cause & Effect and the Law of Attraction. One just carries the old scenario forward to get over and learn from and it will be typically part of the life plan so you have a chance to do just that. But when it is brought forward, you have a choice as to how it will affect you. Once that choice is made, then the Law of Attraction kicks in to seek out a buddy from the quantum field to create the final effect. That choice can be conducted by hard knocks school until you break it working from below, or looking at the issue as something you are bringing awareness to, then energetically doing the same effect from above to set up the parameters for the Law of Attraction to do its work."

"Hmmm, if that is so, then one needs to be much more aware of managing these energies."

"So dear Ed, are you beginning to understand that over your life why you have had such a crappy time of it? Consider the millions of thoughts, visions, words, feelings that you generate without fear of consequence? You have paid very little attention to the energies of fear, hate, conflict and some unscrupulous business ethics that my dear brother has always stuck in your conscious mind."

WHO CARRIES THE LOAD?

"Do you understand who carries the karma?"

"Me, I get the crap."

"Well, you may feel you are the one with the burden but that is because you believe there is only you in this life of yours and no one else is there. In reality it is me, the Soul that carries it for the soul purpose of overcoming it. You as a vessel in the form of Soul, mind and body are my partner in doing this. Because I am pure consciousness, I cannot do this alone without a human vessel. So you are really made in an energetic way incorporating me. The problem is that you did not believe or remember this and so the partnership has not existed. If you believed this then we would share the karmic load and quickly work it out."

"So the stupidity of this is I feel alone and take all the brunt while you have the load and can't work with me as a partner because I don't recognize the partnership?"

"Exactly. You do not even know about the karma you carry that continues to haunt you."

"Hmmmmm, probably not. I must have financial and relationship karma to deal with. So what changes if we become partners?"

"What changes is the awareness of the partnership that addresses these karmic problems from a higher mind. That is why this has opened to you now; to reinstate the partnership so we can work above and below at the same time and change your balance sheet."

"I guess I create karmic crap on autopilot. I must have a crappy balance sheet to put it mildly! But I am still having trouble believing these thoughts, images, words and emotions can do that."

"But, dear Ed understand that the laws we have discussed are the old model of the consciousness norm, not the new. The Law of Cause and Effect is the Newtonian 3D model. The Law of Cause an Effect is the new mind outside the box."

"Ok, can you give me some advice of how I change the ledger on my crappy karma and institute a new model of shifting the balance?"

"Of course, but let us first discuss how you create your reality."

3

DO WE ALREADY CREATE REALITY?

Reality begins by intent of the mind, degree of vision clarity, strength of emotion and persistence of deeds.

CREATING REALITY IS ON GOING

"Ok, let us look at your reality. The process of creating reality is an ongoing process. This process goes on differently depending upon the place of instigation, but nevertheless originates through the intent of the mind. In the material world the instigator process of creating reality is the process of bringing a thought into awareness, creating a vision of the desire, stating that desire clearly as a plan, surrounding that vision and words with passion, acting upon it to seek out the relationships and resources, and persevering to materialize the desired vision."

"Yes, I got that. It's a pretty standard business model."

"Well, people are creating their desires as well as their worst nightmares on autopilot the same way because there is not an awareness outside that global box of the physical world. Energy is just energy until you attach emotion to it as positive or negative. The process is reflected by a global consciousness of beliefs. The belief box has had its effect on you the same way. You cannot be convinced to believe that energy, regardless of its material or nonmaterial state works the same way in consciousness."

"You mean that thoughts actually create reality? I suppose I am stuck in the box like everybody else."

"Yes. In normal activities where you create thousands of thoughts and emotions every day, the ones that you create as the clearest in terms of thought, vision, words and the ones that carry the highest charge of emotion (bad or good is not relevant) are the ones that attract similar energy signatures the fastest. Of the thousands you create, how many are clear enough to fetch a like energy?"

"Not too many I am sure. Because no one pays attention to that possibility."

"Right that is part of it. You also do not naturally correlate the time and relationship between a Cause and an Effect so you do not believe there is a relationship. This may indeed be difficult if the cause and effect straddle lifetimes. So you just work within the lower plan rules of working hard to get what you want within the scope and limits of the global consciousness rules. But what if you believed the cause of thinking, words, visualizing and emotions were out there looking for buddies? Would you think differently? Now that you know about the Laws of Cause & Effect, Karma and Attraction, do you still deny this correlation of how you create your reality?"

"No, you are right. But not my total reality, only some. Do you mean these out of the box things like miracles?"

"When situations venture outside of the global box, such as a health miracle there are instructions that occur from pure consciousness where we are now to the subconscious, then to the brain and body to adjust the programs for the cells to change the issue in the body. This must be done in accordance with rules which operate under a higher intelligence of design encoded in

DNA from outside the box, not inside it. But yes, that is indeed a change in physical reality."

"When situations occur in an external miracle that needs to take instructions the same way, it is the vibratory strength that attracts the results and the brain updates the hologram under the guidance of a higher intelligence governing the rules, processes and purpose of the greater scope."

"What is this higher intelligence that listens and directs?"

"It is me and a higher aspect of you, both outside the belief box. What you are having difficulty with is an easier way to achieve the same effect by working in the higher energetic expressions of self, in accordance with those rules of higher intelligence with me, not my brother who doesn't give a crap, as you put it, about higher energies. Perhaps you are beginning to understand that word crap and its energy? The stark difference is best illustrated by whether you believe you need to pay the bills by working hard in the lower plane like my brother tells you, or playing with me and the energies in the upper plane and letting the means of paying the bills come to you by a managed strategy of Cause & Effect coupled with the Law of Attraction."

"Ok, I get it. I am creating all the time and I get really serious about it so how come I can't just think about something and get it?"

"There are several answers to that question but first understand that you are doing it all the time; it just gets harder and harder to get the big things done. That should be no mystery to you as a businessman. It is because of your physical and mental makeup and it is because of the clarity and emotional strength that you give it when you create something in your reality. Just consider that if you can generate 70,000 thoughts a day, only the clear and persistent ones are going to find a buddy."

WHAT IS YOUR ENERGY BALANCE?

"Ok, I understand everyone has 24 hours in a day to create energies, like 70,000 a day, 60% of which are negative or redundant. It is simply our culture. The underlying belief you are pushing is that these critters called thoughts, visions, words, and emotions are lethal and toxic when they are given life and charged with negativity."

"Considering that this has been going on all your life that creates a tremendous inventory of stuff that is registered in the energetic disc drive of your consciousness. So consider that if at age 50, there are 70,000 X 365 X 50 = 1.27 billion pieces of energy all tagged with your name. They are all causes, many charged with emotions, some clearer than others. Some have already come into reality having found a buddy. Others are still looking and some may be so unclear, they may never find a buddy. Some are similar, some are large, many are small. But it is safe to say that there could be a whole lot out there that are still coming into your life because you created them as a cause and the effect is still out there to come to you. Then add to this unbalanced karma."

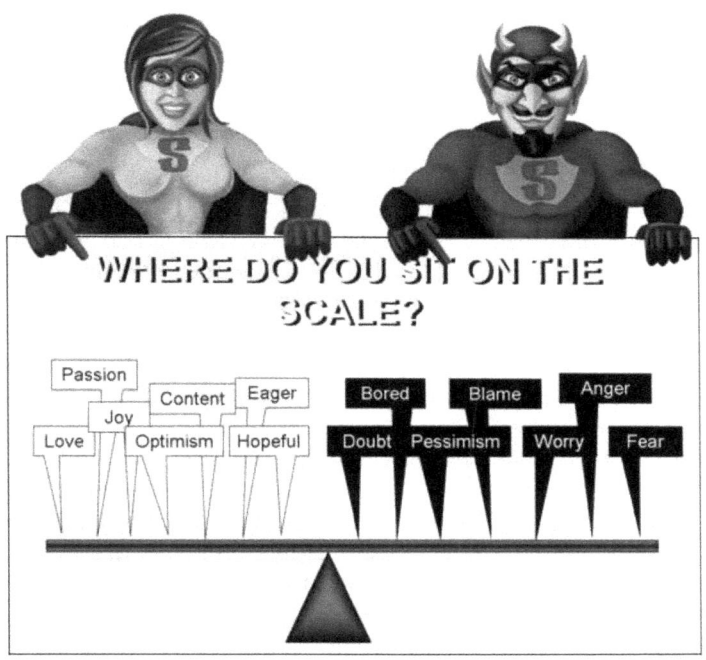

"Look at this image I am projecting into your mind now. What side of the balance are you creating energies on?"

"Jeez, I think I am mostly with your brother?"

"Exactly, and you wonder why your life is as it is? In fact there are so many of these out there you haven't got a clue what they are, when you created them, and what they are going to surprise you with and when. But let us look at these as an inventory that has not been balanced out. Look at it as an energy fund for you to manage because there could be a whole lot of surprises waiting for you."

"Energy fund?" You mean that I have to stop creating more crap and also have to deal with the stuff I created. I need to balance the ledger, then start creating a new inventory of good stuff instead of crap?"

"I will tell you about an energy fund because you associate with this lower process. But you have to believe and accept this as a higher solution. Then you can act accordingly with a great tactic; one of setting up a human subtle energy fund where you take full responsibility for managing four portfolios that include the crap in inventory. Take the management of the fund away from the usual broker - namely ego as Supernocebo. He is really not too caring about your body or anybody or anything else because he is your survivor consultant. I will explain this to you later but because of your business conditioning, you can relate to this energy portfolio."

"Ok."

"You must take responsibility for managing it with your new Consulting Advisor; the Heart and me as Superplacebo. We will guide you on a great growth scheme. The Heart is going to help manage energies of thoughts, images, words and emotions on the positive side of the balance."

"So bad critters that would come back to bite me in the ass never get a life! Are there other reasons to manage these energies through the heart?"

"The heart is the center of emotion and the positive energies like peace, love, gratitude, forgiveness, joy, and bliss are centered there. I am connected to this energy field as you have discovered. I will teach you later about these emotions like compassion, forgiveness and gratitude that are the most powerful energies you can create on the positive side. I will have to teach you also that I am best contacted in the brain wave state of Alpha or lower. What can you lose by deploying these? I will explain later the chemical, physiological, and physical consequences of creating these unmanaged negative thoughts, images, words and feelings. But understand that these can be severe."

"Like what?

"Let me give you a summary. First, they instigate the brain to do things in the physical body that affect biochemical, chemical, physiological process to create dysfunction, disease and dis-ease, as well as affect mental health. This place you will come to understand is where Supernocebo takes reign in the first 12 years of life through the conscious mind and brain development. He is concerned with developing the programs to help survive, all being stored in the subconscious."

"Second, they go into inventory to find more of the same likeness. And the stronger and clearer they are, the more likely you are to clear them out of the ledger sooner than later. But either way, they get registered in the subconscious as programs of behavior, just like you store a program on the hard drive of a computer."

"Similarly, there are consequences of creating positive energies because they also instigate things in the body and mind. This area you can say is governed by the heart, the emotional center to relate to me as Superplacebo in the subconscious. That is my domain. The conscious brain and the big frontal lobe and neo-cortex is where Supernocebo hangs out."

"I will explain this later, but before we get into the physiological processes of the brain and body to create programs, let us continue on the assumption that these energies you create as thoughts, visions, words and emotions are negative or positive and they **do** create and affect your reality."

"I am still wrestling with this business of thoughts causing things and attracting like buddies in a morphic field."

LET US TEST YOUR MIND POWER

"It is because of the belief box that limits you just as the global belief box limits most others. Thoughts are vibrating energy. They are made of words to represent your reality. Just because you can't hear or see thoughts, do not discount the notion they are live energy in a sea that understands energy. That is your old norm talking."

"So before we leave this topic, you do understand that you already create your reality by the actions and decisions you take. As long as you reside within that group reality, you can only create within the rules of that reality that you have accepted as your beliefs. Yet there are many workings of energy that are working in subtle ways. And you are certainly free to move your own personal beliefs outside of the group consciousness at any time. Within the belief boxes energies work diligently under the laws of Cause & Effect and Attraction but as I have said, you seldom make the correlation of the Cause to the Effect. It is because you produce so many thoughts and emotions each day that their clarity, consistency and their repetitively is a huge variable controlling when they may manifest. These go into the quantum field as a pattern of frequency and will attempt to attract a match because in this field all is one field of shared information."

"Yes, I get that now. The exactness of the match and its emotional signature will then determine how and when the Effect will collapse into my reality. It can be a moment, a day, a year, a lifetime, or several. The Law of Cause and Effect determines a Cause that the Law of Attraction attempts to satisfy. This process is at work continuously without regards to any judgment as to whether it is good, bad or ugly as it is just waves of energies and possibilities. But tell me, how is it that people break records that are outside of the belief box?"

"Living consciousness like your own mind is designed to evolve and improve according to its limits yet there are portals in its belief to perform outside of it to improve. Those limits include a belief that one can be better and improve but it is still within the rules of the norm that it must convince the norm to modify."

"Ok, I get it. I certainly understand that a thought or act or emotion that is repeated begins to form a belief which then forms a pattern of physical and mental behavior, even a physical process or change in physicality itself."

"Yes, over time as you develop these, they become the effect in the body registered against signature of emotion by the brain and the subconscious.

Continued indulgence of thought and emotion strengthens this behavior in the physical vessel and its lower mind until it becomes the body and this addiction of the body begins to control the mind rather than the mind controlling the body. The exception to this we have seen in health miracles."

"The process is a self auto-conditioning cycle of old habits and beliefs that become more and more difficult to break because these get hardwired and entrenched stronger and stronger. The correlation between the Cause and the Effect is lost as we have discussed. But when a match of energy signature is further and further removed from reality as a possibility within the norm, it becomes necessary to instigate a new mind from a higher energy perspective."

"Ok, I see this loud and clear. If I am constantly thinking about issues and surround these with feelings of fear and images of the consequences as my future possibility, then they are most likely to manifest in some way. I will continue to draw that possibility into my current time of awareness and then reality."

"Similarly if you are constantly thinking about good stuff in my heart space and surrounding these with strong feelings of love and gratitude then these are also likely to manifest in some way."

"Ok. But if these are poorly defined, vague, fragmented with mixed emotions, then the matching energy signature that will be drawn to you at some time can be just as screwed up."

"It is the stronger ones that will win out. That is simply the way you were designed. You may want to reinstitute something about this process of Attraction and Cause & Effect that brings you back to a new reality of belief in energy and how you create. If you really believe that your thoughts, visions, words and emotions were out there hunting for their buddies to bring to you, you may consider more carefully what you think, say and feel; then manage them more carefully."

"Can I test this?"

"Of course. Because you have not considered the connecting cause with effect or you have just relegated the idea to the hogwash category, the way you analyze this is to conduct your own field study on this using some simple energies. The idea is that you are going to make a very simple clear instruction as a cause that will go into the quantum field with me at the heart looking for the effect. You will create a cause and look for the effect that will be attracted from the quantum field of infinite possibility. The big thing here is that you will set a time constraint and carefully document the cause and effect."

"That's a cool idea."

"Now, you can do this at a specific time, and meditate, as you're doing. It does not matter because you are already doing it albeit perhaps fragmented. What you want to do for this experiment is however, to take the time to create clear consistent instructions with time limits that you are sending into the quantum field of infinite possibilities. To maximize the result and to minimize the time you should sit in a peaceful silent space and think clearly several times on your instructions. Not usually very cohesive for good instructions is the incoherent field of stress. The clearer and simpler the better, unless you want to send clear stress energies out there! The more emotion attached the better. For these experiments don't try to make them complex and look for huge desires like 10 million dollars! It may be possible but reserve that for later when your beliefs have shifted as a result of simple realization of the power you have."

"So the best way to do a bit of a clinical study is to get into a peaceful meditative state? Why if I am doing it anyway?"

"Because not all thoughts and words are doing it. The ones you make clear, repeat, and energize work best, quickest. That is all. Why do you want to test attracting unclear or negative things?"

"No, not really"

"First, there a few things you can do that give you an awareness of energy and intent that you already project as mind energy and body energies."

"What do you mean?"

"Your subconscious is where you hold as your repository of your truths and your physiology will react differently depending on whether it is truth or lies. This experiment will make you realize that your subconscious can actually respond to you. Take a needle and 10 inches of thread. Sit quietly holding the thread end between your first three fingers. Place your other hand palm up under the needle. When it is still, ask it to 'show me yes'. Concentrate and allow it to swing back and forth. Then let it settle. Then ask it to 'show me no' and allow it swing, then let it settle. Then ask it 'Do I believe in miracles?' and see the response."

"Hmmm, that will be interesting."

"You can understand that your heart field is energy and reacts to positive or negative influences of the mind. Take some wire like some coat hangers about 10 inches long and create two 90 degree bends to hold them in your hands. Hold them in your hands like a pair of guns in front of you. First, think about a really good experience. They should rotate out as an expansion of your heart field. Then think about a really bad experience. They should rotate inward as heart energy field contracts. Then with someone in the area, say: 'Show me ….' And watch them point to that person's energy field."

"Can I specify a flower or something else?"

"Yes, anything that has a live energy field within your close proximity. There are several experiments that take you into thoughts and their energies. You will do this for a set number of days, say 5 days. Sitting in a quiet peaceful place in the morning and while lying in bed before sleep to be consistent do this every day for 5 days. When you begin, take a few deep breaths and place your attention on your heart beating. Once they are launched you want to note of the results. For each day of your experiment, you should repeat the process several times. Try to keep these simple and clear. You can select whichever interests you from the list."

"Ok, I got it."

"Much of your world is filled with negative news from media that you react to sometimes unknowingly. You can do an experiment that sees the effect of this by simply eliminating it. The world of negativity creates thoughts and emotions that go out and find buddies. You have to pay attention to what happens but ban media from your awareness and occupy yourself with outside natural things."

"What about movies?"

"Movies generate thoughts and emotions so for the test don't watch movies. For a subsequent week, only watch happy movies and see the difference."

"You are constantly seeing various events, people, situations that may come to you in your daily activities. These cause you to react with judgments of emotion and even trauma and can create strong energies. In this experiment, you will stop any negative reaction and see a different interpretation of what you call crap. In truth it could be a blessing in disguise. Look carefully each day at some situations that come before you that are perceived as bad. Extract the good part of it and document these."

"That will keep me busy! It should be interesting."

"There are also several ways to test your proactive energies."

"You mean the ones I purposely create?"

"Yes, you may spend personal time thinking about your day and other situations where you are generating many thoughts of your life, self, family, and work. You sit and think 'it's been a crappy day', or 'life sucks', or 'I don't have enough money', or 'I am pissed at so and so'. In this case, whatever you focus on can expand and will draw more of it under the Law of Attraction. Catch yourself when that happens and stop it. Switch it to a positive thought and see the effect over the week."

"You can also focus attention and intention on a simple outcome that you visualize and verbalize it. Make it simple, you want to meet interesting new people, or see a lot of red cars, or some such wish. You can also engage yourself in the philosophy that the more you love, the more you are in alignment with the heart field. Spend the days sending love bombs to everything and everyone. Monitor the results."

"What about questions that I want answers to?"

"Ok, you are already doing that but your connection to the field provides accurate unlimited guidance. So ask for guidance on a specific question or issue you need to get answers on and see what comes forward. Your beliefs and expectations draw from field of potentiality so you could draw up a list of what you would like to see."

"It must be you that answers?"

"It is but you have to listen through intuition or a niggling of thoughts. In this case we are looking for results in the material world. It can come from anywhere in any form. Another test is to shift your perception to see that the universe is limitless, abundant and accommodating is to make a conscious effort to look for goodness, beauty and abundance all around and keep track of these."

"What about things like money?"

"I wondered when that would come up. In this process believe money is nothing but energy and a reflection of beliefs so each time bring yourself into the statements and mindset that if I give money away, I will receive even more; and money is easy to come by."

"Another tactic that shifts the energies is to believe and act in accordance with the more fun you have, the better life works. Do great things for 5 days and see how many great things come into being."

"Anything I can do to show that my thoughts actually influence things?"

"Of course, you already know how what you say can affect others but there are some experiments that you can do to see how you can influence matter. So because words have energy, issue only thoughtful loving words to plants or people and monitor the results."

"Another way to see that your thoughts have power is to create a glass of water that you infuse with healing energy from the heart to accomplish a physical placebo change in something not right in you. Drink it each morning and night and document changes. Another test of your thoughts and consciousness impacting matter can be done by setting up two containers of the same type of cut flowers. Put them in two separate areas. For the days of the experiment, go over to one, focus on it and tell it you hate it, it is crap and it is ugly. With the other tell it you love it, it is beautiful. After the 5 days inspect the quality of each one to see the difference."

"In this experiment, you can see the impact on yourself; your thoughts and consciousness impacting your physical body. State you will lose 1 pound in 48 hours by projecting positive loving thoughts into your food before eating it."

"What about higher abilities?"

"You can believe you are connected to everything and everyone else in the universe through the greater consciousness. Send a telepathic message 3 times a day to someone and see if you can get evidence of its receipt."

"But adding emotion is key to getting results faster?"

"Yes, of course. It is an emotional signature that heightens the strength of vibration."

"Ok, I will try this. Can we get back to this energy fund you spoke of?"

"Indeed. In our next session it will be so."

4

HOW DO YOU MANAGE THESE CRAPPY ENERGIES?

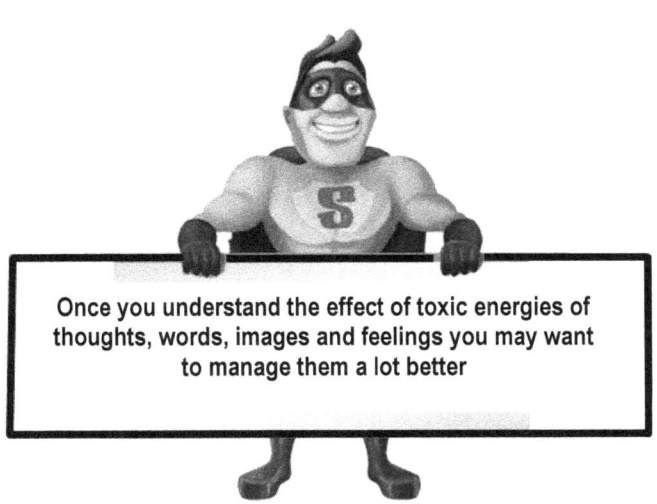

Once you understand the effect of toxic energies of thoughts, words, images and feelings you may want to manage them a lot better

THE ENERGY PORTFOLIOS

After my conversation on these energies I was creating and the experiments, it really woke me up. I was thinking about where my mind had been with Supernocebo and I was clearly understanding why his business type philosophy was like being unconsciously creating all these energies that were coming back to me. All the time in the business world in trying to make a company work, make profits, satisfy directors and shareholders there are so many times you just become a real asshole without ever considering the consequences of energy creation.

I was really interested in what Superplacebo mentioned about managing an energy portfolio. I was quite preoccupied about this as I launched my meditation so it took a while to finally settle in. I wasn't even sure if he was there but then I sensed his presence.

"Ok, Superplacebo, how do I structure this energy portfolio?"

"Let us recall all those experiments on energy. Many of them would fall into your portfolio. And once you clearly understand the toxicity of many of the energies you create, you will begin to pay attention when they come up as a thought. As we continue you will come to realize that they create more toxic energies and they also have a toxic effect in your body. It is your thoughts that are the initiation to many other actions."

"I am really beginning to understand this now. But you say there are some kinds of body processes that are also causing me to generate unwanted energies?"

"That is quite intuitive of you. There are indeed things that are occurring without your direct awareness – both through the heart and the brain minds. We can discuss this after if you like."

"Ok, let us talk about these energy portfolios."

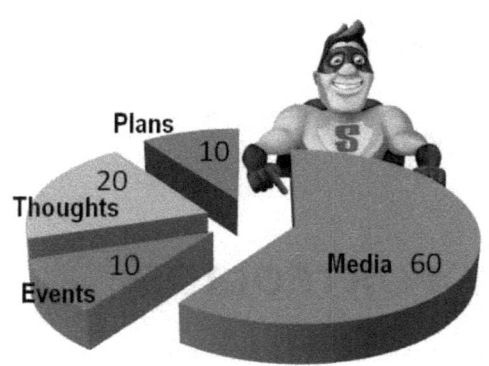

"Yes, with a business inclination you will relate to this. We are going to create a balanced energy management plan. That plan will have four types of investment portfolios that reflect different types of energy generating activities. This will relate to the energy experiments we talked about. Two would be Reactive and two would be Proactive energies. Let us call these Media, Plans, Thoughts and Events to make it simple and allocate a percentage to them. I will explain them individually."

"Ok, I see the image. 60% Media, 10% Events, 20% Thoughts and 10% Plans."

"Yes, these are energies you are creating all the time."

"Ok, that makes sense."

"The first two portfolios are **reactive** energies. One is a result of thoughts created from the news, the media, television, papers, what others said, things that were outside. We can call this the **media portfolio**. Here one listens, hears, sees, reads and reacts, creating energy. Perhaps 60% of your total time in the 24 hours is of this nature. These are the ones that cause the cells and the brain to go into the negative reaction mode that inhibits growth."

"These are like the experiment where I cut myself off from the media."

"Yes, you see this constantly in the negative world you live in. The purpose is to not react in a negative way. No negative thoughts, no adding of negative emotion, never getting angry or saying things shooting from the ego's lip, or doing things that would not be in alignment with the heart. Yes, it is not an easy task in such a negative world."

"Tell me about it."

"So here you stop a thought before you give it life and remember it is there to teach you what you do not want or focus on, not the reverse. If you react instantly in rage, it is ego, probably dear brother goading you on. You simply stop the thought for three deep breaths, let ego subdue and let the heart take over. Then you create a new reaction that saw a good reason for the issue, or do not react at all; keeping it neutral. Rise above it and simply observe it. You have to be mindful the objective to invest in a future life of goodness, so the more goodness you can energize, the more you can build up the value of the portfolio and the return on investment."

"Of course. Otherwise these reactions and actions will manifest later on. At some point good reactions will return through the Law of Attraction. Positive grows the asset, negative diminishes the value."

"Indeed. The second portfolio to set up also comes from outside as part of the reactive process. It has to do with events that happen seemingly not under one's control. This is the **events portfolio** like if you had a dreadful accident, or you got involved in a terrible situation. This may be about 10% of the energy fund. If you carry a lot of unbalanced karma or have been active in creating big conflicts and issues, this may be more karma coming forward. The immediate ego instinct to clash, react, or do something that one could be sorry for later is the issue. The focus is NOT to do that; not to create a huge energy action that is negative. Try to see some reason why this occurred and read something good out of it. Take a higher perception and see it as a lesson of what you did not want or find what is good about it."

"Yes, I have had several of these and wondered why."

"This is really where you need to resist my dear brother's yelling and shouting into your conscious mind. It may well be the case that this is a result of some cause you created before; even in a previous life. Or as you will see later on, it may have even been something that you as a Soul planned in a Life Plan to work off some karma. If this is some terrible thing that would create anger and vengeance you still have a choice. It is a choice to go ballistic but if the portfolio is to build rapidly, this is the place you can make huge strides. Even though many of these could be a result of old karma or negative energy in escrow from the past, the tactic is to create a perception that if it was a terrible problem that brought fear or hatred, ok but then leave it alone for three days to get the ego out of it then you have time to look at it with the heart in mind more calm and collected."

"Yes, I can see this. Boy can I ever! If I react to these and don't learn my lesson then I just set the scene for more of it to happen until I learn my lesson."

"Or understand the consequences of the energy you are creating – with a lot of emotion added, I may add. The next two portfolios are **proactive**—those energies that you create in your own time, purposely and with positive purpose from *inside*. The first is easiest described as **free thinking.** It is the time you would spend letting the mind simply generate thoughts about whatever is on the mind. This could be about 20% of the time, or 20% of the energy fund."

"These are like the 70,000 thoughts I have during a day?"

"Yes but these are not reactive. These are what you choose to think about. This is like when you created a thought about personal affairs, like about a feeling of inadequacy, doubt, fear of the future, crisis from the past, not enough money, or feeling sick. Perhaps it was about how great the world was, what you had to appreciate, what is good. The focus here is to add to the positive investment energy in the fund and with purpose and intent add positive thoughts. Any negative thoughts like '*it pisses me off*', or '*I hate this*', or '*I feel crappy*', are not allowed to enter the portfolio. You learn to stop this and convert it; not give it any negative life with emotion or a following act."

"So turn these around and make them creative. Learn from them and just feel good about them or don't engage them if they are negative?"

"Precisely. The last portfolio has to do with plans. It is the **plans** portfolio, also from *inside*. This could constitute 10% of the fund allocated toward it. These energies are for investing in major desires, solutions, and passions to create in the longer term. Here, rather than being focused on the problems, like not enough money, having to work hard, do this do that to get more money, you change the focus to the solution to feel the energy of completion, add the emotion of enjoyment, be grateful for it being done, and put the positive energy of completion out to the greater consciousness field to attract the solution. You would place this energy in the fund. This could be a very small part of the fund but it could have an immense effect on the positive energy of joy that could come back into the fund and its future value. This is where you implement new mind, new plans on developing mind over matter for health and wealth miracles."

"I like that. Will I see immediate results?"

"When this is instituted, you will begin to see a dramatic change in life as the fund grows from positive energies. The objective is learning to generate new positive energy or converting more and more negative energy until there is no room for negative events and experience to enter each day. It is like a business where you take old energy companies that are failing, then put new energy into them to be successful."

"And clean up the residual energies in the pipeline. What have you to lose except my brother's niggling?"

"Well, I can see the merit but these may not be so effective in managing people in a business."

"Are you sure about that? Perhaps you are stuck in your own belief box that tells you this is so. Perhaps you must reevaluate your business tactics and find that there is much better productivity when your employees are treated from the heart, not Supernocebo's head."

"I understand what you are saying. I have to think on that one. But tell me Superplacebo, how did your brother get all this dominance over my conscious mind?"

"You choose to listen to him as he speaks louder than me. As you say, your world of commerce has a belief that supports his 12 rules, not mine. Do you remember those?"

"Yes, I do."

"There are several reasons, and part of this is about your human design of the brain and your purpose of living as an organism. Let us go there now. You must first understand the process of human evolution as it was designed in DNA."

5

THE STAGES OF HUMAN EVOLUTION

We dwell in your subconscious, the brain being the mental vessel and heart being emotional vessel.

"Understand that you and I are here as partners to engage in a life to evolve the greater consciousness which we are all a part of. To do this, you and I plan a life, choose an environment and a physical vessel to engage in mental and emotional experiences. The process of engagement begins in the physical material world and evolves to the spiritual world. To achieve this, everyone evolves the brain and body a certain way as encoded in the DNA. Everyone is familiar with this process of physical and mental evolution from a newborn to an infant to a teenager, adult and so on that follows what is your normal belief of a birth to death mortal existence. Also familiar are the processes of mental growth to maturity. Through these stages, new functions and abilities can be developed and stored as programs of behavior."

"You mean like learning to walk, talk, eat and so on."

"Yes, even earlier, a newborn must rely on DNA to get all of the vital mechanisms installed first. Then what you mention is followed by learning an occupation and earning a living, raising kids, as guided and determined by the different levels of consciousness and their belief systems. As you develop physically and mentally, the process is guided by DNA which has an encoded blueprint of how the human is engineered to evolve and grow."

"Just as I have done and everything that has life follows a DNA template."

"But seldom are people aware of the complete evolutionary process beyond what is believed to be the end point of adult maturity usually around the late twenties. Your group consciousness is concerned with this first phase of your evolution through matter and that is what carries on into middle age."

"You mean being focused on our physical world as reality? What else is there? Humans are mature by that age, aren't they?"

"Yes, mature perhaps physically as they see it. But this is really the tip of the iceberg in terms of evolution. Just as you are now learning there is a whole different reality that you do not see or feel. And that reality makes up 99.9% of everything that exists."

"Oh? How do people miss this other part?"

"My brother does a great job of eliminating this as being of any significance. It happens to be about the age of 28 where a physical maturity shifts to a spiritual evolution that can evolve or begin. Through that first phase only 1 of the 12 pairs of DNA is deployed. It is in the next 28 years that the rest of the DNA can come into the process. DNA is a repository of the sum total of human evolution. But you are using only 10% of DNA and calling the rest junk. You thus only develop 10% of your spiritual enhancements that are part of the body. These are simply believed to be of no significance as so accepted as the belief of the larger consciousness."

"I think I can see where you are coming from. If you do not choose to develop, learn or continue to evolve according to the plan, then that ability, process, simply atrophies or stays unused as it never reaches the awareness of the mind. Just like if you don't want to learn to walk, you will eventually lose that ability. But what is it that I and the rest of us are missing here?"

BRAIN WAVE PATTERNS

"You are missing your true potential while immersed in the lower material world. You are not aware of the higher spiritual world and the subtle energies that make up the Universe – 99.9% of the rest. The brain is the link between your mind and your body. It has two really big responsibilities of using its neurological processes to sense and present your reality, plus managing your body in a way that helps you adapt to that reality. It has to go through a physical evolution of mind and body which goes from birth to adult in 28 years giving you the equipment you need in the physical reality. The process is one of stages where my brother and I share the responsibility representing the conscious mind and the subconscious mind. He is rooted in the energy consciousness of the big brain, while I am rooted in the energy consciousness of the heart brain as well as a special part of the brain, and subconscious. Unlike him, I am your subconscious part of the greater consciousness and depend upon the spiritual evolution to continue beyond 28 years of age."

"If we consider the morphogenic process of growth as it unfolds in the brain and body we can say that the brain is like a CEO of the body. It has the dual responsibility to sense and evolve within the external reality, and to control the internal reality of the body. To do this it uses a neurological system to evolve and adapt programs that become stored in the subconscious."

"What do you mean by morphogenic process? We already talked about the morphic field but what is this?"

"Morphogenic relates to what you may call natural order, process and purpose. Some call it a divine or greater intelligence that automatically follows a development or growing purpose, from being seeded or born to maturity, and then completion. To you, from the time of conception to the time when your body dies is a morphogenic process of growth. It is a natural process which for humans is encoded in DNA. So morphogenesis occurs when a call to activate programs needed to grow towards a mature state, that process being a set of programs that begin by being loaded from DNA into subconscious even before you are born and certainly in the first year of life."

"So all living things are evolving through a morphogenic process encoded in DNA."

"Yes, these are like computer programs and subprograms that define specifically how something grows, evolves and interacts with its environment. And if you look at the brain that is also a morphogenic process, it is made up of billions of brain cells called neurons which use electricity to communicate with each other. The combination of millions of neurons sending signals at once produces an enormous amount of electrical activity in the brain, which can be detected using sensitive medical equipment such as an EEG or ElectroEncephaloGram, measuring electricity levels over areas of the scalp. The combination of electrical activity of the brain is commonly called a *brainwave* pattern, because of its cyclic, wave-like nature."

"Yes, I know about that. The electrical activity in the brain will change depending on what the person is doing. The brainwaves of a sleeping person are vastly different than the brainwaves of someone wide awake. But what does that have to do with anything?"

"You will see this shortly. Over the years, more sensitive equipment has brought your global consciousness closer to figuring out exactly what brainwaves represent and with that, what they have to do with a person's health and state of mind."

"Yes, I am aware of the brain state of Delta which has a frequency of 0.2hz - 3hz. It is deep, dreamless sleep. Delta is the slowest band of brainwaves. When your dominant brainwave is delta, your body is healing itself and resetting its internal clocks. You do not dream in this state and are completely unconscious."

"It is this delta that evolves first. I will explain but let us continue this because these states are part of the evolution in terms of the chronological morphogenic process of brain, body, mind and consciousness development."

"The next brain state of Theta is from 3hz - 8hz which appears as light sleep or extreme relaxation. Theta is also a very receptive mental state that has proven useful for hypnotherapy, as well as self-hypnosis using recorded affirmations and suggestions."

"The state of Alpha is from 8hz - 12hz. It is an awake state but relaxed and not processing much information. When you get up in the morning and just before sleep, you are naturally in this state. When you close your eyes your brain automatically starts producing more alpha waves. It is also called the hypnogogic state common to kids when they are being programmed automatically."

"The state of Beta from 12hz - 27hz. It is a wide awake state. This is generally the mental state most people are in during the day and most of their waking lives. Usually, this state in itself is uneventful, but don't underestimate its importance."

"Finally, the state of Gamma is at 27 Hz and up. It is associated with the formation of ideas, language and memory processing, and various types of learning. Gamma waves have been shown to disappear during deep sleep induced by anesthesia, but return with the transition back to a wakeful state."

"What does this have to do with human evolution?"

THE BRAIN'S EVOLUTION

"The brain and its states evolve from childhood to adulthood, each having a purpose in evolving the human body within the environment. It relies on a stimulus response system where the engagement of mental and emotional systems select the best ways to learn the appropriate way to behave and survive in the environment. The first 28 years is when the *physical equipment* called body and mind come to the first stage of maturity. This is based upon survival in the material reality. After that we see the evolution of the immaterial reality kick in. Within DNA are 12 layer pairs of encoding that allow this to draw the required programs out to evolve into the *spiritual equipment* each is endowed with. In order for this to occur, a spiritual awareness is required. Otherwise only 1 layer's pair of DNA become the means of evolving because they form the blueprint for the physical morphogenic processes. Ok, now, with these brain states in your mind, I can answer your question of what this has to do with evolution. There are five stages of human evolution."

"Is this where the difference between mind over matter and matter over mind can evolve?"

"Indeed it develops best from this point of 28, but it can be present from an early age if it is part of the gifts that have been planned in your life plan, or they can certainly be developed earlier by choice. However, this schedule is the way it proceeds for all."

"You mentioned life plan before. What do you mean about a life plan?"

"I mean that before you agreed to work with me and my brother, you developed a plan of your life. Don't get too excited about this because we will talk about this in great detail later."

"Ok, so if I get this, I was a Soul, worked with you to create a Life Plan and then there is this growing body that evolves according to set processes of evolution."

"You and I were one mind. You can say that as the human, you began to establish your own mind forgetting that we were one. That is a necessary step of incarnating into a physical body that can hold my consciousness. You see me as Superplacebo for the sake of representation in your mind. Really, it is your Soul that is evolving and growing and I am the Higher Mind or Self that links between the higher and lower forms. Remember I am pure energy of higher mind and consciousness whereas the body is lower mind and physical counterpart. But these names all are just constructs for convenience to understand what we are as a Soul."

"Ok, we won't forget to talk about this later. That sort of screws my belief system pretty bad!"

"I promise. Now, look at this picture that I am going to present to you as an image in your mind. Look at it very carefully because you will see age and the evolution of the brain as researched by many people on your plane and the stages we just discussed."

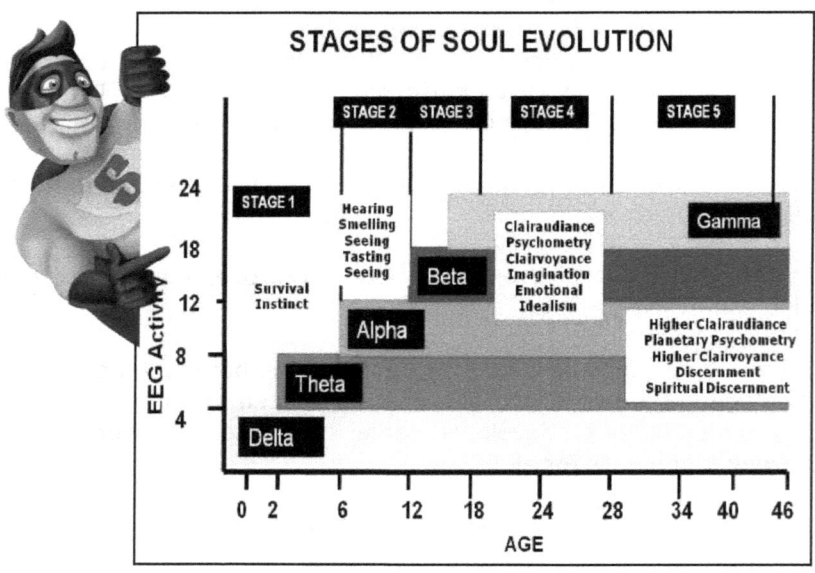

"Wow! Holy Macaroni, did I ever miss the boat at 20! Those are those woo woo metaphysical para normal freaky things!"

"That's because you chose to listen to my brother and pursue a path in your Life Plan that was commerce and embrace his philosophy. And who is it that says these are freaky woo woo things? You or the consciousness box you have accepted?"

"I hear you."

"You chose to select from that belief box what you would place into your subconscious. But that's ok, these things never go away, they just have to be brought back into your awareness and sure it may take more effort and concentration but that's no problem now that you are listening to me. But forget about the woo woo stuff because that reflects the fringe of the greater reality that sits there waiting for you to open."

"Ok, like the rest of DNA?"

"Yes. Notice the first stage is during Delta and Theta before the age of six. Here as you would say, the brain must get its program library together to develop the hard core environment survival habits through perception and response. It has to get this done as a foundation before the self-conscious awareness kicks in to add the ego and the intellect. You will understand that from birth to age 2, that baby is effectively filled with divine love energy – a morphic field where most people, especially women just have to hold these babies and love them without question. It is also the time when their programs of physical and physiological behaviors need to be created and of course the brain is learning all this and programming them into the jurisdiction of the subconscious."

"So in Delta all of the programs from DNA needed to sustain chemistry, biology, physiology need to be engaged internally. It needs this to activate as critical functions that a baby needs to survive before Theta kicks to survive in the external physical environment, like eat, sleep, walk, crawl, cry and so on."

"Yes. From the outside environment, particularly when the Theta state kicks in, just about everything the child encounters is being programmed into subconscious. The perception and response is on auto pilot drawing from DNA what is required to set internal things of growth going and then into external to survive and cope. This is required to allow evolution into the second stage."

"Yes, now the second stage from 6-12 occurs during the Alpha and Beta phase, the self identity matures, as does the education received become discriminated upon before it enters into the belief and perception-response behavior. The primary senses of hearing, tasting, seeing, smelling and perception are dominant because they are key to development of the next set of programs."

"Ok, so now the kid is getting to learn things about his family consciousness, culture and so on. He has to learn how to mobilize, read, write, arithmetic, and develop his creative mind."

"Yes, through these two stages the child is developing his five senses and becoming familiar with them. So if he touched fire and gets burned, the brain fires and wires neurons to create a stimulus response program so the kid now remembers the effect if he engages in that cause. During this time my brother starts to come in to assist in the evolution."

"Is this where he becomes the bad guy?"

"No my brother is an upper Alpha and Beta frequency. Although the brain is really his domain and jurisdiction, he also has little to say until the conscious mind and brain are ready for him. It is when the self awareness is needed in the morphogenic process and ego gains a life. His duty is to teach survival at a mental and physical level of the material reality. So he begins to influence the thinking and behaviour through thoughts. And he does a great job. The issue comes when he will not relinquish that responsibility and share the transition. That becomes clear in the third stage where he has built the identity and ego to such a strength and filled subconscious with the programs of the family, education, cultures and global consciousness, the process of evolution becomes slowed."

"Is that when he becomes the devil?"

"He can easily as he has formed a stacked deck of belief and behaviour programs that limit expansion to my jurisdiction. He becomes the devil when he continues building the ego mind at the expense of the body as I will explain later."

"Well, I know that well. I can see that now, as his 12 laws are pretty draconian and if he comes into the conscious mind nattering away like he has done to me, you create shitload of causes that draw a lot of crappy effects."

"This is where your schooling, experience and engagement shaped your belief system. The third stage occurs between ages 12-18. Here is where the self-identity and ego begin to flourish. It is also one where physical changes to complete the reproductive system occur. The physical body and mind begin to take on a maturity. The primary senses of hearing, tasting, seeing, smelling and perception become heightened and well developed in alignment with your developed identity and character. But here is where the discriminatory process of free will to perceive and make choices should become balanced between my brother who is hell bent on developing a strong ego with negative energies, and me and my sister that brings in a softer spiritual aspect of a life of positive energies which I continuously radiate through my jurisdiction of the heart chakra and its morphic field."

"Hmmm, I see where he who talks loud gets the ear of the crowd! So the devil comes forward because he does not really care about losing control."

"Well, there are many at the extreme end that take on some rather evil traits and that is why he has been branded as Satan in religions who teach sin. He doesn't have to give up control; he has to learn to share the control and allow the conscious mind to evolve and begin to hear me from the unconscious mind. When this happens as time progresses, those parts of you that are quantum in nature such as the brain, consciousness, light body, chakras, heart, DNA, cells, and so on, begin to show themselves to open up your true potential."

"More woo woo stuff?"

"These subtle energy fields are what control those none woo woo physics. The issue is that you do not come to understand these are the powerful forces of the heart, namely love and compassion. If this evolution is curtailed by the choice of low energy components of the chakra functions, these are blocked and rendered dysfunctional. The attributes and abilities, like psychic abilities as part of the chakras and DNA for example cannot develop and the appropriate connection channel to me and the quantum space of infinite possibilities of your higher mind cannot be opened."

"And once Supernocebo takes control, he always instigates protection of ego through the conscious mind and as he dictates the programming in the brain, you can go kiss your butt goodbye to the fourth stage?"

"Well, he does not totally control the brain's process. He obviously had first dibs on programming and he works hard at maintaining that dominant posture which is in sync with the local and global copiousness of matter controlling mind. My mind over matter becomes difficult to believe because society thinks it is silly and the majority can't hear me. It is just like you and your woo woo!"

"I can relate to that. I certainly never heard you. You can't survive in the business world and feed your family if you are quiet and peaceful because the rest aren't."

"That is so, but it still does not eliminate a softer choice in your affairs. Remember what I said before. Either you want to believe you work your ass off struggling in the material world, or you learn to work with me, follow passion and have wonderful things come to you as mind over matter."

"Ok, what's the fourth stage that I missed?"

"The fourth stage occurs from the ages of 18-28 which takes you into the awareness of the other energy bodies that make up your anatomy. Typically this is where you are deciding to engage in a profession and are pretty occupied with professional schooling so you can have a family and a comfortable life according to your norm."

"I am sure your brother has a heyday here, strengthening ego with power and money and nice expensive goodies."

"Indeed he does. The global consciousness supports that need so spiritual, metaphysical wisdom is relegated to the same place the miracles are in. It is simply the choice of the many that override the few. And of course there is nothing wrong with ego as it is needed to develop in the environment but it is an equal partnership with the heart that is important to balance. If this stage is allowed to develop it is where you can meet me or your Soul and talk a new business to re-establish that lost partnership. One of these places to meet and greet is meditation into the astral plane where you are in your mind now. And here resides many of the higher abilities waiting to open."

"What are these higher abilities?"

"When you become aware of me and your higher bodies then you can open to clairaudience which is astral hearing, psychometry is astral touch and feeling, clairvoyance as astral sight, imagination as astral equivalent of taste and emotional idealism the astral equivalent of smell."

"I don't even know what those are. But those are all crap, no one believes that stuff. That's these weirdoes and nutcases that can tell the future, read minds, and are telepathic with ghosts!"

"Well, Ed, Supernocebo and the consciousness box have been effective on you haven't they? Yet you are talking to me. Why is that?"

"Oops, sorry! Ok, I am back in the box again. What is the fifth stage?"

"The fifth stage opens and develops at 28 to 46. It is where you enter a midlife shift when family and relationships become paramount. The heart is a major part of this. But, dear brother by this time has entrenched his programs of survival and the heart is a concept of protection and love for family, not your fellow men. It is about accumulation of material wealth, prosperity, power, greed and money."

"Yes, I do know about those ups and downs at the expense of my health! But how can one have a good life without all this material things to make you happy?"

"It is only because you do not understand the power of managing energies from a higher place of the heart. But I see that you will. It is at this stage that your true spirituality evolves and matures. You learn how mind over matter really works and you begin to open to the rest of the potential of DNA, to the other 90% of the brain, to your higher energy systems that take you into a higher world. During this stage assuming the Astral awareness is perused, new five senses of the mental body begin to open, leading to a much greater inventory of abilities. These then open to the Higher Mind and bodies."

"What are those higher bodies?"

"We will talk of those later. Let us finish this topic."

"Ok, but this is still open to us older guys isn't it?"

"It is so but it becomes more difficult to dismantle the old programming and to step outside of the belief boxes. Having taken the tour of life through the first four stages of Delta, Theta, Alpha, and Beta, one would have to develop the stimulus-response systems to be able to live in all four as if they were in the Theta range to thus be a properly evolved human totally aware of its me and the energetic bodies that are the overlay on the physical that gives it life, and directly connects with the Higher Intelligence or Force through what its makeup is as love."

"So just like me. I atrophied the possibility at the third stage where one has a tendency to deprive oneself of the next steps of evolution of the Light Body-Being. It is stunted because it evolves to the level of self-awareness as ego-intellect by choosing limiting negative energies and limits its final entry into the heart brain and the quantum field?"

"Exactly, you choose to listen to my brother who prevents your spiritual awaking, compromises your body health, mind and life. But do not believe they are stunted or lost. They just need your attention to vitalize. Now here is the crux of the matter."

"At the age of 28 one may easily become stuck in the mud within the physical plane with the limiting beliefs of the global community. In a world of negativity, and accommodation to the lower self of ego totally dependent on the advice of thoughts from Supernocebo and the brain at the top of the body. And the body may become fully trained to run on all the subconscious programs of the past. That is the old mind as it becomes stuck in the lower expression of the body anatomy. The next stages and the awareness of the heart brain and the Astral step of the Soul's evolution simply stay undeveloped."

"Well, I had to take responsibility and make a living so I did not want to be a monk on the mountain top chanting with nothing except a robe or be one of these silly priests who can't have a family and listens to these super religious dudes that say god speaks to them."

"That is an interesting reason. Those monks and priests are a whole different topic for later. But how do you know that if you had not pursued this different path that you could not have achieved family and happiness a different way?"

"I don't but I certainly don't want a life like theirs."

"You have determined a certain model and prototype as a prejudgment. How do you know that is what spiritual evolution means? Perhaps you are not so content with your reality right now either?"

"Well, that's true, I don't know. And I am no shining example of success."

"Well consider that once your evolution takes you to that place around 28 when you are fully developed, you really become like a new kid in the kindergarten school of the immaterial world. That world that allows you full creatorship with your mind, from a higher energetic self simply is not developed, the system goes into default awareness and you create the way you learned; hard work manipulating matter with those primitive tools of creation. Until the new kid at 28 learns about who he really is, how can the lower primitive mind be able to handle the ability to instantly create reality without learning the ropes? You simply defaulted to the Supernocebo way of trying to manipulate matter to make a living. Now you have come to a place where you are seeing it differently and you see the folly."

"Well, true, I suppose seeing an occasional unexplained miracle occurring is a reminder of those that have touched the fringe of this level of evolution. It is what the group consciousness appears to have entrenched in its subconscious mind."

"Let us leave this for now and complete this topic as I want you to understand another aspect of this evolution which is centered on another disbelief of your subconscious minds of the collective. It is about your energy centers and Downward and Upward Causation."

"What is that?"

"Downward causation is my domain of mind over matter; the process of mind that controls and creates matter in the philosophy of 'as above so below'. Upward Causation is Supernocebo's domain of matter; that matter controls the mind."

"The seven human chakra energy systems interconnect with specific functions and organs within the body to the etheric energy body and to the astral. Don't worry about this as I will explain this later. In the beginning of a life, we see the process of Upward causation starting from the bottom (Root) to the top (Crown). We see each stage of evolution taking about 4 years."

"Are you going to explain this chakra system better?"

SUBTLE ENERGIES NOT SO SUBTLE

"I wasn't but if it helps you to understand, I will give you a quick summary now as chakras will come up in our conversation constantly. Do you recall when we talked about your energy balance in your portfolio? Chakras are subtle energy centers that are invisible vortexes linking your physical with your non-physical bodies. They are like energy antennas that pick up astral frequencies and link them into the physical apparatus through your vital or etheric body."

"You are speaking in a foreign language."

"I will explain in detail later."

"Good."

"These subtle energy centers are known to have a direct affect on seven major groups of physical organs. These organs control the physiological and psychological functions related to the *verb* actions on the left. On the right are the resulting *subjects* from the use of the verb. Here is a picture for you."

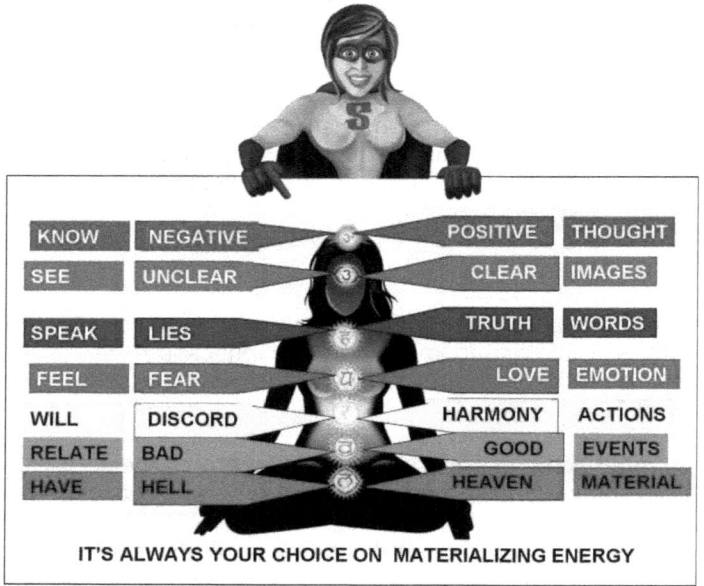

"So each of these can have a negative or positive impact on my organs?"

"Yes. I want to have a separate session on these energy systems but you need to understand several things before that. Look at the top chakra. It is the crown starting in a non-physical world, you *know* a *thought*, *see* an *image at the third eye*, *speak* some *words at the throat chakra,* and *feel* an *emotion at the heart. These are the basic functions of these above chakras.* Assuming an action is prompted below, from that point, you move into the physical world. By using intent, you *will* yourself into an *action at the solar plexus,* which will allow you to *relate* to others and physical *events at the sacral*, thereby allowing you to *have* a *material* experience in the root chakra. Look at this image that tells you what key organ and essence of your personality it affects."

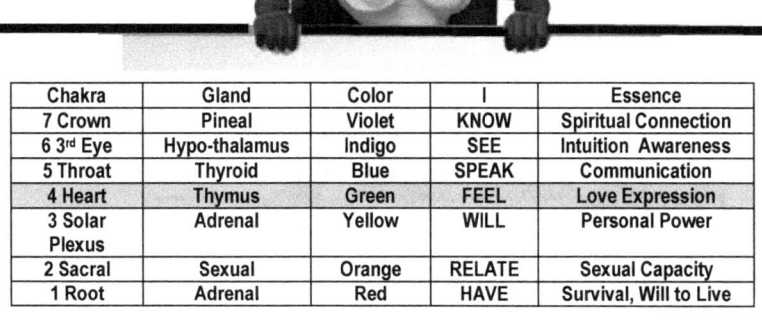

Chakra	Gland	Color	I	Essence
7 Crown	Pineal	Violet	KNOW	Spiritual Connection
6 3rd Eye	Hypo-thalamus	Indigo	SEE	Intuition Awareness
5 Throat	Thyroid	Blue	SPEAK	Communication
4 Heart	Thymus	Green	FEEL	Love Expression
3 Solar Plexus	Adrenal	Yellow	WILL	Personal Power
2 Sacral	Sexual	Orange	RELATE	Sexual Capacity
1 Root	Adrenal	Red	HAVE	Survival, Will to Live

"Ok, I get it. This is what you mean by spiritual from crown down and material from root up. The balance point is the heart of matter! How did you like that pun?"

"You can be funny!"

"So the first 28 years are to get a good handle on Upward Causation. Then you transit to getting a handle on Downward Causation?"

"Exactly, because when you reverse these processes that are balanced by the middle one of the heart the process of thought, vision, words, emotion, action, relationship and material world are the way to create reality under downward causation of mind over matter."

"And that is why you don't have be a monk or a priest to control your reality. That is the alternative to Supernocebo's way of manipulating material reality to cause happiness. In the 28 year process of evolution, these 7 chakras get developed from the root up as in this image."

Age 0-4 Root Learning to be earthed, walking sense of stability, resilience without fear of isolation

Age 5-8 Sacral Learning relationship with others and security, understanding personal boundaries, attaining balance from harmonious relationships

Age 8-12 Solar Plexus Learning to be unique and special, make judgment calls as to what is correct for your personality

Age 12-16 Heart Learning heart love and devotion, through the seat of emotions. Learning to balance and express emotions freely to love, partnership and understand roles as giver/receiver of love

Age 16-20 Throat Learning throat expression following the passion to the heart. Becoming balanced to act in faith in an energetic way and achieve full maturity

Age 20-24 3rd Eye Learning insight intuition, intellectual. Moving into the world then the seeing through the spiritual eye as deductive, rational, and loyal

Age 24-28 Crown Being One with cosmos gaining a rich insight into who we are. Replacing desire by will and a sense of comfort as to who you are

"Then as a fully developed physical and non-physical human vessel at age 28, it becomes your choice which way you want to deal with your reality."

"And your brother keeps you occupied in the lower matter over mind consciousness."

"Yes, and as long as you listen to him, he will keep you in that limited reality by aiding the process by which you create your beliefs, abilities, actions and reality. These are encoded as programs in subconsciousness."

"Ok, I get it. Now how does this programming in the brain take place?"

6

THE CHIEF IN THE ATTIC

The power of creation by emotion is through your mind and brain and they don't know if it is caused by fact or fiction. So be careful how you deploy it.

SO WHO IS IN CHARGE?

"To answer your question about programming, let us go back to the evolution of the brain and its different stages of development. You can understand that as the brain is developing in the first years it is important to evolve the physiological abilities, physical abilities, the sensory systems, and the means of optimizing survival in the external reality."

"Yes, I got that but where do you actually come in?"

"In this development, my brother and I share this development to keep the balance between the material and immaterial realities. When a child is born, it is already totally in the spiritual light as it knows nothing else."

"That must be why everybody loves a newborn without condition or qualifications."

"You don't see it but it is pure light of Soul radiating field of heart energy. Once the child starts adjusting to the material reality it has been born into, this spiritual glow begins to fade. Because it is primarily interested in the material reality survival and adaptation, it takes on the greatest responsibilities of evolution in the first 12 years. Supernocebo is guiding survival in the material world. There is no such thing in my world so I am not of much use at this point as my 'glow' becomes superseded."

"Ok, how exactly do these programs of behavior get created in the subconscious?"

"During the first year the brain and nervous system must interpret environment stimuli and send signals to cells which integrate and regulate life sustaining functions of the body organ systems to support survival. Then it shifts to external environmental stimuli. Notice I said regulate and integrate, not analyze and decide! For this purpose, the brain dedicates vast cell numbers to catalogue complex perceptions. It remembers millions of these experienced perceptions and integrates them into a database to give them consciousness or more like self-consciousness which is through the prefrontal cortex – the neurological platform to realize personal identity and experience the quality of thinking. So the brain has a direct connection to consciousness and self-consciousness."

"What's the difference to the brain; these different consciousness states?"

"In general, consciousness can be divided into three categories. Consciousness can process 40 nerve impulses per second that enable assessment and response to environmental stimuli at that moment so one can participate in life. Self-consciousness allows one to factor in the consequences of past and future as self reflection through free will. Subconscious can process 40 million nerve impulses per second and monitors and controls automated stimulus-response as well as unconscious programs. It is like an automated record-playback systems of recorded habits. It has no creativity, once learned it is automatic."

"So subconscious controls body behavior not attended to by the self-conscious mind."

"Ok, I am going to have to repeat some brain stuff for you but you will see more clearly how the system of brain evolution develops. With this in the back of your mind, let us look back into how kids develop their brain wave states as they evolve their automated stimulus-response programs so they can engage in life. During the lower brain waves of 4-8hz, kids are in a highly suggestible state almost like hypnosis."

"You mentioned hypnogogic, right?"

"Yes. There are three primary sources of this process. The first is programmed perception through inheritance such as instincts and nature. These allow the basic survival as encoded in DNA to be brought into the subconscious database. The second is the nurture type or experiential memories downloaded from the emotional and mental/physical patterns of the mother. This is the time when the child is in the womb and the brain activity is in Delta. The third is a result of actions of the self conscious creative platform of perception by imagination that generates unlimited beliefs and behavior patterns through free will. That's when you have a full brain wave card deck to work with so you can build your personal identity and survive with this free will that you are given. To better quantify this process, have a look at the following interesting graph that my brother will place in your mind."

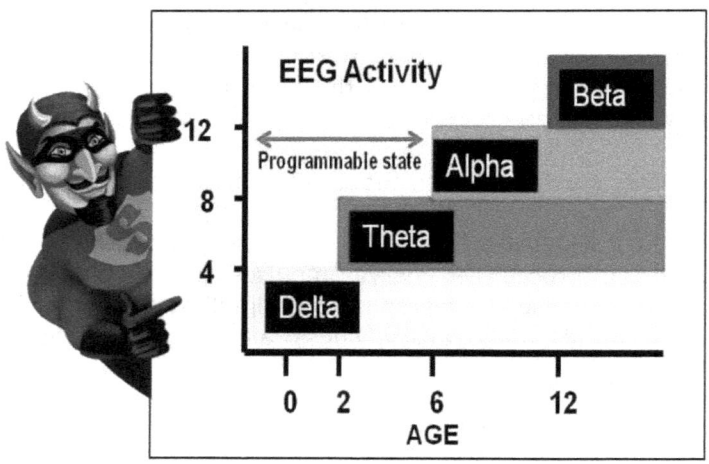

"Now the stages of brain development as related to the programming that is going on starts during pregnancy. The human brain is in operation in the delta range of .5-4hz. This is the unconscious region. From ages 0 to 2, the brain is recording all experiences, motor functions, speech, running, collecting information about the world, learning behavior patterns, acceptable or unacceptable. These shape life automatically because Alpha consciousness has not yet developed. What is added in awareness at age 2 is Theta."

"So here Theta mixes the imaginary world with the real world."

"Yes. Then from ages 2-6 the power of suggestion is prominent as the kids in Delta and Theta have rapid downloading of parent and cultural wisdom to be stored as suggested programs of behavior. The infants quickly pick up skills by observation. These become hardwired synaptic pathways in the subconscious to control biology and behavior. To the subconscious, because the purpose of the life form is to learn to adapt and react as quickly as possible so as to survive, these truths they pick up as suggested become facts, beliefs, truths, and programs needed for their survival. At the age of 6 the brain develops Alpha of 8-12hz. Where calm consciousness like in meditation is added. Alpha brings about the brain activity that opens conscious processing but before it can the brain must acquire a working awareness of the world into the subconscious. That's its duty up to age 6."

"So the kid's belief boxes are quickly being loaded up in these first years."

"Yes, they are. That is the best time to program the brain and subconscious because they need to develop these outside world skills. That's why they are in a hypnagogic trance."

"But then they also need to learn many other skills."

"Yes, and from ages 6-12 as Alpha develops these kids become less susceptible to outside programming as it is where the usual five sense observation systems interact with consciousness. This phases into the mode of discernment where the conscious mind's ability to make a decision by observation before the belief is stored in the subconscious becomes more prominent. It is where the prominent development of self-consciousness begins."

"And this is where Supernocebo enters the picture, right?"

"Well he is always there guiding survival. But at 12, there is focused consciousness where more academic activity is prominent and the Beta kicks in to the consciousness pot to take on life. Here the brain adds focused consciousness. It is here that a new mode develops, that of Gamma where after 12, the brain can go to 35Hz during times of peak performance. It's a great place for my brother because the ego is being nurtured for survival and self identity."

"So kids are in heightened programming mode right out of the starting gate and even in the womb, wow!"

"Of significance here is that Delta and Theta are below consciousness and thus called that hypnagogic trance which is the same state hypnotherapists use to download new behaviors. So kids up until the age of 6 are in a semi-hypnotic trance where perceptions are downloaded without discrimination or filtering of analytic self-conscious mind. It simply does not yet fully exist."

"I was not aware that these five stages of brain wave activates with special purpose are not given to us all at once. They are additive by age, exactly the same way the body develops by age."

"So you must understand that the hard core perception-response programs as well as beliefs are set in the first 6 years. This has relevance later when using the conscious mind to rewrite programs of behavior; it is like talking to a tape recorder. This can sabotage the conscious by limiting programs that are queued for consideration and entry!"

"The other point to this is that by the time you are mature as adults, 5% of cognitive action is through the self-conscious while 95% is through the subconscious. This means that decisions, actions, emotion behavior, for example are directed from unconscious serial processing of the subconscious. So part of the mind imagines who you are as 5% while 95% is controlled by subconscious to be who you are."

"Aha, that is why positive thinking and assertions may not work if the subconscious does not agree. So you might say that fate is based on recorded programs many of which I don't even have an awareness of! Holy macaroni, how does this programming actually occur?"

HOW DOES THE BRAIN PROGRAM?

"Two very important processes are part of the usual programming process that creates programs. The first is the process of conditioning where a past memory is associated with physiological change. For example a pill gets rid of a headache. The pill creates a specific experience to produce a conditional reaction inside as associated memory."

"Ok"

"The second is expectation. There is an expected result that is associated with the condition and it could be an old outcome of pain if the pill is not believed to work. If a different outcome than what is current is anticipated you accept the pill as a suggestion for a new cure. A new possibility and a different outcome becomes expected. If you automatically accept and embrace the new outcome then a new experience and a new trigger is created to override the old program."

"Can you explain that with an example."

"Your brain and body do not know the difference as to how that experience is engaged in. An example is a traumatic event like the fear of water. This could be created because one may have almost drowned, particularly as a kid. At that time a whole cascade of chemicals and physiological reactions in the body occurs as a result and this conditioning process becomes a program. That strong emotion of fear embeds itself into the brain`s neurological filing system and then after that the very thought of water automatically conjures up the reactions as expectations; as does the sight of water, or immersion in it. To overcome this fear and to rewrite the program, you have to believe and accept a different outcome until you get into the water, face the fear, feel the heightened emotion of actually succeeding in being in the water, and reprogram a new sequence. Or just persevere until you get rid of the phobia."

"I see, that is Supernocebo's job to create these programs as survival processes."

"Yes. But brother does not really care. He is just making sure the lesson is learned and the kid keeps away from water. The way this occurs is that brain fires the same neural circuits that became hardwired into the subconscious when the original state of conditioning occurred. It will do so until our state of mind changes."

"Like a new drug is used to release pain when the old does not work?"

"Yes, otherwise it will continue to produce the same expected result and release similar chemicals into the body by way of a simple thought that triggers the result. That's how eventually the programs get to be fewer and fewer that are created. You just don't believe you need more programs as the old are adequate."

"Wow, I see this now. And slowly but surely, through the process of education at an early age, family, people around you and society's common beliefs, the subconscious gets loaded with a lot of belief box programs. What is the actual physiological learning process?"

"The brain is 75% water and has 100 billion neurons suspended in an aqueous environment. Each nerve cell looks like wiggly branches and has root systems that connect and disconnect to other cells where there could be anywhere from 1,000 to 100,000 of them depending on where it resides. In the neo-cortex this is 10,000 to 40,000 per neuron. Each is like a biocomputer with huge amounts of Read Only Memory to process 100's and 1,000's of functions per second. As you learn things, neurons make new connections, exchanging electrochemical information called synaptic connections. If learning is making a new synaptic connection then remembering is keeping these connections wired together to create long term memory. The creation of these connections and the ways they change over time alters the physical neural structure of the brain. As the brain makes changes, your thoughts produce a blend of chemicals called neurotransmitters to do this."

"So these fire up the program creating reactions."

"Yes. When you think thoughts, neurotransmitters at one branch of one neuron tree cross the synaptic gap to reach the root of another neuron tree and an electrical bolt of information is fired. The same thought keeps firing the same ways to strengthen the relationship between the cells so they can more easily convey the signal next time they fire. This way the brain shows physical evidence of learning and remembering. This is the process called synaptic potentialization or selective strengthening."

"And this is recorded in the subconscious?"

"It is but the brain also has access to this through a commonality. When jungles of neurons fire in unison to support a new thought, an additional chemical protein is created within the nerve cell and it makes its way to the nucleus, then lands in DNA to switch on several genes. The job of the genes is to make proteins that maintain function and structure of body. The nerve cell then makes new proteins to create new branches between nerve cells. Repeated thoughts or experiences also affect the physical structure as the brain becomes more enriched microscopically. Creating new thoughts can therefore change you neurologically, chemically and genetically. You gain 1,000's of new connections in a matter of seconds from novel learning, new ways of thinking and fresh experiences. So by thought alone you can activate new genes right away just by changing your mind."

"Aha, so this is your domain of mind over matter?"

"Yes, but there is much more than that. These are all normal functions and process through the human design in DNA but as you have learned it gets harder and harder to institute new programs. I am about opening the other 90% of human potential in that design. The brain does not know the difference between imagination and your so called reality. Thus anything that you can imagine is possible but you have to evolve through that second stage of evolution to be able to do it, and work with me as you in disguise."

"Are you telling me that evolving into the next stage opens to the external reality being imagined?"

"I am indeed, but it is much too soon to understand that. Leave it for now. Many of your earth studies show repeating strengthens neurons to remember next time but the synaptic connection soon disappears and the memory is erased if this is not reinforced or continued. It is important to continually update, review, and remember new thoughts, choices, habits, beliefs, experiences to solidify these neurological patterns in the brain. The brain will keep using the same hardware of physical neural networks and will create a software program as an autonomic neural network. That is how programs are installed in the brain. The hardware creates the software and the software is embedded into the hardware and every time the software is needed, it reinforces the hardware."

"That is how the group limits get embedded in your own subconscious to create the limitations that I have!"

"Odd course. Your old circuits are hardwired. Your new science states that *neuron cells that fire together wire together*. The fixed pattern becomes a finite signature of automatic programs called your identity – like a box in your brain limiting you inside that box that holds all your beliefs, perceptions and related programs."

"So is there an easy way to create new programs?"

THE PLACEBO AND BRAIN IN ACTION

"Let me explain how this is normally working. In this case we have someone who has a horrific event that occurs. In this case it is a public speaking situation that turns out to be a horrible experience. It becomes a situation that creates reactions all through the body; heart rate, fear, sweating, nausea, and a cascade of emotions that one can well imagine if the speaking engagement went badly. The autonomic nervous system that functions subconsciously below conscious would of course be on the spot to memorize these emotional chemical signals to create automatic physiological changes and record this as a program in subconscious ready to be run on demand. From then on all you would have to do is bring a thought of the event into the conscious mind and it would trigger the same chemicals and physiological changes automatically."

"You would not even consciously know what the brain and subconscious were doing."

"Precisely. You automatically and autonomically associate this with the future or current thought of the event with past emotional meaning of the event so it becomes a conditional response to execute the program to create that feeling. One then lives in the past because you can't replace the program and even the thought of it makes you sick to your stomach. It will continue until the time you take charge of the mind and issue a new state of mind that would result as a new possibility like a wonderful presentation and this means you need to change the perception about future events. The event was embossed and patterned neurologically as a physical memory physically wired in brain and programmed to create chemically and physical processes. So a new event that overrides the old would have to be created so as to delete the old program in subconscious."

"That is like carrying this load of karma."

"That is perceptive of you. Because feelings and emotions are the end products of your experiences, and it is your emotional energy bodies that are here to engage through the body, feelings are the true direct doorway to the subconscious. In this case, your five senses capture the event and relay this to the brain. Mobs of nerve cells organize into fresh networks to reflect the event where circuits gel the brain makes a chemical to signal body and alter physiology through the chemistry like feeling or emotion. The event created a cause and effect and the memory of it created your conditioned process. So as you recall the event over and over in your mind it produces the same chemical and same level of mind in the brain and body to reaffirm the conditioning process."

"Until you deal with this issue and overcome it."

"And there are several ways you reprogram. As body acts as your subconscious mind, it does not know the difference between actual events and that created by emotions, or the emotions you created by remembering the event. The body believes it is living the same experience over and over. You fire and wire the circuits of the brain creating long term memory. Now the conscious mind has no control for as you think about it again, in seconds, a host of conditional responses from the brain and body pharmacy manifest the same effect – all from a single thought – the same as the placebo. You have enslaved yourself by the body as it has become the mind and trapped you in that environment lost in past time."

"Ok, so it can be the mind alone that chooses the consequence in the body. It fires up the brain to trigger the chemicals and physiological cascade of effects. It is like the placebo or the nocebo that you are choosing."

"Yes. You can choose to keep trying until you succeed and the emotional glory rewires the program. Or you can convince your subconscious by seeing and feeling your success. One is matter over mind, the other is mind over matter."

"I see. But it may not be easy to change the belief of failure."

CHANGING YOUR MIND

"That is the thinking that limits you. In order to create new programs you must think outside this limiting box – change your mind and know and feel the new possibility. The process of growing, changing, and adopting is called Neuroplasticity. It is where the brain fires different sequences, patterns, and combinations as new choices, or thoughts outside the boxes that lead to new behaviors, experiences, new emotions, and a new identity."

"That sounds pretty hard. But we still learn new things even as an old opinionated fart."

"Indeed you do. You continue to create your reality within the consciousness box you have created and within the global box. But to really change the old one you have to work harder at it. And to do something outside the box means you really need to change thinking to dissolve the limitations of the big box and your own. To change you have to become conscious of the unconscious self which is just a set of hardwired programs and not make the same choices every day. You must begin to break old habits and create new ones. You must think about and perceive reality differently to see life through the lens of a new mind. Leave the same predictable self connected to same thoughts, choices, behavior and feeling and step into the void of the unknown. You do this by repeated firing and rewiring. The old self must die then you have the power to embrace the new."

"But to what? What is a new self?"

"Well, remember what we talked about in managing energies. Remember what we said about placebo power? You have to start thinking and behaving outside the common belief boxes that you reflect and continue your graduate school out of the physical world my brother has you trapped in. As we continue, this will become very clear."

"I will tell you this. The frontal lobe is behind the forehead and is your big creative center. It learns new things, dreams new possibilities, makes conscious decisions, sets intentions and basically is the CEO of the physical world. It allows you to observe who you are, evaluate what you are doing and how you are feeling. It's all about consciousness. In the process of learning new things, the frontal lobe becomes a problem because it gets too opinionated about the old stuff in the box. It can be used for learning new things about your physical world and creating your identity as your lower self but it will sabotage anything that is not part of the norm because your own mind has accepted these as your belief system."

"Ok, I see, that is where your brother carries on and hogs the evolution to create a strong ego and build great survival tactics. This is why the process like meditation gets you into an altered state where your brother can't be heard?"

"Exactly. The beta brain-mind becomes his paradise of yelling and screaming into your consciousness to become tougher and more powerful using that great place for his view of creativity called the frontal lobe. His job is to develop your Lower Self. He gets carried away but you do have to understand that it is still your choice to listen to him. Of course he directs that CEO of the frontal lobe that has connections to all other parts of the brain. It creates intention (say to be healthy) and starts selecting networks of neurons to create a new state of mind to respond."

"But he is not totally in charge. It is the subconscious that directs him."

"Yes, but through this frontal lobe he can orchestrate neural nets to fire in unison. As you focus on clear intention there will come a moment when thought will become the experience in your mind – where inner reality is more real than outer. Once thought becomes the experience you begin to feel the emotions of how the event would feel in reality. This is how a trauma is programmed instantly. Emotions are the chemical signature of experiences. The brain makes that chemical messenger called a neuropeptide and sends it to the cells in the body, looking for the appropriate docking receptor so it can deliver the message to hormonal centers then DNA to get the message a new event has occurred. DNA turns on genes or turns down others to support this new state of being. When a gene lights up it is activated to make protein, when diminished it deactivates and does not produce proteins. Here you see the effect with measureable changes in the physical body."

"Is this also part of creating the impossible?"

"Stem cells are partially responsible for the impossible. These undifferentiated cells become specialized as raw potential when these blank states are active they morph into whatever kind of cell the body needs; like muscles, bones, skin, immune system, for example in order to replace the injured or damaged cells in tissues organs and systems. For example in a cut skin local trauma sends a signal to genes from outside the cell. The gene turns on to make the appropriate proteins to instruct stem cells to turn into healthy functioning skin cells. Millions of these processes occur all the time. Healing attributed to this type of expression has been documented in liver, muscle, skin, bone marrow, brain, and heart. In fact, the brain and body create the perfect pharmacy to alter the internal condition – a new state of being as mind and body work together as one. This is particularly evident in so many cases that medicine says are impossible to heal."

"A new state of being is one outside the box, and that means the frontal lobe, right?"

"The frontal lobe will sabotage things abnormal to its lower reality. You understand that in your world these miracles outside the boxes happen all the time. The one that is the most dramatic as you know, is the placebo. We will discuss this later. The midbrain is actually your miracle maker. You do not create miracles now because most are caught up in 'cause and effect' and time bondage. You cannot experience anything without time and effect. Understand that currently, miracles are being disallowed by the neo-cortex which includes the frontal lobe. This is the part of the brain that disallows anything instantaneous to happen."

"This midbrain is your brother's territory, right?"

"Not the midbrain. He dominates the neo-cortex where all the action of logic, ego, and power to survive reside in a time based reality of past and future which he is always nattering about. In the midbrain there is no time construct or difference between reality and imagination. That's why you have to get out of that brain wave territory of beta. So let us turn our attention to this brother of mine and his domain."

7

THE HOME OF SUPERNOCEBO

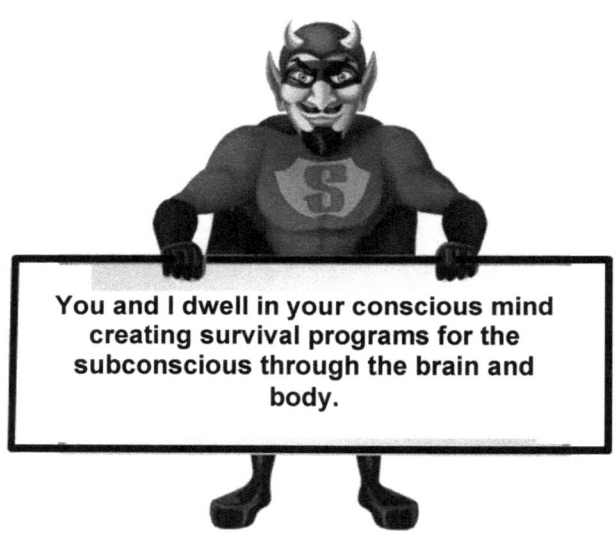

You and I dwell in your conscious mind creating survival programs for the subconscious through the brain and body.

"Now as I understand this, your brother has the responsibility of evolving a strong ego and Lower Self able to survive in the lower physical reality."

"Yes, and he becomes particularly active in the selection of programs necessary for survival in that lower physical environment. When the Beta brain becomes activated in the normal evolution of the human vessel, he is always their guiding thoughts and actions that develop that self identity according to his 12 rules that we talked about before."

WHERE SUPERNOCEBO GETS CARRIED AWAY

"Supernocebo has certainly created a Lower Self in me as ego. I have most definitely been listening to him."

"Hence you have received what you created. Your brain performs a multitude of sensory, vital and physical tasks that it learns in order to guarantee survival in the business world. It is a complex information processing and control system dedicated to controlling how the body and mind function and adapt to its environment. The nervous system, the senses, the mobility, the internal functioning are automated environmental stimuli-response systems that fire-wire these programs. And this is what Supernocebo is dedicated to guiding."

"Also, although the brain is in charge of the physical body, and is very engaged in creating the stimulus-response systems at an early age, it is not in charge of the subconscious; it takes directives from the subconscious and the cell membranes. It is designed to sense and respond so as to create a database of perception-response functions. It holds its own database to remember and execute these on conscious and subconscious command. A copy is held in the master disc drive of the subconscious mind."

"And in the early stages of Delta and Gamma, that subconscious is like an open book, easily programmable from the perceptions created by the child."

"Exactly. Now, when the child reaches 12 and the beta consciousness of the rational thinking mind comes into play, Supernocebo now gets his name because he will not give up his fight for ego, profit and power. He dominates the conscious mind at the expense of the body and is in love with commerce and kingship."

"Hmmm. I can recall our talk about his 12 rule philosophy. So he does a great job to help the human body survive to develop the ego and a strong self identity as unique but obviously there are many consequences of that negative stuff as I have learned. One of the ways he does this is to support the idea of one against the world to develop habits and programs that help the ego prosper. To him a state of well being means surviving well in a world of severe competition. That has indeed been my philosophy."

"And that is fine when the evolution is with a young strong resilient mind that wants to be a unique identity. But he does not share the development of a softer identity full of love, peace, harmony and spiritual being."

"Of course I have a whole different attitude of wellbeing. As he lives in the beta consciousness, he is always niggling and enforcing the need for a state of his wellbeing, you need to be aware that in highly emotional negative states cells do not get signals clearly."

"I know, this is where he gets his name. His name of 'harm' makes sense because I can tell you, this ego is concerned about the material world and those rules that he takes to extreme."

"Yes, he does not balance it with me. But it goes beyond just triggering emotion and physical consequences like in our examples of public speaking and fear of water. Unfortunately there are consequences of this as he pushes the sequence of automatic subconscious fight or flight programs at the expense of the body and that then escalates into a selfish non spiritual realty. Fight or flight is a programmed stimulus response system in you that is there for your very survival."

"This is where you get a rush of adrenalin, right?"

"Yes, but listen. This auto-program tucked away in subconscious causes stress and when activated creates automatic cascades of interfering processes that create a whole scenario of negative things in your body. For example this forces healing to take longer."

"Is that why in a hospital they insist on rest and wellbeing in a less stressful environment!"

"Yes, because if the body and mind are dealing with beta, and consequences of anger, conflict, fear and causing interference which prevents coherence for turning on stem cells into useful cells. So healing is restricted."

"This process is an example of what is known as downward causation. The thought triggers the neural networks that create neuropeptides which embark as epigenetic signals to the cells. This creates activation of cell receptors sites and then activates DNA selection and regulation processes. This creates the expression of proteins to influence the expression of life for a healthy body which is all about the autonomic nervous system managed by the brain."

"Technically, the autonomic nervous system is under control of the limbic brain which is the emotional or chemical center responsible for subconscious functions. Emotions activate this brain and as it exists below consciousness mind control, emotion activates the autonomic nervous system and bypasses the neo-cortex. As you move beyond the thinking brain you move into an area where health is regulated, maintained and executed. This is the way to enter the operating system and make a program change because you are now instructing the nervous system to begin creating the corresponding chemistry. The body becomes the mind emotionally."

"So fear, anger, futility won't signal the proper genes because they turn on flight or fight survival mode. Trying to do something repeatedly may bring stress as the same struggle attempting to force an outcome knocks you out of balance."

"You are saying that the more analytical, the less is the suggestibility to this programming process?"

"Exactly. Polarity as good-bad creates conflict and stress and pumps chemicals to further the analytical cycle more. If you are calm, it works for you. Ego as an extension of the conscious mind is designed to protect you so it will derail the process with a rush of addictive emotion to get more power and move further away from the operating system. The exception occurs when that elevated emotion has an impact to create trauma programs of response."

"Whoa! I can now understand clearly why you need to meditate into an altered state to get this problem and Supernocebo out of the way!"

"Cells are unconsciously driven to the fight or flight reactions to service a hostile environment. His very philosophy of what he calls higher development is one of conflict and stress. These cells have moving parts as proteins as building blocks to generate the cell's behavior. Each has 150,000 parts as pathways as assemblies of proteins for breathing, digestion, and so on. These behave as switches in the cell's membrane and get proteins in motion. Then biological gauges convert information via sensations to produce chemicals. For example when threatened, immune cells release messengers into the blood. When these are recognized by the membrane receptors on blood vessel cells in the brain, they forward a byproduct molecule into the brain which activates fever pathways to produce shivering and high temperature."

"And the signals that cause this can be both energetic and physical like air, food, or news, and they all activate protein movement to generate behavior. The way this is triggered is by a coupling of protein molecules with complementary environment signals. It causes a shape change expressed by movement in the cell membrane which animates the cell, bringing it to life."

"The brain of this operation is in the cell membrane where these switches respond to environment signals thus relaying information into the internal protein pathways. Some respond to estrogen, adrenalin, calcium, or whatever their design calls for. There can be 100,000 switches in a cell. Each membrane switch is a unit of perception with receptor and effector proteins. So a receptor receives signals through the senses for example and moves to bind the effector. A second signal is sent by effector into cytoplasm that controls specific protein functions and pathways. So once again, perception controls behaviors. These switches also activate genes in the nucleus to draw out a needed blueprint from DNA if it is required."

"Are you saying that dis-ease and dysfunction is because of defective proteins or distorted signals from trauma, toxicity and thoughts that misinterpret the environment in a negative way?"

"Of course I am. Consider that cells, tissues, and organs do not question information from the nervous system. Once triggered, the brain and supporting nervous system are the regulating mechanism that coordinates all these pathways. These pathways will include using genes as blueprints to make protein parts. But it had to get through the cells of the brain first."

"That's a lot of stuff to understand. Can you give me an example?"

"Yes. Let us work through an example. Cells accept or reject food by membrane perception switches them on like histamines for example. A body wide system emergency response like this is the adrenalin - alpha (protection) and beta (growth response present) switches. When both histamines and adrenalin are released by the nervous system, adrenalin overrides histamines signals that are local."

"Now consider the power of thought as the system does not distinguish between real and non-real. The placebo effect studies prove mind over matter is real just through positive thinking. Similarly the nocebo effect of negative thinking is possible the same way."

"Like when the Doc says you have cancer, and have 3 months to live?"

"If you accept and surrender to that belief, then yes, it will be so. It is so programmed in the subconscious and the society's belief system, so it is easy to accept that fate. Negative thoughts can truly manifest disease. That is why my brother begins to harm people with his incessant survival thinking that you accept as your thinking. In your world it is reported that one third of medical healings are placebo. But what percentage is nocebo when 70% are negative thoughts brought on by fear or doctors?"

"But let's get back to our example. Protection mode inhibits the creation of energy, growth, and vitality. This is controlled by the nervous system in response to stress. This happens through external process called HPA or hypothalamus-pituitary-adrenal process much like the fight or flight reaction where stress hormones are triggered in the body suppressing or inhibiting normal function everywhere."

"Where?"

"The three key ones are the immune system to fight disease, the visceral digestive area, and the ability to think. This is why if you are frightened you are dumber. Obviously the built in firmware doesn't think you need to waste any resources on eating, thinking or internal immunity when the issues occur. Trouble is, this system doesn't know if the issue is imaginary or real."

"So if you are scared, upset, in conflict you don't care to eat, your immunity is screwed and you are dumber! Wow, we live in a world of fear and threat activating HPA and releasing stress hormones continuously. If 70% of our thoughts are negative, that's a lot of negative stuff going into the process of screwing up body health!"

"It may not be evident when young and healthy but over time you get more and more vulnerable. Many are finding that almost every illness has now been linked to stress. Subconscious is an emotionless database of stored programs that creates hardwire behavior response with no judgment; a programmable hard drive into which your experiences are downloaded. The subconscious does not decide whether an order is bad or good, positive or negative. It simply checks its disk drives to see what is ok (belief sub-drive) and does it without question. If it is already there then it is the belief system and emotional intensity that can make the change."

"The two mind components are like a dynamic duo operating together. Subconscious takes over the moment conscious is not paying attention. To alter the program one has to change the belief because it is the program that creates patterns in realty. The universe of thought and emotion changes belief because they are already working at a higher energy or quantum level; ready to put input into those micro chip cells. When you really know, and really believe you deserve something, then you can have it. You simply know it to be true so it will happen."

"The state of stress and negativity either physical or emotional suppresses many biological processes that inhibit normal functions. Wow! This is why a state of well being of peace and love are enhancers of these biological functions. I can see why it is so important to have a state of well being that is positive rather than negative. It is because my inventory of negative crap just builds and attracts more of it. And at the same time I am stressing my physical biology; and halting my progress in the spiritual evolution. If Supernocebo is ignored with his I harm philosophy, then I see you as Superplacebo begin to take the reign in the evolution. Then I can watch my portfolio of energies and fill it with good stuff. My body will feel better and I can begin to open up to higher abilities."

"Well said. Plus you begin to get access to the other 90% of those programs tucked away in DNA. Always remember that gratitude, love, and appreciation opens the heart and lifts. The emotional energy of gratitude is one of the most powerful emotions to lift the level of suggestibility. Giving thanks shows gratitude for already happened events. Gratitude is the ultimate state of receivership; selfless as a creative emotion versus selfish survival emotions."

IMPLICIT AND EXPLICIT MEMORY

"But we have not finished this story if Supernocebo continues his incessant babbling about survival. The conscious mind makes up 5% and represents your will, logic, creativity, and reasoning. It is called the explicit or declarative memory dedicated to semantic (learned) and episodic (experience). But that conscious mind is the vocal one and that is the one that everybody has been programmed to listen to so Supernocebo has done a great job to fill the subconscious mind with a lot of programs."

"The subconscious mind takes on the whopping 95% as implicit or non declarative memory as the programmed operating system. Here is where those first years as a kid and teenager have programmed skills, habits, emotional reactions, hardwired behavior, conditional responses, associate memories, routine thoughts and feelings, attitudes, beliefs, and perceptions."

"Implicit memory is developed from emotions of experience, especially those that are highly charged one-time emotional events that get branded into memory. The other way is through a redundancy of emotions from consistent experiences that keep firing the same way to hard wire the neural networks."

"So any high charged emotional event opens the door to the subconscious?"

"Yes. Thoughts, images and words are the language of brain and feelings are language of the body. Together they open the door to the operating system. To take from the hypnotic process, you are more suggestible when thoughts match feeling. So when you feel emotions you activate implicit memory and the autonomic nervous system."

"You mean you turn your brother to the off position!"

"That extreme fight and flight or serious emotional stress opens the programming door because as you age, it gets harder and harder to trigger the programming process. It either has to become a continued enforcement of new habits, perceptions and beliefs, an extreme trauma, or situation dramatic enough to override the old program. And like in the case of doing something more and more challenging – like an Olympic ability - it is simply less possible because the ability of the muscles is past the peak."

"If you look at your research in this area, you will see that to increase suggestibility you have to weaken the analytical mind. The best examples are cases of physical or mental fatigue and limited exposure to social, physical, environmental cues in sensory deprivation. Also common are extreme hunger, emotional shock, and trauma."

"That must be why so many rituals and cleansing practices stop eating or create intense rituals."

"Correct, except they rarely understand why they are doing it. For example, we see me as Superplacebo working best where the thought of something is enfolded with elevated emotion like the joy of being healed, hope or inspiration to a new possibility without analysis. Extreme fear acts the same way. Then the level of suggestibility influenced by feelings allows entry in the operating system and is reprogrammed in the autonomic nervous system with new orders by thought alone. Crucial to this process is to get beyond the analytical mind of the Supernocebo beta consciousness. Trauma bypasses the analytical mind. Once again, with reference to brain waves, this means getting out of beta because that is where the analytical mind lives. It forms a barrier between Low Beta and Alpha."

"That is why Hypnotherapists bring the patient down to Theta to do their work. What the hypnotist is doing is starting to shut out the conscious world of noise and bypass the process where the conscious mind gives directives for loading bio-programs at the subconscious level. Again this is in the lower Alpha to Theta range. Now the hypnotist starts suggesting things like you are very relaxed, you are going to have heavy eyelids and not hear anything but me, etcetera, etcetera. It is called getting present to self in the now. It eliminates the outside noise. They are effectively taking you down into those more programmable levels of Theta just like when you were a kid and did not have Supernocebo influencing your beliefs, actions and habits."

MIND AND MATTER ARE NOT SEPARATE

"Now you can understand the mind and matter are linked and not separate. In Supernocebo's world it is simply matter that controls the mind and he certainly has trained society to do just that with power, money, goodies to play with – all satisfying the ego. I offer the reverse; how conscious and unconscious thoughts and feelings are the blueprint controlling destiny. The perception, conviction and focus to manifest any potential future lives within the human mind of infinite potential in the quantum field. Both minds yours and mine must work together in order to bring about any future reality that potentially already exists."

"In Supernocebo's world conditional response is a subconscious program housed in the body that overrides the conscious mind and takes charge. Over time, the body is conditioned to become the mind as conscious thought is no longer in control. For example the autonomic nervous system creates internal changes in the body by associating past memories with expectation of internal effect through associate memory until they actually occur. The stronger the conditioning, the less conscious control and more automatic is the programming."

"It is known in the study of Neurobiology that if you keep taking the same substance the brain keeps firing the same circuits the same way memorizing what the substance does – conditioned to the effect by familiar internal change from past experiences. Because of this conditioning, a placebo activates the same hard wired circuit. Associate memory elicits a subconscious program that makes a connection between pill and the hormonal change in the body and signals go out to make the related change."

"Ok, that's all pretty heavy stuff. What I find so fascinating is that these religious, ancient wisdoms and even new age practices create so many processes and beliefs that try to get around Supernocebo to heal the mind and body. So Supernocebo is branded Satan because he's the evil dude keeping you in sin when he is just doing his job."

8

THE HOME OF SUPERPLACEBO

You and I dwell in your energetic copy of your physical body as your subconscious mind

"You have a much better understanding now of where my brother dwells. But remember that he has a job to do and even though he gets carried away, each individual still has a choice on the acceptance or rejection of the philosophies. The spiritual path is simply not of interest to the majority. You yourself have been on that lower path."

"I am well aware of that now."

"My brother has the rotten image of Supernocebo because he has been branded by many as the devil who makes you sin. It is true that he takes his job seriously and will not let go to let me do my job but he is focused on self preservation and growth in the world of matter. There are also those who take these to extremes that want to have an evil experience. These are subgroups of consciousness. But his philosophy is what forms a group consciousness, so I have to be ok with that because everyone has a choice. Now to look at where I dwell, are you familiar with your energetic counterparts?"

"What do you mean?"

"Let me now test your constitution with the information that has always been in your ancient and current metascience world. It is about where I dwell as pure energy."

"Ok, you may find I know quite a lot about this. After all, I found you in the depth of silence and peace of an altered state. Meditation is not foreign to this kid and I am knowing now of the chakra energetic system and have heard of the light body. Is that what you mean?"

THE ENERGETIC BODY ANATOMY

"Good. Part of this belief shift is to understand where I live, which is in the energetic world of the non-material. The thing is that the human form also has more to it than its physical body which is all Supernocebo cares about. Anatomically, it is made up of many different bodies that all function together. And these are the ones that open new abilities for anyone willing to go into the second phase of spiritual evolution. If not, then Supernocebo holds the reigns; that awareness, that power, and those capabilities resident in the higher vibratory energy bodies is simply not developed and it gets harder and harder with age to awaken these."

"When you say live or where you dwell, you do not really have a physical organ or place you dwell. You are both really in the mind which is not really anywhere."

"As you come to understand this, yes, your mind is not a physical thing. It is quantum being everywhere and no where. There are places of quantum interfaces like the heart and the brain but these are energetic counterparts. There is a perfect copy of the physical body in these higher vibratory parts, everything that is created in the physical below has a copy above. But as you will come to understand it is the above that can cause an effect below if you can get out of the limiting box of your personal conscious mind and the limits of the global or community consciousness."

"Are you going to explain this quantum thing which appears to be the new scientific rage these days?"

"I will. Your norm is used to seeing the anatomical side of your material bodies as atoms and particles. But what about the subtle energy parts which are just energy? One of the bodies is described as the enveloping Causal or Soul Body which appears to many as a golden orb. That is how I would appear to you. It is the subtlest level of personal individuality, the enlivening source of life and consciousness for the current personality, all past life personalities, and all future life personalities. It is commonly called the Higher-Self but it is really me as Superplacebo."

"Well what are you, really?"

"You have to answer the question of what is consciousness. What is your mind? It is really no thing and everything, no where and everywhere. It has a form that your mind or consciousness decides to attach to it. If anything it is simply a sea of information which is now called a quantum sea of energy that has intelligence, purpose and encompasses everything that was, is and will be. To your mind which is here in this sea of higher or greater consciousness, you simply create in your mind what we look like and that can come from you, or from what others may believe. You take it out of your awareness and form an image and I can look like an orb, a ghost, an angel, a shining light, a deity, or Superplacebo. For your purpose, you can just say that I am a Soul as a piece of that greater consciousness and the Higher Self is a descriptive means of connecting the higher and lower bodies. But consciousness is unified as one so really it becomes an awareness at your end that determine how you use and understand the oneness. It does not really matter what it is called as long as you get the idea that it is consciousness that does not die and is pure energy, the same as your quantum mind."

"And as we communicate telepathically and I see these pictures and hear these thoughts, I am in a place where these higher abilities allow this."

THE ENERGY BODY HIGHER PLANES

"Yes. There is much discussion and many interpretations of these different planes and bodies that make up the anatomy of the human, but let us attempt to go through the more common names in order to gain a basic understanding. The number and names of the layers vary according to different spiritual models and theories."

"Your whole energy body system is luminous light made up of layers like an onion. These are interrelated energy fields with special purposes and the ones that are more visible that glow closer to the physical body are commonly referred to as auras. The Energy Body is a vehicle of consciousness that exists as frequency levels on these subtle planes."

"Would that be like ice, water, steam as different vibrational levels of the same thing?"

"Yes. There are many energy bodies. Each has a specific purpose and each, from the high to the low, reflects levels of frequency vibration. These become denser and denser as they progress from above to below, from what is commonly referred to as higher dimensions or planes."

"What plane am I in now talking to you?

"You are in the lower part of the astral plane which is an interface plane and it is easy to communicate through using your energetic chakras."

"Ok, show me a picture."

"Here is a picture I am bringing into your 3rd eye awareness for you see the bigger scope of these bodies. There are three basic groups."

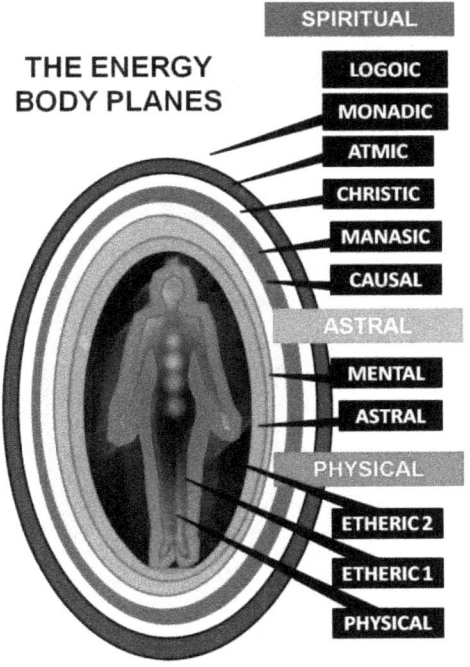

"Wow, that's a lot of bodies!"

"What we want to talk about are the bodies from the causal down into the physical. In a sense, we are showing the progression or what we can call Downward Causation of as *above to below* as key energy components of the total human anatomy at different levels of energy vibration. Because I reside here and you are here now with me, these are the key bodies to understand in how they relate to the human physical body. Do you understand the idea of dimensions?"

"Yes, commonly, many forward thinking people refer to these stages of body energy as being in the 3rd dimension which is our lower plane of reality."

"Above that are 4D and then the 5D place of higher energy state that resides in the quantum field. Here there is no space or time and everything is connected as one. It is a level where you and I as a Soul or Higher Self reside as pure consciousness. That is where I as Superplacebo orchestrate the spiritual connections for those who can attune to them. This is where I experience your engagements of emotions. This is where I deal with my karmic needs. Now let us look at the different bodies proceeding downward from above to below from nonmatter to matter. Each has a specific purpose becoming denser and denser in frequency vibration."

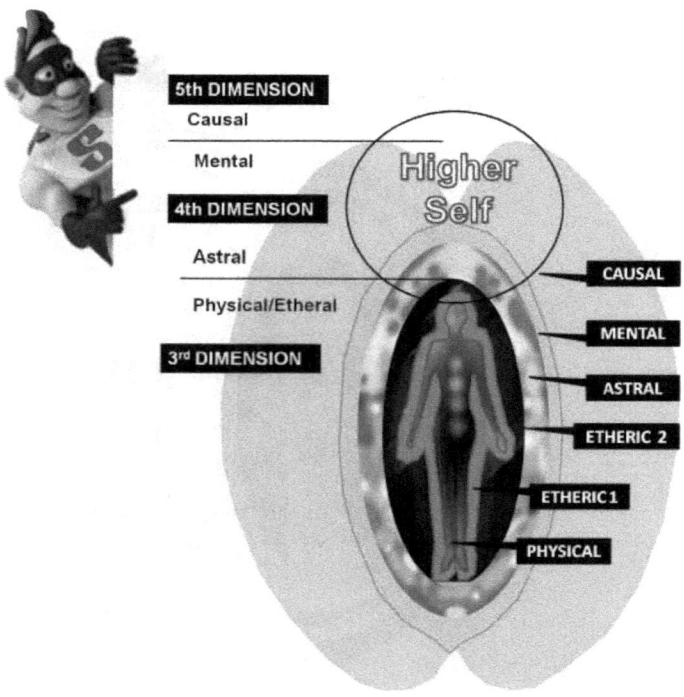

"This is where we are now."

"You are at the lower end of the Higher Self bubble compartment that encompasses the 3rd, 4th, and 5th dimensional levels as pure consciousness. Let us say it is the Astral level. I as Soul straddle all levels of consciousness which is why I can chat with you when you are back in your usual awareness."

"Each body is integrated with the next one down, totally interfaced. The Causal or Soul Body is named *causal* because it is the originating source of each personality that incarnates in each lifetime. It is the source of your personality, causing it to be and exist. When your personality ends, the essence of you is absorbed back into the Causal Body. It is the first level of your individuality that is relatively immortal as the Causal Body exists permanently recording your journey as a human through many incarnations or lifetimes."

"Is this one of many lifetimes?"

"Yes. Although this may give you a conundrum now, understand that these many lifetimes are simply multidimensional journeys occurring without time at the same time."

"Yes, that does give me a 'don't compute' signal. I am sure you will explain."

"The next is the Mental or Intellectual Body seen as a blue for those who can see it. It is the vehicle for understanding, for beliefs, thoughts, knowledge, and cognitive processes. The Mental Body is my higher mind and interfaces through the lower bodies of Astral or Emotional to use the Etheric body as what provides the vitality of spirit to support life. That then interfaces to the Physical for experiencing the Personality. The mental body and the emotional energy bodies use the body for the engagement of my purpose to evolve my spiritual essence as my contribution to the whole. The key, however is that the higher mental is rooted in the energy of the midbrain while the higher emotional is rooted in the heart chakra. The means of me thinking and feeling is through language and feeling."

"Yes, I remember the heart chakra as the balance point of above and below. Is that where Supernocebo is rooted in the bottom chakras while you are in the top?"

"That is partially true. We are more focused on these areas of responsibility true but as you learned in the stages of evolution, the real responsibility is for us to balance these upper and lower through the heart. The Astral body is also called the Emotional Body as it is the vehicle for emotion, desire, imagination, personal power, and has a focus of expressing and experiencing feeling. Again, I am rooted here in the Astral as it is the emotional center that gets expressed through the physical body and its sensory systems."

"So are you saying that mental and emotional bodies are the two key things used by You as a Soul to engage the physical body through the brain and heart?"

"Yes, it is so I can express and experience these through you as mind and body. It is for me to work away at my karmic balance sheet. The Astral Body gives you the ability to feel desires, emotions, imagination, and psychic abilities. It lends power to thought and mental abilities which is the Mental Body's territory essential for effective action and manifestation. Thought is the language of the brain while emotions are the language of the body."

"What about images and words?"

"They actually are the language of the midbrain encompassing the third eye and the throat chakra."

"Really? Are you going to tell me about that?"

"Of course. We are leading up to that. The next body is the Etheric or Vital Body. It is the vehicle for energy and vitality, the subtle basis for the physical body. It is where the chakras and meridians and ley lines of the upper energies connect to the specific area of responsibility in the physical body."

"These chakras keep coming up all the time. Are you going to explain these in more detail?"

"Indeed, as soon as we get through this more general anatomy. As we follow the progression, we get to the Physical Body as the vehicle for stability, separation, and individual focus. It is the human physical vessel that is designed to be the engaging party for the Life Plan experience. The higher mental expression is through language and the brain. The higher emotional expression is through the body and the heart."

"As you now understand the brain has the responsibility of maintaining the body in accordance with DNA evolution, process and purpose, and it has the responsibility to create the holographic reality where you and I are able to play out the Life Plan."

"This thing you call a life plan and my individual personality seems to be all orchestrated and preset. Is this true?"

"It is because it is me that needs to work off my karma and attain a higher evolution through you as my partner. So we made a plan to do this. The personality is composed of the mental, emotional, etheric and physical bodies as a unit. The personality is very temporary and is changed or recreated every lifetime, effectively erasing past life memories on a personality level."

"I hope you will explain this plan deal. But you say that all past life experience, knowledge, and developed ability is retained in the Causal body which is your individual consciousness."

"Mine and yours if you open to the awareness of it. The Soul Body level as the Causal Body is eternal. The interface to the physical plane is through the Astral and Etheric bodies which insures character, behavior and physiological/chemical processes conform to the contracted design formed by the astral substance at birth."

"Astral substance at birth? Really!"

"We are getting there, be patient and open minded. The Higher Self and Soul exist as pure timeless-spaceless consciousness. They are a non local part of the quantum field as one consciousness meaning nowhere and everywhere, yet all interconnected as one sea of greater consciousness. The aspect of nonlocality allows all Souls to be one and know about each other at any instant; so what occurs in one occurs in the other as instant communication. It is like the cells in your body all know what to do instantly. In addition the Higher Self and Soul are interconnected and interfaced to the energetic bodies to the brain of the physical brain. In this way, they not only oversee all the stuff going on in the bodies, they have a connection to the physical brain via the quantum part of it linked between the quantum field of non-matter and the physical matter. It is through this connection that I maintain connectivity to you and your affairs below."

"This is where I need to be to effect changes down below? In this interconnecting astral place?"

"When you get into this astral territory you then are straddling the place of interface between non-matter and matter. It is what you know as 4D. In this place consciousness becomes one mental faculty because now the distinction between reality and non-reality does not exist. It is simply consciousness without bounds. That is why, upon entering this place of nowhere land, astral experiences, like some of the near death experiences, dreams, fantasies, out of body experiences, hallucinations, imagination, and visions, a whole new world opens."

"And this is where you develop the higher abilities?"

"They are only released from DNA which already has them. But they need to be opened from this higher place of awareness otherwise they lie dormant like in the stages of evolution. This is so because it is limited to the consciousness and beliefs of the lower plane where the physical world exists. But you are correct; this is the place where you open to your greater potential as a human being. You will see in many Near Death Experience cases new abilities that are all part of the astral inventory come with the return. We will talk about this in another session on Astral Projection."

"What are these abilities?"

"In your lower world you see tastes of higher abilities that some have. These are energy healing, bilocation, materialization, clairvoyance, seeing the future, remote viewing, to name a few. These all come forward because you are entering a place that is outside the box that says such things are crazy. But at the astral level, we are looking at expansion of the old five senses. These five astral senses are clairaudience or astral hearing, psychometry known as astral touch/feeling, clairvoyance or astral sight, imagination as an astral equivalent of taste, and emotional idealism as the astral equivalent of smell."

"How large is this astral energy field?"

"The Astral Body has a figure form in the shape of the Physical Body and an aura usually in an ovoid shape pointed at both ends. The aura extends about 4 to 9 feet from the Physical Body. It has 7 major energy centers, 21 minor energy centers, and many smaller centers, just like the etheric body. It is constantly changing color, dark to brilliant colors depending upon your mood."

"The mood being these chakras again?"

"Yes, as we discussed, they can be negative or positive. They are the way I feel through you."

"Can these abilities be awakened easily?"

"Astral and emotional consciousness is primarily awakened through the stimulation of desire. Awareness of the Astral Universe is awakened by meditation, psychic development techniques, out of body travel techniques, shamanic practices, lucid dreaming, drugs - especially psychedelics, certain pranayama practices, certain types of trauma, biochemical imbalances, and certain types of energetic stimulation can do this as well."

"These are all metaphysical and ancient practices."

"True, but it is this ancient wisdom that has been ignored. What I want to say here is that there is much more to awakening these higher vibrational qualities than a simple statement that it is possible. Those who have accomplished these higher vibration states have not sat around simply dreaming. Others have them as gifts they have decided to bring into their Life Plan. Many have in some way trained themselves to get into the right state or environment and have become familiar with understanding and experiencing the Out of Body consciousness where they have discovered a new empowering world and reality to be available. It is through astral projection into that place of astral interface. Many refer to this as astral projection because it is the astral part of us that straddles the physical and nonphysical reality."

"And this is where I need to be?"

"In order for you to evolve as you were meant to, yes. Your bottom line is that this is a desirable place to be if you want to link with the void of the quantum field and pick up some very cool abilities and begin to more proactively control your life from out of your box. When you have a visit with me as your higher counterpart and understand our anatomical nature, you can understand we are consciousness as pure energy, residing in the quantum world and consciousness as part of everything that is, is interconnected to it and resides within a quantum field of infinite possibilities. It is just like your mind and imagination do but are incapable of reaching outside the box to utilize the powers. This is the place you want to go to get access to that Life Plan I created and to change reality below from above. All you have to do is go here and speak to me as your partner in human and spiritual evolution."

"Yes, I understand, I have to talk to myself in a different form and open a soul-heart mind."

"I want you to understand a very key part of the energy bodies. It is about the process you call as above so below and Upward/downward Causation. It is a process origination from the Causal Body facilitated by me in the emotional and mental bodies."

"From above, together, you and I cause a change in reality to occur below in the material reality?"

"Yes, it does not work the other way around. Supernocebo is designed to function in the lower mind in the material world and uses upward causation of matter over mind. This is your usual way of creating in your life being constrained by the limits and constraints believed in by the local and global consciousness. In this case matter is what controls and influences the mind as upward causation. I am in the nonmaterial world as mind over matter and there is no constraints and limitations. The true meaning of *as above so below* is executed from the higher mind in downward causation."

"Is this the only way to execute mind over matter?"

"No, but it is the most effective way to attain the proactive ability to create miracles and reality that are outside the boxes. Remember you become more and more limited by the limitations of your subconscious programming that is a reflection of the boxes."

9

AN ASTRAL CONNECTION

Your connection between above and below is the astral body of energetic

A WORD ABOUT CHAKRAS

"I promised you to look more closely at these chakra energy systems that you and I work through. Is your mind open enough to think astral?"

"Yes. Great. I am ready!"

"Chakras are subtle energy centers that are invisible vortexes linking your physical with your non-physical bodies. They are like energy antennas that pick up astral frequencies and link them into the physical apparatus through your vital or etheric body. Here is an image for you."

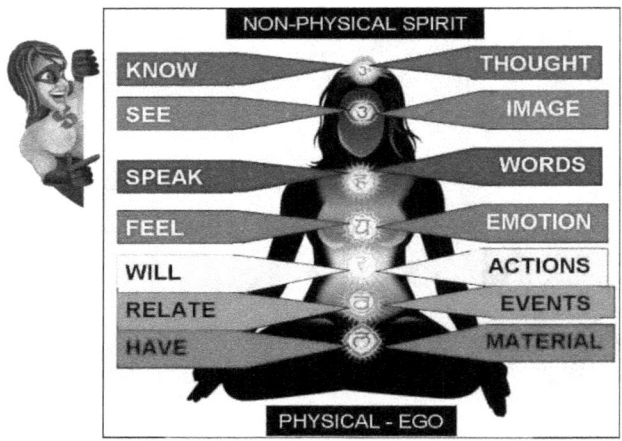

"Look at the top chakra. This shows a simple representation of main responsibility in each chakra. From the top it is the crown chakra starting in a non-physical world, you *know* a *thought*, *see* an *image at the third eye*, *speak* some *words at the throat chakra*, and *feel* an *emotion at the heart*. *These are the basic functions of these above chakras.* Assuming an action is prompted below, from that point, you move into the physical world. By using intent, you apply *will* into an *action at the solar plexus*, which will allow you to *relate* to others and physical *events at the sacral*, thereby allowing you to *have* a *material* experience in the root chakra."

"Ok, but how does this relate to physics?"

"Every part of you has an etheric double. Your heart chakra is one you have come to understand. The heart energy of emotion is not a quantifiable physical thing, but the physical part of it as the heart is quantifiable in material terms and it has specific functions in the body."

"Like the expression '*I love you from the bottom of my heart*', and '*heart of a lion*'?"

"Yes, most seldom understand this physical energetic connection. But all your important organs like the heart, having both energetic and physical qualities can be divided into areas of expression and responsibilities. More easy to understand is a heartache. It is not the physical heart giving you that ache, it is a feeling emanating from the chakra."

"So each of these can be negative or positive?"

"In terms of verbs, it becomes a choice on how you think, see, speak, feel, act and relate to others does it not? That is your free will. This image gives you a better summary of that."

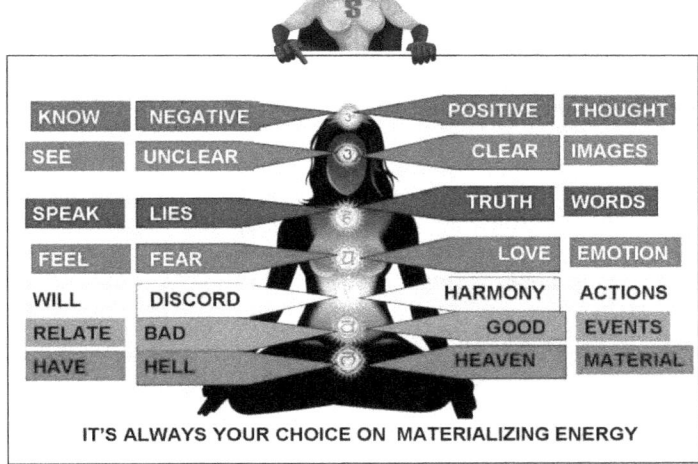

"These subtle energy centers have a direct affect on seven major groups of physical organs. These organs control the physiological and psychological functions related to the *verb* actions on the left. On the right are the resulting *subjects* from the use of the verb."

"Ok, but what does this have to do with you?"

"You can look at these as my sensory equipment that connects to you as the physical, mental and emotional expression and experience. Much like your nervous system, this is my equal to your nervous system which is energetic. This is how I am able to experience you."

"Ok, that's cool but how does this relate to the organs?"

"Look at this image that tells you what key organ and essence of your personality it affects."

Chakra	Gland	Color	I	Essence
7 Crown	Pineal	Violet	KNOW	Spiritual Connection
6 3rd Eye	Pituitary	Indigo	SEE	Intuition Awareness
5 Throat	Thyroid	Blue	SPEAK	Communication
4 Heart	Thymus	Green	FEEL	Love Expression
3 Solar Plexus	Adrenal	Yellow	WILL	Personal Power
2 Sacral	Lyden	Orange	RELATE	Sexual Capacity
1 Root	Gonads	Red	HAVE	Survival, Will to Live

"What is the Lyden gland?"

"Much like the pineal gland which is the portal of the Soul, it is where I connect to the midbrain nervous system, the Lyden gland situated behind the gonads reflects the seat of creation. It has been relegated to mysticism and of no useful function. The current norm brands these two glands as paranormal, of no significant function, or things that suggest insanity."

"Oh, there must be some hidden secret then!"

"Indeed. These two are sealed or open doors that are related to the Soul. The Lyden is a reproductive system as a motor that functions like a switch that turns the motor of creation on. It is not located in the reproductive system but its activity stimulates or activates the reproductive organs. Both pineal and lyden are doors within the body that can be opened to allow access to higher states of consciousness and creation. It is also called the Leydig gland for the one who discovered it. Both males and females have this gland."

"Are they important to understand me and you?"

"Very. You will see how as we proceed in the process of creating reality."

"So I don't get how these glands are influenced through astral. You mean Astrology don't you?"

"Well first you understand what these gland do, do you not?"

"Yes, these are part of the endocrine system; a system of glands that involve the release of extracellular signaling molecules known as hormones. The endocrine system is instrumental in regulating metabolism, growth, development, puberty, and tissue function. They also play a part in determining mood."

"Good. These endocrine glands correspond to and operate within the interetheric level of mind and matter. They are the bridge or connecting link between undifferentiated mind or spirit and the physical body. This connecting link is what explains the idea mind is cause and the physical body manifests the effects of the thought held in the mind or consciousness. You could say this is the process of how ideas or thoughts held in the consciousness affect the body and the body thereby mirrors the mind whether in health or disease."

"As above so below, the process of downward causation! I got it. And I can see the negative and positive choices of mind affecting the mind and body as an effect."

"Not only that, it is how I get this effect above that gets registered in the causal body. Hormones are chemical messengers released from endocrine glands that travel through the blood system to influence the nervous system. This regulates behaviors such as aggression, mating, and parenting of individuals. They travel to every organ and tissue in your body. What happens when there is too little or too much of a particular hormone in your body?"

"It is going to create an effect in personality, physiology, chemistry, growth, everything!"

"Good, now here is a new image for you."

PLANET	Effect on the chakras left side of the nodes' axis, influencing the receptive function of the chakra	Effect on the chakras on the right side of the nodes' axis, influencing the emissive function of the chakra
SUN	lots of high quality energy on that level both naturally and received from the others in life	increased control, mastery of that level
MOON	increased receptivity on that level, the native easily absorbs energies and information from the other or from the nature	deep feelings and a clear inner perspective on the energies of that level
MERCURY	mental receptivity on that level, the native is easily energized, fascinated by specific information, either read or heard from others	mental control, understanding, mastery of that level
VENUS	interests / hobbies / passion on that level, meetings of persons that offer him/her psychological support, the feeling of being loved	seduction power, erotism, the successful use of the feelings in order to gain control on that level
MARS	energy, dynamism, activity on that level, courageous friends	courage, dynamic action, good energetic control

JUPITER	lots of energy and resources, open interest on the level, exuberance,	power of accumulation of energy, wise, spiritual use of that energy
SATURN	few resources and lack of energy	very controlled manifestations, contracture, strategy, economy
URANUS	energy outbursts alternating with low level energy, fluctuations	spiritual, higher consciousness of the energy on that level
NEPTUNE	low physical energy, but good contact with the other worlds	spiritual use of the energy on that level
PLUTO	passion, deep understanding and feeling of the energy on that level	transformative potential, occult interests and use of the energy

"Ohhh! Planets! What is emissive and receptive?

"It is like the yin and yang, masculine and feminine but it goes further as it should be viewed as negative or positive. These are two primal polarities of astrology. The Yang pole is called Emissive, in that it emits or radiates energy outwards, whereas the Yin pole is called Receptive, since it receives, reflects and transforms the energy sent out by the complementary Emissive polarity."

"Planets that are in the projection area of one chakra will influence that chakra according to their nature and the side of the nodal axis where they are located. Those on the left side called waxing will influence the receptive part and the function of that chakra, while those on the right will influence the emissive part and function of that chakra.

Chakra	Gland	Color	Planet	Astrology House	Essence
7 Crown	Pineal	Violet	Sun		Spiritual Connection
6 3rd Eye	Pituitary	Indigo	Moon	Leo/Cancer	Intuition Awareness
5 Throat	Thyroid	Blue	Mercury	Virgo/Gemini	Communication
4 Heart	Thymus	Green	Venus	Libra/Taurus	Love Expression
3 Solar Plexus	Adrenal	Yellow	Mars	Scorpio/Aries	Personal Power
2 Sacral	Lyden	Orange	Neptune	Sagittarius/Pisces	Sexual Capacity
1 Root	Gonads	Red	Saturn	Capricorn/Aquarius	Survival, Will to Live

"You are telling me that these planets are actually setting up an independent and combined vibration that influences my behavior?"

"Indeed I am. The chakra system functions like antennae that picks up vibrations. These planets are vibrating at certain frequencies and as they rotate into the different house that create a mood, tendency, or let us say a mind of attention. Do you understand that music can set your mood?"

"These energy centers play their own songs for their particular area of physical, physiological and psychological responsibility in the body. The organs governing hormones and other critical chemistries are the audiences they play to. The communication network they use is subtle impulses. When the songs and impulses are in harmony and balanced so is the audience – the body and mind is synchronized with the symphony of many subtle energies."

"So in order to take advantage of these vibrations, I should pay attention to what signals they are emanating?"

"Yes, that is what the art of Astrology is all about. Unfortunately it also has been relegated to the woo woo looney bin category but when you align with a specific vibration you are in a better position to reap a beneficial aspect of it."

"That would be like tuning into any kind of energy that is strongest at a certain time. Or being aware of one that could strain your mood."

"Exactly. What is important for you to understand is how the chakra system has much to do with your personality and characteristics, and it is the astral interface between the 3D and 5D worlds, situated in 4D."

"Yes, I got that. But this is pretty far out. These vibrations I can understand are emanating either independently or together to send stuff out that is picked up by the chakras, then picked up by the glands to secret hormones affecting behavior. Wow! But I am not getting how this astral body and this astrology come together."

"The astral substances or forces around Earth come from the surrounding planets. The planets are the physical bodies of some very large beings that have incarnated as planets. These beings have an astral body which is an expression of them in astral substance. Consciousness expresses itself through various dimensions of light with astral substance being the lowest dimension of this light. While the light of the higher dimensions vibrates very fast, the astral light has been slowed down significantly so that the consciousness from the highest dimensions may incarnate into matter which vibrates slower. The dimensions of light come from the higher dimensions of consciousness and so this light is an actual expression of the higher consciousness. It's just a slower vibration."

"You say all these planets are living entities?"

"Yes, they are simply a different form. Earth is a living being like you and it also has a life plan and is subject to her own evolution. She agreed to provide a place for beings to evolve and she is therefore subject to the global consciousness on her planet. Her consciousness is referred to as Gaia or Mother Earth and is separate but still effected by people consciousness."

"Like the family or group consciousness effects me? Or like my mood of stress effects the billions of cells in my body?"

"That is a good analogy. If you really think about this, it is like you carrying a certain type of vibration or emotion with your friends and family. If you are hateful or loving, it is an emanation that you create in your field of influence. In this case the planets are also beings that have such responsibilities and their own plans of evolution."

"Just like you, all the planets have different characteristics of vibration. They have their own life plans and they as a Soul group provide the setting for the greater hologram. Earth is situated with surrounding planets which all have an astral body which is an expression of the being that has incarnated into a planet. These beings are sometimes called gods and the Ancient Greek, Roman and Hindu mythologies of the gods do well in depicting their personalities and interactions. As the human's astral body is made up of the astral substance from each of these so-called gods, the interactions occur both within the individual human and between individuals and groups. The human-being collects astral substance from these so-called gods on the way through the lower dimensions before incarnation. Depending on the positions of the planets in relation to Earth and each other the astral substances acquired will differ and hence the science of the horoscope."

"And as they change their rotational configuration they induce vibrational configurations into the etheric field of the chakras to effect behavior of individuals depending upon their vibrational makeup?"

"Yes. So when the incarnation occurs, a consciousness like in you has a home. I, a spark of Source as a Soul can through consciousness of high dimensional light body gradually descend into lower vibrations and gather astral substance around the light body and then incarnate into the physical and energy bodies of the baby. The actual incarnation occurs at birth as this is when the being is brought into the 3rd dimension. During the pregnancy the spirit has a connection to the fetus and so is partially incarnated but its main substance is waiting in the higher dimensions. It is when the baby is born that the spirit has really begun its incarnation into the 3rd dimension. Although birth is indeed the beginning of the incarnated life it takes time for the various astral substances, light and consciousness to merge with the physical body."

"I get it. It takes a normal person about 28 years to evolve all of the astral energies they have brought with them. They tune into celestial influence and also express outward through chakras."

"You are remembering. The astral substances have characteristics as they are an expression of the beings which they belong to. The consciousness and higher-dimensional Light Body which has incarnated is therefore experienced through this astral body."

"The Higher Self of the baby is an extremely sensitive and loving being. It has come from a place of absolute love, safety, wisdom, intelligence and sensitivity. Life on Earth is very different to the place of its origin. As soon as it is born a huge disconnection from its home occurs, leading to immense heartbreak, fear and need of nurturance. When the being feels nurtured and secure you can clearly see the higher aspects of its spirit. When it does not feel these things from its environment you will clearly see the pain and grief that the baby feels. Whenever this pain is felt by the baby the disconnection from the spirit's essence (home) is increasing. The only treatment for this pain is for the astral body of the infant to begin to crystallize to shut out the pain which in effect shuts out the higher energies as well. When the baby was first born the astral body was like a colored lens but as parts begin to crystallize it's like putting scratches on the lens which further distorts and blocks out the higher light. This is the formation of the ego. Every time the baby feels unpleasant emotions the astral body crystallizes further to block out the pain. Eventually the astral body has become a crystallized structure which successfully blocks out the pain of the spirit's disconnection from its source."

"As a baby they are pure unconditional love and radiate it. Yes, now I see why regardless of shape, size, appearance, they are just loved by everyone! Then it all gets screwed up!"

"Once the astral body has become crystallized to this point, it is a fully fledged ego structure. This structure reacts to the world depending on its inherent astral forces or horoscope and the way its structure was formed as everything that is experienced becomes shadowed by emotional traumas and conditioning. The more emotional pain felt by the individual and the less nurturance, security and love received during infancy, the more crystallized will be the ego structure and therefore the more distorted and blocked the incoming higher light from the Higher Self."

"Wow. Parents and environment can really impact a kid's life. How does it actually incarnate?"

"The astral body incarnates into the physical body through the chi body and the chitta which are both greatly involved with the central nervous system. These include the brain, spinal cord and all nerves running throughout the body. You can simply refer to this life giving essence as spirit or breath which ignites earthly life. Remember that is what I as Soul use to create life. You feel emotions throughout the body because of this interaction. Your Heart Chakra is in the middle of your chest within the Light Body; the emotions felt here in the astral body transfer into the chi/etheric body and then into the physical body through the nerves. That is all the life force or spirit. When you feel broken-hearted you feel physical pain in the area even though the emotion is located in the astral body because of this interaction. The structure in the astral body can be seen and felt in the physical body as tension because the crystallized astral grasps the etheric which in turn affects the nerves in the area. The ego structure in the astral body always affects the flow of etheric/chi energy which in turn causes stress/tension in the physical body which leads to poor health, weakness and rapid aging of the physical body."

"Yes, thanks to your brother!"

"He is not totally to blame as others and environment add to it. In ordinary individuals the ego structure created during infancy remains until death, being the base of personality through which life is experienced. At death the astral body leaves the physical and etheric bodies and begins to rise into higher dimensions. As this occurs the crystallized parts shatter under the pressure of higher vibration. Once the astral body has shattered the parts of the higher consciousness and light of the being that incarnated will go back to the higher dimensions from where they came."

"Am I in my light body now?"

"You are. The difference here is that you can see and sense it. You don't sense below in the lower plane because you don't believe it exists, even though it is sensing all the time. All beings have light bodies which are made of the light from these higher dimensions. While in the awareness of your light body you are in touch with your true self and most essential nature as it has not been distorted by the lens of the astral body or the physical body. You know who and what you are and are at one with the Universe. You can travel to almost any dimension in your light body."

"So not only are your characteristics determined by the astral substances at the time of incarnation by the astral configurations, the chakra system continues to provide the overall setting like in a horoscope to offer you tendencies and environments as you live. Wow, I can see why I have to be mindful of these things to be able to manage that energy portfolio better."

"Yes, these planets and houses are instrumental beyond your norm. I will leave you with this image of how these imbalances relate to these chakras."

The Seven Major Chakras

	Location	Sanskrit	Main Issue	Areas	Health Problems	Balanced
7	Crown Chakra	Sahasrara	Spirituality	Brain and Nervous System	Separation from Source	Unity Consciousness
6	Third Eye Chakra	Ajna	Intuition/Wisdom	The Senses	Sense Related	Calm & Focused
5	Throat Chakra	Vishuddha	Communication	Throat, Mouth, Jaw	Thyroid, Speech	Inner Directed Self
4	Heart Chakra	Anahata	Love, Relationships	Heart, Lungs, Shoulders & Arms	Heart, Respiratory	Unconditional Love
3	Solar Plexus	Manipura	Personal Identity, Ego	Stomach, Liver, Small Intestine	Digestive	Healthy Social Roles
2	Sacral Chakra	Svadhisthana	Emotional Balance, Sexuality	Reproductive, Pelvic Area	Reproductive	Healthy Sexuality
1	Root Chakra	Muladhara	Survival, Physical Needs	Eliminatory System, Legs & Feet	Joints, Skeletal	Groundedness and Safety

"These invisible centers vibrate in unison with the bodies surrounding subtle electromagnetic fields, communicating between universal energies and body functions. Such centers are given life by the Spirit that, like the analogy of a battery, provides the source of operating energy to the subtle system. If the communication becomes disharmonious – with negative energy – they suffer dis-ease, then disease, possibly even die."

"Wow, I can see how the engagement in mental and emotional energies not only creates imbalance and disease in the body, it is also sensed by you and thus recorded. But why do these planets create these environments that add to the issues?"

"That is their duty, to create the environment setting for all to choose their way in. How you take advantage of this or ignore, interpret, perceive is simply your choice, just like everything you encounter in your life plan. Look at the other bodies and beings in your life. They all interact with you to create your environment of engagement and experience."

"It is just difficult to believe that planets are also living beings with a purpose."

"You will eventually get over that. The human subtle energies of thoughts, words and emotion are like combinations of notes that become songs with the assistance of the heart instrument. The planets do the same. All of it is just vibrations. Not only do they serve to play the right music for harmony and balance in the mind and body, they create a resulting energy form that once activated vibrationally by the energy centers of the body, become a signature that is then projected out by a conductor to attract energy that can produce a similar experience. That experience becomes an event similar to a song or a concert."

"So at this astral level, there is still negative and positive stuff?"

"Of course, so I can experience these and deal with my own plan and karma. Astral consciousness includes the full range of emotions from fear, hate, and sorrow to love, happiness, and ecstasy. It also includes the full range of desire from totally selfish and destructive desire to common personal desire to high spiritual aspiration to selfless servicefull desire. You as my partner are here to engage so we can both evolve the greater consciousness by way of our own."

"That is a lot to digest, especially this astral stuff. What I am beginning to feel however is a knowing of what you are presenting that feels the truth of it."

"That is because you and I are in truth one mind and you are beginning to feel that. It should come as no surprise to you that you are actually talking to yourself as one Soul mind. Your major lesson here is to understand the environment you are in and how it is designed by many other factors to provide you with the greatest experience and expression possible."

"Yes, I am beginning to see that more clearly as I disband the illusions of my upbringing and training. But let us continue on this talking to myself so I can understand the connection to the heart. The heart energy field of emotion appears to be the major center for balance and love. Can we go there now?"

Be so mindful of the mood you're in
It may be coming from beyond your realm

10

THE ROLE OF THE HEART BRAIN

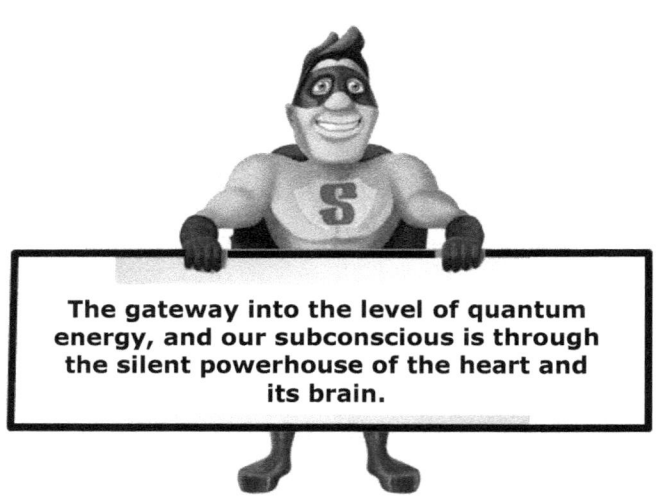

The gateway into the level of quantum energy, and our subconscious is through the silent powerhouse of the heart and its brain.

YOUR HEART ENERGETIC SYSTEM

"Superplacebo, you mentioned a second area as your physical counterpart in the human body."

"I did indeed and it is a powerful place to be in if you are aware of it. The heart is the energetic balance point of the chakra system and it has a mind of its own."

"What do you mean by the balance point?"

"The heart is in a position of 3 chakras above it which are let us say energetic. Thoughts, images and words that emanate from them are the creation energy that is acted upon through the lower three chakras of action, relationship and manifestation into 3D reality. The center of these at the heart is where emotional charge is placed upon the action that begins above. So in a sense it is downward causation of as above, so below. At the balance point of the heart, you are free to attach the degree and type of emotion that you choose. Chakras above are paired below as they essentially are a spiritual and material energetic essence. So the crown chakra balances the root chakra with the heart by positive engagement in your reality of matter. The 3rd eye of how you see things balances through the heart with your relationships at the sacral chakra by love for all you engage with. The throat balances the solar plexus by how communications are presented from the heart by way of your actions and deeds."

"And this is a balanced spiritual-material engagement?"

"Yes. To most the heart is just an organ that pumps blood to keep them alive. The sayings of loving you with all my heart, heart of a lion, broken heart, from the bottom of my heart, cross my heart, bleeding heart and heart of gold are not silly. They come from the negative and positive choices and characteristics of the energetic heart chakra. If you want to believe it is the physical heart that you feel when your heart is broken, think again. It is the heart chakra sending its message to the body; and even the tight chest or angina may not be a result of the physical heart malfunctioning, albeit the two are linked. To most the heart is an expression only as the center of love so reflected in the love for the special ones in our life as in *'falling in love'* and *'I love you'* as a descriptor of special emotion."

"Yes, I understand, we are here to experience emotion and the heart is the powerful center of emotion."

"And to engage mental abilities to facilitate that. What most do not understand is the heart is much more than just a physical organ that pumps fluid. It is the universal soup of all that is and the heart-brain is the access point. The heart has its own nervous system, its own heart-brain and heart-mind that does not take orders from that big brain in the attic - the head brain that my brother likes to dominate. And it has its own special subtle, powerful energetic fields."

THE ENERGY VORTEXES

"Go on."

"Your heart, like the brain, generates a powerful electromagnetic field. It generates the largest electromagnetic field in the body. The electrical field as measured in an electrocardiogram is about 60 times greater in amplitude than the brain waves recorded in an electroencephalogram."

"Wow!"

"The heart is a sensory organ with a mind and acts as a sophisticated information encoding and processing center that enables it to learn, remember, and make independent functional decisions. The heart's electromagnetic field contains certain information or coding that is transmitted throughout and outside of the body. One of the most significant powers related to this field is that intentionally generated positive emotions can change this information coding. The heart's magnetic field in size is 5000 times greater than the brains. This field is a torus – like a big donut – and can reach 6-8 feet in diameter or even much larger. It can actually reach miles in size depending upon its intensity. And understand that this field can influence other heart fields and brains."

"Aha! This is how the Law of Attraction can attract other energies!"

"Indeed, it does. That means the field information transmitted from an individual who is angry, fearful, depressed or experiencing some other negative emotion, takes on beneficial properties when it is influenced by positive emotions coming from another heart. Care, compassion, love or other positive emotion is not only transmitted throughout an individual's body as the cardio electromagnetic field radiates through it, but it is transferred externally as well to people in close proximity and even over long distances like miles."

"So it goes way beyond just the actions. Just the electromagnetic signals generated by the heart have the capacity to affect others around us?"

"Yes, regardless of what they are. For example when a mother places her attention on a baby, she becomes more sensitive to the subtle electromagnetic signals generated by the infant's heart. Remember how we talked about a baby that everybody simply 'loves' regardless of what it looks like. It is its baby heart that emanates love that has the power to transcend everything else. A mother in a psycho physiologically coherent state becomes more sensitive to the subtle electromagnetic information encoded in the electromagnetic signals of her infant."

"That's how mothers simply sense something not right with kids?"

"Yes. The Energetic Heart creates the bioelectromagnetic interactions within and between people. When you're not consciously communicating with others, your physiological systems are interacting in subtle fields in surprising ways. And the electromagnetic signal produced by your heart is registered in the brain waves of people around you. You already know how your physiological responses sync up with your mate's during empathetic interactions. The heart's electromagnetic field acts as a central synchronizing signal within the body, an important carrier of emotional information and a key mediator of energetic interactions between people."

"Is this where you take up a secondary residency?"

"Well, like the midbrain, it is not so much a residency as much as a quantum connectivity. This is where I can be felt as pure love and you know that I am directly connected to the subconscious, not like my brother in the conscious. His brain state is Beta. Mine, to synchronize with the brain is Alpha."

"You mentioned a place in the brain a few times."

"I do have a connective place in the brain. Remember the pineal and leydig? It is the midbrain that has been relegated by science and my brother to the primitive mammal brain. It is in the pineal gland that is also a brain and is what you call the third eye. We will speak of this later but it also is awakened by and tuned in to Alpha waves."

"I won't forget to remind you. What are these vortexes all about?"

"There is more to this energetic center of the heart. Centered on the heart chakra is a torroid or a double vortex of energy. A vortex is a mass of energy that moves in a rotary or whirling motion, causing a depression or vacuum at the center. These powerful eddies of pure earth power manifest as spiral-like coagulations of energy that are either electric, magnetic, or electromagnetic qualities of life force. Vortexes are areas of high energy concentrations, originating from magnetic, spiritual, or sometimes unknown sources. Additionally they are considered to be gateways or portals to other realms, both spiritual and interdimensional. Many vortexes have been shown to be associated with ley Lines and have been found to be extremely strong at node points where the lines cross in your bodies. At each chakra there are vortexes reaching out perpendicular to the axis of the body chakra system."

"Is this the heart field that attracts?"

"It is a part of how the attraction works, yes but all your energies are attractors. The heart field is a morphic field which surrounds you and vibrates with emotions emanating outwards. So it can be felt by others but it also is a nucleus within the quantum soup of infinite possibilities drawing likeness. Your emotions are drawers as are images with quantum signatures of emotion. Exact replication is not possible this way, only likeness."

"What about this donut torus?"

"Known as the double torus of infinity centered on the heart, it is the engine of energy, the center of singularity. It means your heart is the central engine to provide a portal to the love soup of the quantum - that place of infinite possibilities. Inside this torus is your pillar of life, your chakra system that is not only the transference vehicle between DNA and biology from above to below, but energy transmutation from thought to form."

"So the torus is the spiraling engine that does the actual transmutation of energy. The double torus is like a funnel of energy that spins down the funnel becoming more and more concentrated to reach the singularity point at the heart. Then the funnel inverts itself at the heart and the energy then spins down and expands. This why it is a double torus?"

"Yes. Each chakra has a function to interface between 3D and other D's within this torus. Your thoughts, images, language, emotions, intent, relationships, existence move down the pillar from above to below and are deployed for the expansion and expression at the choice of consciousness. They are the receivers and transmitters talking to DNA because all these subtle energies are in the quantum world. You have developed a knowing about this."

"The thoughts, visions, words, emotions that drive intent constitute the torroid process downward to the heart at the point of singularity that then drops into the bottom torroid of intent, relationship and 3D expression of manifestation, and eventually materialization of matter."

"It is so. And whereas Supernocebo lives in the past and future, the heart as the point of singularity has no time, space or identity, only the present."

"So when Yogis talk about being present, getting into an altered state, it is the heart that they want to become coherent with?"

"Indeed. The emotional balance of peace, silence, stillness and no time are key to that state. The way the pillar is deployed is by choice and intent. It carries the communication of information between consciousness of mind between your first layer of DNA of biological-chemical and the other 11 DNA pairs that constitute your being. As you know, this interface is not working at full capacity. It has atrophied through fear and your choice to not develop spiritually into what you are. So it sits stagnant in your DNA. The manifesting processes you have come to know as resident transmitters in your chakras are the thoughts, visions, and the language of emotions. The choice is whether these are sourced from the essence of the heart - love, or the essence of ego - intellect. To open to the full library of DNA, the full abilities of the chakra psychic library, and the portal to infinite possibilities, you must shift from that know all ego brain and my brother to the heart brain. It awakens in an aura of well-being, love and compassion. That is the electricity that turns it on."

"Is it the same with the midbrain?"

"Yes, there is no time or space in the midbrain, it is entirely quantum. All are interconnected. All that is you, in your DNA, of karmic lesson, of Divine, of your total records, and all that is, all sits awaiting your awareness and intent. You now have a knowing that the best interface is positive thought, visions of completion, words of the language of creation, emotion of love and forgiveness. This is speaking, listening, feeling with the heart. For all this means is that the choice of your seeing, speaking, listening, feeling and thinking is always in the light, not with the traditional limited physical sensory system. The portals of access to the DNA is the communication medium of love. And the ability to optimize the toroid's process is the bringing of these positive attributes into the singularity of heart, the heart of all matter. This is simply your knowing that it is so, and however this works is not relevant because you acquire the faith and trust that this is so, and all you have to do is accept and be it. The true power of this process is keyed to a specific vibratory range that is what the energy of love is."

"Is this torus common to all life?"

"The torus, or primary pattern, is an energy dynamic that looks like a donut – it's a continuous surface with a hole in it. The energy flows in through one end, circulates around the center and exits out the other side. You can see it everywhere – in photons, atoms, cells, seeds, flowers, trees, animals, humans, hurricanes, planets, suns, galaxies and even the cosmos as a whole. A torus is the only energy pattern or dynamic that can sustain itself and is made out of the same substance as its surroundings – like a tornado, a smoke ring in the air, or a whirlpool in water."

"The torus also applies at the human level. Each person not only is a torus – bodies are a continuous surface (skin) with a hole through the middle (intestinal tract). Each is surrounded by a toroidal electro-magnetic field. Each individual's torus is distinct, but at the same time open and connected to every other in a continuous sea of infinite energy. It is the same energy field you can feel with a magnet. It is usually invisible, but by scattering iron filings loosely around a magnet you can actually see the toroidal shape of energy."

"How is it positioned on the body?"

"The Heart's electromagnetic frequency arcs out from the Heart and back in the form of a torus field. The axis of this Heart torus extends from the pelvic floor to the top of the skull, and the whole field is holographic, meaning that information about it can be read from each and every point in the torus."

"Just like a holographic plate."

"Yes. This also connects on the sacred geometry level where your heart chakra is composed of a star tetrahedron. It connects the energy together. Also the way the kundalini flows within the chakra system, this energy flows within the same way, the rising serpent of the ida (feminine) and pingala (masculine) join together through the Nadis.

"Can you put a picture in my mind? I still am having trouble seeing this. What are these nadis and energy lines?"

"Here is an image for you."

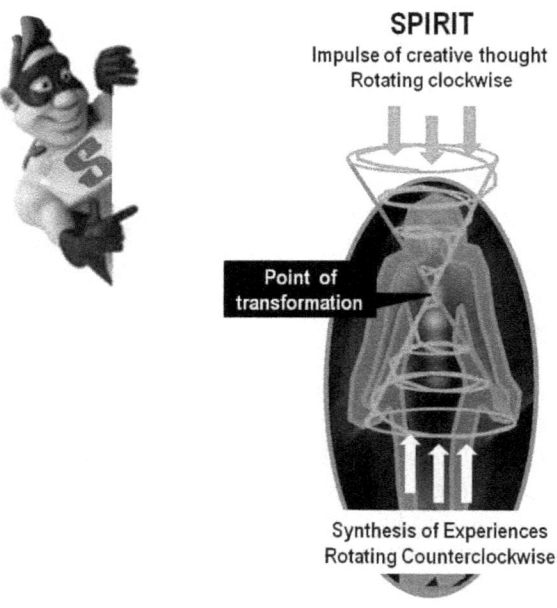

"The Nadis are your subtle channels that heighten your psychic abilities through the network of energy. The ida and pingala rises up to create a central channel called the Sushumna where they are joined. In your ancient wisdom these were not secret. The Kundalini will then awaken and rise up

Sushumna, energizing the seven chakras that create your aura and your aura field of energy which is the torus."

"Most torus dynamics actually contain two toruses – called tori – like the male and female aspects of the whole. One spirals in one direction toward the North Pole and its opposite spinning toward the South Pole. This is also referred to as the Coriolis Effect. Examples are the weather on the earth and the plasma flow of the sun. In the heart torus, the spin down the top center is clockwise, down into the point of singularity at the heart, then to the outside of the lower torus, around to the inside of the lower torus, back through the heart then to the outside of the upper torus, then back down."

"The underlying structure of the torus is called the Vector Equilibrium, or VE. It is the blueprint by which nature forms energy into matter. It is the only geometric form where all forces are equal and balanced. The energy lines or vectors are of equal length and strength. They represent the energy of attraction and repulsion, like you can feel with a magnet."

"So when you place energies into this quantum field, they try to find a match. Cool!"

"They are also concentrators and dispersers of thought energy. You can't actually observe the VE in the material world because it is the geometry of absolute balance. What you experience on Earth is always expanding toward and contracting away from absolute equilibrium. Like a wave arising from the surface of a tranquil sea, a material form is born or unfolds from the plenum as fullness of energy. It is ironically referred to by physicists as the vacuum and dies or enfolds back into it. The VE is like the imaginable – yet invisible – mother of all the shapes and symmetries we see in the world."

HEART BRAIN EMOTIONS

"But what I want you to now understand is where I really have influence through the heart brain. You understand the head brain where my brother likes to rule and understand how stress and beta activity can cause lots of problems for your body but there is a whole lot of things that you also need to know about the heart."

"Yes, I see how the perceived environment can cause the flight or fight syndrome and the HPA axis to affect the immune system, the visceral system and the intellect. Is there another process?"

"Well, you have another process where I live that can cause havoc. You see the heart has its own brain that communicates with and influences the head brain through the nervous system, hormonal system and other pathways that affect the quality of life as well."

"Ok, the brain gets communications from the neurological system of nerves, the biophysical or pulse waves, biochemicals like hormones, and energetic or electromagnetic information. Is there something else?"

"The heart has its own brain that can sense, remember, learn, feel, and process information independently. Signals go from the heart to the survival centre in hindbrain where blood pressure and heart rate, and respiratory rate are controlled. This part analyses information and makes changes. These signals also affect your feelings and emotional memory center in midbrain or amygdala. The cells here synchronize to the pacemaker in the heart. If the heart rate or HRV is chaotic, it matches that to negative emotional experiences and automatically recalls what negative feeling correlates."

"What's HRV?"

"Heart rate variability is the physiological phenomenon of variation in the time interval between heartbeats. It is measured by the variation in the beat-to-beat interval. Brain waves in cortex are also affected by powerful chaotic heart signals coloring how you think and perceive. This alters top level functions like calculation, planning, creativity, and communications – all from the big signal generator in the heart."

"So be aware that stress feelings alone activate a stress response that is emotional and psychological. So a simple thought recalling anger will provoke a response but it is nowhere near the intensity of the physiological and psychological process of the stress response of emotion. Where have you heard this before? In our discussion about the cells. My dominion is emotions so you have to choose these wisely because these contribute heavily to stress on the brain and it can be real or imagined and whether you are aware of this or not. The end effect is the same. There is no difference."

"So this is why meditation, yoga, and prayer help."

"Exactly but you cannot just meditate when you are fully engaged in your life. As soon as you are aware of negative energies of stress or negative things hit, first focus and neutralize – time out. Shift attention to the heart area away from noise and stress. Stop the emotion or thought. Take three deep breaths slowly by counting 5 in and 5 out. Feel the breath through me in the heart in a steady rhythm while you disengage thoughts and feeling. Then engage a positive feeling emotion by thinking back to a positive situation of love and care. This coherent pattern overrides negative emotional programs. Positive feeling is not a thought process alone. You want to be genuine in thoughts and feelings. Learn an inventory of these positive thoughts and feelings matched and your awareness/control increases so the threshold is reset. It is like our bedtime practice in our energy management plan."

"So, there is a lot of stuff in me that is a subtle sensing systems through subtle energies and the energetic body that is working away clogging up my chakras. If I am not mindful, I am aiding dis-ease and disease as well as clogging those higher abilities. And If I cause a negative reactive procession in my body, my heart field is also doing the same thing. Geez! How does this actually work?"

"The emotion creates a reaction in the brain that affects the body. The ANS, short for Autonomic Nervous System, kicks into action upon any threat and it works in two parts. You are already familiar with the flight or fight syndrome coming from a different source. First is the fight or flight situation where the sympathetic system causes the body to constrict blood vessels, raise blood pressure, raise heart rate, constrict skin arteries, move blood away from organs, dilate pupils, and raise neck hairs for starters. And this is all done automatically in a few seconds to prepare you. The orders are made by the brain to do this."

"The second situation is when the threat is only perceived like when you walk into a dark alley and feel threatened. Then the parasympathetic system kicks in. It causes the heart rate to go up, you get a sweat, or chill, and the blood pressure goes up in readiness. The hormonal system then starts a long sequence of reactions of nervous system signals to the glands so as to increase chances of survival. These actions take a few minutes but they last for hours. Once this starts, there are some 1400 reactions that occur in the body."

"Wow! Can you give me an example?"

"For example when you get wounded, there are a lot of things happening that the body does to protect you. But the major trouble maker is cortisol released from adrenal glands when you perceive stress. It goes into the blood to raise blood sugar so muscles have more fuel. Adrenaline also increases to make the heart beat faster, and it also raises blood pressure by constricting arteries and interacting with kidneys to save salt and water. So this is what the protective system does automatically."

"But this same process is also triggered by negative emotion like anger and depression. This then creates a feedback loop of stress, cortisol, bad mood, more stress, and more cortisol feeding on itself. This can rise to levels that can reach a burnout condition. To add to this mayhem, cortisol also inhibits memory, clarity, and higher functions of the brain."

"That's what you get by engaging in your brothers' philosophy, right?"

"Yes, but again it is a choice. There is, however, another hormone that I speak with. It is called DHEA or Dehydroepiandrosterone produced by the adrenals. It actually counteracts the effects of cortisol. It is produced by positive emotions of love, compassion, reverence, gratitude, and joy. But this hormone declines with age. So increasing stress with age can make a stress button get stuck in the on position for good."

"Well, the obvious conclusion is that things like finances, job, conflict, and anxiety problems are stress triggers that accumulate on an ongoing basis and the body gets used to a new threshold. If this happens, and the cortisol and adrenaline are stuck in on positions, you get heart disease, raised blood sugar, hypertension, high cholesterol, obesity, arterial diseases, and diabetes over time. So what happens is the body functions get set to a new higher threshold as the body simply believes this is where it should be."

"Precisely. You need to reset the thermostat down to a normal level again because the stress can become an addiction. Like we discussed before a diet of positive feelings resolves this problem and this is how you can reset the thermostat. The heart is where you feel strong emotion because it is the core of emotion and it is where I offer a better choice."

"So the real control center is the heart brain, not the brain. It ain't the real boss! So these sayings like heartfelt emotion, heartbroken, put your heart into it, the heart of the matter, heart to heart, and from the bottom of my heart are not just sayings. They are reflecting a real process from the heart center. Ow!"

GET INTO ALPHA PERMANENTLY!

"Well, get to listen to me. Listen to the heart. It is a heart mind talking to you through emotion and the head brain is also talking to you in a soft voice. Listen to the heart, not the ego which can create false fears and demands. Shift emotions and change HRV by reversing stress. Events can create an auto response which equals HRV in chaotic mode. This then goes to the brain to produce anxiety, panic, and anger. But when signals from the heart are coherent, the brain's three parts synchronize to create cortical facilitation of improved function. It is called heart intelligence."

"The key then is to create the heart-head entrainment that is brought about by appreciation and love. This creates a strengthening of all of these communications as they get synchronized. But how does this relate to the brain waves of the head?"

"Remember Alpha brain waves? They were the first waves discovered in 1929 using an EEG machine. They were hence named after the first letter in the Greek alphabet – Alpha. Alpha brain waves have electrical frequencies between 8-13 hertz. Alpha brain waves are most present in a wakeful state that is characterized by a relaxed and effortless alertness. Alpha states have been described variously as sublime, flying, floating, lightness, peace, and tranquility and they are not always present. For example, if someone is in deep sleep or in intense anger there are almost no Alpha brain waves."

"Yes, I have read this. Alpha brain waves are important for creativity. Scientists have shown that highly creative people have different brain waves from normal and non-creative people. In order to have a creative inspiration your brain needs to be able to generate a big burst of Alpha brain waves. The brains of creative people can generate these big Alpha brain wave bursts, and do so when they are faced with problems to solve."

"Yes, that is true, but normal and non-creative people do not produce Alpha brain wave increases when they are faced with problems, and so they cannot come up with creative ideas and solutions. Any time you have an insight or an inspiration, you know your brain just produced more Alpha waves than usual. Increased creativity is helpful for everyone. One way to increase creativity is to increase Alpha brain waves."

"I know the answer to that. Your dear brother keeps them active in Beta and they are too busy in stress or conflict, or feeling stupid."

"Yes. Peak performance is another activity for which Alpha brain waves are helpful. Increases of Alpha brain waves precede peak performance. One key difference between novice and elite athletes is in their brain waves. Just before their peak performances, elite basketball players, golfers, and marksmen will produce a burst of Alpha brain waves. Novice and intermediate athletes do not have these Alpha bursts. The Alpha brain waves seemed to be essential for peak performance and were increased."

"But what does this have to do with the heart brain waves?"

"Alpha waves of the brain like those produced in meditation are synchronized to the cardiac cycle. Hence meditation, yoga, and prayer help create coherence. When you learn to shift attention to heart area away from noise and stress, you stop two culprits; emotion or thought. Alpha is the state of coherent communication between us at the heart brain and the head brain. It is like opening the wellness channel with the body."

"So the heart is not only the source of emotion, courage and wisdom, it has its own brain that communicates with and influences the cranial brain through the nervous system, hormonal system, and other pathways that affect the quality of life. The heart and nervous system *do not* follow brain's direction like everyone believed. The heart has its own brain that can sense, remember, learn, feel, and process information independently."

"Exactly, and do not want any negative emotions to create disorder. You want real positive emotions to increase mental clarity, creativity, balance, and effectiveness. And the best way to keep this going in the conscious state is to be in Alpha all the time."

"I will tell you something else. When people touch or are in proximity of each other, one person's heart beat signal is registered in the other's brainwaves. Have you ever felt uneasy about somebody just being in their presence?"

"Yes, one can pick up these from their morphic field around the heart. And that can infect your field?"

"That is not all. Your relaxed brain waves are the same as the frequency of the earth! This background frequency is known as Schumann Resonance. The phenomenon was named after W.O. Schumann who first predicted and discussed it in the 1950's. The Schumann resonance resonates with your alpha brain waves."

"Wow! Alpha is how we 'tune in' to the planet!"

"It is called reverence."

BEING IN THE HEART BRAIN

"So the bottom line is this: The focus is becoming present and centered in the heart mind - in Alpha every moment as I am always there to guide you. I reside in the present where there is no time while my brother resides in the past and future in the Beta brain."

"The coherent Alpha pattern overrides negative emotional programs. Learn an inventory of these and your awareness/control increases so the threshold is reset. It is like our bedtime practice in our plan. *'Have a good heart'* as in Buddhism, which means *"care deeply without hidden agenda"*. The heart is the mind's Powerhouse – center of wisdom, mediation between Heaven and Earth."

"By focusing attention on the heart, you increase synchronicity between heart and brain to calm the nervous system and deactivate stress response so the body conserves energy for growth. Love feelings generate measurable heart field coherence; negative emotions create incoherence and disharmony."

"And this is all about the silence and altered state that we talked about with miracles. This brings another common practice which has to do with going inside, or being present to the heart. Many meditation methods take you into that altered state, as does hypnosis. It is to bypass the conscious mind that is hooked to the beta brain. What is most important is to get into this state by becoming present to the heart brain, and that has to be done in a state of peace and love to open the portals. It is a simple practice but places your attention away from the higher interfering brainwaves of consciousness into the lower state and centering your attention to the heart energetic center. But to do this outside of the altered state, the secret is to be in Alpha by going back to what we talked about as managing my energy portfolio!"

BEING IN THE LOVE CENTER

"When you fall in love, you feel your heart flutter, beat loudly or leap for joy; when you're rejected, your heart breaks. You are called heartless or cold-hearted when you show no care or love... and big-hearted when you extend your concern to others. You *'take things to heart'* or *'talk heart-to-heart'* about deeply personal issues. You love someone *'from the bottom of your heart'* but are *'half-hearted'* about something when you're emotionally uninvolved. You experience your heart as the center of your feelings, as seen on Valentine's Day when love-filled hearts abound. You know this instinctively, as you always physically point to your heart when you say *'I'* or want to express your deeper feelings."

Alpha keeps fully aware coherence. Remember the need for a feeling of love emotion with prayer or it does not allow miracles to work! In the same way, when faced with a decision or conflict, your mind may come up with numerous, different and quite logical reasons why you should act as it advises, but if you listen to and trust your heart - however illogical or irrational it may seem - it is usually right and you are happier as a result."

"There is great brilliance and beauty inherent within the mind, because it is capable of understanding the most intricate scientific and mathematical theories and can make complicated corporate decisions. Yet the same mind can get caught up in trivia and nonsense, becoming upset or even unglued over a seemingly harmless remark. It runs your life, pushing and pulling you in all directions, from attraction to repulsion, creating endless dramas in acting out your insecurities and fears, because it is not in touch with your deeper feelings. Living inside your head all the time is actually not much fun!"

"While the mind is the content of who you are, your heart is your essence. Your true heart is not subject to chaos or limited by pain, fear and neuroses, but is joyful, creative and loving. But it will *ache* as a red flag when something is not right. That is the heart intelligence telling you to smarten up. Some believe the heart can be too uncertain and even misguided, but that is the head talking! It is actually a source of great richness, and this wealth is one that cannot be squandered or lost. It is the core, the essence of your being, a reservoir of joy, powerful love and infinite compassion that lies within you. But you have to listen to these aches."

"When you honor the wisdom in your heart, then you act from this core of your being which is the Soul mind. You experience it in those moments when your needs and worries quietly dissolve and confusion or pain no longer dominates. Tears may spontaneously arise and there is a sensation of great warmth and peace. It is the letting go of fear and the need to control. Try a meditation of your own to get more deeply in touch with this loving center of your being."

"What you are telling me is to pay attention to the prime residence of your higher energetic self and its counterpart in the body – the energetic heart mind. The Lower Self and ego occupy the brain mind at the top. It is concerned with the past and future for survival and lives in beta consciousness. The Higher Self occupies the heart mind and is not concerned with time at all as it is focused on the present moment looking for positive emotions to be generated. It lives in the state of Alpha or lower. The power of emotion and all those energies of love, gratitude, forgiveness, compassion, joy, and bliss are very strong program writers that simply bypass the head brain to the subconscious."

"Yes. Don't think that it is your conscious brain mind that you have to train into new programs, it is that unconscious heart brain that really rules the roost. The real power is in emotion and if it is equally charged with negative power from fear, hate, conflict, it is equally effective in the program conditioning process like in severe trauma which is the opposite of intense positive love and gratitude."

"But you have also mentioned the midbrain as a place of quantum power."

"It is but it is not so much a thinking brain like the neo-cortex. It is an acting brain that is highly responsive to the images and words that are the expressive vehicles of the 3rd eye and throat chakras. It is a means of getting changes made to your reality and health issues but once again you need to get away from the meddling beta mind. It is a place of alpha - no time."

"Are you speaking of imaging and chanting?"

"Yes. We will reserve this for later. Let us first see what people on this Earth know and do to bend reality outside the box."

"You mean health and wealth miracles?"

"Yes, are you interested in that?"

"You are kidding of course!"

11

CAN WE CREATE HEALTH MIRACLES?

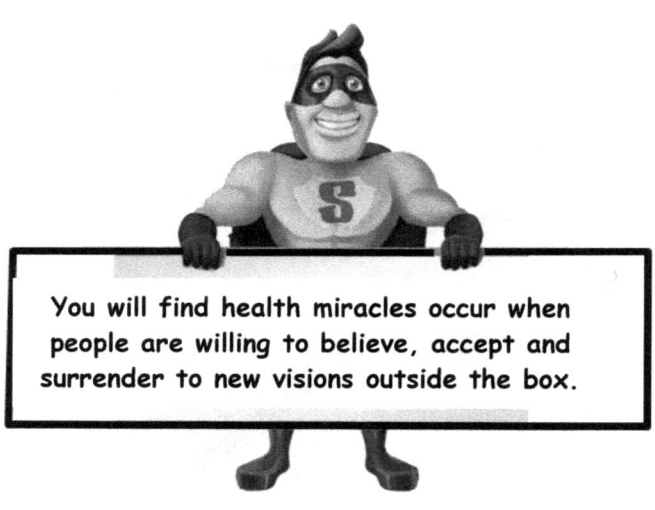

You will find health miracles occur when people are willing to believe, accept and surrender to new visions outside the box.

I can tell you that the illusion of a fake reality and life plan comments stuck in my mind. But I also felt that it was not time to pursue that topic yet. I was much more interested in how wealth and health miracles could be created with this new wisdom of going out of the box. I had heard and read about many spectacular health miracles. History was laden with these as unexplained phenomenon. Religious Saints, Faith Healers, Energy Healers, Yogis, Near Death Experiences, Native Rituals, even placebos reported incredible cases of healing. And of course there were many New age gurus who promised fantastic wealth rewards – if only you bought their books and took their seminars. As I digested our last session on where Superplacebo lived and the waiting abilities in these higher bodies, I wanted to know more about this and understand exactly how I may be able to create these miracles in my life. I certainly could use some help on both issues as I seemed to be going nowhere.

As I drifted into what I thought was theta in the morning, it was time to find out about what people who went outside the boxes of belief were doing. After our last session, I still was not sure what state my brain was in and it was really hard to completely get rid of all thoughts. But I knew I just had to let go of this analysis and it would eventually happen. I wanted to know how to have something happen that was not physically explainable; something not believed by the group belief system. The most obvious was healing miracles.

"Superplacebo," I said this morning, "I am ready to talk more about these boxes and how some people do things like healing miracles that do not conform."

"I mentioned that there is a state of consciousness that is like a family, community, or global consciousness. Because consciousness is quantum each is tagged separate but part of the rest. So the beliefs and behaviors are limited within each consciousness. In other words, your own consciousness may find limits from your family beliefs, your family may fall within community or cultural belief systems and so on."

"I understand that. It is like my own mind that is unique and separate yet it is part of a family mind that has a life of its own. And that is what creates my inventory of subconscious programs. But obviously some get out."

"Precisely. In many cultures, we find that people do get outside of the limits of all these to create or to be part of something that does not fit within the limits of the prevailing consciousness. Many are small groups that purposely combine their beliefs into out of the box practices. The most obvious are cults and religions. The out of the ordinary miracle creations are where I come in to the picture to assist in this process when it is asked for."

"Obviously just asking or praying does not work all the time. Yet these occur all the time."

"Of course they are not accepted into the box of beliefs because they cannot be explained. But many miraculous things have been done to the physical health by stepping outside of these boxes and allowing me to do my job from above."

"I do not understand how this happens and how to ask properly yet. Who does these things and how are these being done?"

"I understand why you ask this way."

"What do you mean?"

"You want references and examples. If I just told you, which I have already done, and you believed it, then you would already know the answer. In truth you already know but your lower mind needs to relate this to your logical brain to look for evidence that convinces it. At some point in this you will bypass this analytical process and simply know and remember this truth. So the best way for us to proceed is for me to use examples in your own reality."

"Yes, it seems to be difficult for me to simply get out of that old belief mode."

MIRACLES ARE OUT OF THE BOX

"Let us back up then. Miracles of health, even though they occur all the time, are not believed because the belief box of the prevailing consciousness is not ready to accept them. It is as simple as that because your own consciousness defaults to that programming of subconscious forming the same limits, relying on programs that are already there. However, there are many people who have broken away from this limit to facilitate this process in others."

"And eventually, there will be enough people who will tip the scale and it will be accepted, right?"

"Yes, that is the way it will evolve. That is the way all living things including consciousness evolve."

"But obviously there is always a portal out of the old to bring in the new."

"Of course, you are in that portal now, free to accept or reject it."

"Ok, as you said, it would be best if you use as examples some of the miracle healers and explain what they do."

"Yes. Here is a list of the most popular and successful methods. My sister is going to put a vision into your mind. These are methods that all have created many spectacular health miracles. They cover some of the more famous and are from very diverse backgrounds."

1 QUANTUM TOUCH	7 JOHN OF GOD
2 REGRESSION THERAPY	8 FAITH HEALING
3 NATIVE MEDICINE	9 ANCIENT PRAYER
4 DIVINE CONNECTION	10 MATRIX ENERGETICS
5 ADAM DREAMHEALER	11 CREATOR-CREATRIX
6 ANCIENT HO'OPONOPONO	12 ENERGY UNBLOCKING

"I have heard of some of these but relegated them to woo woo stuff."

"If you believe they are woo woo and discount their existence then you will never bring one into your life by conscious action. So drop this. We will use these as examples. There are two reasons why I want to use others as examples. First, it is to allow you to shift your beliefs out of the box. Second is to illustrate that although there are common processes, their success varies because of some very intangible variables."

"That is wonderful. I am going to just reconfirm I am in the proper state of letting go of doubts."

"Good. I sense the heart connection. Now you must understand that although they all work and have produced extraordinary results, they do not work every time. When you look carefully at the methods that these miracle workers use as healing facilitators, you begin to see a pattern of processes and steps that are common. None of them will admit that they did the healing. They suggest it was done by some other force – usually divine intervention. It is because they cannot explain the healing. Keep in mind that there have been some very spectacular healing miracles that these people have created for others. What you find is that there are variations of these similar practices."

"I bet belief is a key that determines the success."

"Indeed. Belief is a variable. The brain wave state is another, as is the depth of entry into the higher mind of away from the belief box. The depth of programming in subconscious is another. The state of wellness and being is another. The recipient's belief system must be one that believes in the healing process and is aligned with the subconscious belief that this is possible. That aligns the conscious with subconscious and then it becomes possible. It immediately takes them out of the box. And if it is not, then subconscious, whatever has been put there, wins out."

"Ok, they have to get by Supernocebo and his nattering, right? It is where you get into the lower brain wave states of Theta just like I am doing now."

"Yes, the recipient must be in a programmable state where the brain does not interfere and the subconscious mind says it is ready to accept a new program. This is through methods of guided meditation, regression, becoming present, and many other variations to lower the brain wave interference of the conscious mind."

"Then the state of well being is also important, right."

"It is, however, you find that there is great variation in setting the environment where this is to occur. It is dependent on the culture and local belief system. It could be a ritual, a gathering, a noted authority, a process by the healer is important in creating the focus and attention for the intention of healing and reprogramming to take place. This creates a morphic field of energy that enforces the belief so as to allow the reprogramming to occur and the new reality to manifest itself. You find that combined beliefs and emotion assist in the process."

"Yes, I can see that. A religious faith healer and a native Songoma, or an energy healer, witch doctor, or an Indian ritual, or a doctor's office all have different environments to do their stuff in creating the morphic field that assists the process."

"Yes, it sets the external morphic field and environment. Also, the focus is on the internal environment of well being. The internal environment of the recipient and the healer is one of love, forgiveness, compassion, peace and harmony as the morphic field of energy around and in the body."

"So the elimination of stress is needed here too as to better entrain the body and mind into a higher state of vibration and settle the physiological and chemical processes that Supernocebo is always pushing. It is like tuning into the right channel, right?"

"Precisely. The next common practice is to bring into awareness of mind a focus and intent. By triggering the intention, the issue is identified or located so as to direct the process of healing to that location. At this point, the clear vision of the correct state becomes the focus as surrounded by the joy of its completion. This is done through words, prayer, emotions, or guidance, and it brings into the consciousness the new possibility being considered. It identifies the directive to the subconscious to correct the issue."

"But the Healer is not the real healer."

"No. That is done by facilitation. It is to engage that process by looking to a Higher Power, God, Spirit, Guides or whatever the belief system outside the norm supports. That is some form of Divine engagement to assist in the process of correcting the issue and instigating the subconscious reprogramming. Another aspect that creates the strong belief is that the healer is believed to be a credible authority acts as the conduit for some form of Divine Intervention. That is triggered to actually replace the program in the subconscious mind. The process of reprogramming convinces the brain and the cellular community is to respond by instituting a new action overriding the old program; load and run from DNA inventory."

"Is it really divine outside the norm?"

"Well, first of all you actually are Divine so you have to give consideration to the possibility that it is really you that is the healer. The vast majority of you humans do have a belief of some superior deity or god or divinity and there is no logic here. It is a simple belief that is personal and you know how strong this personal opinion can be. These are outside the norm, science, or anything else that attempts to describe or quantify it. So yes, it is outside the norm and this is why you find many successes part of religious or socialized belief systems."

"Secondly, in these cases, everything is presented as one and connected. Some of these cases like placebos have no divine involved. It is a matter of belief and that is typically from an expert or higher authority that facilitates the process and the brain does the rest with the cells. In these cases, a common denominator is that a Healer creates a **Belief** to be an appropriate authority or facilitator so the patient **Accepts** an outcome outside the box and **Surrenders** to the new outcome. In looking at a process where you wanted to get healed, you could summarize these simple steps."

0. Create a setting where the patient is in an altered state
1. Bring into thought the belief of being healed
2. Bring into vision the image of the issue corrected
3. Communicate to find the source of the issue
4. Bring in the power of emotion to surround the corrected desire
5. Launch the intention to correct the issue
6. Surrender control of the correction to a higher power
7. Be grateful for the Higher Power to materialize the correction

"Now, Ed, let these sink in and tell me how would you deploy these steps if you were doing it?"

"Ok, that's cool. It looks simple enough. If I wanted to do this myself and say heal my screwed up knee, I would first have to bring myself into an altered state by imagining a peaceful place, breathing softly, and becoming present to myself in the heart."

"And then?"

"In my thoughts I would assert my beliefs that I believe in miracle healing, I can heal myself, believe I am worthy and I believe in a higher power that will assist me."

"That is the way they do it, yes. I will modify this later for you."

"Then I would visualize clearly in my mind a picture of the healed desire a situation where it is healed. Having a clear vision I would state that I am asking for Higher Divine Intelligence assistance to manifest the vision."

"And then?"

"I would bring in the heart emotion. In my imagination I would feel the result of the knee being completely healed and I would surround this vision with the joy and bliss of it being so."

"Good."

"Then, with strong clear intent feel the completion I would accept that a new state of being would take me to that wonderful feeling of the healing being done. In my mind, I would connect to a higher power to feel the energy flow into my total being and into my cellular structure to the area of healing need."

"Yes."

"And then I would sit quietly and feel the gratitude of completion and thank the higher power or those I called to assist me."

"You must be mindful, Ed that this does not work every time. Why do you suppose that is?"

"Because there are many intangibles here. The degree of clarity, the height of emotion, the depth of altered state, the strength of belief, the belief in higher power, the acceptance of a new fate and the surrender to it. It all varies."

"Yes, you have learned that it is the brain and the subconscious that are the culprits too. The subconscious holds the inventory of chosen programs to execute and the brain executes the programs that make the appropriate changes in chemistry, physiological and physical. And it is the mind not the conscious beta mind, but the theta and alpha mind that speak the right language. You have learned that that mental mind of Beta is not going to let the program through easily when it is limited by the nested consciousness of self, family, society and global. And it gets more difficult with age and conditioning to create new programs in an inventory that has a whole life of stuff in it based upon all that history of programming."

"Yes, I understand, the exception is to train harder or repeat this more, be persistent longer, use greater emotion, or have a trauma occur to convince the brain fire-wire system to get recorded in the subconscious."

"There is one important variable related to success that you have not considered. See if you can pull it out of your mind."

"What is that? The midbrain and sound? I can actually see that the place that these guys are taking the patient to is the heart mind and the midbrain mind. Here the vision equals the word or mantra that when repeated creates a resonance that the creative center of the brain responds to. Is that right?"

"Aha! Brilliant! But the truth is that it is not so much the place or process used to visit me or your Soul, it is the conviction to the intent, belief, clarity, and charge of emotion. But there is something else that sabotages efforts."

"You mean ego?"

"Partly. The big brained ego will come into play when you undertake these processes and steps. Someone else who you have faith in is leading the process so your mind lets go properly. You will have difficulty at first getting beyond the analytical mind that will be concerned with the correctness of steps, the conditions, the doubts, the mind chatter that occurs when you are trying to get rid of the mind, yet use the mind. This is why most healers cannot heal themselves and it is why it is best to use hypnosis and be led by a facilitator in the beginning."

"I can understand that. I would be analyzing to see if I am deep enough, using the right step, looking for results, feeling doubts and interfere. That would most likely sabotage results which I would be looking for and cause an endless cycle of doubt-failure."

"What about recording the process and steps?"

"That would be better but still not as effective as being led to truly let go of the lower reality and big brain interference. At some point you will overcome this and simply know that you and your Soul mind as me are one. Then your thoughts all come from one source of mind and in your conscious state you learn to be in Alpha."

"I understand. Do these steps also apply to the Law of Attraction Gurus who sell people on the idea of changing their external reality?"

"Let us look at that in our next session."

12

CAN WE CREATE MIRACLES OF EXTERNAL REALITY?

Reality changes by intent of the mind, degree of vision clarity, strength of emotion and persistence of gratitude.

This was pretty cool and I was looking forward to writing my own process for recording it. This time, my mind was bubbling with questions about changing external reality... money! It was interesting to know that the brain and body do not distinguish between reality and non reality. So imagining a crisis has material-physical consequences in reality. But it was also interesting that the mind as imagination can create anything from the sea of infinite possibilities but it does not create that directly in the physical world all the time. Or does it? Then there was the comment that reality is an illusion that was bugging me. Was that how these miracles actually manifest into reality? Are these wealth miracles somehow bending reality or controlling the Law of Attraction? Are we talking about proactive control of Cause & Effect and Karma? I had to get some answers.

So after my usual morning process, I entered what I was believing was the heart mind and what I thought was the quantum void. I was becoming more relaxed about doing this without incessant questions about whether it was right or wrong. I called Superplacebo forward. I knew he was always there even though Supernocebo was saying otherwise. I was still not sure how to listen to him in the daily beta chatter of Supernocebo. There were still a few nigglings about how well I was doing at getting into the right frame of mind and letting go properly but I was getting much better at stopping those thoughts and becoming centered and present.

"Superplacebo," I said, "what about changing the reality outside of your body? Can people actually do that?"

"Well, they already do this as a natural process as long as it is within the consciousness of the norm. The problem is that with 70,000-90,000 thoughts, images, and emotions per day you lose track of any connection or correlation between a Cause and Effect. It is because the when, where, how are not evident. The limits of the consciousness boxes simply believe such a correlation is what you call crap. But yet everyone who succeeds in changing their business reality is very familiar with these steps."

"What steps do you mean?"

"Here is an image for you. Let us say your business manifestation objective is to make a million dollars on a new business venture of selling chairs. Look at these steps."

1. We form the thought of making a million dollars
2. We form a vision of a company that sells chairs
3. We make a business plan of the company and product
4. We get emotionally excited about the plan/company
5. We launch the intent to execute the business plan
6. We engage others, money, relations to make it happen
7. We create the chairs/company that enters our reality

"Yes, do I ever know those! The truth is that only a small few actually do it when it is a big objective like that million dollars."

SO WHO'S CREATING NEW REALITY?

"True, and what does that success depend upon even though you are working within the limiting reality of the norm?"

"Clarity of vision, depth of passion, strength of intent, getting financing, lots of business stuff."

"Here again, is another lost correlation between these steps and the energetic nodes of the physical body – the chakras. These same business steps are reflected in the 7 steps of the above to below functions of the chakras. To quantify this process from the top down as above so below. Here is an image for you."

1. In the Crown Chakra, *form a thought,*
2. In the 3rd Eye Chakra, *see an image,*
3. In the Throat Chakra *speak words,*
4. In the Heart Chakra *feel an emotion,*
5. In the Solar Plexus Chakra *create intention to act,*
6. In the Sacral Chakra, *engage in relations needed to assist,*
7. In the Root Chakra *indulge in the material reality.*

"Wow! So the clarity of vision is like creating a clear business plan at the throat chakra, the passion in the heart, the perseverance in the solar plexus and the money from relationships in the Sacral? To believe this has anything to do with the process of manifesting reality just does not register to the global consciousness or anyone else. It is just fantasy."

"Yet, you all do it within the box. And now you are aware of it outside the box. Outside the box has been well documented in metascience that these chakras have higher functions and abilities that are dormant. Unlike the hardwired nervous-sensory system that is sensing things more physical, the wireless chakra system is sensing via the metaphysical and therefore has a direct impact on the state of psychic abilities. The other consideration is that each of the chakras has a vortex projecting out of the body into the auras that surround the body. These vortexes reach out perpendicular to the body axis and behave according to quantum mechanics, also there are non-matter to matter concentrators, located at each chakra."

"What you are saying is that these subtle energies are already working and can be proactively managed to work for you under Cause & Effect and Attraction to bring a new reality into existence."

"What you are struggling with is whether it was the energy you created that attracted the result or whether it was your hard work of action that created the result, right? That is the in versus out belief."

"Well, in the cause of miracles, the effects were created by the mind out of the box. No one had to work hard, it just happened. Can the same type of miracle occur outside of the body?"

"Here is an image of some of your expert Gurus on this topic, starting from the matter over mind process to the more spiritual of mind over matter process. These are some of the people who have been noted as creating those financial miracles."

"Ok, what do these Gurus report as the way they teach their clients to do this?"

NAPOLEON HILL: THINK AND GROW RICH
WAYNE DYER: THE POWER OF INTENTION
JOE VITALE: THE ATTRACTOR FACTOR
ESTER HICKS: THE LAW OF ATTRACTION
JOHN KEHOE: MIND POWER

"If you look at the process of changing business reality, you have to look at the work of Napoleon Hill who surveyed 100's of the wealthiest business men of his time and wrote one of the best sellers of all time. He was very clear in outlining the same 7 steps for making the million dollars with chairs. This is the traditional way inside the box. He stated that these things did not suddenly happen it was continued focus and perseverance that he observed had to be taken in the last 3 steps rather than having a Divine Intervention assist."

"I see that clearly. But the new idea outside the box is like the placebo that begs the question was it the pill or the mind that did the miracle. You have to ask was it the energy or the actions that attracted the miracle. So who are the main proponents of changing this external reality in a proactive way and what are their steps?"

"Ok, just as you are doing now, get into that environment of well being, believe you are worthy, and find your Divine Intervener. Before you start, get a clear idea of what it is you want, and know clearly the feeling of what it would be like emotionally to have this done. Here is another image for you."

0. Bring yourself into an altered state by imagining a peaceful place, breathing softly, and becoming present to yourself in the heart.
1. Assert your beliefs that you are worthy of your desire, you believe you can change your reality, and that the Divine Intelligence will assist you.
2. Visualize clearly in your mind a picture of the desired result.
3. Speak out stating that you are a believer in your ability to manifest your desires and ask for assistance.
4. In your imagination feel the result of the desire being completed and surround this vision with the joy and bliss of it being so.
5. With your intention send the request for the desire/visualization to be completed.
6. In your mind, connect to a higher power to assist in the completion.
7. Feel the gratitude of completion and thank the higher power or those you have called to assist you.

"But that is exactly what we saw with health miracles! And it falls back to these chakra steps again!"

"Why are you surprised? The processes instigate the intention and attention to a new possibility under the Law of Cause & Effect giving life to an energy with a clear signature of mental and emotional vibration. It is the causal process of mind over matter, as above so below, as done through the chakras. To make this clear and strong, you must go to this place of infinite possibilities every day and in this environment of continued well being, faith and trust, enforce the vision and enfold it with the emotion of gratitude, repeating the process until you begin to see the Law of Attraction responding with people, events, situations coming before you. You then act on these as they attract into your energy field."

"I am familiar with the Napoleon Hill book. He very much follows a softer version of the brothers 12 rules and there is nothing spiritual about it. These steps are exactly the same as Napoleon Hill stuff. The only difference outside the box is you are asking the higher power to do it."

"Yes, that is so. The real difference in the processes is that Napoleon Hill assumes the higher power is you and your mind but you still have to work your butt off. The others assume that some other higher powers were the forces that answered. The big deal is that this process is one of being proactive in creating your life in a way that you bring forward with grace and ease. Isn't that what you want – to unfold your passions and get the crap out of your life?"

"The difference is whether I work my butt off with physical energy or sit on my butt and let the energy find a way to get the same result?"

"Yes, one is within the norm of the global belief box, the other is outside of it."

SETTING THE WEALTH ENVIRONMENT

"Do they follow the same practices?"

"Yes, there is a consistency. Belief, trust, love, acceptance, surrender, faith, desire, worthy, miracle minded, positive outcome, compassion, and trustworthiness of a Higher Force is repeated over and over in different ways. So in view of what you have learned, what can you suggest as the type of environmental setting that you should be in?"

"Clearly well being is a natural setting to be in because the cells, the brain, the heart all can be fooled. They do not know the difference between imagined and real. And we don't even know when negative thoughts and emotions are toxic environmental stimulants that chain react affecting the body in a cascade of negative problems. Being constantly in Alpha assists and we have to be mindful all the time of our energy portfolios."

"Indeed, being present to me in the heart is crucial. It is a simple practice of moving out of beta into alpha that first places your attention away from the higher interfering brainwaves of consciousness into the lower state and centering your attention to the heart energetic center. Here is the gateway to that Higher Power which is represented by me representing your Soul."

"The next is the energy of love. It has to be the common catalyst to all the systems of miracles. It means using and feeling the high energies of forgiveness, unity, compassion, gratitude, faith and trust. It is a surrender to a higher power to bring your desires to you, to manifest from the quantum field a new possibility to be collapsed into reality."

"Yes, this process is common to all of the Gurus' processes. It is one that the desires go out into the morphic fields to attract likeness. That means the altered state takes you into the heart, the center of the quantum void of infinite possibilities."

"The next is the altered state that drops below Alpha into Theta where there is no identity and means totally letting go of that which is the normal interference of the mind stuck in the limiting consciousness boxes. It is the entry into a true state of self, one with you and the Soul. It is a place where Supernocebo does not exist."

"From what we have spoken of, how would you now relate this to your chakra energy centers?"

"Well at the top of the process or 'Above' is thought initiated in the Crown Chakra. In the altered state of pure consciousness, it is here that the scene is set to affirm my beliefs as I say. '*I believe in changing my reality. I believe I am worthy of my desires. I believe I am the creator of my life, and I believe in me as Superplacebo a part of a Higher Power that will assist me.*' As I am in an altered state, in control of the conscious mind, we have a direct access to the subconscious. Here it is best to affirm what I believe in case it has some other ideas about sabotaging my process."

"And then?"

"I must create a clear vision in my 3rd eye chakra of the desired result. In my now higher conscious mind, I create a clear picture of what the desired result would be."

"And the next energy center?"

"I would activate the throat chakra by communicating words that affirm out loud to the heart, you and the Universe what I desire in simple concise statements. I would be clear and concise, aligning the words with the energy of your the vision."

"And in the heart?"

"Dropping into the heart as the center of emotion. I would infuse the vision of the desired result clearly in my higher mind as being completed and me enjoying it. I would bring in the emotion of my total being vibrating in a state of bliss and joy. I would form a clear picture of this and be surrounded by that joy. I would linger here in a field of total peace, love and harmony as

I gave strong life to this vision infused with an emotional signature, placing this into the morphic field of the heart."

"What about the Solar Plexus?"

"At that point, I would launch clear focus and intent thus initiating the process of intention energy for manifesting the desire. Being centered on love, I would create a resonance with emotion of completion making it strong using the vision of completion strong and potent, feeling and enjoying it over and over. This would open the communication channel to the quantum field of infinite possibilities and you would assist in its manifesting into reality."

"At the sacral level, it is where the faith and trust in me as you energize the vision into the relationships needs to bring the result forward into my reality. It is here that I would substitute my beliefs on the Higher Power to be you and me now coherently attuned to bring forth that which I am already enjoying, in whatever way it can. It is the formal request in the completion of the desires. This is a release to you and Universe of a greater intelligence and a detachment from the results."

"And finally?"

"Yes, here the condition is released and I surrender to the Higher You and the Universe to do what it needs to do to entangle and collapse into the desired reality. Or it works towards attracting that result initiated by the cause. At the 7th Chakra dedicated to the materialization, I hold on to the truth of completion, with an unfettered faith and trust. It is fulfilled by the powerful feeling of gratitude that surrounds the vision of completion. This is where the vortexes will attract various energy signatures, people, events and situations into my reality."

"That is very good. You can see the difference of being in and out of the box."

"Yes, one is enforced that this process needs repetition. These super dudes all say you are leaving it to the Universe to bring the results to you, and depending on the complexity, many choices may be brought into your reality to act upon."

"I can see an analogy to this is with the Law of Cause and Effect. If you put into the field that you want to win the lotto, then when you have a ticket counter come before you, it may be a wise choice to buy a ticket! If it does not work it is because something is still not right, and it is the repetitive process that will entrench beliefs and strength of conviction and intent. Strong positive emotion and intent in a field of well being and love is crucial."

"Well, if it was the lotto, you would have received an intuitive niggling to buy a lotto ticket! But there are other reasons we will get to later. Regardless, always be aware that it is repetition, clarity and strength of desire and emotion that are your allies. Love and well being are paramount. Your morphic and subtle fields need to be pumped with passion of completion. When it does not appear to work, check your beliefs with your douser and continue. You have no idea when something will manifest, nor in what form. Have faith and allow the power of the mental and emotional energies to resonate and attract. You will see a difference."

"It is not a coincidence that we are looking at the same steps in health miracles, wealth miracles and chakras. It is an indication that you need to think outside the box and get help from me. And whether it is a miracle, is cellular reality, or one in attracting the external reality, there is no difference because either way the brain is the dude that needs to be told what to do. The brain is also the guy in charge of projecting and sensing your material world as a second main responsibility."

"Ok, let us continue on that comment. I am still curious about this other place you dwell in the midbrain. Is this where reality actually changes and miracles occur? Is that where I can get some fast action?"

"You are always looking for an analytical shortcut, dear Ed. It is an interesting question and I will answer these. But in your new knowing, you must first understand how your reality is currently working against you to understand how it works for you."

"You mean change the laws from the matter over mind of cause and effect to mind over matter of cause an effect?"

"You have been listening."

"Well, I can understand these steps very well. I am amazed at the simplicity and that they follow the functions of the chakras."

"You will find that if you study the cases, there are many variations around these steps. The fact is that that they all work, but not all the time."

"Yes, I can see that now because it is the mind that needs to be convinced of the belief it can be done. But it seems that the process of getting into that place where it can be launched energetically is a pretty big variable. Can we talk about meditation and the program portals?"

13

THE PROGRAMMING PORTALS

Fundamental to the manifestation of all miracles is the self induced or the assisted state of consciousness outside of the conscious mind. This altered state is where your Soul lives, listens, and communicates the instructions pertaining to what you believe is your reality.

BACK TO THAT BRAIN AGAIN

"So you know now that the brain has the job to create programs so you learn to survive. The way it does this is by firing and wiring neurological pathways that connect neurons in a way that encodes the appropriate condition and expectation as a program that creates chemical, physiological, and physical results. The emotional signature is key to creating the program that can be reactivated by a thought alone."

"And when you have a new experience that provides heightened emotional feelings, these simply get branded into the neurological circuitry in implicit and explicit memory and are available for recall any time as a program ready to enter the operating system of the subconscious providing orders to the brain and cells to act as set in the program or retrieve the appropriate program from DNA."

"In order to change this from the conscious state where it has 5% of memory allocation dedicated to your will, logic, creativity, and reasoning it really does not have much hope in changing the explicit declarative memory dedicated to semantic learned and episodic experience. As you understand now, the catalyst to change programs in the implicit is emotion, especially highly charged one-time emotional events. They also get branded into memory by repeated emotions from same experiences that keep firing the same way to hard wire the neural networks. In order to trigger programming processes outside of the normal beliefs there is the need to get rid of the conscious mind of will, logic, creativity and reasoning."

"Yes, I get that now. That is where Supernocebo gets carried away with his duties and sort of fills the subconscious hard drive up with a lot of this negative crap of survival and it gets harder and harder to get by him to add new stuff."

"Yes, but it is not that you can't create new programs; they just take a greater emotional charge and assertion. You still learn new things if you want to. As you get older, you just don't believe you need to learn more things and the programs you use are on auto pilot. For example if you wanted to quit smoking or drinking – habits that Supernocebo says are good because it makes you feel better – it may get to be harder and harder to break as you age or get the body addicted. Then the body controls the mind which is ok to Supernocebo because the body is expendable; there to suit your desires. But it may take perseverance of months of actions to reprogram and break the old habits."

"Superplacebo, what you are saying is a striking paradox that the process of healing may not be because of some divine intervention or power that did the healing, it is because the mind became subconsciousness and instructed the brain to get its shit together and open up the pharmacy to instigate the healing with its troop of cells all containing a different set of programs from DNA. Now you are talking! That is the placebo, isn't it? We have determined that our brains that are responsible for managing the chemical and physiological changes in the body do not know the difference between imagination and reality. So it is the mind that convinces you as the programmer, but not the regular beta mind."

"I am your mind. We are just in a different state of mind. Most would say you have to be out of your mind to believe these things. Ironically that is true. You will see it is the same place, just from a different perspective. As we have seen, external and internal miracles show clearly that this reality we live in can be instructed to change dramatically once the directives are issued. In your current state of awareness inside the box there would seem to be a hierarchy that needs to be convinced to change the program code, recompile it and replace the old version. The conscious, subconscious, the brain, the heart, and the cells all take instructions to respond to such an order."

"I see that there are many ways to institute the appropriate directives, and they all use an imaginary vision of the mind, a new possibility of a physical state of being that manifests itself into physical reality. The strength of emotion assists in collapsing waves of possibility in the mind to physical reality. But in many cases of health and wealth miracles the most direct, and dramatic being the placebo that issues a mind over matter command, there is no divine Intervention, it is simply the mind."

"It is so because the ultimate director of the code change sits above the domain of the subconscious where the code can be instigated, changed, retrieved from DNA, and recompiled into the programs that control the version of reality. That is what you are as me. And from that position of higher vibration, we are one with the subconscious. It just becomes more difficult to institute the change as age and stubbornness to believe inside the box becomes rigid. But on the positive side, as you grow old it can be easier to become one with me."

"Ok, but what is particularly perplexing about this is that we are engaged in this process of creating reality all the time. We all have control over our imaginations. We have seen that we create programs of habits, new beliefs, and behaviors all through life on a reactive and proactive basis. We are already engaged in this programming hierarchy in some way. We have also seen that sometimes we can, through these miracles, create more dramatic proactive changes that are outside the norm of our belief system. So there is something I am missing here as to why I can't do this all the time."

"There are several ways that you can create these new programs or updates to old ones. To change a program, you have to create the emotional intensity and habits supporting the new vision to be greater than what's already a program. The example of addictions is a good one. Similarly if it is a new physical ability, it requires consistent training, especially if your body is older and worn out or dysfunctional. As you know, it becomes more difficult to create new programs like Olympic abilities when your body is not capable anymore. Similarly, the box always allows people to think outside and to convince the rest if they can. The box of limiting consciousness reflects the same process. The other way, as we have in the case of miracles, is to concentrate on the vision and get out of the conscious conformity box by executing from above to below which is not limited to the box below."

"But, regardless, you have to get the brain and Supernocebo out of the way. That is how you reach me as your buddy out of the box, now issuing orders from your higher mind. Call me the Divine programmer if you like but it is simply your mind in my jurisdiction of energy that issues the directive to the subconscious, then the brain."

"And this is why hypnosis and meditation do this part of getting around your persistent brother?"

THE POWER OF MEDITATION

"Exactly, Ed. Like hypnosis, meditation bypasses the critical analytical mind to move into the subconscious system of programs beyond analytical interference away from the outer world of body and time. Here you can pay attention to the inner world of thought and feeling. It moves the mind from selfish to selfless, from being somebody to no body and no one, some place to no place, materialist to non-materialist, from survivor to creator, imbalance to balance, from limiting emotions to expansive emotion of love, and joy; known to unknown."

"If the neo-cortex is the home of conscious awareness like intellect and planning you must move beyond it to meditate. You must move into the limbic brain or the midbrain where I am represented. You have to declare a cease fire on all neural networks. The neo-cortex uses the 5 senses and is preoccupied with the body, environment and time. This is ego surviving so nobody, no thing, no place and no time is a serious threat to it."

"Meditation is about navigating brain waves to effect how suggestible we are at the moment. The EEC measures how neurons fire together since they create electromagnetic fields. The slower, the deeper we go, the higher the wave the further away from the normal operating system which can be the belief boxes of consciousness. The worst place is where all programs familiar are running at the same time in the high state of Beta created by stress chemicals."

"Ok, we went through this. You have to get out of Beta and Alpha in some way. Are you going to tell me the best ways?"

"Yes, you know this now. High Beta is focus crisis mode where my brother loves to take you. Mid Beta is focused attention, learning and remembering. Low Beta is the start of a more relaxed state of awareness, interested attention like reading a book. Here is where you activate the frontal lobe. In Theta it is like twilight where there is no analytical mind and high suggestibility. That is where you really want to be to institute change."

"I understand that to increase suggestibility you have to weaken the analytical mind. Is this what happens in cases involving physical or mental fatigue and continued exposure to social, physical, environmental cues in sensory deprivation. The altered state works the same way, doesn't it?"

"Yes, an extreme hunger or emotional shock and trauma are extreme emotional signatures that create instant programs – once again as survival firing-wiring of neural pathways. The altered state is common because it bypasses Supernocebo and goes to theta where the suggestibility to the subconscious is higher and without trauma. The state of well being is vital to stop things that are going on in you that are on auto pilot. This makes it easier to suggest a new mode of behavior from a new state of mind. And that state of mind must be a mind where no time, space, identity or thoughts exist."

"But still, this is no guarantee because the subconscious may not agree, right? Is this where hypnosis can help?"

"In many cases yes. But if the subject has too much analytical-mental activity, getting into that empty space will not work. If the suggestion is inappropriate to the limited programs of the subconscious, then it will also not be accepted. When the hypnotist knows he has you in that state, he checks to see if you - now the subconscious - agree to listen. You are now under his spell as he is able to suggest things to the subconscious mind. He makes some suggestions for later when you are in the conscious buzz state. He may suggest that when someone claps, you will bark like a dog. Now be aware that the subconscious mind simply takes orders and responds - if it has been given the orders properly and it does not have something encoded that is in conflict."

"Like if your true belief is that this hypnosis is crap."

"If you believe hypnosis is a joke, your subconscious will protect you and not let the suggestion through."

"And in many cases the process works because that suggestion has now been programmed and loaded into the bio-computer of subconsciouness to be run at a specific time by the operating software. So suddenly 10 minutes later, when someone claps, you start barking like a dog in your seat. Of course everyone laughs and applauds the hypnotist. Your subconscious is doing this all the time - filtering what comes in on the basis of your belief system."

"So, the Hypnotist bypassed the consciousness to input into the bio-computer of the subconscious what he wanted to. There was nothing there in the belief system to negate it. In self-hypnosis one does it by themselves. It works but not all the time of course."

"Now be aware that this process of hypnosis is done all the time by some medical doctors, psychologists, psychiatrists and energy therapists. Some serious and spectacular issues have been solved this way. Some cases have even bypassed surgery. Does it work every time? No. Why not? Because, what is already programmed, and in agreement with the belief system, does not agree with the new information."

"I am aware that in the profession of psychiatry, the hypnosis process goes a step further. In regression therapy, a patient is brought into a hypnotic state and is slowly taken backward in time to a point where a problem like a trauma or a physical injury occurred. In the case of a trauma, once the patient gets to that point and it is revealed, it is released simply by saying and believing it to be so and it gets erased! There are millions of documented facts of incredible trauma healings. Likewise, there are millions of documented cases that have eliminated serious illnesses like cancer, AID's, and other problems. In the physical case, a patient is regressed to the point of injury or before. The patient imagines, and is aided by reinforcement from the therapist to see the issue gone. That is it, and in many cases, poof, it is gone. The belief it is so gets the subconscious to make it so and it is. A miraculous unexplained anomaly happens instantly."

"It is not erased as much as it is re-perceived. Are you not seeing the same idea coming forward here? When these patients surrendered to a higher authority and accepted a suggestion, they were outside of the belief box that constrained them. Then whatever was impressed on subconscious expressed as a condition to experience an event occurred. The subconscious is the objective responsive process while the conscious is subjective."

"You may be interested to know in comparison to a computer the subconscious mind can process 20 million environmental stimuli per second. The conscious mind can process 40 environmental stimuli per second. The conscious mind can look back and forward, but while the conscious mind is out dreaming and playing, the subconscious mind is always on duty dealing with the moment now. It effectively is the manager, the overriding authority and manages things the way it was trained. In simple terms, if the subconscious does not agree with the conscious, guess who wins? One follows energy instructions, the other makes them up and uses imagination. When thoughts are conveyed to subconscious as energy, impressions are made on brain cells and as soon as subconscious accepts the idea, it proceeds to put it into effect."

"I can see the reasons to get out of mind so to speak, in a peaceful state, in direct communication with the subconscious and you. Otherwise it is hopeless."

"Not hopeless. You are still creating within the operating system of the group mind or consciousness. Karma, Cause and Effect, Law of Attraction are all at your service here. You have done this all your life. The subconscious does not reason and compare and decide. Yet it can act by suggestion if you persevere under the rule of the operating system. And it can revise programs that control biology like in the case of miracles."

"But if you control the subconscious why do you agree to execute these horrible norm programs?"

"Because that is what the partnership is all about. We are here to learn together and experience things. You choose these and you choose to load them. I do not choose them when you command them by way of your free will perceptions, mental abilities and emotional engagements. I can whisper into your conscious mind but you may not listen. If you can't form a partnership, then those programs are on autopilot. It is we not you or I that control things."

"And if there is no partnership, then you can't act either. What a strange partnership! Let's talk more about hypnosis which helps the meeting of the minds."

HYPNOSIS - A PROGRAM PORTAL

"Indeed, hypnosis does provide a way of getting out of your normal mind to where the subconscious is. Hypnosis is an easy way to launch the intention that takes you into the domain of the theta brain waves and the subconscious. Over and over, as you have mentioned this process has become more widely accepted and used to modify unwanted behavior. It is simple and can take you to that most preferable state of theta if you want to modify behavior and make suggestions for reprogramming reality. Even self-hypnosis has been shown to modify behavior, emotions and attitudes. It can be used to increase confidence and develop new skills. It can help to reduce stress and anxiety, and can even help people overcome habits such as smoking and overeating. Self-hypnosis is also used by sportspeople to enhance their athletic performance."

"I remember that kids, ages 2-6 are primarily in this state of Theta because their brains haven't yet developed the Alpha capability. It is when they are most susceptible to programming what they need for survival. It's where the hypnotists make suggestions that you don't even remember. It's where the unconscious and the subconscious open up to being programmed. The Altered State through meditation attempts to get you there. Sometimes prayer and rituals and trances enter this area that gives access to the programs and then the hypnotist, the healer, the doctor talks to the higher mind to submit a change in the reality. But, like in the case of the placebo, I can bypass the consciousness and all these other parties to submit the change in the program."

"It is true but the state and strength of emotion is what dictates. A child has no preconceived biases or perceptions. It has no concept of time or space or identity and is effectively living in the greater consciousness in an altered state. It does not need to be induced into the state. As it develops within the operating system of the global belief box, it acquires its biases and identity that begins to interfere."

THE ALTERED STATE IS KEY

"The altered state or some form of it is directly correlated with the state of the brain's vibrations. It is apparent that the brain in a usual conscious active state of Alpha developed at age 6 then Beta at age 12 interferes with access to the subconscious which vibrates in Theta as developed at age 2. The need to be in the state of lower Alpha and Theta as in the case of young children up to age 6 offers the time of greatest programming opportunities as the brain has not yet developed the Alpha and Beta to interfere with the programming."

"So the key is to be a kid again and get into the same state of mind."

"It is not that you cannot create and modify programs in the subconscious, it is that by design and evolution, you develop the programs for survival and adaptability through evolutionary stages and these form the primary basis not easily dislodged when in the beta state of consciousness. As you know now, to gain access to the computer code and the operating system you have to be in a state outside of Beta where analysis, intellect and the decision making processes do not exist. And the best state to be in is Theta just like a kid. That is what hypnosis leads you into and that is why it is so effective in what people call 'letting go'."

"What I find so interesting is that the state of well being is not just a New Age or Religious practice to talk to a superior God, gods or archangel that can assist in the process of creating miracles. There is a biological, physiological and chemical process that interferes with the ability to move into that state of communication with the subconscious mind. The state of stress and negativity either physical or emotional suppresses many biological processes that inhibit normal functions. This is why a state of well being of peace and love are enhancers of these biological functions."

"I can therefore conclude that if you are an adult, where Beta and Gamma are dominant in consciousness, it is the Theta altered state brought about through some process like hypnosis that would be the most effective way to get back into that programmable environment in order to optimize access to the subconscious where physical changes of reality are instigated and directed."

"Within the confines of your global and individual consciousness operating system, this is what you already do in some way or other. You just do not understand how, but you will as this higher wisdom sets into your new mind. What you really seek answers to is how to move out of the box and create miracles at will."

"Yes, it seems that the placebo effect directly bypasses any requirement for the Higher Power of Divine intervention to make the change in reality. How does the placebo bypass Beta?"

"The most successful examples are those that supercharge the vision of a new state of being healed with emotion, then totally surrender to that outcome as already done without analysis, question or thoughts. Within the confines of your belief box, in order to achieve this, the entry into the altered state is a prerequisite as is a state of wellbeing."

"Understood. Otherwise, the brains subconsciously through both physical and mental interference can create cascades of chemical, and biochemical reactions that interfere with being in that programmable space".

"Indeed, you will not be successful unless it is so. You find it more difficult with age because 95% of the subconscious is on autopilot with Supernocebo drawing from the past experiences and programs already solidified. They are time based habits of addictions to the past. And as he is also concerned about the future security he draws from the past to develop tactics for the future. These are strict limitations preventing anything new from entering the boxes of belief. It isn't that there is no space left. It is because the process requires more and more repetition to get through and you believe there is less and less to learn."

"Unless it is highly emotionally charged or traumatic?"

"Yes, one of the best examples of this is where people have a Near Death Experience and come face to face with me as their Higher Selves. Let us talk of that afterwards."

A SELF HYPNOSIS PROCESS

"Is the process of hypnosis difficult to do?"

"Not at all. It is very simple. But letting go of the reality around is not. The purpose of course, is to get access to that place where the programs are stored in the subconscious mind. It is here that I am able to receive instructions from you to have this temporary partnership. And even though you are the best one to execute self hypnosis, you are best led by someone else first, or create a recording to follow."

"Why?"

"Because the mind needs to be silenced. And how can it be silenced when you are speaking, thinking and placing attention on the process? Once you are trained in this and can stop analyzing the process and outcome, then it may be easy. Your mind needs to see and feel results otherwise my brother begins to tell you it is all foolish. The intellectual loop you create as you try steps and look for results may feed doubts. It is therefore best to be led into this space of no mind, no identity, no time, no thoughts."

"That doesn't make sense. How can you create thoughts and visions in that void?"

"That is the secret you must learn to be comfortable with. When you can feel the experience of the void and be in it totally, and know this, then the greater mind will open to you. Is that not what you have attained here?"

"Well, I can tell you I was never sure that this is so. And it is still hard to determine what is my thoughts and your thoughts. But I have developed a sense of it being true."

"Hypnosis can make this easier as you let go slowly and are led into the state of suggestibility. That degree of suggestibility will determine how well the new program is accepted in subconscious."

"Yes, I understand. If the subconscious does not agree, it won't happen. But if you are the subconscious why not just do whatever I ask? I am doing this anyway."

"I will when you and I are truly one mind and your belief system is in total alignment. The real question is why you as ME and YOU do not just do what you ask. Then we step outside the rules of the box. Are you there yet? If you do not have a belief that it can work, then it won't. That is why it is so important to have the faith and trust in the facilitator so you let go of the beta and alpha mind. But to go direct, you need the same faith in us as one."

"Ok what are the basic steps?"

"Once you are in a seated position, have settled into a quiet still mind, you can become present to yourself and leave time behind. By simply focusing on your breathing in and out slowly, you will shift your mind into the now. Soft meditation music can help here as the senses are becoming detached and the auditory one is simply listening softly slowing any body activities, creating an environment of well being, peace and comfort."

"How long?"

"At first allow at least 5 minutes to truly settle into this space. It's important to drop deeper and deeper. The usual way is to use a counting process. This is done by the facilitator asking for you to act physically to know you are consciously responding and becoming more open to suggestion. He can say: *'raise your right hand to your chest and now you are going to place your mind onto your heart. With this attention, feel the heart beating and he will go deeper and deeper into your heart energy of pure consciousness. You will now drop deeper and deeper into the heart energy as I count from 5 to 1. Are you ok with this?'* "

"After a few minutes of feeling this with your raised hand, he will lead you into the count. *'We will start at 5. Are you ready? We are now dropping deeper into the heart. Can you feel the peace and love? 4, we are dropping deeper now, 3, we are now deeper. 2, we are very, very deep into the heart and you can feel the total peace, silence and love. 1, we are now deep, deep and as you drop your hand onto your lap on the count of 0, you will be one with the heart field of total stillness, love, and peace. Now drop your hand. Do you feel the wonderful energy?'* "

"OK, that's cool. I could record those steps and play quiet music. But should I do this myself. What if I get stuck there?"

"Well just believe you won't. You are always conscious just like now. You are letting go of the 3D stuff that interferes."

"Ok, will I be in the void through this?"

"You can be, but it is best to do that as a next step. The facilitator would ask you to linger here and feel the space. This may take several minutes. Then he would use some visualization process, like a tunnel or a beam of light to lift you away from your physics of the reality and your belief consciousness. Which do you prefer?"

"Let us use the light."

"The facilitator would say '*Imagine a bright light from above coming down to the top of your head to fill the body. See it, feel it and let it become reality. Do you feel it now and can you sense it?*' Your response would confirm you are opening up more and more."

"Ok."

"Then he would take you into the next step of entering the void of infinite possibilities and the higher mind. '*Imagine an aura of pure light from heart region emanating out to surround you, protecting you. See it, feel it and let it become reality. Now only your Higher Self and highly evolved loving entities who mean you well will be able to influence you during this and other sessions. You are totally protected by an aura of pure white light*'."

"This would help my mind become at ease, right?"

"Yes, this can be repeated by you to confirm it into your mind so not to have fear or doubt enter. The next part would take your heart based consciousness of pure mind and lift it out away from the body and environment: '*I am now going to count to 5 and as I do you will visualize and feel yourself rising up to a higher and higher state of superconsciousness as your Higher Self. Are you ready?*' Your confirmation would allow the next step."

"Soft music for a few moments could be used before the question are you ready?"

"Yes, of course. Then the facilitator would begin. '*5, we are beginning to feel a separation as your heart mind is being allowed to lift. Do you sense this? 4, we are now lifting slowly as we separate lifting along the beam of light. Do you feel this? 3, we are now lifting higher to feel the beam of light drawing you upwards higher and higher. 2, you are now above your body which is below you. Can you sense, see or feel this? 1, you are now separated as pure consciousness. You can linger here and orient yourself.*'

This may take some time and you can float around becoming familiar with your surroundings'. This is a space where you may be led to look around and respond to what is sensed, or seen."

"That sounds pretty scary!"

"Is it scary now? You obviously have not done this yet?"

"No I have not and I understand that this separation is a key part of rising higher. You are communicating with me in the lower end of this consciousness."

"Exactly. Now let us go the next step: *'You are now going to float through a tunnel as pure consciousness and at the end you will see a light that you will enter. Here you will meet your Higher Self or Soul as pure soul consciousness and enter the quantum void of infinite possibilities. I will count you along the tunnel from 1 to 5. Are you ready?'* When the answer is yes the countdown would begin."

"Does it have to be a tunnel?"

"No, not at all. I am using this because it is becoming more of the norm from so many near death experiences. You can use anything you like to do this; a beam of light, a set of steps, a rising of vibration, an intensity of light, a silver tube, whatever. Now the facilitator would begin the count: *'You are now at 1, entering a dark tunnel. Feel yourself, moving into the entrance with a feeling of peace and love. Can you feel this? 2, you are now inside the tunnel, floating gracefully forward. Can you feel it? 3, now you can see a light at the far end. Can you see or feel this light? 4, you are now floating through the light. Are you through? 5, there is a light at the far end. Can you see or feel this light? 6, you are now floating through the light. Are you through? 7, you are into a burst of bright light with a feeling of peace, love and silence. Can you feel this or see it? Now you can linger here and feel the essence of this space. In your mind, ask your Higher Self to come forward.'* Here you would feel the empty space and allow it to permeate your being for several minutes."

"This is the real way to get into that higher consciousness with you isn't it?"

"Yes. Now the next step would be to understand the void and what this is. The facilitator would lead; *'You are now totally in the quantum void of pure higher consciousness, a place, like your imagination that has infinite possibilities. You are no one, no where, no time. There is only pure thought. Feel the wholeness of being the true You and being whole with who YOU really are as pure consciousness. Can you sense the presence of your Soul?' I want you to linger here and feel the love and the light.'* In this place you would linger for several moments."

"Now you are truly out of the box into the quantum void of infinite possibilities. This is becoming the more common way to let go of the reality and enter a new mind."

"Ok, what would be the next step?"

"From here, it would depend on your purpose; answers to questions, instigating miracles, changing your reality, dealing with issues, looking at previous lives, looking into the future, travelling interdimensionally, there are endless possibilities, remember."

"Ok, I want to look at this past, future stuff. I take it that in our discussion of miracles, this is the place I want to get to before I follow the steps we talked about, the thought, visualization, words, emotion and seeing the vision done?"

"Precisely, the truth is that where these miracles have worked, those people would have most likely been led to this place of infinite possibilities. Of course the processes would differ but it is here that the divine intervention would be asked to do the work of instruction of the subconscious. This process will assist in increasing your chances of being totally out of the box."

"Ok, let us continue on the basis of what I have already gotten used to; asking a question on some issue."

"The facilitator would then say: *'Ask a question directed at Your Soul. Ask about the past, present or future, state your desire for information or an experience. Once you ask, you will let go and have the faith and trust that your Higher Mind will work this out for you in the best way that assists you. Then allow this to flow into the void. Can you feel the flow of energy into the void?'* Here is where a few moments would be taken."

"That's it?"

"In this case yes. You are already doing this, are you not? You may not have gone through the same steps but You are communicating with me. You have found a portal at a lower energy level and that is the beginning of opening the infinite mind of possibilities. Now we are looking at graduating you into the higher planes from this point."

"Ok, how do we close this off?"

"This would be a place to linger with soft music for several minutes after the facilitator would ask you to repeat: *'I now open up channels of communication by removing obstacles and allowing the receiving of information and experiences to help me in the present life time. I ask this of my Soul to open communications at all times',* or something like this."

"From this point, you would be led back through the tunnel and back down to re-engage into your body. This would be a simple process of the facilitator telling you *'We are now going to turn back into the tunnel and feel yourself floating out the other side. Then as we count down from 5 to 1 your consciousness will drop down and re-engage with your body in the present and remember everything'.*"

"So this is the same process used for out of body experiences and astral projection, isn't it?

"Yes, this is a common practice of getting deeper into the altered state where anything becomes possible. It is where you execute the downward causation process of as above, so below, or what we have been discussing as mind over matter. It is a similar process to that used in future life progression, between life regression, past life regression and opening up to your true superconsciousness. It is also similar to near death experiences and the process of getting a life review."

"What happens when you die?" Can we talk about that?"

14

WHEN YOU NEARLY DIE

It's easy to understand who and what you are; just go out of your mind and have an encounter with your true Self.

WHERE AM I IF NOT DEAD?

"I find this whole business of near death really interesting because I know a bit about these strange cases. You said the process of getting into the void and meeting a Higher Self is similar to a near death. But I met you and I did not have a near death experience. I know that those who practice deep meditation will tell you they also meet a higher fellow filled with wisdom and love. I seemed to have met you through meditation as well. The other thing is the people who come back to living after their experience are sometimes changed dramatically. Can you tell me more about this process?"

"Do you not feel you are also changing after several of our sessions? Yes, they are of interest to your analytical mind because the process of these near death experiences or NDE's is one that does not require any assistance or steps. No mind meddles with it. It illustrates clearly how consciousness separates from the physical world and lets go of absolutely everything. So, yes, there is much wisdom to draw from these documented experiences. This is where it is uncontrived by anybody and you absolutely and totally get rid of that meddling brain and that interfering physics of reality. You take a trip to visit the other side, your Higher Self as your Soul."

"I can see that this is good for those rational brains like me that are trapped in the belief box; if these are well documented."

"Yes, these cases are for the rational beta brain demanding evidence for these beliefs. These are totally non-planned by your mortal self and they reveal many things about dying and your true self. It is so common, so researched and has so much consistent evidence about the nature of the journey to the other side that has not been planned by the conscious mind. It is a wonderful repository of information for us to look at."

"Can I get a better picture of what typically happens, who NDE people meet, and how and why they decide to come back after being pronounced dead? I have heard there are millions of people dying this way all the time - then coming back to tell about it. I know there are many professional, medical and research people looking into this particular phenomenon."

"Yes, it is so. Yet the consciousness norm is still resistant to acceptance so these do not get registered in the global subconsciousness. And even though, according to the norm rules of the person being clinically pronounced dead, gone, dead for some period of time like 4-60 minutes with the heart stopped, cells dying in the brain from lack of oxygen, and it is coffin time, these cases receive little attention. That tells you how you all form the belief boxes that limit you. So I will tell you about these cases."

"And do these cases reflect the truth?"

"Yes. You will find in our talks that I will seldom bring information forward that is not true. Upon dying, your consciousness leaves the body. But you can still see, hear, think, move, communicate, float, tell jokes, and retain senses regardless of distance from the body. In fact the senses are even better because you have come through the astral plane. They are heightened just like in the case of miracles. Everything that was ever learned, experienced, and felt - along with all of the senses are left completely intact."

"Sort of like now talking to you? So obviously it had nothing to do with the brain. That brain was pronounced dead. Consciousness, which clearly includes the life giving force, leaves the body, goes on a little trip, then comes back and da-ah, the body has life again. All the dead cells are cool again. Rigamortis has no say here - the white face gets pink again, and it is wakey, wakey time! Right?"

"That is so. The brain, as you know, is a relay station, not the controller. When you die, you are simply higher consciousness, a state of pure thought without any relation to the brain and its conscious mind. It does have its own copy however. That is exactly the state that these meditative and hypnosis practices attempt to get to. You can research these for yourself, but I will tell you what these stages are. Not all are the same because each individual has different beliefs that influence their experiences."

THE STAGES OF NEARLY DYING

"Yes, I am aware of this and I have seen books on this topic. I know these excursions have been recorded independently from many different places, independently by different unrelated people and cases."

"What you will find with many is a word that can be used to describe many people's experience. It is ineffability - a difficulty in describing the trip with any real justice. It is unexplainable and beyond their comprehension."

"The first stage is an *out of body* experience. You find yourself looking at the physical body, watching and hearing things as a spectator. You will feel like pure consciousness that is indescribable. This is your spiritual energy body lifting away. But because you are pure consciousness energy you cannot touch other bodies or material things. No one will hear or see you as you are weightless, floating, going through things like a cloud. What you will look like will be from your own mind. It could be a cloud, a ghost-like entity, a ball of light – it is totally dependent on what your pure consciousness decides to present you as. When you practice the hypnosis steps I gave to you, you will experience this."

"And I understand that I should not go further until I do, right?"

"Yes, otherwise you may easily delude yourself as the lower mind is still in charge. What you will feel is extreme peace and quiet. That is what the void is. Even if there is severe trauma or pain you will experience wonderful feelings of comfort, peace, quiet, relief, and no pain."

"Well so far, I have not achieved this but I will work at it, and record my steps."

"Another common stage occurs as you hear the news of dying from the people in the area, or those that may appear in the vicinity of the parting. It could include the doctor, others around your physical body, as well as events around it."

"It may be possible in the next stage to hear unusual auditory sensations of buzzing, ringing, and clicks. This will vary as well but it is a sign that you are embarking on a journey typically through a transition into a special place. Here you get pulled rapidly through a dark space, tunnel, valley, pipe, or some such thing in a wonderful worry free ride."

"I see the similarity to the steps in hypnosis."

"Yes, you will enter the void of nothing where you are pure thought and consciousness. Here the pure consciousness has different abilities and senses so it can bring forward into your awareness your Higher Self and other spiritual beings that are part of your pure consciousness. These may be people that you had known before, like friends and relatives would come to greet you. You would see everything filled with white light and beautiful - like a feeling of coming home. These beings will not have a physical body and the types of people you encounter will depend upon your belief background of pure consciousness which now holds all your information about all lives. It will be dependent upon the purpose of your dying. There will be no speaking as thoughts are communicated as a direct transfer - no language totally telepathic."

"What do you mean the purpose of my dying?"

"We will explore that in another session but you will learn that your life has been planned by me, your Soul and Spirit Guides that work with your soul family to create a plan. A Near Death Experience could be a planned exit point and those that assisted you in this plan would be there to assist by having a reality check with you."

"Really?"

"At this stage when the appropriate entities have assembled there will be typical questions that come forward telepathically like: `Are you ready to die? What have you done in your life that is sufficient?` Here there is no condemnation or judgment, only total love and acceptance coming from the light."

"Is this where you get the review?"

"In the next stage you will bring into awareness a bright light being which is your Spirit Guide or me looking the way you remember. We will present a high speed video panorama review of your life. Here the intent is only to provoke reflections. There will be a rapid display of temporal memories in chronological order that occur almost instantaneous. The images generate emotions as they flip by. You will be asked what you have done with your life, stressing love, and pointing out things. Here there is no time and you could have your whole life flash by in a moment - instant replay of consciousness."

"Wow! A movie of life with emotion! And the Plan of my life?"

"Yes. But let us finish this first. After the review stage, there will be a need to make a decision as to whether you feel you have fulfilled what you came for, whether you still have work to do, or whether you want to continue on and allow the physical vessel to die completely. At this time you are still connected through what is the astral light connection which will disconnect upon complete physical and energetic death."

"Is this the astral connection to the pineal and the lyden glands?"

"Yes. Through the channel of the heart. There will be some limit like a fence or border where over the line there is peace, tranquility, golden light, and joy. It is your true Greater Consciousness of Home. If you decide to come back, and there may be a lot of discussion, more review, and even a look into the future of your Life Plan, then you will not go over this limit and go through the last stage of total disconnect from the physical reality."

"At that point, if you stay, death of the body becomes permanent?"

"Yes. If the decision is to come back, you will come back spurred by some being which will be in your higher beliefs. It may be God, Spirit or anything familiar to you alone as the representation of a Higher Force or Being. You will then be sent back for obligations, or pulled by relatives or soul family members who helped you develop your Life Plan."

"Life Plan. That's really interesting. I can feel truth coming forward about it."

"Good, we will discuss this next. At the next stage you will once again come floating back into the environment and feel a re-entry into the physical body. Depending upon the nature of the death, you may or may not regain consciousness but you will nevertheless be alive according to the medical definitions. The key is you will not forget this experience."

"So when I came back, I would have some pretty shocking stuff in my awareness. I would have realized that I am not just a body. I would have realized that I as pure consciousness or Soul do not die. I would meet other entities that were my soul family, Guides, even my idea of what a superior being is."

"Plus you would have seen a panoramic holographic movie of your life. Do you think that this would change your life?"

"Big time!"

"It all depends on the life plan and the purpose, but most who come back after this experience created a totally new attitude in life. Some report enhanced senses, some pick up on others' feelings better, express a need to cultivate love of others, seek knowledge, become morally purified, and create new clear goals, mostly in service of others. The bottom line is that their belief systems and behavior changes dramatically. Some have miraculous things happen as well."

"Like what?"

"There are many cases where healing miracles took place. It can be terminal patients with cancer, any incurable disease, physical disorders, blindness, and disfigured bones. There are no limits to these. These people will tell you they have come to realize the powers they have of being love, and their true magnificence of each and every human being. Realizing that they are love is usually the most important lesson they learned, allowing them to release all fear; to shift their faith to love, not fear."

"Ok, I get the out of body thing very clearly as I am engaged in this myself right now. That is how I met you, without having to die. And you are the field of transpersonal experience that is the source of knowledge and memory - not the brain. I am independent of the conscious physical mind. Whole consciousness is stored with you as the Causal Body not in the brain. The brain serves as a relay station for connecting to our bodies when we are in a conscious state of being awake."

"The other lesson here is that death is a passing, a simple shift of focus in vibration from one state of energy to another. The physical body of particles dies and the consciousness as waves of energy leaves. The body is a temporary vehicle to have fun in while you are on the Earth in a movie that was created carefully and purposely, then recorded for review. It was pure consciousness separated from the brain and body that held it."

"The one that is extraordinary for me is that this business of a recorded movie of my life and a plan to follow that is discussed by my Soul Family and a Spirit Guide. That is pretty heavy."

"I understand. You will come to acknowledge all this as we proceed with your personal revealing of what you already know. I as your Soul created this movie to learn and expand and evolve. It was to develop new virtues and to learn from my karma of other lives. Let us talk about that now. Are you ready?"

"Absolutely!"

15

YOUR IMMERSION MOVIE OF LIFE

The life you engage in is a virtual holographic movie which you as a Soul directed and produced so you could engage in the mental and emotional joy of its experience.

THE REVIEW APPEARANCE

"Alright, Superplacebo, let us continue on this movie of life. First, I now understand that I am creating my own crappy reality and how to change it. But now you are saying I as you actually planned this crappy reality. Come on! Since we are here, I get the idea of this bright Light Being coming forward in a near death situation because that seems to be how you and I are speaking now. But please explain this high speed video panorama review of life."

"We need to clarify something first that you may not be understanding. I am really you. You are simply communicating with your higher mind that is not bound by the beta brain or its interpretation of reality. Remember the picture I showed you of where I live? We are all one consciousness of one mind. In your lower form, the mind you are aware of is simply an individualized sub compartment of your larger mind. You have become aware of the larger compartment where my mind as Superplacebo is simply the greater consciousness of pure thought within the quantum void of infinite possibilities. The rapidly awakening people on earth right now see me as a Higher Self living out a life in a lower plane. A Soul is actually orchestrating this life and a Higher Self is just a convenient handle for you humans to use. The Soul is a unique part of the greater mind which is most often referred to as the divine mind - what you may refer to as the Creator. All of your Soul's lives are recorded in the Causal body. But really at the level of the Soul mind, it is just one mind. Your awareness and access to its contents; everything that was, is, and will be, is opening now as you are really communicating with yourself."

"You mean I at my lowest level have access to and potential awareness of the mind of the Creator?"

"Yes. As long as you continue to ask me why I don't do something we are polarized because it is really YOU that should be asked that question. Even at a lower level you have your imagination which is not limited. Within it you have only to bring forward a thought, vision or word from the vast sea of infinite possibilities. It is from this quantum void that you bring ideas and thoughts into your local consciousness. Your problem, however, is that once these are brought into your awareness for manifestation into your reality, they become subject to the rules of that consciousness that formed the reality because you cannot truly believe you are more."

"Ok, I hear you. And to get out of that box where the rules are different, I need an awareness of a new mind of consciousness where the rules are different and imagination can become more widely expressed?"

"How have you managed to come to this next level of awareness to speak with me? You have really only learned to access a higher vibratory segment of the total mind. In truth you are simply talking to yourself."

"The others that I meet such as Spirit Guides and Soul family are just made up in my mind?"

"No, they are not made up. They exist in the higher reality just like you do with your physical counterpart in a lower reality. This reality is not as dense as where you physically are. They are as real as you in this state right now. You have become aware of them."

"And they helped me create a movie that you call a life plan?"

"In the review process for those who have had the near death experience there is indeed a rapid temporal play out of all people, events, emotions and effects in chronological order that occurs instantaneous. The images generate emotions of all parties as they flip by. The being doing this would be me with the Spirit Guide. We ask you if you are happy with the sufficiency of your life, stressing love, and pointing out choices. It is a visual recording that concentrates on the mental and emotional life that you have lived."

"And when you say you, you mean my Soul, my Spirit Guides and the other actors in the movie that are my Soul Family?"

"Yes. The Soul and Soul family determine the Life Plan which you live out so as to learn and expand your spiritual evolution. In truth you are part of it, you just forgot. You as the Higher Self take responsibility for engaging in it as do the higher selves of the other players. The vessel that allows experience and expression is the human body."

"But how come I don't remember any of it and I certainly have not been aware that I actually am my Higher Self. I am just a big dummy actor in your movie and I don't have any control if the life plan is set!"

"Well, you did as a baby and kid but you made choices or were influenced to forget. There are many reasons for this but it is primarily because you chose to do so. But you have overcome this now, haven't you? It is your choice to be a big dummy actor and live a life plan on default. But you are learning that there is more to this proactive control of reality, aren't you? Consider what else you can overcome as you evolve your being into the higher and higher state getting more and more access to the total mind of the Creator. Why did you not do this earlier in your life? Because you chose to listen to my brother – perhaps because that is what your Soul intended to do to learn and expand?"

"Ok, I can sort of understand that. But we are talking about a movie that was planned and another movie that was recorded as I lived! Wow, that's ineffable!"

"In this state where we are now there is no time or space. Your life movies are like a stack of DVD's on the shelf. They only have time associated with them when they are played out by a device and that is only a few hours. Yet that few hours can represent a lifetime. On the disc it is not only reality, it is information and it means nothing until it is played on a DVD player. Your brain is the same kind of device, playing and recording information which resides in a compartment of consciousness, ultimately part of the Causal energy field."

"You mean where we are now there is no dividing line between the real and the non-real worlds and I can change both. I can change the frames of the stored movie that result in a new frame to be created in the mental, emotional AND physical bodies?"

"In your imagination there is no dividing line. If you impose your illusion of real world, you immediately create a dividing line."

"But…"

"No buts, it is the same process. Indeed, is that not what the miracles do? It is an instant correction of broken bones or diseased tissue, there is a re-write of the movie frames now and moving forward. Gaining access to the causal, mental and emotional bodies allows one to change reality through the interface of etheric to the physical body. The two realities are accessible and both realities are interactive from the power of the mind to change. Bear in mind you do not change what has been recorded, you learn from what has been recorded to move along a different path of moments to present a different picture. Even your brain does not know the difference between the different 'realities'."

"But not all the time?"

"Not all the time because of what we have spoken of. Everybody is different, just like you and it is back to the belief boxes that limit that interactive ability. It is what you choose to impose upon you mind."

"Ok, this is a pretty mind blowing thing that the reality we see and the life we live is a virtual movie. It must be like a holographic medium understood and viewable when we are pure consciousness not limited by the physical body and the Beta bothersome brain. Tell me more."

UNDER FREE WILL I CREATED THIS LIFE?

"All Souls create what you would call a contract to engage in a virtual movie of life that is called the Life Plan. This movie of life sets the major parameters of existence in your physical reality. The major events, your characteristics, your plan of life has been created by way of free will by you as a Soul with the assistance of Spirit Guides and with your Soul family who all have the same purpose."

"A contract? Are you serious? What is this same purpose?"

"Your Soul, as is every Soul, is a spark of the Greater Mind or Consciousness. You can look at this as the quantum particle that is the most fundamental unit of light; a photon. It is like a unit of the whole that has a greater purpose of spiritual growth. In order to do this, a Soul chooses the way in which it will incarnate into a body, choosing a soul family to experience this with and sets out a life plan of lessons and experiences to do this. Souls then review the akashic records to determine a new plan."

"What is the akashic record?"

"It is the grand database place in the greater consciousness that holds the record of all lives of all Souls. The Causal body is of course part of it but the Causal is particular to one Soul's life. The players, the character, the events, the script for this life plan is created with the soul family and spirit guides so as to learn virtues and evolve their spiritual growth. The Life Plan creates a contract that is developed through free will. A soul determines the way in which it will incarnate and leave the physical body. It can walk in or walk out when death occurs – a walk in is an exchange."

"And I did this of my own free will. Why?"

"The Soul's true evolution is to turn negative to positive. Each Soul has its own rate of growth and evolution. Without negative it is believed that it cannot be motivated to want positive because it forgets when it crosses the veil into the incarnated plane. Its purpose is to understand that misery is an illusion and that to know this it must stop judgment. It is an understanding that there is something more, that we are love and we have a pre-birth desire to be of service to one another. Without contrast to love we cannot know fully who we are so we script lives and forget true identity to awaken again to attain the greater self-knowing – to know ourselves, as love and only express that."

"Why would I create a plan that has a bunch of ugliness and crap? Why would a Soul punish me as a living entity? Is that how a Soul gets its jollies? Sorry, why would WE do this?"

"There may be several reasons. Why do you sit down to watch a movie that can bring you emotional distress? You are learning now that your body is being tortured by negative emotion in it. Is that how you get your jollies? The Soul may want to simply feel the experience of it just like your movie on your DVD. There may be a bunch of karmic lessons to learn. Just like your own individual consciousness, the greater consciousness is also evolving. But there is no Soul that has to engage in this process, it is a choice."

"Well, I certainly didn't look at it that way."

"Of course. You forgot and that may part of the plan. Anyway, it is your choice of how you get tortured. Once you engage in the life plan to evolve spiritually you must follow intuition not intellect. Intuition is direct communication with the greater mind for the right path and usually discounted by the lower mind. To do this one must overcome the challenges to be able to listen to the inner voice like me, to hear intuition and attention and intention to open paths. You learn to allow skeptics help you to open conviction, overcome fear in a life plan as they go and you grow. So you need courage, a choice open by way of free will. These are all part of your chakra systems. You chose my brother's voice. You deployed the laws of Cause & Effect and Attraction all by yourself. You chose not to develop your 4th and 5th phase of human evolution. You choose to love the great big brain of yours that operates on 10% and let all the other 10 strands of DNA sit there doing nothing."

"Wow! Ok, I get it! What you are saying is that to accomplish this, a Soul has a purpose of creating a Life Plan; to determine body, time, place, events so as to evolve spiritually. The body is the physical vessel used by a Soul that has full access to this plan. The aura and subtle energy bodies are also part of this vehicle so as to experience lives in accordance with the evolutional stages of human development. So what is this primary expression it is trying to learn?"

"It is to develop divine virtues, to cultivate and express on the physical plane."

"I'll bet these virtues are compassion, forgiveness, empathy, kindness, gratitude, reverence, and unconditional love."

"Yes, that names a few but there are many. You construct this plan between lives when you are one with the Greater Mind. Your Soul continues to reincarnate in different bodies and lives each time using free will to make a life plan and a contract to follow it. The contract is to develop divine virtues, to cultivate and express on the physical plane."

"It has a lot to do with karma."

"Your Soul's plan would indeed be to balance karma and heal issues like false beliefs and develop service to others. Many different virtues are developed from karmic patterns by cultivating passion, compassion, forgiveness, unconditional love, empathy, and becoming a balanced Self. The self identity defines what the Soul wants to express. To do this, a series of lives become the vehicles of expression for the Soul who desires profound self knowing."

"So my Soul created a Life Plan designed to experience the opposite karma crap over and over until I learn on his behalf? To do this these virtues need to have a stark contrast so love, peace, and joy can be learned as a result to know who we are. This is why we appear to torture ourselves; to learn to rise above it?"

"Yes. Remember the Law of Karma and Cause & Effect. Many things that you call crap in your life were purposely created by you to experience, or re-experience until you learned to rise above these to learn virtues. Implement your energy portfolio with me."

"Wow! That's a tough way – to torture your lower self to learn to be a higher self!"

"Well, you dwell on this torture. The act of dwelling on it will create more of it. Torture, remember is a choice of perception created by mental and emotional gifts. Learn from this. Your own Soul's plan will involve the development of virtues so as to awaken to come to know there is more to a physical body than just emotions, and personality. Each is an eternal Soul agreeing to come into body to express these divine virtues. Each can change the lesson by increasing vibration for learning to be compassionate, choosing the high road at key junctures in the plan to ascend to a place that holds all records of past, present, future as a compartment of your Soul and all engagements."

"And so I get the blame because I don't listen to you?"

"There is no blame and I feel all you do. You may feel like a big helpless dummy but it can be said it is the same for me. I intuit you all the time and you ignore it. You may say you ask me to help but you don't dial the right phone number so in a sense we are both big dummies."

"Well, I suppose that is changing now."

"Remember there is no judgment. You create a Soul Contract to use Spirit Guides connected to the Higher Mind to create a personality that agrees with the plan. You can express concern and modify it but highest good is for all and each other of the Soul Family. The purpose is to choose paths in such a way as to understand the deep meaning to challenges so you are not victims. Life is not random, as you agree to the plan, and specifically the idea is to come out of victim, helpless, consciousness mentality. If not, these negative energies will become a self fulfilling prophesy executed through the Laws of Cause & Effect and Attraction. When dealt with through the virtues, it all results in the healing power of the soul - wounds can be healed with love. So that which is perceived and felt as torture is simply a way to heal. The true growth comes through emotion. Only by working through the experience does a human understand it."

"And I did this with a Soul Family?"

"To do this Soul groups of the same evolutionary needs incarnate together and evolve their own life plans which integrate into each other's. To assist, one can have several guardian angels who also assist in staying alive by providing the silent guidance. All is in service to each other. To determine the integrated plan and in developing the scripts, Spirit Guides and Soul create the plan together with a Soul Family."

THE PREBIRTH PLANNING PROCESS

"How exactly are these planning sessions done?"

"This whole process will be ineffable for you. At a very primitive level it is much like creating a Hollywood movie or creating a virtual reality computer game. In other aspects it is like a planning engineer who lays out a vast network of people, events, and activities to complete a major project. Sessions are conducted to create a complex flowchart advanced beyond comprehension with decision points where parameters are set up as choices all pre anticipated. Each is shown scenes to upcoming life. The Guide's and Soul's ideas of personality and life path options create the plan in benefit to all of the Soul's family."

"And of course the planning has karma in mind."

"With the karmic balance sheet in mind, major life challenges are set up and exit points are planned. Normally a guide would implant a notion or idea. If it is a prebirth plan they can intervene. Life will end when the Soul decides when the plan is done or when it is futile. Intervention can occur through Soul agreements."

"These exit points are like a near death experience or even death?"

"Yes. Several plans are made as a flowchart that can expand to infinity with choices that are predetermined. Acting in love takes you on a different time line which may take several lives. These plans are conceived for that deeper meaning and purpose. Karma provides situations and events as a range of possibilities as to how you could choose different paths at these juncture points."

"So I could come to a place where I could meet a soulmate, marry and have kids? And all this is preplanned?"

"But if you did not choose to meet and marry, then that path you close off and a new path would open."

"How detailed is the plan?"

"It is up to the Soul but it can be very detailed or it can be general. You find the maturity of the Soul dictates this. All major things are planned, some minor. Free will allows deviation but you may create more issues through the Law of Attraction into low vibration choices that cause the same issue to recur. The free will allows going into joy choices of love, and appreciation to minimize the issues. But to answer your question it can expand like a giant tree to infinity."

"Ok, and the many virtues are learned via contrasts so for example it may be that loving people may have challenges because of this prebirth plan to experience the negative contrast. And these can be extreme like poverty, incest, rape, murder, as serious challenges to rise above and find a virtue?"

"Yes, there is no judgment except by yourself. The Plan may also put others in support of challenge to assist in dealing with these tests. This is part of the prebirth plan. The victim mentality is something that you will overcome by way of setting people and events up to assist. The Soul plan challenges and how to overcome these as a set of choices all agreed to. You will see holographic images so you know what the events, situations, and possible outcomes may be. The planning process shows houses, colleges, places, at whatever detail level you care to see."

"You mean I saw details of scenes to an upcoming life? So it is like writing a movie script and developing the scenes and characters ahead of time. And then somehow this is recorded for me to be immersed in it when I incarnate?"

"Yes. The Guide's and Soul's ideas of personality, life, and physical characteristics are used to create the plan in benefit to all of the Soul's family."

"I designed my personality too?"

"Remember the astral plane? The time, place, parents are all predetermined. The time of birth will determine the astral setting of the zodiac as to what personality characteristics you will take on. This occurs as the higher energies congeal into lower form through the astral interface, as we discussed before. You chose the time."

"Yes, with the Zodiac."

"The planetary zodiac will influence the way stimulus-response process affects your mental and physiological being. The chakra system of energetic to physical interface, remember? To give you another shock, your life plan is written in the palm of one hand and the actual living plan is written in the other."

"Whoa! Really? And it doesn't matter if you are a bad guy or good guy?"

"There is no judgment. Many want to experience evil despite the karmic consequences. Some Souls do bite off more than they can handle to accelerate or deal with old issues of guilt. One can fail at a level of personality but a Soul never judges because of the failure, they just try again. The personality is eternal as is the Soul but each personality is different in each life so a portion of the Soul is placed in each body. Dark roles are played in service to others. There is no judgment by the Soul, however, one may carry a notion of failure as the Soul tries again. Significant people are all part of the plan, each assisting to bump a Soul back on a plan. Each Soul is in collaboration with other Souls and can bring in others to help if the plan is not on track. The Soul's plan can override the Law of Attraction as it can choose location, time, events and people. The law is powerful when you send a picture with feeling and gratitude it is stronger."

"That is how you dissolve karma?"

"These life challenges break the heart open to create contrast so as to learn and heal. At Life Review sessions that occur in prebirth regression, Out of Body Experiences and Near Death experience, divine virtues are brought forward as a test to see how these are scored in a life. One can see progress and determine the extent of healing. When you know this, you will see the reason for these challenges and find the purpose in the future so as to cultivate the virtues. Certain virtues will come up again and again. The Soul may take on too much and Spirit Guides may caution it."

"Then what?"

"It can come to an end because all has been achieved or it may not be achievable but it is the Soul that decides. Various exit points are created, as are support people and events to assist but sometimes the choices may become so horrific that the Soul may just decide to terminate it and try again."

"That sounds terrible!"

"It is a movie, remember. And you are me up here as an eternal being. Look at it as if you got into a nightmare or got so engaged in a movie you forgot where and who you were until someone gave you a shake. That was on your plan. It is the personal search for victim consciousness that is a heavy path, not a painful experience. The virtuous path is to change this by forgiving others, deal with unresolved karma ties, and take responsibility for creating your life in the world of virtues and service, stepping up with the heart, not ego, and to use real emotion with gentle kind intention instead of forced intent and will. It is a process of surrender to it as a real experience. It is the same process as with the Law of Attraction; do not force it."

"There is something that I do not get. The Life Plan details are a prerecorded immersion movie that can be modified or edited. The characters, events, exits, are all known and we just play in them. Wow!"

"All your lifetimes occur concurrently as directed by your Soul. Life plans are like a stack of movies on DVD's. The DVD's sitting on your shelf are like the imaginary movies in your mind. They can all be played at any time, put on hold, fast forwarded, backed up, and if you have the right means to knowing and belief, these can be reviewed and changed by the Soul. In the non physical where you are now, thought manifests instantly into an image where thought creates reality. There are no limits here, only infinite possibilities which already exist otherwise they could not come into your awareness."

"Ok, I see that. We do this in our imagination but it is not real."

"It is not real in that lower reality because the group consciousness and yours does not allow this to be a possibility. You have learned that in the physical thoughts respond to reality, not that thought creates reality. And yet, as we have seen these miracles occur all the time through the placebo effect."

"So we have been designed to play these movies through the brain and just like imagination does, record the plan and become the plan?"

"Look at this like it was a play board of imagination that are like holograms. The thoughts create the play board where story lines and infinite possibilities are drawn onto the board to create a plan of expression and growth. Of course the components are people, events, and scenes, character, choices, situations, places, and so on that are pulled out of an inventory of infinite ideas to form a Life Plan. You then capture this Life Plan immersion hologram played out by the brain. But because the brain itself is a holographic part of it, it can immerse into the movie and change the movie by changing the mind."

"Obviously that is not so easy!"

"But we have already seen people doing this all the time. What you do not understand is how you are doing it and from where it is done so you can do it as well. It has to be outside the box remember."

"And this is not just a simple process if you are stuck in the box with your brother. Can you change a life plan?"

"Once a life plan is set, it is the Soul and You that have to be convinced of a change not in the plan. It may well be that many of the life issues are there for a purpose and not changeable. Only your perception of it is within the scope of freewill. It means you have to talk to your Soul and Spirit Guide because there are other players who have a deal with you to learn as well. Right now you are talking to the Soul so what would you like to change that we haven't covered so far?"

"Well, I have to think about that. In view of what I have learned so far, it is my attitudes and beliefs that are the keys. But can you jump between pathways in the life plan?"

"Life Plans contain an almost infinite network of paths. If you looked at it carefully you will see a high path and low path with a lot of paths in between. These are like branches on a tree that get more numerous. Each path like the branches on a tree are unique and jumping from one to the other is not possible within the consciousness domain even at this level. It is possible to jump time lines yes, but not at this level. What you will find however is regardless of the path, even if it is the darker lower path, you always have a choice to choose the higher place and move towards the highest path as a separate growing path but not through engagement in the set paths. You can however jump to different possibilities on any time line."

"If for example you choose to take a lower path which is filled with torture as you put it and distress and trauma, you may have placed an exit point on it which could be a Near Death Experience. So you would exit, have a review process and determine whether you want to re-immerse or leave and die. You may have created other triggers like meeting someone to activate a part of memory to take you on a specific choice and path. Many exits are planned, triggered by soul agreement. Souls create impulses, thought, intuition, to influence, older souls leave many doors open for choice – all have different advancements."

"But yet, from where we are now, it is all an illusion. And I am trapped in it."

"It is because you agreed to do it and trapped yourself. Are you not learning how to untrap yourself and live this life in a more wondrous way?"

"True. I guess it just hasn't hit home that I am the guy who did it and agreed to it. I just haven't figured out how to get out of that cycle."

"But you have. You are now knowing your Soul is the game designer and the moments – like frames in a movie – are pulled out of the mind of infinite possibilities to be captured in the holographic immersion movie. All memories including past lives and time between are stored in DNA, itself a holographic energy form and you are becoming aware of this. If you truly believe this do you not think you will make different choices from now on and take different path away from your torture?"

"I suppose."

"In this process Souls are counseled on self forgiveness. Souls evolve to higher vibration – guides do not need the school. At home, connect, understand or create things they are never without – all divine, no negative emotions, duality only peace. Ascended masters are finer vibrations in all that is love. Through these play boards Spirit guides and Souls draw lines of growth. Souls can exert influence by nudge, suggestion, thoughts even through astrological influences as possibilities to traits, and attributes. Judgment is self judgment as separation from source consciousness believing that the big brain of yours does not need spiritual evolution. That reversal is what is happening to you now. You are opening to miracles, to new awareness, to a new mind. But it is still your choice as to whether you will or will not."

"It seems I have a long way to go."

"You now have a wonderful start as all your answers are coming to you. As we continue this and you have faith in your belief, what will also come to you is how you take your power to create your own reality. You are in a time of worldwide awakening and you have come here for a special purpose even though it is a game. Our meeting is your way of waking up by understanding it is a game and do not need pain in your life to nurture virtues."

"Ok, I see the process that got me here is very important and it is from this point of the greater mind of infinite possibilities that I will launch my next phase of the Life Plan."

"Yes that which you call crap has brought you here into this awareness. So indeed it has a higher purpose. Change your way of looking at it and disengage from the perception of crap; otherwise how can you stop giving life to the same cause that attracts the same crap?"

"Yes, perhaps there is that reason."

"Indeed. Now that you are aware of this you are on the verge of understanding how you change things from the Astral Plane as the interface plane."

"What changes are these?"

"There are many. You can open up your higher powers. You can dissolve karma, you can get rid of the old 3D model of Cause & Effect and use the law of Cause an Effect – mind over matter. You can look forward into your future and adjust life now. You can institute a new life just as if you had a near death experience. As you embrace what you are learning the rest of your higher mind, brain and DNA can open as you get back on track you're your evolution. As you progress you will create miracles outside of the box yet live in the lower planes. You can be the greater limitless mind. Is that enough?"

"Hmmm that's a good incentive. I know we talked about these energy bodies but it seems that the Astral body and plane is pretty important. Can we go back to that?"

16

THE ASTRAL PLANE

When you enter the astral plane of pure consciousness, you are pure thought energy open to the Greater Mind, a place where the mind controls matter.

THE ASTRAL INTERFACE

"You do remember we talked about you being in the astral level of pure consciousness where we are now. What is it you need to remember?"

"This is the space I am now and where I need to get used to being, right? But you said I was on the bottom fringe. Don't I need to get higher up in this space?"

"Yes you do. But as your consciousness rises and expands into mine, we are then both able to rise into the other levels represented by the higher bodies above the 5th dimension. We are unified as pure consciousness of mind here. Let us review this. In your meditations, you need to become one with me in our compartment of Higher Mind. As you become more in tune with this space of limitless mind, it will become easier and easier to remember that which you have forgotten. Let us recall the image part of the Greater Mind as a bubble that straddles all energies and minds. Here is your image again."

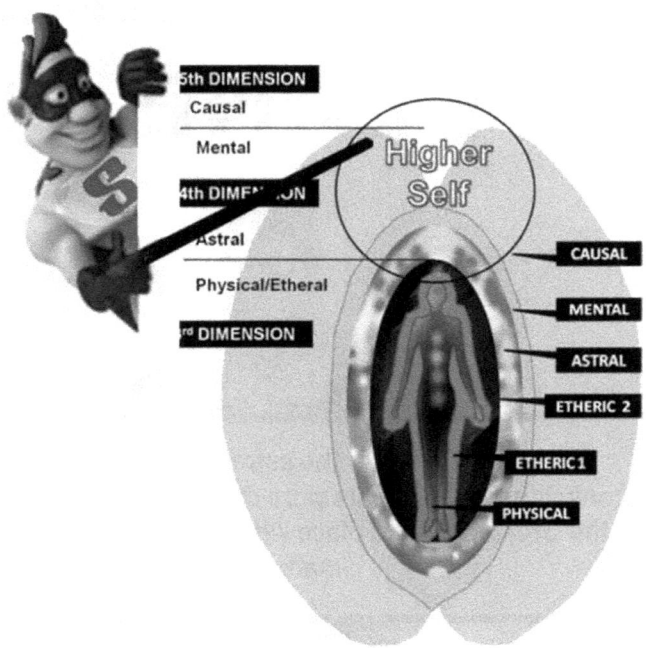

"It is all one. In truth it is really your mind and imagination of infinite possibilities that this reflects. The imagination as used within the lower 3rd plane is not free to create the infinite possibilities, only dream them, or abide by the limits of that consciousness. The manifestation of them, even though they are within the astral mind are subject to the limitations of the 3rd dimension so those dreams falling outside cannot be easily manifested. What you must learn is to be in this mind permanently and the alpha brain can allow this. At the current time you experience the lower vibrational end of this bubble of the Higher Self. You want to train yourself into getting higher and higher in this bubble as more and more opens to you."

"When the higher and lower mind becomes unified I learn to walk in both lower and higher worlds?"

"Yes, when your Soul and you are one unified consciousness. The Astral is the interface between the Higher and Lower planes. It is your awareness of your place in the higher planes of this partition bubble that allows you to change these rules. That is what happens in miracles."

"Because I am truly part of the whole unified with pure consciousness, not an individual body and mind listening to your brother. It is sort of like tuning into the right frequency is it? Like turning the dial to the right place?"

"Indeed. If you are not in the right frequency, you cannot communicate. The Astral Body gives you the ability to have desires, emotions, imagination, and psychic abilities. It lends power to thought which is essential for effective action and manifestation. Astral consciousness includes the full range of emotions from fear, hate, and sorrow to love, happiness, and ecstasy. It also includes the full range of desire from totally selfish and destructive desire to common personal desire to high spiritual aspiration to selfless servicefull desire. It is important to eventually rise above this full range of polar emotions to truly be one with the Soul mind."

"And is this what is called the Light Body?"

THE LIGHT BODY

"A Light Being is made of light. It does not die; it is eternal, and it is a higher form of pure consciousness. Consciousness is pure light and the elemental unit of it is the photon. The photon is one quantum of electromagnetic radiation. It is the smallest unit and the plural of quantum is quanta. The photon is both wave and particle as it uses one to express through the other. The field of the photon is the torroid and it is both separate and connected to everything else."

"So is the photon actually the Soul?"

"The Soul is an infinite point of light, most likely understood as the point of all creation the singularity that it represented by way of the Light Body. The makeup of light and consciousness is the photon so you could say there are a lot of Souls wanting to experience and express but this may not be a choice of any Soul. Each Soul which exists as the spark of the greater mind contains the whole of the greater mind. Each is evolving at its own pace to serve the greater whole and therefore it expresses through the lower form of vibration of particles by creating that reality. The way it gives life to that cluster of photons is through the infusion of spirit."

"And the point of access is in the heart? So the Soul is the Light Body?"

"It is the point of singularity between above and below – non-matter and matter. That is what you get access to when you go into that energetic heart-brain which lives in the space of higher consciousness, and the soup of pure love. The light body is a structure of light from higher dimensions. Like the physical body it is a vehicle for consciousness evolution. As your physical body contains organs and other physical structures to match its density, your light body contains various structures of light to match its higher density. The chakras, the Column and the MerKaBa are all structures of the light body interfacing with the physical body. Between lives you journey in the light body to various places and dimensions and it is the central vehicle used to incarnate into any of the nine dimensions. For incarnation into the 3rd dimension the light body needs an astral body as the interface."

"Yes, I remember our talk about the way I reincarnated from light to matter, from photon as wave to particles and matter."

"As we discussed, for the Light Body to incarnate into the lower physical form, it needs an astral body as its interface. Astral Substance is what makes up your astral body. Before incarnating into the physical body, the consciousness of the descending soul passes through the astral layers around Earth and collects various astral forces to build the astral body that will be used as a vehicle to incarnate into matter. The specific astral forces collected depend on the soul itself and its chosen life on Earth."

"I got that but tell me more about this Light Body."

"Indeed. It is waiting for you for when you leave your physical body. When you die and your astral body shatters, the consciousness and light that you incarnated into during the life will re-emerge with the rest of your light body. You are learning that you do not need to be so dramatic and have to die or have a near death experience. At this point all veils will be gone and you will begin to remember everything. What is important to understand is that there is a Light Body along with many of your higher selves waiting for you after each life and you will re-emerge with these parts. There are many higher selves because there is more than one level of your Higher Self. While on Earth you could become aware of your Higher Self and even partially incarnate it. You would then realize that there is still another Higher Self than this one and so on. You have higher selves in many dimensions with many different perspectives and views of the Universe and even of your life here on earth."

"I thought the Higher Self was you as the Soul."

"I am in this earth dimension experience. Higher Self is a convenient word to describe this incarnation. As a Soul, however, I have a multitude of other Higher Self representations."

"And I can access all this without dying? Cool! But I have to do some repair work on this body, don't I?"

"You will as your beliefs solidify into your everyday reality. The light body includes the chakras a central column and the MerKaBa along with other structures of light that have been described. The Light Body is partly here and incarnated but it is very blocked and is not functioning properly. This leads to the state of consciousness of the norm box-controlled individual. Because of the way you have incarnated into such dense matter, the dualistic nature of the 3rd dimension and the purposes for which you have done this, your bodies are all out-of-whack. Of course dear brother has much to do with this, but he just provided the options for you to choose from so you cannot blame him."

"I hear you. In a nutshell the goal is to purify the astral layer, clear and raise the vibration of the etheric and physical bodies, incarnate more of the light body and get its structures and energy centers balanced and functioning properly. Through this you are able to evolve spiritually better in this plane of matter."

"And you are able to open and expand into a better life. But understand this. It is both of us that carry the karmic load. Both of us need to cleanse and clear this. You feel it manifested physically, I feel it mentally which in truth is the same; we are just using different sensors. Your goal is to go higher, into the Causal level to be in a consciousness totally above this astral level because this in itself can inhibit progress and effectiveness of working from outside the norm."

"Otherwise we are both stuck in lower energies that have allowed your brother to interfere?"

"Of course. That is why you and I need to free ourselves together. That is why the process of love is the proper communication medium, the process of forgiveness dissolves karma, the process of compassion unites you as one and the light is the unification all that is. In the end when you die, you see this reality of yours as just an illusion. You are suffering and are unaware because you choose to be so. It is like anything else on your earth plane. You choose what you want to learn, experience, understand and bring into your reality. And if your lower mind and my higher mind are one then you had input into the plan. You have chosen to deceive yourself from this truth."

"I see that but I am not aware of this karmic debt that you carry and it would be nice to have some warning about it rather than just dumping it on me to deal with."

"Is this what you are not learning now? There are many ways of dealing with this karma which I will teach you. You have your own equivalent of karmic energies that you have created yourself which you may not be aware of. What you must now open to is to cleanse it all and get into a more proactive management of it all. It is really a choice of yours as to whether you really believe this or not."

"Yes, I get it, and stop blaming others. And by bringing my awareness into these bodies and being them instead of the physical carcass limited by its narrow mind and physical body, I am able to know all this and cause a desired effect by my attention, intention and will?"

"Indeed. Cause an effect rather than be subjected to Cause and Effect, and Karma! You begin to remember all and open to your powers of being a creator of your destiny rather than a player in the game."

OPENING ASTRAL ABILITIES

That which you do below in your physical reality is mapped above in your nonphysical reality but that which you create above in your nonphysical reality controls your physical reality; as above, so below.

"Now you are ready to understand how to get into these energetic components of yourself and think, act, and feel from that point. As you now have a better grasp of the place I dwell, you can begin to understand the reason why you must learn to dwell here with me to best instigate changes below. Once you get here, there are many possibilities and destinations to become aware of the same way you can sit and use your imagination. The most common practices are to engage in Past Life Regression, Opening Higher Potential, Future Life Progression, and Internal and External Miracle creation that we have already covered. There are limitless places to go as in remote viewing, worlds to see, and things to learn as it is truly a Greater Mind where limitless possibilities exist. Many of these rely on being led through a process of Astral Projection to reach a place in the higher planes where you, as Me, are within the Greater Mind of Infinite Possibilities. The difficulty for most who get here arises in taking these possibilities into the lower physical plane and maintaining acts of support."

"When some of the NDE cases went to visit their Higher Selves and Souls, they came back with enhanced abilities and a new appreciation for their life. Is that what you are saying; can that be done without having to die?"

"Part of the life review process is to see the opportunities of what could have been had you played it differently taking different choices. What is shown is the full potential richness of human life and how valuable a human life can be. We are co-creators beyond what we conceive – that a human is one of the most incredible examples of perfection; that there are riches within you that are beyond imagination, especially the obsession with material reality. Some of these riches or gifts are part of the processes of awareness of the astral body as that is where they reside – in that frequency. So to begin to attain these, you can do what is called astral projection to visit with me there."

"That is like an Out of Body projection, is it not? Sort of like the Near Death Experience?"

"It is a means of leaving the physical body and meeting me as your mirror self. Indeed there are real-world benefits that come from exploring the astral plane as you are finding now. But you need to learn controlled, self-induced astral projection and reach beyond physical limitations to new sources of knowledge. The benefit is to live and love more fully than you have ever thought possible by tapping your immense unconscious powers and integrating them into your conscious experience and opening to your highest potential."

"What are these real world benefits of this projection?"

"There is quite an impressive list of reasons to engage in Astral Projection to open up your potential. Of course your norm Consciousness assesses these as woo woo para nonsense. But it is like a permeable container of space. It is permeable in that it shares in the space that is everywhere. It is a container in that it is yours to expand within to infinity. Within the container is your bubble of light that is your awareness functioning as your conscious mind. Both light and dark, consciousness and unconsciousness can be found to function within a particular vibratory range that you experience as a body. Here is a vision for you to see that explains what can be done from the astral plane."

To visit the heavenly world while still alive
To experience the continuity of life and consciousness
To feel a confirmation there is life after death
To explore the astral plane and the larger universe
To gain an understanding between the physical and other energy/consciousness levels
To gain an understanding of the functions of emotional interactions between people
To explore the play of electrical and magnetic energies between men and women in relationships
To gain understanding of the relationship between physical world and other dimensions
To explore the role of subatomic particle and quanta in the greater universe
To explore the quantum level of the physical plane and astral plane
To gain understanding of the interactions between consciousness and energies
To have astral adventures in other dimensions
To meet and interact with spirit guides, angelic beings, departed ones, friends and other astral entities

"Are there other abilities as well?"

"Yes. There are also many abilities that are brought forward by engagement in the astral plane."

> To explore the possible therapeutic applications of astral projections
> To do path-working on the tree of life and other guided journeys
> To exercise psychic abilities
> To engage in remote viewing
> To develop clairvoyant and PSI skills
> To actually see chakras, thought forms, astral entities, angels
> To see higher dimensions of sacred sites, healing sites, local deities
> To see the creative visualization of personal goals in action
> To stimulate creativity in problem solving
> To develop fictional stories and seeing the action
> To augment artistic work and seeing things in future motion
> To better design new products trained imagination intensified
> To diagnose health problems
> To augment physical vision with astral perspective
> To work with healing energies, physically and psychologically
> To find missing documents, lost objects, pets, persons
> To prospect for minerals, locate water, rare plants
> To find undiscovered archeological sites
> To research real estate sites for unknown problems
> To augment forensic search
> To augment divination answers
> To time travel to the past and future
> To space travel to planets, water depths inside volcano, deep inside earth

"Wow, that is a lot of woo-woo stuff relegated to the metascience and silly category."

"That is your belief system limiting you again. It is your goal to expand the bubble of light to focus anywhere in the entire container that makes yourself as light to move beyond through expression and experience as an expansion of consciousness. This marks the growth of the ordinary person to become the extraordinary fully integrated with the Higher Self. To achieve this, astral travel or OBE'S are critical to evolving souls, reaching beyond physical limitations for new sources of knowledge and personal enhancement – solving issues and enhancing decision making, to understand life beyond death, gain new insight, awaken new potential, and to engage in healing and rejuvenation."

"I have attempted this but I cannot say that I have felt anything different. What are people bringing back?"

"In the many cases it has been shown without exception that through the engagement in astral projections here are what people report."

- intelligence functions are enhanced
- high positive emotions of joy and elation are common
- states can influence tangible objects
- all senses are intact or expanded
- feelings of weightlessness occurs
- sensory abilities are enhanced
- there is an awareness of a guiding presence such as Spirit Guides
- meaningful interactions with departed and living people are common
- many have a spontaneous OB travel
- many cases show it can be instrumental in preventing physical injury
- many rise above the body, view from above, and travel over terrain

WHERE ARE YOU REALLY

"I truly cannot say I have experienced any of these. Seriously, I am here speaking with you but none of these are entering my list of activities. What is it that I am missing?"

"Let me explain something to you about where you are now. The process of meditation is one that can get you to the lower extremity of where you become aware of me. Can you remember the picture of where the Higher self overlaps the brain all the way up to the Causal body?"

"Yes."

"When you meditate you can change the vibration by the depth of meditation. As you go deeper and deeper, you open to higher and higher vibrations. The depth of meditation relates to the lowering of the brain waves related to the height of vibration, and the attunement to the particular energy body, and the strength of influence over the lower reality that is in the belief box."

"What do you mean?"

"There is very crucial aspect of this that has to do with the statement **As above so below.** Remember this? We saw it in the above to below chakras. Now take that to a higher plane of directing this process. It describes the fact that the higher consciousness always incorporates the lower consciousness. The great secret is that higher always controls lower Causal-Mental-Astral hierarchy to appear in lower planes."

"What do you mean?"

"There are two key principles. First every physical action below is duplicated on higher planes according to the nature of these planes. That is how I as your Soul feel everything you do."

"But you said there is no judgment on what I do in ignorance."

"That is so, I am not complaining. There is no judgment. It is all experience but I want you to understand that what you do below is reflected energetically above and that simply leaves residual karma to work on later on in another life."

"Ok, I understand. So I can end up trapping you too?"

"Indeed. But to me it is not a trap. It is an educational process. Secondly, the Higher or inner heart plane controls the lower or outer reality. So you must understand that you can apply leverage at higher to shape reality in lower once you are able to function consciously at a higher level. The key is to function consciously at a higher level."

"And of course be completely out of the box by being in an altered state and deep in the trance and in the heart mind of peace and silence."

"Correct. They are necessary before anything can happen outside the box. The leverage to change the reality at the lower is from the higher plane. The directives to change reality in the physical plane must come from a higher mental and emotional plane above the astral. This is particularly important to understand how in the case of these miracles, here is where communication is with this Higher Being, divine intervention, the Universe, and so on."

"So where is the divine intervention?"

"Perhaps you do not understand that it is you as a Soul and Higher Self as a spark of the Greater Consciousness – perhaps call that Divine – that is what is referred to as divine intervention. You see the human makeup as learned through my brother is to believe something through some form of rational thinking. When it is not easy, humans like to assign the process of proof and credibility to some higher power that they believe in even though they cannot understand it. Whether it is gods, or God, or Buddha or Christ or a PhD or Doctor or Healer matters not. It is simply the way the Beta mind has been trained to work for survival."

"Hmmmm. So what level are we at when I am talking to the Astral Body?"

"It is about half of the way up all the bodies, remember how many we talked about? Let us look at that again. Remember the astral plane is the interface plane which straddles the physical and spiritual dimensions."

"We did not talk about these higher spiritual ones like the atmic, monadic, logoic, christic and manasic, did we?"

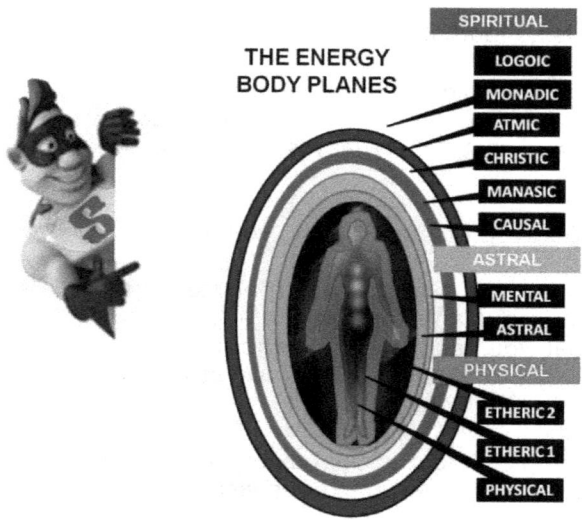

"Not yet, they are the higher spiritual bodies that your anatomy encompasses. These are stages of evolution beyond what we have talked about but to give you a clue, your Spirit Guides and higher beings reside here."

"You mean like angel, archangels and that sort of entity?"

"Yes, they are beyond the need to play the games of life. In physical forms as they are one mind taking higher forms to relate to you in lower form. But let us get back to as above so below."

"Typically people accept their experience to be the physical and the inner experience is an addendum. To take command of astral power it is the opposite; physical is addendum to the non physical. Of course access to this inner world is though an altered state and well being is the key to directing reality changes in the physical from the energetic bodies through the subconscious and the brain down the causal hierarchy to the cells. In the case of external reality, manifesting by way of Cause & Effect from above to the Law of Attraction below energetically is the effect responding to that which has been mentally configured and energized mentally and emotionally from the infinite possibilities above to be collapsed into external reality below."

"When consciousness is centered with physical body, your astral, mental, spiritual attributes are channeled through the physical senses provided by the brain and the nervous system. We can say that this ego-intellect mode makes the mind a slave to the body and it is what is bypassed in the OBE or Astral projection process. Here it is opposite where the body is the slave of the mind."

"I guess that is the way it is supposed to be if I honored our partnership?"

"Indeed! In the Astral plane and up here where you as pure energy thought in touch with your Soul and your Higher energetic Self there are things you can do not possible from the physical. What you do in astral can create a physical correspondence so skilled healing can have effects in physical. This is where the mental and emotional energetic counterparts, as the invisible anatomy of every person becomes the creator of reality."

"So it is because the mind, the emotion, the consciousness, once you dump the Beta mind are one and the same quantum field encompassing all that was, is and will be. But just like you are engaging now the process of Astral Projection requires training and exercise."

"Is that why I have not got there yet? Crap! Does this mean I have to change diet, take vows, be celibate, give up sex, be a monk, and change my job and all that?"

"No, that certainly has been the old way to discipline yourself into letting go. You DO have to devote time to train and build your higher astral muscles. Lower astral merges with etheric below, metal above. The process of engagement in astral projection or OBE is not something that does not have a learning curve and time element. It must be practiced, believed, and developed in order to be effective. Each individual is different in this respect, just like the degree of suggestibility as we have seen in hypnosis."

"Because the etheric energy body is more personal one must gain control of the etheric double to gain more control over the physical to provide a channel and means of control below astral and into the physical. You can use creative visualization that is charged with emotional energy; like that directed through magic, ritual involving physical activities then projected from astral into physical. Examples are prayer, mind power as charged with emotional energy with directives for manifestation – like the power of attraction which is simply activated astral power. It is a place where astral power can change your life and empower you."

"I would imagine that another important conclusion is that the emotional state is critical and can inhibit progress if not right. Anything other than genuine peace, love, joy is mandatory because there is no place here for negativity and confusion from the lower plane and your brother."

"Indeed. It should not be much of a surprise as the state of being must be a precondition in order to be in the love field in order to communicate with it. The lower struggle from karmic baggage and the survival mode of the ego have no place in the planes above astral."

"Astral substance is shaped by feeling and thought to create thought forms seen clairvoyantly. This property is both passive – reflecting feeling, passing thought, day dreams, and active by deliberately created and shaped concentrated thoughts and visualization."

AN ASTRAL PROJECTION PROCESS

"Ok, I get it, I need to take this meditation thing to the next level. Perhaps the lesson is with those guys who create miracles by getting in touch with their Higher Selves through a facilitator, right? What is the best process for me to use?"

"Yes, if you do not get out of the old belief box and into at least the astral level, then you may as well be trying to operate within the belief box of the norm and it will not trigger the as above so below with any degree of strength. You will not move beyond creation in the usual way within the norm. You will simply be subject to the rules of that physical reality of matter."

"Ok, so what are the steps?"

"I will lead you through the steps commonly used to satisfy your mental quirks but you must clearly understand and believe that you have an astral double which provides a complete model parallel to the physical."

"I got that now, clearly."

"Next, understand that when you energize astral parts it is because they are a mirror of what is below. We are in this together. Thus it is the astral parts or systems that need to be healthy with positive astral energies first and foremost. You and I need to institute a Soul cleansing first."

"So both you above and me below are infected by negative stuff?"

"Indeed, but remember above is a copy like a mirror reflecting what is below. There is no physical reality above it is only energy. It is from here that you must channel or infuse healthy images from the greater consciousness of infinite possibilities so as to transfer these to biological counterparts. When the same counterparts are energized, it transfers upon your re-emergence in the lower plane. The real healings, and the miracles start from above at the Soul level."

"And all this time I thought the Soul was immune! And the procedure calls for one to be in an altered state of relaxation and silence in an essence of love and peace."

"If not in this peace and silence, out of the beta brain and within the heart field of love, attempting this is simply a waste of time. The other important consideration is that this is not a 10 or 20 minute affair. At least an hour is needed to truly engage and this should be done daily without any of the daily mind buzz. It is important to feel and know without doubt you are in the right space. You must continue until you know it is so. How much time do you allocate now?"

"Maybe twenty minutes, and I really never know or feel it."

"Then that is part of your procedural limitations. You are not getting deep enough to be out of the norm. There can be no doubt about it. You may have to spend 20 minutes simply getting to this state. It is not to be rushed. But before you begin, you know by now that you require a statement of your purpose. You must formulate your objectives and affirm goals. There is no point to this if your thoughts and desires are fragmented, unclear and do not reflect precise mental and emotional energies."

"Does that not depend on what I want to do?"

"If you wanted to categorize this, you would have 9 steps where you linger each time. It is the 6th step that may vary depending upon the purpose."

1. Setting Objectives
2. Setting Environment
3. Trance Induction
4. Astral Disengagement
5. Astral Ascent into Void
6. Destination examples
   a. Past Lives
   b. Life Plan
   c. Healing
   d. Higher Potential
7. Astral Infusion
8. Astral Re-engagement
9. Enfolding New Reality

"I want to first explain how to best get into the Astral Plane through the first five steps. This process is very different for many but as you have seen with the ones who best facilitate miracles, there is a common set of steps. When you can understand and do these first five and simply be in the void of pure thought and consciousness, we will be ready to discuss the different destinations and purposes."

"Meditation takes you beyond?"

"The goal of meditation is to go beyond the mind and experience our essential nature - which is described as peace, happiness, and bliss. But as anyone who has tried to meditate knows, the beta mind itself is the biggest obstacle standing between ourselves and this awareness. The mind is undisciplined and unruly, and it resists any attempts to discipline it or to guide it on a particular path. The beta mind has a mind of its own. That is why many people sit for meditation and experience only fantasies, daydreams, or hallucinations. They never attain the stillness that distinguishes the genuine experience of deep meditation."

"I can relate to that!"

"Meditation teaches you to systematically explore your inner dimensions. It is a system of commitment, not commandment. You are committing to yourself, to your path, and to the goal of knowing yourself. But at the same time, learning to be calm and still should not become a ceremony or religious ritual; it is a universal requirement of the human body. That is why it is an excellent practice to become familiar with and to get in touch with your true self, as you have done. But we are going beyond that state."

"Okay, I am ready."

STEP 1: SETTING THE OBJECTIVES

"You can understand that by meditation and its practice you have identified a clear objective; the goal of knowing yourself and the inner dimensions. However, there may be other goals to achieve when in these inner dimensions in your true state of being. The very first part of this is to determine several things about your desires and goals. In these procedures we are looking to the higher order as deployed by You as the program instigator to update something in the upper and lower planes. We are looking to get out of the old ways limiting our way of thinking and create a better life by proactive use of Karma, Law of Cause & Effect, and the Law of Attraction; off of autopilot or default."

"But all this clear objective stuff is just holding on to the analytical beta mind. I thought you said I had to let go of that."

"You want to start with the Alpha mind, remember? You do not have to meditate to do that but you do have to settle into quiet thought and stillness. Recall also that when you are in a place of infinite possibilities, you need to be clear. How can you put in an order if it is undefined and fragmented like your 70,000 thoughts? Train your beta brain to be controlled, get the proper desires into Alpha and then go to Theta. "

"Ok, I hear you!"

"It is best to train your Beta brain to be commanded by Alpha and write these down in a concise clear form. By simply being and thinking from the heart of positive energies, you will be in the Alpha brain. When we refer to life, these are about external realities, when we speak of body, these are about internal realities. In any case there will be something about your past, present or future that you desire to change. Remember that there are four key elements of this that reflect every situation; namely the thoughts, visions, words and emotions. So in every case that forms a new desire, write out what you are seeing in this image."

1. What is it that I wish to change about my life?
2. What would that change about life, belief, perception be?
3. What would the change look like as a vision?
4. What would that change feel like emotionally?

"This could reflect a physical disease or dysfunction, a difficult issue, a desire for a better life, an answer to a question, a need for expanding potential, a life review, a better future, wealth and health improvements, and so on. As an example look at this image which looks for changes of health and wealth."

1. I wish to change my belief that I am poor and unworthy
2. I have unlimited financial abundance
3. I am holding a check for 5 million dollars
4. My body is exploding with bliss, joy and gratitude
OR
1. I wish to change by physical dysfunction in my legs and knees
2. I see my leg and knees completely healed
3. I am running down the road like I was 20 years old
4. I am laughing and with great joy and gratitude

"This reflects several things about instituting a new possibility into a new state of being. It defines it clearly what needs to be changed so to replace the old state of being, then creates and registers the new state by way of a strong definable signature of emotion."

"I get it. In this way a signal of intent is being sent to begin the process of firing and rewiring a new set of programs that are tagged by the emotion emanating from the body. It is the intention to think differently about what has become an issue, accept a new definable outcome, believe the resulting vision is done when emotionally charged into awareness as an observer, and surrender to its manifesting into reality. Of importance however is clarity and emotional charge."

"Exactly! As you practice this understand that each state becomes deeper and deeper, further and further away from the reality of day to day life. The longer you meditate, the deeper it gets. We have seen that the initial altered state is best described by meditation where the mind wanders between Beta and Alpha but the best place is Theta. We have seen that in the hypnotic state it can easily be induced by one's self easily. This is the place of the higher astral plane where the access to the programming process is but it is not something that most people can do easily. You need one hour without interruptions. Here is the process that is used by many trained in this."

STEP 2: CREATING THE ENVIRONMENT

"To begin with once you are in a place of no distractions and sitting comfortably, you may want to state verbally your personal objectives. It sends a message out to me and your Soul with your intent. The environment from which you will work has to be one of peace, silence and comfort. There is no escape from this because you cannot have anything of mind, environment or body bugging you. The process can be meditative or whatever you wish to label it but you must be comfortable sitting still and relaxed. If it is soft music, or simple silence that works best, it is the same space, chair, position, and environment that is required to launch your new state of being."

"Should I record this and play it back?"

"Absolutely, as we have discussed, it keeps your mental interference away from the process. Script this out and record it. At each step leave a void to feel and sense. Light music can be played while you do this but it must be more and more a process of quicker and deeper induction into that pure state of higher mind by first entering Alpha."

STEP 3: INDUCING THE TRANCE

"Once you have settled into the environment. You are ready. The next step is called the Trance Induction. It is where you become totally present to the heart mind."

"This is related to two important things that relate to the brains of head and heart. The first which you called being present, takes you out of anything to do with past or future where Supernocebo lives, or the present as NOW into lower alpha and the second is called moving into the space of positive heart energy to get rid of any interference from emotion and letting go of all lower influence, right?"

"Yes. If you want to use the practice of meditation, it would be here and this is normally done for 15-20 minutes to insure a deep state entry to Theta. Until you are practiced and can get into this altered state quickly, there are no shortcuts. This is why in the beginning, it is best to have someone else lead you and take over the suggestion process so your mind does not wander."

"Or alternatively set out the statements and record them to follow them."

"Yes, otherwise you never let go of your lower mind and environment. In this process you would settle, hands on thighs, close your eyes and mentally scan your body from head down to release tension by taking deep breaths;

exhale slow in rhythm for each breath count to hold it for a 5 count, then release it for a 5 count. As you become more and more relaxed on each count. Tell yourself '*I am becoming more and more relaxed.*' Linger here for a few minutes to feel the peace."

"This is like the hypnosis stuff. In a simple sense, feeling love and peace being present in the heart is Alpha?"

"Yes. But feeling negative emotion in the heart is not. The process you are engaging in is to get away from the Beta environment of the brain and into the silence of its influence of the conscious mind of ego and protection. The best state is to reach Theta like when you were a young child and let go of any tendency for the brain and intellect to interfere. This process is shifting your attention and awareness to the present now time as you shift to your body, parts, or functions."

"The time to detach in this way will be variable but it is suggested to be at least 15 minutes as the brain ceases to fire and think in the intellectual space of Beta and higher Alpha. You can begin this part by placing attention on your toes, sense and feel them in the space they occupy. Move to your knees, stomach, chest, arms, fingers, forehead, body, each time sensing them and feeling them in the larger and larger space they occupy. You are slowly detaching from the material world of body and brain."

"Then focus on your hands, noting sensations of tingling or numbness. After a few moments focus on right hand and imagine weightlessness. Do the same for your left hand. Linger here. Imagine a gentle force under it pushing it gently to your chest over your heart. Then bring the other hand up and linger here."

"Now place your attention onto your heart and feel your consciousness and awareness moving inside to be enfolded with heart energy of peace and love. Stay here a while until it is strong. Imagine a wonderful feeling of peace and love by bringing a scene or a loved one and feeling a radiant energy emanating from the heart becoming bigger and bigger, stronger and stronger. Linger here."

"When we went into the hypnosis discussion, you will recall the steps?"

"Yes."

"They are the same here but let us review this again."

"As you come to the world of brain silence, you may institute a self-hypnosis process that takes you into the next state. This is done by you saying: *'I will now go deeper and deeper into my subconscious state of pure consciousness as I count and breathe from 5 to 1.'* Then count and breathe: *5: going deeper, 4: going deeper, 3: very deep, 2: very deep almost sleepy, 1: into pure consciousness* and linger there for several minutes."

STEP 4: PHYSICAL DISENGAGEMENT

"As your hands rest here give yourself permission to enter a deep hypnosis and then leave body. Affirm: *'When I count down from 5 to 1, I will enter a deep hypnotic state and give way to the OBE state. Upon leaving my body I will be fully conscious, safe and secure. I will be enveloped through this experience in the powerful energies of higher astral planes. I will return to my body at any moment by so deciding. Upon returning and reengagement I will exit hypnosis by simply counting 1 to 5 (allow plenty of time to raise hand) then affirm: I am now in hypnosis and prepared to leave my body by simply relaxing my hands to resume original position'.* Let your hand drop."

"I take it that this is not to be rushed."

"You will waste time if you are constantly analyzing this or even following a script in your mind at first. The next stage is very critical. Upon deactivating the intellect and letting go and entering the deeper state of Theta, you will begin to feel the space of pure consciousness of peace and silence. It is here that you would detach your energetic self as you. When you have settled into the altered state you will state: *'As I count from 1 to 5 I will rise higher and higher along the beam of light separating from my physical body'.*"

"With hands down, sense a gentle rise leaving the body below. Facilitate this by visualizing your heart field as a glowing mist lifting gently from body to be suspended above it. Then when ready, begin your count and feel the rise and see yourself rising higher as pure consciousness separating from the physical body; *'1: I begin my rise, 2: I rise on the beam, 3: I am rising higher, 4: I am above the body, 5: I see my body below'.*"

"View your body at a passive state of rest and sense the powerful radiance enveloping your total being then affirm: *'I am now outside my body fully enveloped by pure, radiant cosmic energy. The radiance enveloping my astral being extends to my biological body protecting and energizing it as I travel to higher planes. The highest cosmic realm is now receptive to my intentions'.*"

"This is the beginning of your Out of Body experience or Astral Projection. If you wish to identify yourself as Higher Self, Soul, or Energy Body, it is up to you but regardless, see yourself free of the physical body and the physical world. Linger in this space becoming more and more comfortable."

"This is not so easy now, but I know I can improve this."

"Take time to linger between counts. Feel and see and sense as you lift. This is very important and this is why it is best to be guided by another skilled in this or guided by your own recording. Remember you have spent a lifetime disbelieving any of this as a possibility. Until you know and feel this separation is done, and you can move about to see your lower form and the surroundings easily and clearly, you are not there yet. You must be patient until you simply sense it so."

"What if I don't see clear images?"

"Many do not. But you will sense it and simply know it is there. You need to get used to the idea that it is the very first thought or feeling that 'pops' into your consciousness. If you linger, wait, anticipate, analyze, it will not be from the proper place."

STEP 5: ASCENT INTO THE VOID

"Once you have separated, you will linger in this place of oneness, of love, of peace, and harmony. You will then state: '*I will now proceed along a tunnel by counting from 5 to 1 to the light at the other end and emerge into the void of infinite possibilities'.* Know that you will proceed through a tunnel as in NDE, and meet me, the Creator, God, Spirit Guides or Angels or whomever suits your belief system for assistance. In the OBE or Astral projection you are simply an energetic body of pure consciousness where you have no identity, there is no thing, no time, you are no where, only the space of the quantum field of infinite possibilities is real. Here you will disconnect from the body, time and place and become a thought in the void of infinity. You will be in this space where you will continue to be present and aware of possibilities that you can create. State: '*5: I begin floating. 4: I am moving along the tunnel. 3: I see a light at the end, 2: I float through an open door, 1: I am in the void of infinite possibilities'.*"

"What if I can't let go and be there?"

"Any time you are drawn away simply become aware that you are an observer. Stay present in this void and if you become aware of yourself as

Being of Light, a Higher Form and meet Guides and angels which will be sensed, may appear – it depends on the individual. You will linger in this space, sensing and feeling the presence and peace and love emanating from the beings that have joined you."

"The experience is usually being carried forward first through darkness into a radiant fluid like dimensions of varying colors – corridors or channels. In the distance magnificent light will draw attention as you go to the cosmic core now one with cosmos. This is the void of pure consciousness."

"And then?"

STEP 6: DESTINATION

"In this space you have many choices to deal with the written objectives you created. Depending on whether it is Past Life Regression, Future Life Progression, Astral Projection to heal or expand your potential, explore, get answers, see your life plan, or do a life review. You will look to different destinations which are really just shifts in awareness to different mind environments. But it is at this point that you will begin your re-programming process."

"I don't know much about these practices of regressions and progressions. Can we go over these?"

"Yes, we will. In the beginning, it is most effective to understand that you are now me – Superplacebo – in a Greater Mind that has no limitations of lower minds. As you enter this void, or field of infinite possibilities, you are effectively your Higher Self/Soul form as pure thought and energy within the greater consciousness. With this, your first session would simply leave this purpose as your primary goal; to explore, to look, feel, sense with your astral abilities."

"And when I am done, I just bring my awareness back to my lower form and reality?"

"Yes, as you do now. Let us leave that and consider these 6 steps as Part 1 of your lesson. Now we are going to leave this alone for a while and look into the other common practices that set different objects and destinations when in the void of infinite possibilities."

"Can I eventually do this alone?"

"Yes, of course. Once you and I are one mind and you know it, a quick meditative step connects us. Then we will go together wherever we need to go. You will really enjoy that."

17

WHAT DID I DO WRONG?

Being aware of a past mistake as a Cause which has manifested into physical reality as an Effect allows you to change the energetic picture, then the physical reality.

"You understand how by working from a higher plane we can change a cause to create a new effect on the lower plane of physicality. A common practice is Past Life Regression that can be used to correct an issue recorded in the past. This is particularly useful to deal with karmic issues that you may not even be aware of. Being taken back and having realized a cause, you are able to simply cleanse it and create a different effect in the current time. It is proactive control of the Law of Cause and Effect."

"I have read about this. The thing about this process that has been puzzling is that this goes back to previous lives meaning this information is stored like you would store a show on a video recorder. I understand this now. And then it can be changed; and sometimes the result can be a spectacular healing miracle. And that movie is recorded in explicit detail as engagement in it continues. Are you actually changing the plan?"

"I understand that this is giving your intellect some difficulty so we will deal with this. You know now that these movies are stored in the Causal Body of consciousness. Through the process of Past Life Regression, facilitators are not only gaining access to that information but are able to change it. Now, understand that I can actually change a life plan but that is seldom necessary. Remember that it is the perception and emotion that accompanies these movies. When something has been recorded it is not necessary to change the recording any more than you can change a picture once recorded. But it provides you with an opportunity to understand where the issue came from and change the way perception and emotion will result in going forward."

"Like if I had a serious trauma before that is affecting my behavior now; if I became aware of what happened, I could react smartly when I got hit with it as karma or it is effecting me now."

"Yes. That is what your Psychologists attempt to do. Let us look more into this recorded movie of past life and the process that many use as Past Life Regression."

PAST LIFE REGRESSION

"The purpose of past life regression therapy is to retrieve memories and belief systems from previous incarnations that are still negatively influencing a person's life. These old belief systems can create disharmony; physically, mentally or emotionally. Once the past life memory is brought into awareness, deep understanding and insights arise as to how the events of the past are deeply impacting the present."

"Can you use an example?"

"For example, during a session a person may re-experience having starved to death in a past life. They then relate this memory to a current behavior pattern in their present life: a compulsive eating disorder. Often once the connection between the past life and the current behavior is made, the pattern is broken. However, if the pattern still exists, the therapist can apply energetic and therapeutic techniques to release the frozen energy and help free the person from the limiting pattern."

"And you as the Soul too?"

"What is particularly relevant about this is that karmic cycle we have discussed before. You have learned that the Soul purpose is to experience the lower form to exercise mental and emotional abilities; to engage and learn to evolve better through the virtues, to overcome fears by engaging in that which creates it."

"To put it bluntly get over it and learn a positive lesson from it and move on!"

"Indeed. So if you carry a karmic record of being starved to death in a previous life as a Cause, you may have an Effect of overindulgence in food in this life. Obviously the mortal version would carry this karma because it did not learn from it and get over it; so you carry the karmic fear of starvation and have to learn again. That fear generates an urgent emotional and mental need for food as the effect. So the Law of Attraction looks at this highly charged energy signature you constantly enforce until your body is addicted to over consumption. Being consciousness within the infinite quantum field, it buzzes with this energy to attract possibilities that satisfy the energy. But if you had learned to deal with this before, and got over it, it would not occur in a different life plan."

"Therefore, through me, the Soul is always getting into these predicaments designed into a life plan to get over these issues. To get over it, I forgive myself for this state, let it go and learn from it to instigate a new state of being and life that would have been one of the other options of choice in a life plan."

"You forgive me too! Since I did not communicate well enough. What is so very interesting about this is that this possibility is always available to you no matter what life created through a cause, and we can change the effect to break the karmic loop."

"And this is what the miracle workers are doing?"

"Once again we see that the typical procedure to do this is what we saw with some of our miracle healers and the steps we just went through. To engage in this process a person is asked to be in a comfortable sitting or lying position and the person is first asked to set an intention about what they want to heal or change. They are then verbally led through a progressive relaxation exercise until they reach a deep state of hypnosis, preferably Theta where the subconscious mind is open to suggestion. The therapist proceeds to lead them on a guided meditation to an inner sanctuary, where they feel safe and comfortable, and from here, they're guided to journey back to the time when their problem first began. The therapist facilitates the process by asking questions to help them figure out what occurred in the past, and how it is presently influencing their life."

"Once the connection is established, the person is guided to the end of the lifetime and is often instructed to float above their body. In this in-between life state, the person has a broad perspective on the incarnation and they are able to understand the life lesson they learned from that lifetime. The person is then slowly lead back to the present lifetime and given positive suggestions to feel really good, better than before."

"In past life regression therapy sessions, the person is in total control of the process and the therapist acts merely as a guide. The conscious aware mind is always present and can withhold any information at anytime. The person is also able to immediately return to present time awareness if desired. If at any time during the regression process an unpleasant or traumatic memory is recalled, the person always has the option to float above the scene and watch it as if a movie; comfortably detached from the painful situation."

"Most people can retrieve some past life information, and with practice can achieve deeper and deeper trance states where they can access more vivid memories. About 15 percent of the population has difficulty achieving trance states deep enough, to allow past life memories to emerge."

"Are their many dramatic cases?"

"Past life regression therapy has been used to successfully treat phobias, eating disorders, physical aches and pains, fear of death, depression, anxiety, relationship issues, bottled anger, insecurity and migraines. Basically any physical, mental or emotional disorder that has its roots in past incarnations, can be treated with past life regression therapy."

"Some people try past life regression simply out of curiosity to see who they were in the past. But for most, it's a path for personal growth and healing.

With the help of a trained guide, past life regression can help you experience some of the things in this image."

- See personal relationships in a new light
- Energize talents and abilities from the past
- Release fears and anxieties linked to past life traumas
- Release past life traumas at the root of physical problems
- Experience the transitional states of death and beyond
- Understand and align with life purpose

"How do people actually experience this?"

"Past Life Regression can be an amazing, full-sensory experience. You might experience the memory as a vivid movie, or see only vague flashes of images that prompt the narrative. You might hear gunshots or explosions on a battlefield, or music at a dance. It is possible to recall smells too: smoke from a fire, leather from a saddle, or the sweat of a dirty body."

"As the story unfolds, you feel real emotions appropriate to the story. You may cry when you re-experience deep sadness at the death of a beloved child, feel despair in the pit of your stomach as you witness a massacre, or elation at a long-awaited homecoming from war. And just as you can recall strong emotions, you feel the pain of an arrow piercing your body as you are dying, or the heaviness of a load you're carrying on your back. These physical sensations and emotions are very real in the moment, but pass quickly as you move through the past life story and death."

HOW REGRESSION HEALS

"Ok, so how does it actually heal?"

"Past life regression is healing. You were born not as a blank slate, but as a Soul rich with both the wisdom and scars from many lifetimes. You all carry memories from past lives into this life – unconscious memories that carry an energetic charge and continue to affect you. They can be things left undone, vows made, accomplishments, failures, mistakes, success, emotional debts, guilt, gratitude, traumatic and sudden deaths, wisdom, and love."

"These charges from the past set up patterns which are continually triggered and repeated in your present life. These patterns can be positive or negative. They can affect your relationships, behaviors, motivations, and even your physical bodies and health. Positive patterns can feed talents, bestow wisdom, influence tastes, and energize the life purpose. Negative patterns fuel destructive, compulsive behavior, cloud judgment, cause injury, and block your way. By making these memories conscious, you can release the patterns that no longer serve you, freeing you to live more fully in the present. Beneficial patterns are reinforced, negative patterns are neutralized."

"So just like becoming aware of anything I have screwed up, I can change my perception, forgive myself for being such a dork and act differently."

"Also forgive the one who may have caused it. The problem occurs when there are so many behaviors that are karmic or not so obvious as to how or when they were caused. Yet they can be manifesting behavior and beliefs unknowingly."

"Yes, I see that."

"Past life regression is the process of healing the Soul by healing the past. It is gaining recognition as a legitimate form of spiritual healing. No matter what religion you profess - or even if you don't follow any religion - experiencing yourself as a Soul in other lifetimes gives you a profound awareness that you are more than a physical body. You encounter your soul's essence, connected and aligned to a greater universal energy, perhaps for the first time in your life."

PAST LIFE PROCESS

"Ok, I understand, can you tell me the best way to do this?"

"You will have determined by now that there are no rules as to set procedures. It is really your attention and intention that is your guide."

"Because in this mental space of the void, once there is anything that you bring into thought, vision or communication simply is, right?"

"Yes, so the process we have discussed is your guide to get to the void. It is what you determine as a destination and purpose that you must first determine."

"And?"

"Once you have determined as your questions or issues to address, you must seek out the place where the issue occurred. That is where a skilled facilitator is effective because while you are in this state, it is a conflict of minds to seek out the place and time. A skilled facilitator can do this. It may not be simple to hunt out the exact time and situation that caused something. It may be a hide and seek exercise. Do you want to use an example?"

"Ok, let's say I am fearful of something and wish to get this fixed."

"Fine, so let us say you have entered the quantum void. For example, he may say: *'We are now going to move backwards in time as we pass through a doorway. When you walk through you will be in a past life scene or you will be in the past of your current life. You will experience one of your past lives at a time that created an issue of being fearful of drowning. You will move to an event that will be significant in explaining where and why this has occurred. As you float back, you will stop at a point that will answer your question. Let me know when you are there.'* "

"As you drift back, this whole process may be hunt and seek exercise as the facilitator interacts with you. *'As you come to a place and stop, say the first thing that pops into your mind. Do not analyze or hesitate.'* When you come to a place, the facilitator will attempt to interact with you interrogating the situation: *'Orient yourself, focus, listen. Describe where you are, what time? What are you? How do you feel? Take a few moments to let the information flow.'*

"I see, the facilitator is making sure the analytical mind keeps away and the Higher self is actually speaking?"

"Yes, this process of finding the cause can become tedious and the skill of the faciltator is key to finding the place, event and situation. But once found and the reason for it is determined. The facilitator is in a position to clear this away."

"How? Can you use an example?"

"This is highly variable depending on the issue and who or what caused it but in this case, the event is where you fell into the water, could not swim and went under several times to create a deep trauma as the cause. Your fear of water has never been cleared. You have had an issue with this because your friends laughed at this as they watched you scream and submerge. It was an adult that jumped in and saved you but you never forgave these friends and this trauma was deeply embedded into your subconscious as a program."

"So your facilitator would say: '*Now that you understand the issue and the cause, you will forgive those that did not help you and ask that this fear be deleted from your subconscious memory, that it cannot effect you anymore. As you bring this forward into your present, it will be cleansed away so you will not have this fear ever again and will now enjoy learning to swim. Do you agree?*' In some cases the facilitator will ask that this be stated by you to enforce and confirm the change. The facilitator, may have different modes of cleaning, like asking angels or archangels, or a light beam to assist in this cleansing. Again, typically you will see something included in the process to act like the divine intervention depending on the culture within the belief box fringes."

"Because people like to see or believe in a higher power or authority to instigate belief, accept and surrender?"

"Yes. This is a product of my dear brother's analytical influence."

"When the cleaning is done, you will be led out as we have already discussed."

"This way you can go to any life time?"

"Yes. When you open this mind, all the lives in your Causal energy body are available. It is that you come into this life as a Soul impressed with the wisdom and wounds from many other lifetimes. These impressions are encoded in an energetic template that informs your present personality, physical body, and some external circumstances in your life. This template also carries the emotional charges from unfinished lessons from previous lives, and the plans and blueprints for the present life."

"I can see the need for a facilitator."

"With the help of a past life therapist, you re-live the past life story, you understand the full context of that life, and you recall the thoughts and feelings that got frozen in the past life trauma, usually at the time of death. That's where the pattern originated. The process of remembering diffuses the energy around the pattern. You finally release these old thoughts and feelings. You feel lighter. You are lighter. The past life therapist guides you to see the bigger picture, too: to understand why you were born into your present family and circumstances, and to realize that you brought this pattern with you into this life - it's a pre-existing condition of your soul.

With these insights, you understand your purpose and what you came here to learn."

"Can other things happen as a result of this, like in an NDE?"

"When you attain the state of awareness from the higher perspective, many surprising things can happen. You can objectively review the past life just experienced, and gain a sense of understanding of lessons learned in that lifetime, and what thoughts, feelings, and physical sensations may have carried forward from that life into the present. If more than one lifetime is recalled during the session, general Soul patterns can be observed, shedding tremendous insight into where you've been and where you're going in your journey through incarnations."

"And the experience is different for all?"

"Of course. Some people move into a highly energetic state where they experience healing energies coming into their bodies, imbuing information, love, and understanding. These energies may be experienced as orbs, colors, and other amorphous forms. Or the energy can take on the form of spiritual beings that give guidance and answer questions. Groups of souls may appear and act as agents of teaching and healing. This type of healing usually occurs spontaneously, without any prompting from a facilitator."

"I have read of this. These healings have been described by many as one of the most significant, life-affirming events of their lives. For some, it is the first time they've experienced absolute peace and unconditional love."

"In this state of Soul consciousness, deceased relatives can suddenly make contact both viscerally and telepathically. A presence is felt in the room. Their forms are recognizable with telepathic dialogues."

"I see that hypnosis is once again key to get a form of focused awareness that is used to attain the appropriate state."

"Indeed. It is necessary for you to focus inward to access your past life memories – or any distant memories for that matter. In this state you can still be aware that you are reclining in a chair, a bird is chirping outside, or an airplane is flying overhead, while at the same time you are completely engrossed in the past life memory."

"These must make up a lot of the karma that is carried forward to gain lesson and virtues from."

"Some past life memories are of happy and fulfilling lives. These benign lifetimes help us understand and appreciate our present positive attitudes, talents, and good relationships. They are life's gifts. Most memories that surface in past life therapy are of past life trauma, usually a traumatic death."

"It is pretty hard to see these issues as gifts!"

"If you look closely at any situation, you can find positive outcomes and gifts. The fact that many cannot see this does not nullify the choice to see it differently. If that was not placed before you as a gift, how could you ever experience the wondrous side of it? Otherwise you and I do get stuck in these traumas."

"So you have to live the pain to do this until you rise above?"

"It is the past life trauma that continues to affect you emotionally, mentally, and physically, causing difficulties in many aspects of your present life. By exposing these painful memories to the light of awareness, and understanding the context of the past life and death, the emotional intensity loses its grip. You can finally let go of the past and move forward in your life. You will feel lighter, as if a burden has been lifted. This is the heart of your purpose to heal the deepest part of us as a Soul. You will not get stuck in these traumatic memories. Sometimes the healing is immediate and dramatic, or it can be more subtle and noticeable over time. After the regression, you will remember everything you experienced. Over time, new layers of insight and understanding may emerge spontaneously."

"You know what? Since you know all this stuff best, why do I need a facilitator? Would this not be easier to meet you in the void, then you take us back to the problems and karma and fix it?"

"Yes, it is exactly true. So when you know and feel you are in Theta in the void of infinite possibilities, that is exactly what we can do. Your bottom line is that the simple process of loving, forgiving, holding light and having compassion are your key tools. Are you ready for this?"

"Well, not quite but I will be. I can feel it!"

"Wonderful!"

"Superplacebo, is this the same process used in understanding the life plans that are created between lives?"

"Yes. You would be taken to the place in between lives and ask your Soul and Spirit Guides to come forward. After slipping from your body, you travel in the spiritual state between lives and feel the energy of 'heaven'. You get a glimpse of who you truly are as a Soul learning and growing through different incarnations. Some meet guides and make plans. Some dialogue with deceased relatives, and are left with a profound sense of having made genuine contact with their loved ones."

"Do you want to understand this now?"

"Yes, let us suppose I want to change the movie because I don't think it serves a purpose anymore."

18

I DON'T LIKE THIS MOVIE ANYMORE

You can regress to difficult issues in your past to effect change now, so why not progress into your future to make better choices now?

FUTURE LIFE PROGRESSION

"Ok, I will take you to another practice that we talked about - a Future Life Progression. It is a glimpse of your Life Plan. But once again for your intellectual mind, we will discuss what is being used in your 3D reality."

"Yes, that has indeed made me curious about this movie especially after we see people come back from a near death review session to have this instant temporal view of their life flash by to feel all the emotions of all in the movie. It seems that there is a movie being created as the actual life and there is another movie of the possible life?"

"Yes, it is so. It is like the representation of the lines on your palm. One lays out the potential journey and characteristics taken through the astral time and field, and the other is the actual journey you chose to engage in. Both are stored in the Causal energy body and accessible when you open your awareness into this field of pure consciousness."

"Now that is really fringe stuff! It is really hard to accept how these lives are just movies that can be created and then used to one's advantage."

"You have a word that is often used in Near Death Experiences. It is ineffable; the inability to really explain something. It is because your lower intellect and group limitations of conditioning cannot think beyond the box. When you begin to attain the higher senses of the astral, mental and causal fields then it is perfectly explainable and understandable."

"Ok, I obviously have not attained these yet."

"You will as you are in the right out of mind place. Let us begin by taking you to a practice called Future Life Progression which takes your pure consciousness forward in time rather than backward."

"Yes, that is a bit of a chuckle. I get it. I have to be out of my norm mind to be in the right mind!"

"Future Life Progression is called a waking dream therapy. It is a form of hypnosis that relaxes you into a deep yet alert state that also opens your mind to the potential you have at your fingertips. Past Life Regression concentrates on your personal history and how certain events in your life, or past lives, have shaped your beliefs and circumstances in the present day. Future Life Progression takes you forward in time to a place where you can explore the possibilities that extend from your own creation and look at the different paths and different results of that choice."

"Can this also take me on a journey into a next life or future lives and provide insight and knowledge on future incarnations and choices?"

"Yes, you may wonder how is this possible. But if you can wrap your new mind around the therapeutic work being done on In between Life Regression this is not hard to understand. Remember we discussed this and you learned how we created a Life Plan and contract to engage in a carefully laid out plan that suited your and my needs of self evolution in the form of learning lessons. Let us recall that Life Plan included the actors, the scenes, the storyline, key events and multiple situations, choices, and exit points that you saw – before you engaged in it."

"Yes, I recall it. And the detail was up to me and you as the creator of the Life Plan. That was You as me and my Soul with the Spirit Guide in collaboration with your Soul Family."

"It was our guideline to your life as a partnership where you would engage your mental and emotional higher bodies through the interface of the astral body to a lower form."

"Yes, I understand. The brain would be the physical manager and processor deploying mental thought and the body would be the physical means of deploying a feeling body through the heart brain. And the subconscious would be the recording instrument, operating system and link to the higher state of Self as Soul or Higher Self. So how does looking at this plan assist me?"

"The process allows you to peer ahead into those choices and pathways that you created and forgot… silly you! You actually saw what things would be like and what people looked like before you decided so all we are doing is having a look at those situations which are already recorded in the Causal energy body."

"Ohhhh! I can see where this could be used a lot when one feels life is stuck on hold or one has tried, and failed, to remove personal blocks and obstacles. The big question of course becomes one of asking: '*Why can I not overcome this issue; is it because I absolutely have to do it by design?*'"

"It is more than that. Future Life Progression can provide you with the tools to make renewed progress. You can fast forward the Life Plan look at how you would screw up or look at how you would benefit, then come back and make the appropriate choices now. You may have already cleared blocks and now need clarity to build confidence and move forward in the direction that most appeals to you."

"Ohh! It can help me make better informed choices and help explore alternatives. Future Life Progression will also allow me to see how my future could pan out! Holy macaroni, are you serious. You mean I could have avoided my first wife and the calamity it caused me?"

"Yes, you may be able to experience how your life is, given the choices you opt to make, as well as the people you share your life with and the location that it all takes place in."

"How do we do this? Is this one of the destinations we talked about in the process when you get to the void of pure consciousness?"

"Yes. During a session it is like hypnotherapy. The practitioner, or facilitator, will talk you through relaxation steps that allow your body to become naturally deeply relaxed. You will have discussed, beforehand, the areas that you are most interested in exploring and examining and will therefore be lead in that direction."

"Wow, it's the same old procedures again. Is it back to knowing your objectives and purpose?"

"Otherwise how could you know where to start? It is a sea of information and knowing what you are looking for, where to look and why you are doing this is important. This is how you set pointers in your mental mind to take you to specific points in the movie."

"Well once again, you and I can go there directly."

"Well, once again, are you ready? The information that you will receive, during the meditative state, will usually be the most relevant information for you to gain knowledge from in the present time. This means that although you may feel you want to focus solely on career prospects your unconscious mind may feel that it is more important for you to examine another area or issue of your life that is preventing you from living your true potential."

"The process must be similar to the life review."

"It is. Here you are led through relevant images to review your mortal progress. Once again, you are getting a look at some recorded information but this time it is a plan that has not yet become reality."

"Wow. That reality we appear to accept as real illusion is like a readable-writeable DVD that contains a self created movie that can be changed?"

"It's not so much changing the movie as much as changing the choices that are shown in the movie. In the past life regression, you do not actually change the movie, you become aware of the issue and a cause, then change the effect in the present now."

"Yes, of course, I remember you said that."

"After a session, having explored the possibilities of your future life you will return to normal, waking consciousness feeling more relaxed, confident and keen to start implementing the changes you saw clearly in your mind during meditation. These images will be vivid enough for you to interpret them as a memory, because you will have explored happenings that feel true to life, rather like in a dreaming state. This experience will bring with it new insight and personal knowledge that you can tap into during moments of stress or anxiety. This will encourage you to continually make progress towards the path that leads you to the future you have seen and experienced during Future Life Progression."

"So in effect I am changing the real-time virtual movie of now, which has the result of changing things going forward?"

"Not exactly, you will still encounter the paths along the Life Plan as they were designed, but the perception, emotions and experiences may be on different paths than you were on, then recording as you go from moment to moment. There may be karmic needs along a path that you may want to cleanse. That is for you and I to decide."

"So in both cases of past life regression or future life, I do not actually change the movie."

"That is correct. What you have recorded or planned is set. But how you respond, feel, perceive, behave, using mental and emotional gifts is being recorded moment by moment. What path you take is also different. Having learned something from the past or future allows you to respond, perceive, feel and behave differently."

"This means that people have the power to customize and control their destinies. We can all use hypnotherapy to eliminate past and current problems and attain our karmic purpose. Can you give me an example?"

"An example is how the laws of Cause & Effect and Karma work between lives. An effect in the current life is a result say an opposite in a previous life. For example obesity now relates to starvation in a previous life. Desertion now relates to overprotective parents in a precious life. The fear of water in this life relates to drowning in a previous life. A fear of noises now relates to being killed by a bomb in a previous life. Loss of children in this life is a result of being barren in a previous. These cases illustrate the notion of learning lessons that we will carry over and over until we can balance the karma. The key point is that through the process of hypnosis it is possible to overcome a problem, accomplish an objective, have an experience."

"Ok, I get that. But that's going backward but what about forward?"

"Well, perhaps you can better understand those lessons you are about to experience and make sure you do not fall victim to it as crap and horrible! Suppose you can see the life type you could have should you find a partner, job, or take a certain path? This way it is for people to take control of their destiny and create the reality they want and deserve. You can see what happens on each path and become self assured, confident and more direct on the one that works best for you or perhaps when you see a big karmic challenge ahead, you can be prepared you and I."

"Hmmm, that could be cool! But how do you actually seek these out and see them?"

"Again it is about being clear with your intent. I will guide this to provide answers to your questions and link you with future lifetimes and even concurrent lives. You will only see future events that you can influence now, in the present. You will see warnings, see future partners like major events, people, and so on that are relevant. There is nothing that is meant to be hidden here. But you have to open to this awareness."

"Yes, that is the key isn't it?"

"Remember that the future already exists, tomorrow is real only in potentiality. Future has many forms but only when congealed into the present does it exist in actuality. We live in a framework of potentiality and our actions determine final form so we can change the future."

"That is a real tough one to understand. But you and I can do this, right?"

"No question when you feel ready. When you truly get into this space, there is a way that gives you the ability to see forward. It can be tested. You can move to see a week ahead into future, and document the detail then confirm them after a week."

"Ok, that is cool but I need to practice getting into that space first. How do others do this? Can you use an example?"

A FUTURE LIFE PROGRESSION PROCESS

"Let us once again look at the ones doing this as a service. We are simply going to change our destination within the void. Do you remember those steps?"

"Yes. When is the best time?"

"It is best to do this twice daily for at least 20 minutes; best when fresh in the morning and you are alert. We will continue from the destination step. You will see a certain pattern of possesses and steps here similar to what we have already discussed. Do you remember these?"

"Yes. The key components are quiet environment, a mental device, passive attitude, and a comfortable position. When you enter the self-hypnotic trance, you will observe the positive mind of tranquility, peace of mind, experience unity or oneness with environment, sometimes have an inability to describe experience in words, see an alteration in time/space relationships, and have an enhanced sense of reality and meaning. This is a check point to see if you are ready in the quantum void. I could use a self-hypnotic process."

"It is the best way to start, we covered this before but it would be guided by your own recording of the process."

"I understand."

"Once again, you must determine what you need to know. Think back to what you would have liked to know so you could have taken different paths and actions. Make a list of these which can relate to worries, concerns, problems, or future relations. Spend some time thinking about these. Write these down on paper because it acknowledges them and it sends a request for help to the universe and your future self, your Higher Guide."

"This is one way you can do it. First your destination is your future and your life plan so you would ask for your Soul and Spirit Guide to join you. Ask the Higher self for comments or advice with attention to: '*What will facilitate my spiritual growth? What decisions, choices can I make now to achieve highest aspirations? What behavior, thoughts, actions can I implement to accelerate my spiritual path? What am I learning from this scenario?*'"

"Ask me as your Higher Self to assist you. Imagine a specific time in the future. Your need is to see, feel what you are doing and allow thoughts, feelings into awareness. If you were recording the guidance, you could follow these steps."

"Imagine a long tunnel and floating along it, dark but silver lights on sides. Notice cool and peaceful and relaxed. See a curtain at end as a gentle blue cloth and reach out to pull it aside."

"See a large red shiny door with the word Gallery in brass. Trace your fingers on it."

"Note the brass handle, turn it, push open the door into a dim lit room with a few candles. Note a candelabra on a wood table. Light the candle on it and pick it up. Look around."

"See walls covered in huge paintings in this wondrous place. Suddenly you are drawn to one and you realize it is you with the outcome to your dilemma or question you came with."

"The picture will represent a temporal download into your mind. The answer will be here as a picture which you need to study and inspect to see the future. The details will answer your question. Who are, why are you here, are you happy, how do you feel?"

"Step into the picture as the image is a doorway. Feel yourself inside. How do you feel? While inside, have you made the right choice or move? Step outside when ready. Hold candelabra high and look at other pictures. Do you want to step inside?"

"When done, put down candelabra. If you have another time or question, this the place to ask. You will travel to the time that answers your questions but you can say I wish to go to a specific period into the future. For example go six months ahead and ask your questions."

"So if I was contemplating or in a relationship, I could ask: '*will I get along with this person, will my relationship work out? What would it be like?*' and see and feel it?"

"Yes, when you are done, make a conscious note that you will remember this in detail. Walk back through the door, close it, step into the tunnel and glide back to the Void and feel the peace. You are ready to move forward with new information."

YOUR SOUL PURPOSE REVIEW

"So suppose we are back at step 6 as our void. Would this be the place to do a Soul purpose review?"

"It would indeed. Remember it is to live a life that will facilitate my spiritual growth. You can check choices to make now to achieve highest aspirations and determine the best behavior, thoughts, actions to implement to accelerate that spiritual path. It may be that you are off track or some lower path and not learning from this plan. On the other hand there may be things like crap that you do not understand the purpose of it."

"It is to evolve and grow to become one with the universal energy – the energy that flows through everything, is part of everything and governs all things. Each lifetime will teach you and allow your opportunities to perfect yourself until the time you are ready to reconnect with the universal energy – when you have learned all you need to know. The Soul lessons are made by spiritual agreement and we go through life reviews to review progress between lives. But if this is off track then a review process is a good idea."

"You have been listening. So to continue, see yourself stepping into a huge cavern knowing you have been here before."

"See your Guides and know they are here to assist, to show you pieces of lifetimes past and future. They will explain themes, lessons, how you can be aware to move on and release what does not serve you. They will present images of you in thought forms and you will be told of your higher purpose, what you must release, what repeats and how to fine tune your path."

"In your mind and in this place of total void, you have no space, no time, no identity, there is nothing here except you and I as pure consciousness within the openness of the greater mind. Now when you are clear, we together will ask your Soul and your Spirit Guide to come forward."

"You will lose all perception of time as the download is panoramic, 3-D or holographic in increased vividness, as if you were reliving a given episode itself. You will interact with all parties at each point being reviewed."

"Most things will be pleasant to see, some things may make you feel embarrassed, you feel sorry for certain things you have said or done. You will feel the injury or pain of those who suffered because of your selfish or inappropriate behavior."

"It is here that you would ask about your spiritual growth, reasons for your issues, what you were to learn, and whether you are off your path."

When you are finished, you would know that you will remember and come back with a new point of view."

"You would thank all and slip back into the peace of the void."

19

THE MYSTERY OF THE MIDBRAIN

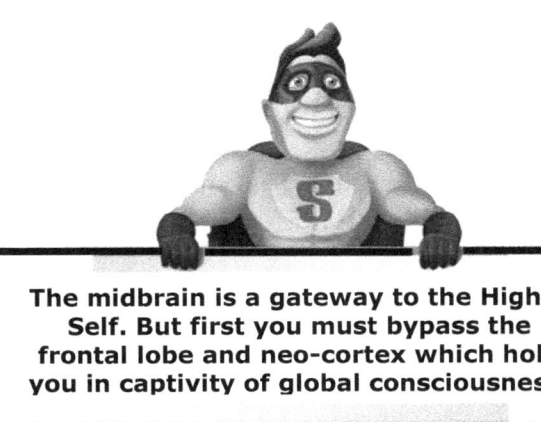

The midbrain is a gateway to the Higher Self. But first you must bypass the frontal lobe and neo-cortex which hold you in captivity of global consciousness.

This was all sort of making sense to me but there were still many questions. Boy I was getting pretty excited about this partnership. Most of this was simply ineffable and I could understand that too. I could understand that there was more to me and even though I never took any notice of religions, there always was an inherent feeling and belief there was something more powerful guiding this universe than anyone could understand. I also was beginning to see the light in this whole thing about managing energies and karma. How else could I explain my life? It made sense. But the idea that we create these movies and that our reality is just an illusion was difficult to comprehend, even in this higher space. Certainly I would listen, and it seemed more and more truthful but there were still things that did not make sense. There was this open question about the midbrain that haunted me. There was also the idea of the game and the quantum research and the big deception that was just a game I was playing out for my Soul as Superplacebo to get wiser and have his jollies. That rattled me. So I made my list of questions and it was time to get deeper into my heart mind.

Not surprising was when I went into what I was beginning to feel and sense as the void Superplacebo already knew the questions I was perplexed with. That's pretty silly when it is all one mind, but it in this mind of mine it was still he and me, not we.

THE SECRET OF THE MIDBRAIN

"I understand you want to go back a bit with several questions. You understand that you are essentially just pure quantum consciousness and represent my Higher Self and Soul in the games of life. You understand that my brother represents the Lower Self as consciousness and takes up residence in the brain. You have questions about me and the brain and how it creates your reality, don't you?"

"Exactly. What about you? Do you have some counterpart in the brain where you take residence?"

"It is not so much that we take residence, it is that we are resident in the mind consciousness that influences the physical counterparts. The Lower and Higher Minds are simply by design able to influence different dimensions of energetic bodies where there are counterparts."

"And Supernocebo is relegated to the 3rd dimension?"

"Yes, he is designed to be a conscious compartment like ego that I relegated to that dimension. You as a conscious compartment have the luxury of thinking outside, but he does not go beyond the 4th dimension. But what he influences below in the 3rd dimension is reflected in the energetic copy above. My influence jurisdiction is much different because I can influence and transcend all dimensions. It is because we are quantum."

"Depending upon how one chooses to listen, right? I also have questions about this quantum stuff."

"Of course, but to answer your question, I do have another preferred point of access and place of influence in the lower 3D plane of the body."

"So that is the heart, I know but I bet the pineal gland and the lyden are also higher brains."

"That is very perceptive of you. The pineal is part of the midbrain which has been shrouded in function over time. Over time, the evolutionary process in the development of the human brain has chosen to expand the frontal lobe and the neo-cortex to be larger and larger so as to create a 3D wisdom for survival."

"Right, I see it. It is because your brother has been so active and loud building the abilities of humans to be so smart and powerful according to his 12 rules."

"Yes, it is the choice of the group consciousness and so the importance on rational thought, logic, power and satisfying the ego in lower matter are the most important means of survival so accepted by the norm. So that is why you are all subject to the laws of matter until the group consciousness breaks out of it."

"So the evolution of the spiritual aspect and the higher Mind does not have a chance? Is that where the midbrain comes in?"

"You are now ready to understand something new about your reality. All we have been talking about is related to attaining a state where you are using various techniques to create miracles from a higher vibration. The norm is a very cumbersome issue in allowing a true development of your true potential. This norm stifles your evolution into the 4th and 5th stages because it is strongly entrenched in beliefs that 90% of DNA is junk, 99% of that which is not matter is of no significance, all paranormal abilities are freaks of nature, the brain is being fully employed, and the reptile-mammalian brains are primitive. It is now time, after you have a fundamental knowing opening that we look into this more carefully."

"Yes, I am sensing that there are other ways to create miracles that we have not covered."

"I can see you are remembering now. The neo-cortex is a limiting brain which makes sense to those that listen to my brother. The neo-cortex's main job is to maintain control, which is essential; so the belief boxes and the brain anatomy respond to the demands in human life. However, it is the opposite of spontaneity and miraculous occurrences. The midbrain, which is beginning to be more comprehensively understood by scientists, is the part of the brain that can give access to miracles. In truth, the neo-cortex kills miracles."

"Just a minute. Doesn't the neo-cortex control your higher order functions, planning, reasoning, judgment, impulses, memory, and motor functions. In fact, much of our brain function happens in this area of the brain – the frontal lobe, the parietal lobe, the temporal lobe and the occipital lobe."

"Indeed it is so, but those higher order functions are higher in respect to other 3D creatures and it is believed that these higher order functions of matter are more important than the higher order functions of non matter. That is the delusion that is reflected as the norm. That is the delusion that believes in polarity and stifles the spiritual evolution as it analyzes it is smarter than the spiritual brain. In truth the higher functions of the higher energy bodies are through the midbrain which has simply been atrophied in neglect and misuse."

"But isn't this what people call the lizard or reptilian brain?"

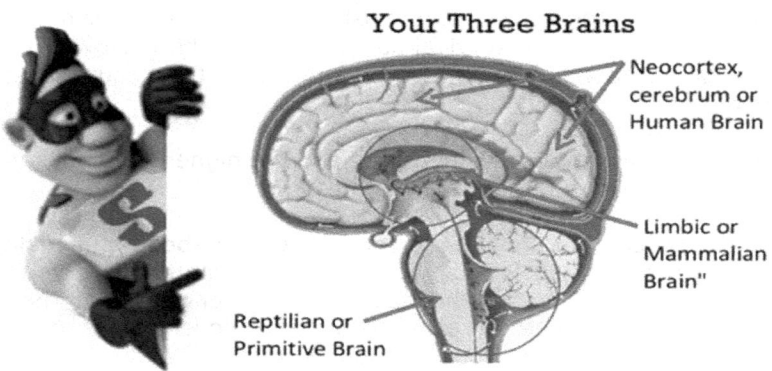

"It is and perhaps this is where it has been branded and accepted as the primitive animal brain that those who actually know the truth of wish to hide as its true function. It is part of the midbrain just as the 3rd eye and pineal gland are. This is one step above the reptilian brain typically branded as the mammalian brain. The truth is that the midbrain is the brain counterpart that has no predisposition to time like the frontal lobe and neo-cortex have. It is the no-time, no-space quantum void as a physical counterpart of your Higher Consciousness. That is why I can occupy quantumly this space."

"I can see that if it is not able to understand time which is important to this reality. Well what is this spiritual brain you talk of?"

"It is the midbrain that is directly linked to me and my brain if you would like to call it that. I have what you would call spiritual intelligence that comes into play as your total conscious awareness that does not need the neo-cortex to think and do. It is then your Soul mind that thinks and acts through the chakra systems to govern your life plan and your behavior, not the falsely deployed giant neo-cortex and frontal lobe."

"But what about the motor functions? What about coping in this fake reality? What does it do?"

"Ok, take this image into your awareness for a moment."

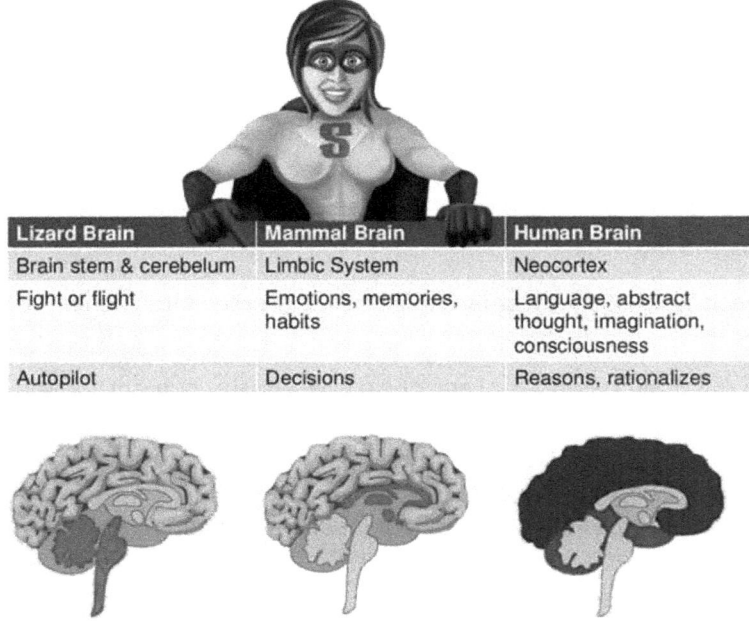

"Got it, we actually have three brains?"

"These three brains are sort of like an onion, each encompassing the other but with special roles. You see the prevailing consciousness has created the big brain to believe it is better than anything else, and is totally in charge of time based reality. It is what, under the guidance of dear brother, that places plans in your minds of what you want to happen, the ways you need to heal, the dreams that you want to fulfill, the relationships we want to create. But the mind is very different from the brain. This is where the neo-cortex and frontal lobe are disallowing anything instantaneous or miraculous to happen in your life."

"Ok, I got that loud and clear. So what is the big deal about the midbrain?"

"The midbrain, on the other hand, acts most notably as the information superhighway connecting the forebrain and hindbrain. It enables your brain to integrate sensory information from your eyes and ears with your muscle movements, thereby enabling your body to use this information to make fine adjustments to your movements."

"What does this have to do with miracles?"

"Take a moment to digest what I said about sensory information."

"Jeez! I get it! This is the place where our senses gather information from that fake reality and give us the physical evolution to act out our roles! Fake reality!"

"You have the key. So in truth this brain is just as well equipped to run your life as the big brain."

"Especially if it is way smarter with that greater intelligence at its disposal! Wow!"

"The midbrain has no concept of time which the neo-cortex and frontal lobe are preoccupied with. Miracles that are outside this belief box are created in this place outside of time and space. It is a matter of moving your attention from the frontal lobe to the midbrain and accepting the Higher Mind as the mind in charge of your affairs. It is like the biological equivalent of the Internet; it's a vital aspect of our neural information superhighway, which transfers visual and auditory input that actually creates your reality."

"But this whole thing about life the way we live it would be totally different! How could we adjust?"

"I did not say it was easy since the norm has gone so far off the spiritual track. It would be a slow evolution but it starts just like you have started now."

"And this is where you are as well?"

"The midbrain is vitally important to maintaining and regulating the state of consciousness, alertness and attention. Remember that is that cool state of awareness called Alpha. The midbrain contains the physical pineal gland, which has similar features to the retina in your eyes and is also a replica of what ancient wisdom called the third eye. It also includes the pons, reticular activating system, the pituitary gland, and the 3rd ventricle. The Pituitary gland is the master gland. The pineal gland and the surrounding area in the midbrain is where your connection to higher thought and reality is. When these areas are activated you open up to the extraordinary and welcome events that begin to manifest in your life beyond what the falsely name superbrain tells you. You do not create miracles now because most are caught up in 'cause and effect' and time bondage. You cannot experience anything without time."

"Ok, so I understand that currently, miracles are being disallowed by the neo-cortex which includes the frontal lobe. This is the part of the brain that disallows anything instantaneous to happen. I can see why you need to shut up your brother and the beta brain. But how does this reality bending occur?"

"This is another topic but in a nutshell, your reality is a holographic illusion; a projection of 3D reality that is created by the brain for you to experience through your five senses and deploy mental and emotional abilities. The main camera of assimilation and projection is here in the midbrain. So to change the movie you need access to the projector and the programmer that reside outside of the belief box consciousness. This is the place where that can be done."

"Yes, I see this. If the midbrain is under the direct guidance of the Soul and does not need the frontal lobe or neo-cortex, it does not really even care about the right brain left brain subdivision because it is simply one consciousness that supersedes your brother's meddling."

"And open you to where you are now, totally aware of who and what you are, what you are doing here and opens the fullness of your DNA. How do you like that?"

"So why in God's name were we not designed to just function that way from the beginning. Who let Supernocebo loose to create this big stupid brain?"

"It was that way in the fullness of DNA. It evolved that way by continuous choices of human. I will tell you about this DNA devolution soon."

WHERE I LIVE IN THE BRAIN

"That should be interesting! So this is an access place in the brain for you"

"Indeed, through the energetic portal of the pineal and the hearts. Both are 'brains' of higher mind representing the higher mental and emotional energy bodies."

"Are you saying this tiny little thing called a pineal that has atrophied over the years can actually replace the big brain? What's the difference?"

"Exactly. It should be the big brain that should be managed by the pineal brain not the other way around. When you enter the energy portal of the midbrain mind, you are directly connected to my Soul mind consciousness and the mental energy body. You are actually there now because no time quantum space is everywhere. Here there is no purpose to what has evolved as the big rational brain because you simply know all that is the higher mind. When you enter the heart brain mind, you are directly connected to the emotional energy body and that is the emotion of love. Remember, in simple terms your gifts of being human give you the mental-intellectual and the emotional energy bodies that are reflected in the pineal and the heart energy fields."

"That seems very simple. You know all and love everything? You don't need a brain?"

"The midbrain is the source projector of your holographic illusion and it does not need to be analytical to deal with time and space. That is an illusion. Your body functions and evolution are all encoded in DNA to be used to grow, evolve, and feel with so what else do you need to experience the hologram? Right now you are not using any of the 90% of what has been called junk DNA. Think what goodies are in their anxious to morph out into reality?"

"Hmmm, that's why you need to get out of the 3D brain, body and environment!"

"Yes, to effect change outside of time and space, you must do this from the outside of the big smart brain. If you want to meet with me face to face you can to tap into the pineal gland. It is truly the portal. The pineal gland is a small reddish-gray pine shaped gland about the size of a pea. It hangs from the roof of the completely dark cave of the 3rd ventricle of the brain and is constantly bathed in cerebral spinal fluid. This gland is the connection portal to me. It is the portal to all that exists. It is the source of all wisdom and knows all that is, all that was and all that will be."

"So what else does it do?"

"Physically, the pineal gland is connected to the thalamus, hypothalamus, basil nuclei and medial temporal lobe. The function of it has been relegated to the controls of circadian rhythms. The focus is the *hypothalamus* that is also sensitive to light and dark and therefore affects circadian rhythms. It's true function goes much beyond that as it is considered by those out of the box to be a master gland (as is the *pituitary gland/hypothalamus*), both being responsible for the *regulation of all the other endocrine glands*."

"Back to these chakra antennas and the hormones. What do these other parts do?"

"The thalamus will process and relay sensory information selectively to various parts of the cerebral cortex, as one thalamic point may reach one or several regions in the cortex. Of course it also plays an important role in regulating states of sleep and wakefulness."

"The hypothalamus regulates certain metabolic processes and other activities of the Autonomic Nervous System. It synthesizes and secretes neurohormones, often called hypothalamic-releasing hormones, and these in turn stimulate or inhibit the secretion of pituitary hormones. The hypothalamus controls body temperature, hunger, thirst, fatigue, anger, and circadian cycles."

"The basal nuclei or ganglia are associated with a variety of functions including: control of voluntary motor movements, procedural learning, routine behaviors or habits, eye movements, cognition and emotion."

"What about this holographic control center of reality?"

"The medial temporal lobes are involved in high-level auditory processing. The temporal lobe is involved in primary auditory perception, such as hearing, and holds the primary auditory cortex which receives sensory information from the ears and secondary areas process the information into meaningful units such as speech and words. You also have the superior temporal gyrus within this area where auditory signals from the cochlea first reach the cerebral cortex and are processed by the primary auditory cortex in the left temporal lobe. The areas associated with vision in the temporal lobe interpret the meaning of visual stimuli and establish object recognition."

"That gives me headache. Can you simplify it?"

"The ventral part of the temporal cortices appear to be involved in high-level visual processing of complex stimuli such as faces and scenes. Anterior parts of this ventral stream for visual processing are involved in object perception and recognition. The left temporal lobe holds the primary auditory cortex, which is important for the processing of semantics in both speech and vision in humans. It plays a key role in speech comprehension. The functions of the left temporal lobe are not limited to low-level perception but extend to comprehension, naming, and verbal memory. The medial temporal lobe are involved in encoding declarative long term memory."

"Jeez, you just described our means of seeing, hearing, sensing and feeling reality!"

"Indeed, you can see that this is the Soul's brain, the physical representation designed to create reality for it to engage in through you."

"Wow! Is this also the 3rd eye?"

"Spiritually, the pineal gland is associated with both the Crown and 3rd Eye chakras. This is used like an antenna or satellite dish receiving cosmic energies through the crown chakra. The 3rd Eye Chakra is located directly between your physical eyes being associated with clairvoyance, which is the ability to see beyond the physical sense of sight. The pineal gland is intimately connected with your physical vision being affected by varying degrees of light and darkness through your physical eyes. *Both light and dark* are necessary for your pineal gland to be healthy and alive, just as metaphorically both light and dark must exist in all of cosmology."

"When the pineal gland is vibrant, there is the potential to make rapid leaps in spiritual development and illumination. The pineal gland is light made manifest in the physical human body. It is what connects you to a cellular DNA level with the unknowable, the great mystery, the great beyond."

NO TIME NO PLACE NO THING

"You mentioned that reality is a holographic illusion, a projection of 3D reality that is created by the brain for us to experience through our five senses and deploy mental and emotional abilities. The main camera of assimilation and projection is here in the midbrain. So to change the movie you need access to the projector and the programmer that reside outside of the belief box consciousness. This is a place where that can be done?"

"Yes, if you are really interested in the technology, as I have said, the midbrain is under the direct guidance of your Soul and does not need the frontal lobe or neo-cortex to live a life of higher mind. It does not really even care about the right brain left brain subdivision because it is simply one brain. The division and purpose has been created by the choices of mankind to evolve away from any spiritual mind. The physiology has the corpora quadrigemina, composed of two parts. There are two colliculi that act as relay stations that take sensory information from the eyes and ears and relay it to the thalamus for distribution to the appropriate area of the cerebrum. The cerebral peduncle and corpora quadrigemina are separated by a canal called the cerebral aqueduct, which distributes cerebrospinal fluid throughout the brain and spinal cord to buffer the tissue, remove wastes, and maintain cranial pressure. It is in this place that by way of proper communication, you are able to create miracles that change the physics of your reality."

"And one of these is time?"

"Yes, as I said, the midbrain has no concept of time, nor does it distinguish between what is imagining or perceived as reality. Time is a construct of the neo-cortex. The midbrain is totally in the now. Both time and space are meaningless. Time is built into your big brain and it can stress you out like when you are thinking time is running out. Time is a construct of the lower mind and the work of my brother. Your mind and its imagination are in the now without any time constraints."

"So the quantum void of infinite possibilities is in the midbrain. What about the heart and the astral stuff?"

"Understand when you are in the void, there is really no particular place or time. How or where you bring yourself into the quantum field of no space, no time is not important because quantum is everywhere and nowhere, no time and every time, all one field so these places we speak of such as the Soul mind, heart mind, higher mind, greater mind, they are all one. If you understand time, you can control it and move it faster. Time will stop if you are in soul intelligence as it is instantaneous time control."

"I can't imagine what this reality would be without the idea of time."

"You can, just sit down and imagine whatever you want. I am going to take you into some information that is really outside the box. It has to do with words, images, DNA, and the brain. This will lead to a new discussion about the nature of your holographic illusion."

THE ISSUE WITH MR. SMARTY BRAIN

"The issue with the big smart brain is that it is time based and matter based. It learns from the past to plan the future. That is what it has evolved to do. The global consciousness, which as a reflection of the billions of minds is a living evolving energy, just like your own consciousness. Your consciousness is always evolving and learning, storing its chosen wisdoms in its subconscious. The global is the same, storing its collective wisdom into the subconscious. Thus the global limits its participants just like yours does because that is where you choose from."

"Ok. So the main issue is preoccupation with matter. I understand that. But what about time?"

"The global mind is conditioned to time. Time governs everything. Time is money, all work to time, you must plan for a future time, your time is limited, history is time, the clock governs life. You worry about it and it governs your life. Matter is the model of life. Matter is more important than mind. Identity and self protection, conflict fear of time, growing old, not being secure is a paramount issue which the big smart brain has evolved to solve. And of course my brother has been active here to assist in evolving this big brain over time."

"So in a place of no time, no matter, no identity, no space, just pure consciousness, this is not a viable thing. So the midbrain has no useful function in this wisdom about matter, right?"

"The norm, the global box, reflects this belief. Most have been hypnotized into believing cause & effect which is a Newton model. Many that are even partially outside the box believe in the Laws of Karma and the Law of Attraction. These are a silly rationalization of the big brain trying to expand out of the box. These choices keep you inside the laws of matter."

"But you told me all about this before."

"I told you how it is influencing your life in the box because you are in the box, struggling to get out. The issue is that you cannot let go enough to really get out of the box. Some temporarily do it through these beliefs but are just drawn back in because they are faced with their reality of living day to day inside the box, unable to really get out."

"So what are you saying?"

"When you succeed in being in the place of no time no mind no identity no place things are different. The rules change. The mind is totally the vehicle for manifestation because what it thinks, it creates. There are no laws to inhibit it. The Law of Attraction is a foolish construct because in truth you create from inside and project to the outside as a holographic projection. I understand that this is not yet comprehensible to you but we will get to this later."

"Yes, I do not understand."

"The law of karma does not need to exist. It can be dissolved by simple awareness and forgiveness. In this place it is not relevant because the game of life and the life plan are totally understood and not relevant, serving no purpose. The way energies behave in other dimensions is different."

"Woah!"

"The Law of Cause and Effect suggests you have no control over your destiny and is an old energy belief. So you need to physically push an object to move it. But the other model is that you move that object with mind alone. The new is that it is all about mind over matter and that you as the creator cause an effect."

"So we have to use the mind to give thanks ahead of the experience. In order to have wealth you have to feel it before hand, feel whole before healing occurs, feeling empowered before something occurs. Your body is your conscious mind it does not know the difference. It is a mantra-an assertion in the mind that repeats over and over. Emotional engagement adds to the power as it better to change the body when a value is assigned to that emotion. Then the physics responds to the mind?"

"That's what all these miracle techniques do."

"Yes. It goes further. People who heal with miracles never cared about the miracle. They were whole, celebrating the occurrence of the emotional engagement. They no longer needed anything. When you add emotional energy you speed the occurrence. You must train your body to experience that future in the present moment as it does not know the difference. You need to train your body to experience that occurrence. Your body will begin to change because it is getting signals from the environment to signal new genes. You signal new genes ahead of the experience. Thought, brain, emotion, body. The more you practice the elevated emotion, chemical, neuro transmitter, hormones and genetic expression, the more you change genetic expression. The result is that body responds to a new mind by experiencing the future in the present moment. A notion ahead of the event is causing an effect in the quantum model to activate a response. You cause a desired effect. Emotion is an end product of the experience, so give thanks for thanks by emotion then it looks like it has occurred and then allow the experience to find you. This is a heartfelt feeling process."

"Why do you suppose that everyone believes they have to work so hard for money?"

"That's the accepted norm in the Newtonian rules of physics so they do."

"When time disappears, no one has to work so hard. Time is not money anymore. The dramatic shift comes when the belief of working hard to make a living to working hard at celebrating the money that your creatorship brings to you."

"That's a tough one, I agree. That's why those who temporarily escape are sucked back into the lower energy vortex of norm dynamics."

"Yes, but you can get used to working from the divine miracle brain so you become very intelligent to get rid of all the negative qualities. They will not go if you do not believe you are a part of God, or whatever your ineffable understanding of a superior force is. It is foolish to fight for a living when you understand you can create what you need by modifying the game called the hologram projecting your Life Plan and the global consciousness life plan."

"Well that is where I clearly do not understand. You still have to work to pay your bills."

"You may call it work if you like but if it is some wonderful opportunity you create or attract by your own mind, your engagement in it is not work, it is passion, bliss and joy. You are ready to understand this and the secret lies in the midbrain. That is why the midbrain has been relegated to the useless anatomy just like the other 12 strands of DNA. Essentially, to simplify things, your mind is already the quantum void of infinite possibilities. What becomes the issue is how your own beliefs create the programs in subconsciousness which set the rules. These rules are no different than the laws humans create to police their behaviors within the consciousness and physical environment. The laws in this case become your subconscious. In simple terms, let us look at three stages of evolution, namely in the world of matter, totally in the world of non-matter, and in between. For simplicity, let us refer to this as 3D, 4D, and 5D."

"We are in 4D, in between, right?"

"Yes, each level has portals to the next and when you reach 5D and higher, as total awareness of your higher energy bodies, you reach a stage where your mind, as one with the greater consciousness is not limited by the rules of the lower 3D and 4D minds. Each has different rules of behavior. At any time you may step through the portal and awaken to or open that next level just by your attention and intention."

"Just as I am doing now."

"Yes. The portal of miracles, which is outside the rules of 3D consciousness, is by that opening of awareness into the next level of mind."

"It is usually just temporary experience as most do not maintain the higher state of mind when they drop back into the lower state. Right?"

"Yes. However, when you do learn to reside in that state of mind. Then the downward causation prevails and your mind, and what it can imagine as a new possibility can manifest below, as you have learned. In that higher dimension, the rules from below can not apply, they are only recorded."

"But there must be certain rules that still apply, like I could not create weird monsters into 3D."

"The point is that when you are the Divine Intelligence, you would not even try to create monsters any more than you would bring harm to a loved one in the lower reality. That is part of totally being in that level and becoming responsible for your actions."

"Has anybody attained this?"

"Many, many have of course. Many have simply ascended to the state of a being of light. Many, like gurus, monks, priests, gifted healers, masters, and yogis have attained these levels and remained on Earth. They have through dedicated training and persistence attained these levels, and continuously exhibit abilities to create miracles outside the box."

"I'll bet in the religious world, these guys are called Saints."

"Yes, they all learned to open to their true brainpower and DNA by becoming the higher mind. Of course they did not know about or care about the process and scientific reasons. When you as a human vessel incarnate, you begin that evolution of the 5 stages. As you physically develop, I explained, you decide whether to choose the spiritual development which will bring you above the 3D world and the survival game. As this opens, so does your mind, brain function and DNA because they can evolve as a spiritual being in a physical vessel."

"In the place where you are now, in between, it is about selective thought manifestation all the time. The key is how to create powerful thoughts in you. There is only one reality of thought. If you know the dynamics of it you can create reality. Those dynamics are now coming forward for you so you can responsibly and proactively change time to no time, live in the present through your midbrain by allowing the higher mind to guide you and begin to master your control over the hologram. In the astral plane you can bypass the need for physical action and time by learning the power of mind alone."

"By feeling and knowing the effect and allowing the cause to be manifested?"

"Exactly, that way you reverse the process. Mind over matter because when you already celebrate the effect, the cause of that effect has to be brought into reality to balance it. So you cause an effect."

"But obviously, one has to get beyond the monkey mind overshadowed by your brother who loves the reptile survival instinct brain and the great big frontal lobe to play games of power with. You have to get beyond time."

"The mind over matter is not just a philosophy. The mind has complete control over how the particles function. You have to instill techniques to do this from this 3D surface level. You have to go beyond to thoughtlessness – stillness."

"We have touched on this DNA and the brain as having greater powers that have been lost or unused. Can you explain this? I have heard we only use a minor part of our brains."

ON THE JUNK DNA

"It isn't so much how much of the brain you are using, it is how you are using it. Ironically, if you use the smaller midbrain plus greater consciousness, it may be superior to the big brain and the smaller consciousness. As we have discussed, by choosing a material versus spiritual path, you do not open the portal during the 4th and 5th stages of evolution. Your DNA reflects what state the greater consciousness has evolved to. It is built into you as a self evolving blueprint. Every soul is on a personal path to expand that evolution."

"Jeezz, if we are only using a small percent of the brain and DNA that is a pretty dismal performance."

"There are not many in your lower conscious world that will agree to your statement. Majority tells you that there is no merit in this thinking. Because these other parts are invisible, quantum in nature, they are discounted as nonsense. Science will tell you about junk DNA and that we are using 100% of our big brains. So this is the prevailing choice of limits in the global mind."

"Ok what is the truth of this higher potential?"

"We have already seen many of the paranormal abilities that open with the higher bodies and the astral plane. These are all reflected in the brain's ability to deploy new programs given appropriate instructions. These programs are encoded in DNA. In the development of the Soul's journey, 12 layers reflect the physical and spiritual state of the art evolution of the human vessel. It is the ultimate record of what humans at some stage have been able to achieve in their evolution. At the current time, you as a group consciousness, have formed a belief box that there are only two strands which are essentially rooted in 3D biology and matter. In beliefs that are out of the box, a new consensus is evolving, one that says the other layers are more quantum and spiritual in nature."

"I suppose you could say this is a reflection of a fall from grace of current humanity; there is a whole load of stuff in there that has atrophied or is unused."

"It has been this humanity's choice and yes there is a whole lot of potential in there that you have not brought into your conscious awareness. However, don't think it is just this earthly humanity because there are many, many others involved that you brand unfriendly aliens. Your DNA is a gift for all to evolve the greater consciousness beyond itself. It is not a reflection of earth's humanity alone."

"Will you elaborate on that?"

"Yes later but mostly it is for you to awaken to your own Soul family that spans other dimensions and realities. As I have told you, the means of access to the rest is rooted in a more spiritual path to evolve our total being which includes both the physical and then the non-physical or energetic components. As you are learning now, primary access to this DNA is through the mind's awareness of a Higher Self or Soul mind."

"What about this junk DNA?"

"Your scientific community will tell you that DNA stores biological information referred to as coded. And a significant portion of DNA namely more than 98% for humans is non-coding, meaning that these sections do not serve as patterns for protein sequences. That 98% is simply classified as junk DNA."

"But this is really just the tip of the iceberg, right?"

"To understand coding and the 2% tip of the iceberg, it is like coding in a computer program. A simple way to see DNA is to understand each cell has its own job, just like humans do. Some cells help detect light and see, other cells help touch, some cells help you hear, other cells carry oxygen around, and other cells help us digest food by secreting enzymes. There are over 200 cell types in the body - that is 200 different jobs. And each cell knows what job to do. It's the same they say as how a human knows what job it has to do."

"Yes, someone tells them."

"Your cells are also told what to do, but not by a person or a computer! Your cells are told what to do by a very special molecule called DNA. DNA is a record of instructions telling the cell what its job is going to be. A good analogy for DNA as a whole is a set of blueprints for the cell, or computer code telling a PC what to do. It is written in a special alphabet that is only four letters long! Unlike a book or computer screen, DNA isn't flat and boring like a computer that has only two codes of 0 and 1 - it is a beautiful curved ladder. You call this shape a double helix."

"So what does the 98% really do?"

"There are 4 groups to the DNA layers. They actually work together but let us go through each layer briefly. Layer 1 represents the biological double helix. It is the master biological record of this life time. Two percent of the instructions in this human genome are for the protein encoding layers."

"That is the one we are all familiar with."

"Yes, the rest is simply your woo woo stuff of no significance. Layer 2 is the human being's life lesson. You understand what a life lesson is and it is encoded here. You come into this planet with it, and it is something that has been constructed for you due to the Akashic Record. That is to say, your life lesson is connected to your past lives."

"I do know now, yes."

"Layer 3 is the ascension layer. However it is only the one which points to the interdimensional layers that really provide ascension status. It is a catalyst that works with DNA layer 6, the Prayer and Communications layer. It is also affiliated with the pineal gland."

"So prayer is important in communicating with you?"

"Yes. Prayer has been believed to be something different than what the ancient wisdom knew it to be. It is a communication channel through the pineal to me and prayer if carried from the heart carries tremendous power to manifest. Of course religions have confused this and so it is part of the norm."

"Are you going to explain that to me?"

"Yes, it will come forward to you at the right moment."

"Ok, what is the next group?"

"The next group relates to Human Divinity. Layers 4 and 5 together are the essence of your expression as this specific life on Earth and how you evolve your divinity on the planet. Together, they can be understood as the primary and most important spiritual attribute of all which is your physical existence as family. Layers 4 and 5 carry your angelic name as core crystal energy, your identification so to speak of your interdimensional Akash. It is your record of who you are in the Universe, and where you have been. It's also your name on the crystal in the Cave of Creation."

"These take you outside of the limited realm of the Earth plane. No wonder they are a woo woo science. These are all spiritual!"

"It gets better. But understand that the tag spiritual is in itself a mislabeling. It is about a total understanding of all that was, is and will be. Layer 6 is about prayer and communication and the Higher Self always involved in everything. Where is the Higher-Self? Well you know that now, don't you? Do you think you are awakening your DNA?"

"And the truth is that the only part that is higher is my perception of its vibration. It's in a place that makes me want to expand and worship my higher self as me."

"The next is referred to as the Lemurian group. It contains two energies of layers 7 and 8. These are the most important, since they drive the engine of karmic purpose. They are responsible for life lessons and they relate to layer six, the Higher Self. They are the creation layers, which are your Akashic Record. That is to say, the record of every single lifetime you've ever had on the earth, everything you've ever done, all the accomplishments, all the talents that you have learned, and the spiritual jar of knowledge that you have filled up along the way."

"Why is it called Lemurian?"

"That will get us into a whole new topic but it relates to the time of Lemuria when great spiritual advancements were made by a highly evolved civilization. Because of this, they have contributed to the inventory of DNA coded wisdom, spiritual skills, and morphic behavior. There is another highly evolved contribution in Layer 7 which is about revealed divinity as an extradimensional sense. It is also part of an important pair 7 and 8 called the Lemurian Pair Layers, one of the two given to us by the Pleiadians as a divine complement to the Earth's normal DNA progression. Its description is of the intuitive interdimensional sense that Lemurians had, and also means Revealed Divinity."

"Is this what is niggling at me now?"

"Indeed it will. Knowing this and believing it are in different stages. Once you believe it and open totally to it, then acting in that extradimensional divine wisdom will open the DNA layers fully."

"But there must be some hitch to that?"

"It is encoded in Layer 8; as wisdom and responsibility, the master akashic record. Consider the power here and what your fall from grace civilization would do with the power if my brother was still in control?"

"I can imagine the power of greed and dominion like in the dark side stories."

"Think about Layer 9 which the healing layer, also Lemurian, but very human not Pleiadian. It is the one that is responsible for miraculous healing, and is the antenna of DNA in an interdimensional way, that talks to layer one and provides a 4D response to the Human body as healing. It is also represented by the Violet Flame. Some call it Intelligent Human Cell activation. It listens for harmony to activate healing. Layer nine is called the healing layer, not because it heals the body – it heals the Akash! All of these layers work together, and some of them have laid dormant for all of humanity's time on the planet, ready to be activated when the earth's energy reached a certain point."

"Or I reached a certain point. Yes, I see why we only get glimpses of this and even so, these miracle workers instantly convert the skill to money and greed of commerce and feeding ego."

"Yes, that has to do with the level of vibration and responsibility. Many choose to serve themselves rather than be in service to others."

"Tell me about it! What is the last group?"

"Here is where it gets woo woo as you call it but you already know this. The last group is the God Group. The basic information is that this layer must be considered as a package with 11 and 12. These last three are then called action layers and are different from any of the attributes of any of the former 9. Layer 10 is your call to divinity as the recognition of god in you. Layer 10 is also called the Divine Source of Existence. It is the first of the divine, God layers that represent the call to understanding your divinity."

"Why are they called action layers?"

"The God layers are action layers because they facilitate the divine within, thereby facilitating enlightenment and remembrance of who you are. Layer 11 is the wisdom of the divine feminine and compassion layer which is not about goddess energy or even about female energy. It is the energy of pure compassion, and is what is missing in the duality balance of the earth at this moment. It is the layer that is the true secret of peace on earth. Human Beings with this layer enhanced are balanced with the masculine and feminine duality energy."

"Boy that is not what is on this planet now."

"You may have noticed this changing. We can speak of this later. Layer 12 is very simple. It's the God layer, the most divine, and truly the layer which is the God within all. There are many divine layers, but this one is the last and highest in vibration of all of them."

"What does it do?"

"Don't look for these layers to do anything any more than your home does something. It provides you with peace, shelter, and a feeling of being home. It is when you have indeed come back home to your fullest light."

"Wow that is pretty heavy! I am curious about these Pleiadian and Lemurian layers?"

"At a point in the evolution of humanity, there have been civilizations that have advanced DNA to higher spiritual levels. Some of these are extraterrestrial. The current level thus reflects these advances of the greater consciousness. Suffice to say at this time, this is a separate topic for discussion. What you will see, however, is the possibility of higher spiritual advancement available and encoded in the DNA you carry."

"That is a long fall from grace."

"For many yes, but there are still those who are advancing. It is for you to evolve to and beyond this."

"It would seem that there have been many civilizations and wisdom that had already figured this out. It is incredible that we have fallen so far from grace and just learn and relearn without actually contributing to the whole. It does not say much for our evolution, does it?"

"Understand that each Soul is evolving at its own pace from different realities and dimensions. Understand that you are engaged in many lives, in multidimensions with no time. In order for you to fully understand this ineffable situation, you must evolve with me. Understand that this Earth is but one holographic illusion of billions so you have no idea of what is going on in the rest of the greater consciousness. You are opening to this as these layers open, but in the meantime, yes, this particular holographic illusion has a long way to catch up. It is accelerating and we will speak of this as a special time in the life of the planet."

"Ok. I still have trouble with this illusion stuff. You also suggested that the throat chakra, prayer and words are a communication channel to the midbrain and the pineal. Are you going to tell me about that?"

"Have you enough woo woo stuff?"

"You know, I am feeling a certain subtle acceptance of this."

"Wonderful, you are re-remembering."

THE GOD CODE IN DNA – REALLY?

"You mention God in the DNA. Is there really a God?"

"Let me tell you about what your world is discovering about God and DNA. It is about what has been called the God Code. There are scientists on your planet that have been studying the basic elements of DNA."

"You mean Thymine, Cytosine, Adenine, and Guanine?"

"Yes and hydrogen, nitrogen, oxygen and carbon as the major elements of life. They show how these letters translate directly to key letters of both the Hebrew and Arabic alphabets to spell the name of God. What is being said in this research is that the letters of God's ancient name YH meaning god eternal and creator are encoded as the genetic formation in every cell, of every life in DNA."

"Ok, this should be interesting. These other spiritual layers encoded in DNA must have something to do with the drive in humanity to seek out themselves as divine beings that are created in the image of God?"

"Yes, 95% of humanity believe in a higher power that they cannot explain, and 50% of these call this power God."

"So did God come down and create this reality?"

"Let us see how this vibrates with your new intuition. The oldest text that has never been found, lost to antiquity is the Book of Adam which describes how YHVH formed man in his image from the dust from the ground, formed the spirit of his breath to place in man and gave him the instructions to '*walk before me and become perfect*' which will explain that subtle quest to seek out and know God."

"If it was lost, how does anyone know it stated that?"

"Before it was lost, it came into the possession of Adam, Joseph, Moses, Joshua Ben Nun and Solomon. In the 18th century it came into the possession of Israel Ben Eliezer who became the Father of Chassiduit Judaism. Here in a town some distance from Israel there was a Rabbi Adam Tzaddik who knew of the book's existence and sensing he was near his end of life he entered a dream state to ask for guidance on his final act of goodness. He wanted to know who should the book be handed down to so as to preserve and continue this truth of man. At night he was led to a cave in the Holy Land where the Book of Adam was buried. Rabbi Adam asked his son to locate the young Israel Ben Eliezer and hand the book to him. He found Israel living in a barn where he would absorb the words of the Torah, the Jewish Holy Scriptures. One evening the son saw a miracle assuring him Israel was worthy. He saw a blaze of light as the inspiration being received by Israel as he read the words of the Torah. The next day he handed Israel the book who based his teachings on the Book of Adam. Israel became the Master of the Holy Name. This was the last time the Book of Adam has ever been mentioned. The Torah is the oldest aspect of the kabala and ancient Sepher Yetzirah that describes this process of creation. Here it has the link between Hebrew letters and elements to describe how YHVH using numbers and letters produced the universe, the world and the bodies of man."

"Wow! Tell me more! How do these guys conclude this?"

"In Hebrew tradition, God is identified by names such as YH as god eternal and the creator. It was held sacred in the Hebrew tradition so 6800 occurrences were replaced with a substitute name to prevent misuses. There are many versions of this now but the original still has never been found. In this book, YH created the world and man from text, numbers and communication"

"Ok, so how can these guys say this?"

"In order for this to be explained, I have to tell you a bit about Gematria. It is the ancient wisdom of numbers that has been brought forward as numerology. Of importance is that the letters of the Hebrew 22 letter alphabet are all assigned numbers; and all alphabets are assigned numbers so although the words and letters may vary the numbers do not."

"In this image I am giving you can see the number relationship with Hebrew, Greek and English letters. These are the way they are pronounced. It starts at 1 to 10, then it continues in 10's to 100, then it continues in 100's and so on.

Here is part of the table."

Hebrew		Greek	English	Gematria
Aleph	·	Alpha	A	1
Beth	B/V	Beta	Bee	2
Gimel	G	Gamma	Cee	3
Daleth	D	Delta	Dee	4
He	H	Epsilon	E	5
Vav	V		Ef	6
Zayin	Z	Zeta	Gee	7
Chet	Ch	Eta	Haitch	8
Teth	T	Theta	I	9
Yod	Y	Iota	Kay	10
Kaph	Kh	Kappa	El	20
Lamed	L	Lambda	Em	30

"Ok, so every number has a corresponding letter."

"Then numbers are always reduced to a base. For example the word soul in Hebrew is NeShaMaH and the equivalent numbers would be 50, 300, 50 and 5 which add to 395. By applying numerology, this number would be 3 plus 9 plus 5 which is 17, which further reduces to 8 as a prime. The word Heaven in Hebrew is HaShaMaYiM with corresponding numbers 5,300,40,10,40 which adds to 395 and also reduces to 8."

"So Soul and Heaven are the same?"

"Each letter of every alphabet can be linked with a specific number value. The primary Hebrew alphabet which has been used for at least 3,000 years has 22 letters, each having a unique sound and number. Within this number code, you are given information about your past and your future. Secrets are encoded in these Hebrew letters and the hidden number code in the Hebrew language offers a link between the worlds of science and spirituality."

"What do you mean?"

"The 118 elements, which comprise everything in your physical world, are each assigned properties that are represented by numbers. These qualities of numbers link the elements of your DNA to the letters of the Hebrew alphabet. This means that the bridge between letters and elements is one of numbers."

"I don't get it."

"The 118 elements are defined on the basis of mass in the periodic table. Now what is DNA made of in terms of elements?

"That would be Hydrogen, Nitrogen, Oxygen and Carbon."

"Let us look at H, N and O for the first three. They would have an atomic weight of 1.007, 14.000, and 15.99, right? In numerology, the decimal is ignored so H is 1, N is 14 reduced to 5, and O is 15 reduced to 6. By taking these numbers and converting them to Hebrew you get YHV. In the book it says He chose 3 letters from the elementals and he set them into His great name as A M Sh which equals YHV."

"OK, that's bizarre!"

"Now what are the most dominant elements?"

"Why H, N, O and C."

"In ancient alchemical terms these are Air, Water, and Fire that reflect those three elements."

"So YVH created the universe from these three elements in his Hebrew Name? What about Carbon?"

"In a minute. In the text it says all was created form A, M and Sh that became Y H and V as Fire, Air and water. The text says from the three (air as breath, fire and water) he founded his dwelling (home, body earth). It says YaHWeH formed the spirit and put it into man formed from dust from the ground. He then gave instructions to walk before him and become perfect."

"Wow, that is really something. But what does this have to do with DNA and what about Carbon?"

"Carbon has mass of 12 which reduces to 3. Yod Hey Vav are 1 + 5 + 6 = 12 =Earth or 3 the major earth and body element Carbon. So in the name YHVH, in Hebrew YH means eternal and VG means within the body. This means that YHVH is the name of God, YHVG is the name of man – not quite God."

"So God is made of gases and he added carbon as the material earth?"

"Invisible colorless, odorless gases that are a super consciousness. Can you try to define your own consciousness? Why would this Higher Intelligence be different? What is your mind that contains all this quantum information?"

"That is really tough to answer."

"You will. Now, the structure of all life is made from different combinations of only 4 DNA bases with each base made of the four main elements of life hydrogen, nitrogen, oxygen and carbon same as Hebrew letters YHVG. He made man in his image and gave the gift of DNA. All life is formed of combinations of four chemical compounds in DNA and it contains all information required to produce every form of life, from the smallest single-celled organism to the 100 trillion cells of a human being. Every program to describe life in your reality is there. So in every cell of every life the name of God is revealed."

"Huh? How?"

"Through various combinations of the four DNA bases, it becomes possible to create the substance of life from the name in your bodies. TCGA are letters scattered along strands (C T A G) as the 4 elements of life. The DNA double helix is held together by hydrogen bonds between the bases attached to the two strands. The four bases found in DNA as you said are adenine (A), cytosine (C), guanine (G) and thymine (T). These four bases are attached to sugar/phosphate to form the complete nucleotide."

"So if we replace elements with letters we get YHVH = God = eternal = within the body meaning God eternal within the body. This works in other languages as the cement of traditional spirituality. So the suggestion is that every cell has everything coded into it – the complete library. What if you use the sounds of vowels to unite the name? What would this sound like? There is a code that instructs us to intone a Divine name as the sound of YHVH."

"This gets even more interesting in that all carbon life bases contain some message/code. Our name as a human is YHVG as different than God YHVH but all the tools are there to be chosen to be like a God YHVH. All you have to do is look at our section of the other 11 layers of DNA presented in a previous chapter."

"And also, this greater consciousness which you represent has no carbon in it, that is what humans are made of."

"So God is a bunch of intelligent gasses!"

"Look at your mind. What do you suppose it is made of? How do you as a mind distinguish yourself from other life?

"I can use words, numbers and communicate."

"And does that describe your complete reality?"

"It does."

THE POWER OF PRAYER

"Now let us go back to prayer. It is important to discuss this before we talk about the power of words. Prayer is a very interesting phenomenon because it has been mis-interpreted and mis-directed. Prayer itself is a powerful process because surrounding it is the power of the placebo. The prayer is a request for something issued to a higher being or authority so it carries with it the belief and acceptance in the form of faith and trust in this higher power. It would be considered a power word that carries special communication powers to the Creator. The configuration of bowing to the Creator to receive a blessing and placing the hands together at the heart energetic vortex concentrates the energy of the prayer. The actual prayer then creates the intent and attention in the heart center that assists in the altering of reality in line with the request. It is a process that surrenders to the higher power. What do you see that is missing in the prayer *What so ever ye ask thy Father in my Name, he will give it to you'* from the King James modern condensed version of the Bible?"

"It's just talking to yourself in the lower plane. There is no emotion nor is there the gratitude of it being done."

"Exactly. There are other version like *'Hitherto have ye asked nothing in my name: Ask and ye shall receive, that your joy may be full'*, but from the original version we have a whole different concept. Here it says: *'All things that you shall ask straightly, directly… from inside My Name you shall be given… be enveloped by what you desire, that your gladness be full'*."

"That's a whole lot different. This prayer invites us to feel as if our prayer has already been answered. It is different than feeling powerless and needing to ask for help from a higher source through desperation. It is the quality and depth of feeling that does, in fact, *speak* to the void or quantum field that connects us with the world. So enveloped with emotion of gladness is a key not in the modern versions."

"Yes. Through prayers of feeling, you are empowered to take part in the healing of your lives and your relationships, as well as your bodies, and your world."

"There is other ancient wisdom on this revealed in the Essene's Gospel which is 2500 years old. It says: *'When three become as one, you will say to the mountain move'*."

"What do you think are the three items?"

"I would say thought, words and emotion. It is the feeling of already accomplished as key. It requires a faith that acknowledges our power in creation - it happened. You created it or the seed. Then you give thanks after you felt it. So you don't just pray for something, you have to feel it to really give it life. That is what creates the vibratory possibilities that draw and attract it out of the void of infinite possibilities. Feeling is magnetic energy movement through us and around us."

"So if you can make thought, words, and emotion one, you can '*move mountains*' and create miracles."

"Yes. If you look at the old edited version it says: '*ask*' when the real version says: '*be enveloped by what you desire, that your gladness be full*'. It is all about visualization and feelings. The Essenes also said: '*First, seek peace in your own body (emotion) then seek peace in the feelings, then seek peace in your own thoughts, such can shape the Heavens*'."

"Of course. Peace is the key. Demonstrate love and compassion. It is an anchor point."

"Then the Essenes said: '*go to Nature to nurture peace - reverence will help create peace*'. The Essenes said peace is the most powerful component. We can create it in our bodies through thought."

"But this has all been re-written and presented in a rather useless way. Why?"

"There have been those that come here to play roles of dominion and power that have followed the masculine dominion over others. They have kept these secrets to themselves."

"Your brother again."

"Yes, it is a story we will unfold later as this dominion is in the process of shifting during what is the End Times. Let's now continue on our discussion about the word."

20
THE IMPORTANCE OF THE WORD

Words, numbers and communication are the building blocks of the form of conscious creation that the midbrain projects as your reality.

IMPORTANCE OF SOUND WAVES

"So let us move into that topic now. There has been much wisdom even in your own civilization but unfortunately it has been relegated to the metaphysical silliness of fringe science. You are now more knowing about 'in the beginning was the word'?"

"Yes, of course. Now you are going to link it to the midbrain, right?"

"Indeed. Let us look more into this since you are now aware of DNA and the midbrain. There are many new discoveries of the wave information nature of DNA that overthrow the old understanding that you are genetically fixed. This is led by the new science of wave genetics that shows DNA functions like a holographic computer, part of the larger hologram of the information wave reality. Your DNA has the capabilities of hyper-communication - telepathy, remote sensing and remote feeling, along with other psychic abilities. They say you also have the ability to reprogram our genetic blueprint with simple words and frequencies."

"Is that what you say too?"

"Yes, but I know you are a very pragmatic scientist stuck in your left brain so I will use your own earthly examples. For example, Russian researchers' findings and conclusions are that DNA is not only responsible for the construction of your body but it also serves as data storage and communication. The Russian linguists found that the genetic code, especially in the apparently useless junk DNA follows the same rules as all our human languages. To this end they compared the rules of syntax; the way in which words are put together to form phrases and sentences to functioning of DNA. They look at semantics as the study of meaning in language forms, and the basic rules of grammar. They found that the alkalines of DNA follow a regular grammar structure and do have set rules just like our languages. So human languages did not appear coincidentally but are a reflection of our inherent DNA."

"Wow! This would explain why affirmations, autogenous training, hypnosis and the like can have such strong effects on humans and their bodies."

"Yes, it is entirely normal and natural for your DNA to react to language. While western researchers cut single genes from the DNA strands and insert them elsewhere, the Russians enthusiastically worked on devices that influence the cellular metabolism through suitable modulated radio and light frequencies and thus repair genetic defects."

"Boy that is out of the box!"

"Now think about this. In order for DNA to do all of the things that we speak of esoterically and quantumly, 300 trillion pieces of DNA must all know something at the same time! There has to be a communication that takes place in the microscopic DNA of your toenail at the same time as the longest hair on your head. They both have to know about it instantly. Then those trillions of pieces must agree, must have one energy absorption of consciousness. This all must happen in a 3D construct – that is, within your reality. There is no word in science for this process unless you consider the one created for a description of photons called entanglement which is a rapidly emerging quantum term."

"Quantum entanglement is a quantum mechanical phenomenon in which the quantum states of two or more objects have to be described with reference to each other, even though the individual objects may be spatially separated."

"Yes, they are one unified whole. There is instead, a confluence of energy so that they become something else, a oneness. Science doesn't see it within DNA yet, but at some level they know it must exist. For how else can the human body do what it does?"

"I intuit that this is somewhat the way all these Soul photons work as a unified field of consciousness yet can be individual evolutionary units of the whole."

"That is very perceptive of you. Cellular structure is specific and unique. Like the linear machine, it is specialized, and you have heard of stem cells carrying that specificity. But DNA is identical all over the body. It's not specific. You don't have toenail DNA or hair DNA or heart DNA. You've just got your own unique DNA. Trillions of copies of the same Human quantum blueprint must talk to each other instantly or you would cease to exist. How did they do it? No name in science truly has been given to the process of communication between DNA loops, but it will. It's a quantumness within the soup of magnetics."

"Indeed just like all souls, each loop of DNA has a magnetic field that overlaps the loop next to it, which overlaps the loop next to it. Hundreds of trillions of overlaps equals one consciousness. This then represents a magnetic imprint, which the Human carries around with them. Magnetics is an interdimensional energy, a quantum energy, and this imprint creates the Human aura. An aura is not a magnetic field and you will not be able to see an aura with magnetic equipment. An aura is the result of a confluence of DNA communication within the Human body, a quantum imprint, a melding of energy to create a quantum field not measurable by anything on the planet, yet."

"So what happens in DNA happens all at once within every energy layer of it. Think of the coordination, the puzzle. If you're going to have some kind of esoteric activation that is new within your DNA, think of what must take place! Hundreds of trillions of parts all receive it at once. What does that feel like?"

"I see it now, DNA is always evolving on a self improvement cycle, just like the global consciousness is supposed to. My own is being activated and upgraded."

"You are already active. You are not running the appropriate programs. If you want to get an idea of how this DNA works in practice let us use a simple example. Let us say a species – say a seagull – somehow learns to pick up a clam off the shoreline, fly up with it and drop it to crack it open on the rocks. That is not a normal programmed behavior in its neural networks. Because it satisfies its desire to survive and the clam is yummy, it does this a lot and it gets hardwired into its neuro pathways. Then some buddy seagulls see this and copy it. At a certain threshold the number of seagulls doing this causes the DNA to take this on as a permanent behavior encoded into the group DNA. When this occurs at a certain threshold, all seagulls get their DNA upgraded even if they don't have any clams in their environment. Because DNA is quantum, they are all nonlocal and the effect is immediately updated throughout all whether they need it or not. From then on it becomes a hardwired instinct of behavior."

"And is that the way DNA has evolved to the 12 strands?"

"Yes, but let us get back to these words. You now understand that DNA is called upon by the subconscious and the brain to repair or maintain things in your body – absolutely everything right down to the smallest details. You have also seen that DNA is quantum and you can call on it to trigger these extraordinary things like miracles of healing through activating these stem cells."

"And that seems to correlate with the DNA healing layer that is being accessed to create the healing miracle. So where do words come in here?

THE BIBLE CODE LIFE PLAN – REALLY?

What I am going to tell you about now is how these words carry much more than meanings. The whole reality of yours, and the way of communication is through words. All that mental intelligence of yours and all that is your reality is described with words and combinations. But do not forget words are vibrations representing reality. When YHVH created human beings - Adam and Eve - he created them in His own image. This likeness unquestionably included the ability to engage in intelligible speech via human language. In fact, as the story goes on, God spoke to them from the very beginning of their existence as humans."

"And he obviously manifested this Book of Adam. So obviously they possessed the ability to understand verbal communication and to speak themselves. So?"

"Again, the language used was original Hebrew. It was formed into Arabic and Egyptian. Biblical Hebrew is the oldest language still in use today as 5000 years old. Hebrew is the basis for half of the religious traditions. The Kabala is a collection of this wisdom. And these books confirm God created the universe with text, numbers, and communications."

Ok, we talked about that."

"YHVH created the Universe by engraving the letters in all that emptiness by choosing three letters for his name. Then he handed down the operating manual called The Book of Adam from which the inspiration of the Torah came about. To continue on this special encoding in the Torah, let us look at another word phenomenon called the Bible Code."

"What is that?"

"The Bible code is also known as the Torah code. In these original texts studies are being conducted to suggest a set of secret messages encoded within the Hebrew text of the Torah. This hidden code has been described as a method by which specific letters from the text can be selected to reveal an otherwise obscured message. Although Bible codes have been postulated and studied for centuries, the subject has only been popularized in modern times because of computer technology."

"How does it work?"

"By creating one long string of letters from the complete Torah, you have to employ a computer to search through the whole sequence for these "codes" that are allegedly written by God the author of the first Hebrew Bible. The primary method by which purportedly meaningful messages have been extracted is the *Equidistant Letter Sequence* (ELS). To obtain an ELS from a text, choose a starting point (in principle, any letter) and a skip number, also freely and possibly negative. Then beginning at the starting point, select letters from the text at equal spacing as given by the skip number. For example, the bold letters in **t**his **s**ent**e**nce **f**orm **a**n EL**S**. With a skip of −4 (that is, reading backwards every fourth letter), and ignoring the spaces and punctuation, the word *safest* is spelled out. Often more than one ELS related to some topic can be displayed simultaneously in an *ELS letter array*. This is produced by writing out the text in a regular grid, with exactly the same number of letters in each line, then cutting out a rectangle. In the example below, part of the King James Version of Genesis (26:5-10) is shown with 33 letters per line. ELSs for BIBLE and CODE are shown.

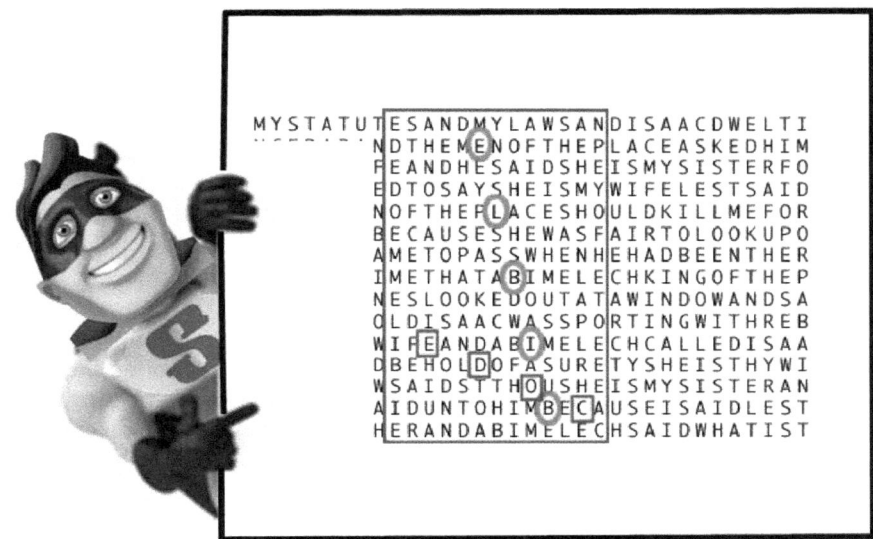

"Normally only a smaller rectangle would be displayed, such as the rectangle drawn in the figure. In that case there would be letters missing between adjacent lines in the picture, but it is essential that the number of missing letters be the same for each line. Although the above examples are in English texts, Bible codes proponents usually use a Hebrew Bible text. For religious reasons, most Jewish proponents use only the Torah (Genesis–Deuteronomy). This is undoubtedly because the subsequent texts have been edited and changed by mere mortals".

"Once a specific word has been found as an ELS, it is natural to see if that word is part of a longer ELS consisting of multiple words. Code proponents Haralick and Rips have published an example of a longer, extended ELS, which reads, 'Destruction I will call you; cursed is Bin Laden and revenge is to the Messiah'. ELS extensions that form phrases or sentences are of interest. Proponents maintain that the longer the extended ELS, the less likely it is to be the result of chance."

"It is said that there are many predictions here that are thus coded into the bible. These name people and events that could not have been known – unless the writers were in charge of the overall Life Plan! Armageddon is encoded in the Bible with the name of Syria's leader, Hafez Asad. In fact, the name of the actual site of the long-prophesied Final Battle appears with his name in a single skip sequence: Armageddon, Asad holocaust. At the current time, there are many things encoded that has created a renewed interest. Syria is encoded with World War. It is the country that stands out, because it is not expected. Russia and China and USA all also appear with World War. Barack Obama is prevalent."

"Do these have predictions in the past that can be verified?"

"Many code proponents assert that names and events hidden in the Scripture can only now be revealed, in this modern Information Age, through computer searches of the Hebrew text. Supposedly, these codes contain secret predictions of events that have already come to pass, including the assassination of Egypt's Anwar Sadat and former Israeli Prime Minister Yitzhak Rabin; the Jewish Holocaust; the 1995 earthquake in Kobe, Japan; the first Gulf War; and the emergence of diseases such as AIDS and diabetes. They even predict an earthquake will strike Los Angeles in 2010."

"What has sparked today's mushrooming interest in prophecy? Sensing that something is terribly wrong, many believe the world has reached what the Bible calls the end-time - or last days. Millions routinely discuss prophetic terms such as Anti-Christ, Great Tribulation, Millennium, Armageddon, Beast, False Prophet, God's Wrath, Abomination of Desolation, and others that are written for the years 2015 and 2016."

"Are you telling me this is true? Are we going to talk about this?"

"Let me ask you. Do you believe there is a Life Plan for the planet and the planet consciousness?"

"Hmmmmm."

WORDS DESCRIBE REALITY

"We can talk about this book of Revelations later. Let us get back to words. Why is this important?" It is to understand that these words from the beginning have energetic power and significance that you are just beginning to understand. Some people believe that there is something to these Bible codes while others consider them to be a total load of nonsense. Of course this is all in dispute because the belief box is not yet ready to accept this information, despite the evidence."

"Numbers are universal. They are related to the numerous alphabets as a common denominator. A word has a description and that description gives us the vision of what it represents. A word is a vibration. Everything is described, perceived and understood through words or combinations of words. It is the mental body's means to experience reality through the senses and the brain so as to derive emotions centered in the heart. That is what the Soul does. Every word or combination also describes a morphogenic process of chemical, physiological, physical birth, evolution and behavior encoded in its DNA or determined by some higher intelligence. Is it surprising to think that the 95% of people who believe in a Higher Power can also believe that it started with the word? What are our thoughts? Combinations of words that represent images – all energy vibrations."

"And is it surprising to think that this midbrain of yours that houses the Soul mind, responsible for creating and presenting your reality can adjust that reality by the repetition of a word? The words may be different vibrations but the image presented attached to the word is not. If it is in charge of this holographic reality, it simply needs instructions to change the form of the projection and integrate it into the larger hologram. There is nothing new here. Your computers do this all the time. And where do you need to do this program change? In the place where the neo-cortex has no relevance; in the space of the midbrain where there is no time, space or identity to interfere with the Soul mind of infinite possibilities."

So is all this true? Are there codes in the bible, in DNA and in these ancient writings?"

"The answer is yes. It is all a structured system of sacred geometry above to create that measured as geometry below. If you can understand that the Life Plan of Mother Earth – Gaia is created like yours, then it should not be surprising to see that the bible code can prophesize what that likely plan is. And if you can understand that words and language are used to describe everything in your reality, then it should not be difficult to believe that words, sentences, paragraphs, stories which are simply five sense representations of something taken from the infinite mind of quantum possibilities, then why wouldn't words be the key to creation?"

"I can understand that but the more difficult is the first premise of Life Plan and in the beginning was the word."

"You do not have any difficulty in understanding how simple patterns of bit and bytes of 1 and 0 create all these complex images that represent reality, do you?"

"Hmmmm, yes, what you are talking about is just a more complex ineffable system that is using the midbrain as its processing device?"

"Yes, let us save that for our next topic. I want to tell you more about the midbrain and miracles first."

MIDBRAIN MIRACLE METHOD

"Ok, let us get to these words and midbrain and 3rd eye. In all of these techniques to create health and wealth miracles, what have you seen as common denominators?"

"Well, there are hundreds of documented dramatic cases that have created unexplained miracles. The issue is that they do not work consistently all the time. Clearly, by now, you will have realized that the degree of belief, the depth of letting go, the degree of love, and the amount of clarity, vision and emotion are key variables that affect the success of how and when a miracle may occur. The belief, acceptance and surrender are vital to the process. It will be realized also that we already launch the creative ability all the time but within the limits of the prevailing consciousness. What appears to be important is the intention and action rather that the exact science of procedure."

"Yes, that is so, what else have you learned?"

"What is consistent in all these cases is the process of engaging thought, images, and words in the creation of a new possibility. What is also consistent is the need to let go of the usual ego mind and the lower reality. This can be recognized as the above part of as above so below. Regardless of whether it is a miracle, this is always the case and it happens to be coincident with the top three energetic centers called chakras. This is totally within the power of the mind and is purely a mental ability. The other major component of this process takes you to the heart and emotion and the need for joy of completion to enfold that which is created in the mind. This is purely an emotional ability. At that juncture it is a choice as to whether we as mental and emotional beings decide to create within the box of prevailing consciousness as in the case of Napoleon Hill, or outside of the box, as we have studied here."

"Yes, and the usual engagement?"

"Regardless, the usual way is to engage by way of the passion and intent activated at the 3rd solar plexus chakra, seek out the appropriate relationships and work hard to create that desired reality or vision."

"But I have also seen that the other way is to work hard at thoughts, visions, words and passion to activate the creation and intent through a different relationship – that of Source and Soul to get the body of the projection of reality to adjust to the desired reality."

"Now, dear Ed what is it that has to do with words and visions that has been a bit sketchy in these techniques?"

"Well it has to do with 3rd and 4th chakra. That is still a bit hazy. I can see that to place a vision in the 3rd eye and the summary of words from the throat chakra have something to do with the midbrain and the pineal brain but that is not clear. Intuitively I feel there is something I am missing, especially now that you bring up the power of words and numbers."

"That is very perceptive of you. You are beginning to fill in the blanks through a knowing or re-remembering. The chakra of the 3rd eye is about vision and the throat is communication and words. These are very much a part of miracle workers that embody sound and mantras into their processes. These have been responsible for hundreds of thousands of miracles. Thoughts are combinations of words and numbers tagged to images. This is your COMPLETE reality."

"But sounds and mantras have not been a part of those popular miracle workers."

"That may be so but if you look at some of the ancient wisdom and what Yogis, Siddhas, Songomas, Masters, and ancient priests use to create miracles it is a whole new story."

A SCIENCE BEHIND MIRACLES?

"Because you are still a bit stuck in your lower intellectual mind, I am not just going to tell you what you already know, I am going to use examples for you. In your reality, one such worker is Dr. Bascaran Pillai who calls himself a spiritual scientist, academic scholar, philanthropist, and world new thinking leader dedicated to the study of mind science. He lived as a poor monk but obviously that was not his true calling. More importantly, he is a well known and practiced Yogi and Siddha Master based in the ancient and spiritual wisdom of the Indian tradition. Through the combination of both the Western and ancient Yogis' understanding of the brain, Dr. Pillai provides the world with uncommon solutions to common modern day challenges."

"Boy that has my attention. This guy uses ancient methods and merges science! Has he done a lot of healing?"

"Yes, you can find many miracles in wealth and health that he is responsible for. He reports making several millionaires through his service of bettering humanity. To Pillai, a miracle is anything from receiving the exact amount of money you need, at the exact moment you need it, being in the right place at the right time, to physical healing of something doctors said was impossible. These are things that he facilitates to happen outside the realm of logic, something that doesn't fit into the framework of what all have been told is possible."

"Boy, you have my attention! What does he use?"

"He has created the Midbrain Miracle Method as a step-by-step process that will allow you to activate the powerful midbrain under his guidance. What he has undertaken is to merge the ancient wisdom with newest technology of brain science to cultivate miracles and make significant changes in people's lives."

"Oh boy, now that's cool, tell me more."

"Why did I know your senses would be aroused when I mentioned money? He states that a part of your brain called the neo-cortex is disallowing anything instantaneous or miraculous to happen in your life. The neo-cortex is a limiting brain, which attempts to make sense of things. The neo-cortex's main job is to maintain control, which is essential in human life; however, it is the opposite of spontaneity and miraculous occurrences. Does that sound familiar?"

"Sure does. What else has he found out?"

"The midbrain, which is beginning to be more comprehensively understood by scientists, is the part of the brain that can give access to miracles. He states '*Miracles are easy, it is a matter of moving your attention from the frontal lobe to the midbrain.*' He confirms that the neo-cortex controls higher order functions, of planning, reasoning, judgment, impulses, memory and motor functions."

"Beta brain Supernocebo who thinks he is smarter than all this wisdom!"

"Yes, but he also reports the midbrain is vitally important to maintaining and regulating the state of consciousness, alertness and attention. He affirms the midbrain contains the physical pineal gland, which has similar features to the retina in our eyes and is also a replica of what Siddhas call the third eye."

"Ok, back to the pineal and the master pituitary gland!"

"The pineal gland and the surrounding area in the midbrain is where your connection to higher thought and reality is. When these areas are activated you open up to the extraordinary and welcome events that begin to manifest in your life. He confirms that if you don't expect a miracle, it will not happen."

"By higher thought you don't mean the neo-cortex, you mean the Soul mind. What exactly does he say this activation does?"

"He holistically deals with five areas. Health; you learn to open yourself and invite restoration from illness. Relationship; you learn how to attract and experience the highest form of love in your life. To resolve the loneliness and abandonment you feel – and open your heart. Creativity; you discover ways to tap into your own divinity, to find places of unlimited, effortless creativity. Timelessness; you receive the knowledge you need to transcend time and make instantaneous changes in your life. Divinity; Divinity is the ultimate ability to move from a limited reality to a limitless life."

"Wow, that's an impressive list. It is like opening up those higher layers of DNA! Is this timelessness what we are talking about in the void of no time?"

"Yes, he explains to his people that there are three aspects of time that are programmed wrong. He tells us that **Time Economics** is relative to getting paid. We relate to time and money. All you need to do is put this in consciousness. There is also the **Biology** of time that can change DNA of aging. The programming is wrong. The brain can influence the nucleus, DNA and the gene. The brain is most important as you can program DNA to process in a different way to not get old. We change DNA through brain by changing time. The **Futurology of Time** is also mis-programmed. You can know about it and change it if it is not good."

"That is so because we have had your brother influencing the programming for thousands of years."

"Ok, now listen carefully to what he explains: 'The neurology of time is in the parental frontal lobe. If you are poverty stricken it is a brain issue. You can put a mantra there and use science to see what happens in the thalamus and cerebral area. If you understand time, you can control it and move it fast. Time will stop if you are in soul intelligence. We can jump time lines and be given new life to do more. Time line jumping means there are several opportunities available at any moment. Jump and see the parallel line opportunity'."

"Timelessness is the most important. It is a matter of being thought free, then there is soul intelligence that comes outside of time through intuition and through timelessness. Bypass the effects. Do not waste a second. You are a master of time and can jump into a parallel of time. If you are in timelessness, you are omnipotent as you will see what you are capable of instantly. The secret is in the timeless domain where all possibilities exist and soul intelligence is there. Our mistakes reside in the past as negative experiences in the mind living in duality. You must move to only timeless experience from quantum level where there is no polarity or victims. Get beyond this past to get control of time where there is no time."

"It is about thought manifestation all the time. The key is how to create powerful thoughts in you. There is only one reality of thought. If you know the dynamics of it you can create reality. In the astral plane you can bypass action of effort. That is because the astral plane is where you find your soul but you must get beyond the mind to help manifestation of thoughts. Get beyond the monkey mind; we all only know about developing the mind; no one teaches getting beyond time. That is how we can have powerful thoughts that can become reality."

"Mind over matter is not just a philosophy. The mind has complete control over how the particles function. This is not your mind consciousness because that is a surface level. You have to learn the techniques to do this. Logic and sequence is a primitive process of cause and effect to manifest little things. You have to go beyond this into thoughtlessness – stillness not a divine coma and a vegetable in constant meditation. That is just a step you need to get beyond into a new state."

"Sounds create meaning. You cannot have a Mercedes without thinking about it. Words are the building blocks of universe. Vibrations are a fundamental reality, not particles. In the beginning there was the word. It is simply a matter of creating words of meaning in the form of mantras. A mantra carries the energy of the reality to manifest. A mantra is a unidimensional reality in the form of sound waves capable of creating a 3D reality. If you go on saying something over and over, it manifests. Whether it is $100 or $100 million there is no difference to the cosmos. There is only one time; NOW. But there are two choices; now negativity and cosmos now. The cosmos now is the Higher Self beyond the mind. The secret is to get into that now. If you wait, you create time so get in the now of Higher Self beyond time. Keep putting information into the cosmos by believing in the higher now where everything is possible."

"As a Yogi, my mission merges ancient wisdom and modern technology. Things happen naturally, not through strife and now many people come to me for miracles. The energy of the brain is available for others to pick up from Gurus. These Gurus are able to take a thought manifestation into reality. I am in the science of miracles and I say the idea becomes the object. You need a divine mind to mediate the process into the material. There are three models or steps that are key:

1. Think about it all the time to manifest something – repetition;
2. Speak a mantra to become as you think;
3. Only the object remains as reality."

"You have to activate the midbrain to create miracles. It is the answer to creating your reality. It is the primitive or reptilian brain. It has been ignored and the neo-cortex has been believed to be the important part. But it is full of logic, negativity, and questions so it stops the miracle as we try to satisfy our desires. It will not allow miracles to happen. Other areas like the Parental are not the focus. Yogis only look at cause and effect without time. As soon as you get the frontal lobe into the idea, it kills it. The midbrain does not care. No complex process is needed. From the level of the midbrain you can manifest but it is not easy with the rest of the brain in the way. Yoga is actually a brain science. First you must stop the brain. Now brain scientists are saying this. When you enter this place, you know the soul intelligence not the mind intelligence."

"Powerful thoughts are the simple key to changing your life. The name of God is a powerful word as it vibrates you into a new state of mind. Regardless of religion, each has a name for God. In the Indian tradition it is a science to repeat the name over and over and you will have everything you need. For example Namah Shivaya is the most powerful mantra for self realization as it represents the five elements. Na ma means earth, Mah is water, Shi is fire, Va is air, and Ya is space. Manifestation takes place in no time so it is instantaneous. The Sun and Moon are involved to transcend time. Sun and moon create time through calendars as movement of time cycles. Sun moves through zodiacs. If you can arrest the movements you are in a timeless space. Sun is left brain and moon is right. Meditation is to have them converge in the heart. See the sun in heart, moon merging into the heart. Just have this image in consciousness and time will come to an end you will see the external reality as an illusion."

"Wow! That is heavy!"

SOUNDS CONTROL CONSCIOUSNESS AND MATTER

"And what do you say about this? Is it true?"

"Well, dear Ed, would I bring this example forward into your awareness if it wasn't. If I just told you this, it may not sink in as deeply through your belief systems than if I use an example. Would it? The real question is whether you believe it to be true. How does it feel?""

"Well, I have to say it does ring true!"

"Good. You will like this. Let me go on. In a special study, Pillai is engaged in scientifically verifying what the Yogis have known for centuries. The key purpose is to validate that sounds can change the brain by the use of mantras, and also that the science of sounds controls consciousness and matter. Pillai has said there are 51 sounds that can produce significant results and effects in the brain. In his work, he has had extraordinary results with the learning skills of kids by using sounds and the midbrain. These sounds are the ones being tested in his research. Pillai states: *'The answer to poverty lies in your brain. A person's socio-economic environment influences the development of their brain. Growing up in a poor neighborhood can impact a child's learning ability and their mental and emotional well-being in the long run. Phonemic Intelligence can improve the social behavior of children, reduce mental stress, and enhance their ability to memorize, retain and deliver'.*"

"What he has researched is what he calls Phonemic Intelligence that can help overcome such negative effects of poverty by changing the neurology of the brain for the better. *'It involves using specific phoneme (smallest unit of sound that contrasts with another sound, in any given language) sounds in different parts of the brain, by which it is possible to enhance the functioning of those parts of the brain. Our study done at a leading brain laboratory shows positive effects of these sounds on the brain'.*"

"A lead researcher Dr. Anbarasu Annamalai, while introducing the methodology of the study via Video stated *'In this pilot study, the participants were made to listen and vocalize 4 sounds focusing on different parts of the brain. Using EEG (Electroencephalography), we recorded electrical activity in the brain and found profound changes with the use of each discreet sound'.*"

"And the results?"

"As an example of the work, the image here shows the effect of one of the mantras on the anterior singulate. It is deep and unrelated to sound but you see it here. This is where it controls how the world should work and if it does not, a signal goes off. The Anterior Singulate shows focused activity. This region is involved in decision making and emotional regulation as well as vital to the regulation of physiological processes, such as blood pressure and heart rate. The research shows that these sounds can erase thought patterns and create new ones to have profound effects. Sound is the basis

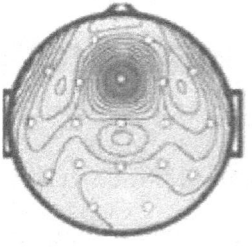

for consciousness. You think something and it is a sound. The brain is empowered by consciousness. It creates matter through sound. They reported the following:"

"Our consciousness is created out of sound waves and our emotions are determined by the sounds we continuously repeat in the form of words or thoughts. Sound waves thus play a very important role in determining the level and nature of our consciousness. It is the thoughts, emotions and consciousness we have created that determine our happiness or sorrow, so, it is very important we are aware of what we say to ourselves on a regular basis. If you aspire to a better job, your positive thoughts and attitude will allow you to see better opportunities than a negative attitude will allow. The sound waves used by the Pillai Center for MindScience are words/power sounds, which are found in divine ancient languages such as Sanskrit, Hebrew and Arabic. These power sounds contain high vibrations that help elevate consciousness in ways ordinary words cannot. Through his research in the fields of spiritual sciences and technologies, Dr. Pillai has discovered numerous sound waves that help transform the mind, body and soul, thus bringing in manifestations of your desires."

THE PILLAI MIRACLE METHOD

"Holy Macaroni, that is profound. So what does Pillai teach as his miracle method?"

"An important part of his work as derived from the Yogis and Siddhus is that karma is the root cause of all current sickness and must be cleared at the Soul level. Forgiveness by the Divine is a blessing that clears blocks and karma which is a record of services as deeds and virtues."

"Is this true?"

"Yes. But you have to stop asking me that question. Answer it yourself. What he from a Yogi perspective has also come forward with is that the Yogis knew about the brain as a subtle brain which they could see as the etheric double like in the astral plane. So they did not see it as a physical thing but it is the mid part of the brain. It is really not separate from physical but when you activate it you will have a tremendous understanding about everything. In Pillai's midbrain activation process, he tells us that Ommm is a key name for God as the midbrain. Ahhh activates left brain and Ohhh activates the right brain. Ommm is the sound that opens the midbrain."

"Words and sounds again. That is what you have been telling me."

"Yes. He also enforces the need to cut out the noise from neo-cortex. But as we know, shutting it down completely is not easy as it keeps coming back and distracts. He says that the Yogis accomplished this through discipline. As soon as one meditates, the thoughts come. The true state when it is attained is reflected by the Yogi who said: '*it is hard for me to find a thought*'. That is the level needed because here is where all thoughts can manifest if you are in the Soul mind. The goal of meditation is not to have a negative or time condition. When you are empty, you are full. Pillai states that repeated practice is key."

"That is a state that I have not yet found. It is lower Theta."

"You must work on it. When you seek a PhD do you attain it in a day? If you seek to be a CEO of a company, do you attain this instantly? You must do it step by step and graduate. This is no different, is it?"

"Why not, should I not just be able to create being CEO? Is it not just mind power?"

"You are funny, Ed. It could well be so but it may take another lifetime to manifest. No time remember? And if it is this lifetime, then the opportunities to attain that position will arise step by step which you would choose to engage in."

"Ok, I was just being sarcastic. Sorry."

"I understand. Now here is his method for opening up the midbrain. Let me tell you what he says about this method."

"*You will see dramatic results within the midbrain. This is the way to empower the brain. You have to know the higher brain. If you have problems in life, blame it on the brain, it is responsible not anything else. Sound is the building block of consciousness. Ommmmm my lord is the sound that can open the midbrain. It opens the channel from the brainstem because the life force prana connected to breathing is here so when you put attention on the brain stem then it comes alive because you put attention on it as life itself. Yogis do this ommmm on their brain stem. You see the energy floating up to the top of the brain. The sound exchanges in all parts such as the thalamus, pineal, singlet, cortex and goes to the parental but it is not the physical brain. Yet it does affect the physical brain.*"

"Here is an image for you that gives you the steps since you like steps."

1. Close your eyes and focus attention on your right eye.
2. Visualize a powerful light from right eye shooting into left brain.
3. Focus on your left eye.
4. Visualize a powerful light from the left eye shooting into the right brain.
5. Focus on the right nostril.
6. Visualize a bright light entering it.
7. Focus on the left nostril.
8. Visualize a bright light entering it.
9. Visualize the light from left and right meeting between the eyebrows.
10. Again visualize a light in the right eye, shooting into left brain.
11. Again visualize a light in the left eye shooting into right brain.
12. Again right, left nostril light meeting between the eyebrows.
13. Visualize your entire body filled with light.
14. Go to brain stem and focus on it as here is where it converges to mental mind energy.
15. Go up to thalamus, parental lobe and visualize a column of light through them.
16. Ommmmm, ommmmmm, ommmmmmm.
17. The whole body is light.
18. Focus on the midbrain.
19. Ommmmm, ommmmmm, ommmmmm.
20. Visualize the sound rising to the top of the brain.
21. Ommmmmmm, ommmmmmm, ommmmmmm, ommmmmmm.

"The focus is not in the cortex. Focus is on the stem as this is where the life force begins. Breathing is only conscious energy of prana. Focus on the thalamus on two sides of the brain attached to the stem for in-between is the pineal. This is where the miracle will happen. Yogis say put it into 3rd eye and it will become an object. The thalamus controls everything in the center

of midbrain and does not know the difference between illusion and reality. Keep the things you want there and it will make it into real. This way you are making a tremendous impact on the brain. You do not have to meditate forever. A repeated thought affects the brain by changing nerve cells."

"When you put a light into the midbrain starting from the stem and moving up, you allow it to go into the infinite sky. The consciousness of the midbrain is connected to several heavens and you are acquiring this by putting attention on them. It is connected to the highest heaven with a tremendous amount of vibration. Just the light from the stem through the midbrain opens it. You can put into the midbrain area of the thalamus what you want to manifest; car, business, whatever. Put it into the thalamus and pineal. Just imagine it and chant Ommmmmmmmmmmmmmm repeatedly. When you open in the midbrain thalamus it does not know the difference between object and image. It is the cortex that makes a differentiation of the object. Work with the astral not physical brain."

"Of note is that Pillai gives us his wisdom on why he is dedicated to eliminating poverty. He is saying that the most powerful place of the soul to manifest is the midbrain. So that other human brain is dumb because you have to work hard. The cortex is the stupid part that will organize your life and keep most in poverty. 99% of the time we think stupid, survival, anxiety, money, relationship. It is an anatomical abnormality. The mind should be peaceful."

"Cool! I believe it."

"That is a rather harsh interpretation of your big brain but that is true. He also says: 'But you have to take responsibility for what you do and the defects in your life. To identify the part of the brain that creates these problems is key. Then there are the negatives; what if I can't open my midbrain. It comes from the frontal lobe. It creates crazy people. We want this science to stop this and everything is rooted in the brain, not the mind that is not allowing what you want to manifest. The neo-cortex needs to be shut down and the midbrain activated. Then use power and intelligence of the Soul mind and go back to the frontal and empower it'."

"Does he say there are separate parts of the brain that have separate responsibilities?"

"Indeed he does and these areas and words are key to activation. You will find a correlation between the astrological houses. The key thing about sounds is that there are sounds and areas of brain responsible for money, relationships, and health. I will tell you this, however: when you begin to correlate the responsibility areas of the chakras, their physical counterparts, the zodiac houses of responsibility, and the characteristics of the planets you will see a dramatic correlation."

"What is interesting is that these sounds go back to original Hebrew and Sanskrit. Can you tell me what he uses to activate the money mantra?"

THE PILLAI MONEY MANTRA

"Yes, of course. I knew you had to know. The SHREEM BRZEE money mantra is offered freely by Dr. Pillai in his quest to eliminate poverty. As an enlightened master, Dr Pillai (Baba) teaches that SHREEM BRZEE is the ultimate and most powerful quantum sound to attract money, wealth, prosperity, abundance, joy and material happiness to you. This mantra he suggests originates from Hebrew and Sanskrit. SHREEM is the seed sound for Lakshmi, the archetype who gives money and prosperity. Goddess Lakshmi is the aspect of the Divine that gives you money blessings and material miracles. BRZEE is a sound that was revealed to Dr Pillai by an ascended master known as Visvamitra who meditated on this sound on a different plane for 1500 years. BRZEE is an ultimate sound which can attract untold wealth and riches to you."

"He suggests that the quantum sound SHREEM BRZEE is the ultimate money magnet - it carries deep within it the power and potential of pure gold. Just like how an oak seed has the potential to grow into a large oak tree, and thereafter multiply into a forest of oak trees, the sound SHREEM BRZEE once implanted into your consciousness and very soul, will turn you into a pure money magnet that attracts wealth and prosperity to yourself. BRZEE will also bring more Divine Light into your Soul."

"He does say that the meditation is offered for free to download and that the mantra must be from someone who is attuned as there is a power from receiving this sound from someone who has received this consciousness. It is from a higher consciousness."

"That must be a marketing tactic to get business."

"Perhaps but what he says is true. You must be in that divine space. Listen to his tape and then he should be the attuner. Here is the process he teaches when leading a group."

Close your eyes for a minute.
Put your attention on your 3rd eye for a minute.
Chant Brzee (25 times).
Allow the sound to go deep into your 3rd eye and then into the entire brain and pervade the whole body.
Chant Brzee (5 times).
You have no responsibility. You have given total control to Brzee.
Chant Brzee (30 times).
Join me now.
Chant Brzee (40 times).
Allow the sound to permeate the mind and the complete body and soul.
Chant Brzee (8 times).
Now mentally keep repeating Brzee in the 3rd eye.
Ommmmmmm shati shanti shanti, shati shanti shant hi
Slowly, slowly you can come back.

"The chant is done 108 times. Pillai offers some advice on this mantra: 'You do not have the burden to check out what will work for you. Brzee will be like a watchdog to keep wrong projects away from you. She will spontaneously spring the right thought in you and the right project will show up for you. You have given your financial plans and future to her. Let her take over you and control you'."

"There is another aspect of this that relates to the areas of responsibility I mentioned. He tells us that the best time to do this is during the 11th moon."

"What does that mean?"

"The word Ekadasi in Sanskrit means *'the Eleventh Day*,' which occurs twice in a lunar month - once each on the 11th days of the bright and dark fortnight respectively. It is known as the *'Day of Lord Vishnu''* it is a very auspicious time in the Hindu calendar and an important day to fast according to the Hindu scriptures, Ekadasi and the movement of the moon has a direct correlation with the human mind. It is the time when you get the attention of the coherent forces to address wealth issues."

"Hmmmmm, that's pretty heavy! I am sure that will begin to sink in for me to better understand."

"Indeed. There is much that is 'sinking in' for you. Have you had enough?"

"No. I am enjoying these examples you bring forward because they totally wipe out that neo-cortex. Are there others using mantras?"

"Yes, of course. Let me bring into your awareness a Master Sha of the Chinese ancient wisdoms. You will get more insight into chanting and the correlations of areas of responsibility."

MASTER SHA MIRACLES

"Awesome. Ok, who is Master Sha?"

"Master Sha carries into the current time the Chinese ancient wisdom. He reveals how the sacred Source meditations and mantras have been so successful for him. He is a medical doctor, doctor of Chinese medicine in China and Canada, as well as Qi gong, tai chi, kung fu, and a feng shui master. He is also engaged in advanced cellular healing research in China and has his own TV show on the power of sound. He has had 10 years of healing and reports hundreds of thousands of miracle healings. He has trained thousands of followers. His sole mandate is in service as the purpose of his life; to make others happy and healthier through empowerments in three ways. He is here to teach universal service to be unconditional unusual services. Teach soul secrets wisdom, knowledge to soul healing miracles, and to teach to reach soul enlightenment."

"That's an impressive background and purpose. What does he do?""

"Master Sha teaches that the Soul, mind and body are the key areas of healing. In order to heal, karmic blockages must be removed from three areas: soul blockages are bad karma and must be removed first; mind blockages are negative beliefs, ego and attachments; body blockages are energy and matter blocks. Compassion boosts energy vitality, immunity in all life, and Light transforms. To Sha everything has a soul, mind and body. In all his work, he uses five key techniques of Body, Soul, Mind, Breath and Sound power."

Body Power puts hands on place to remove blockages. Where you put your hands is where you receive healing and rejuvenation.
Soul Power opens to healing and blessing to invoke inner souls of body, organs, cells, DNA and invoke outer souls of divine.
Mind Power puts your mind using creative visualization on what you are to receive. Thinking and what you visualize is what you receive blessings from.
Sound Power chants sounds as what you chant is what you become. Mouth mantras are sacred sounds from pure land of service which is the Soul's journey.
Breath Power breathing deeply in and out drawing in the Source Light and exhaling with the appropriate chanting mantra.

"I really love Sha because he focuses on Soul healing as he states that when you first heal the Soul which is spirit, then healing of mind and body follow. The Soul is a golden light being, the essence of life, boss of human. When you get sick, the Soul gets sick first then sickness of mind and body follow. Healing first removes karma blockages from Soul, negative energy from the mind and negative matter and energy from the body."

"I see why you love him. This all sounds very familiar. Where do the ancient wisdoms come out?"

"In his healing practices, he brings ancient wisdom into his procedures. He states there are five elements in ancient wisdom that have responsibility areas in the body. These are Wood, Fire, Earth, Metal, and Water. They correspond to the 5 senses and are balanced or unbalanced by positive or negative emotions. To offer healing to the organ within that group is to offer healing to everything connected to that element."

"An example of part of the table he offers in his book is the body organ of the heart which belongs to the Fire Element."

Element	Yin Organ	Yang Organ	Body tissue	Body Fluid	Sense	Unbalanced Emotion	Balanced Emotion
Fire	Heart	Small intestine	Blood vessels	Sweat	Tongue Taste	Depression Anxiety	Joy

"He tells that the heart is the authority (zang - yin) organ of the fire element, and the small intestine is the fu (yang) organ. The meridians of these are internally and externally connected. The heart is the driving mechanism for the blood. The heart houses the mind and soul, connecting with soul's activities, consciousness and thinking. The tongue is the governing organ for taste, blood and sweat as they come from the same place. Depression and anxiety results in imbalances and joy balances."

SHA MIRACLE HEALING PROCESS

"What is his healing process?"

"Sha applies his 5 power techniques as an example of healing the heart and all related parts of the element fire. First is his body power where he instructs the individual to '*Sit up straight, place tip of tongue against roof of mouth. Place one palm over heart and other over lower abdomen*'."

"Why?"

"Sha explains that there is a specific hand placement, one where the healing is to be received, and the other at the area of the sacral chakra that is the seed or origin of the energy manifestation. The tongue is a key ancient wisdom area of central sensory energies."

"The Leydig gland!"

"Yes, the seat of creation. The next is his soul power where he opens to the mind body and souls to instruct what he calls the inner souls."

"*Say hello to inner souls.
Dear soul, mind, body of my heart, small intestine, tongue, blood vessels and emotional body of the fire element.
I love you, honor you and appreciate you.
You have the power to heal and rejuvenate my heart, small intestine, tongue and blood vessels which include big and small arteries, capillaries, small and big veins and to heal depression and anxiety.
Do a good job.
Thank you.*"

"Then he opens to and instructs the outer souls."

"*Dear Divine.
Dear Tao, the Source.
I love you, honor you and appreciate you.
Please forgive my ancestors and me for all the mistakes we have made in all lifetimes related to the heart, small intestine, tongues, blood vessels, capillary system and depression and anxiety.
In order to be forgiven, I will serve unconditionally.
To chant and meditate is to serve.
I will chant and meditate as much as I can.
I will offer my unconditional service as much as I can.
I am extremely grateful.
Thank you.*"

"In this process Sha is following his table items, addressing the areas of healing, the issues that caused them, all of the inner and outer souls to address and issuing the words to bring love, forgiveness and compassion into the process. He issues gratitude, faith and trust it will be done. Of note is the necessity to clear karma by forgiveness."

"In the next step, he opens to what he refers to as mind power as he instruct to '*Visualize bright red light shining in the heart area*'. Central to the healings is light which carries the powers of divine; namely love, forgiveness, compassion within light itself. The type of light is as in the table which in this case is red."

"Well so far this is pretty consistent with all the other methods. So where do the mantra and chanting of words come in?"

"It is the next part. Then he deploys the sound and Breath Power where chanting and breathing are used. He instructs as follows:"

"*Chant silently or out loud.*
Visualize red light in the heart as you breathe in and silently chant: Heart circulates perfectly.
Visualize a golden light throughout the body as you breathe out and chant: Da Ai or Greatest Love.
Visualize red light in the heart as you breathe in and chant: Complexion is glowing. Perfect tongue.
Visualize a golden light throughout the body as you breathe out and chant: Da kuan shu or Greatest Forgiveness.
Visualize red light in the heart as you breathe in and silently chant: Clear Mind.
Visualize a golden light throughout the body as you breathe out and chant: Da Guang Ming Greatest Light.
Continue to chant and visualize 10 minutes (two hours for life threatening conditions)."

"What is this Chinese stuff? These are not ancient sacred words or sounds are they?"

"They are simply words that have been given energies or associated with a vibration representing an action and result. You see that there are ancient vowels yes, but like a special personal mantra or affirmation that you can create meaning for and that is what will buzz into your midbrain. We can talk about this later."

"And you say he has healed hundreds of thousands?"

"Over a period of 12 years, he has trained many to follow his procedures and attune them to the energy. That has indeed resulted in many miraculous healings. But what I want you to understand is the simplicity in the process. Have you noticed this?"

"Yes, of course there is the light, love, forgiveness and compassion. He simply says I love you, I am sorry, you know how to heal, do a great job and thank you. Then the golden light and the chants to enforce the process."

"Did you note anything about karma?"

"Yes, both these guys are onto the Soul's karma and the need to heal the Soul of karma first. I asked you if this was true and you said yes but did not elaborate. Can you tell me more? Is this perhaps why healings and miracles don't work all the time – your state of Soul karma?"

THE KARMIC CONUNDRUM

"Indeed, that is very perceptive of you. We are becoming united in one consciousness. Karma is the root cause of all current sickness and must be cleared at the Soul level. Forgiveness by the Divine is a blessing that clears blocks and karma which is a record of those services and if that record is not clean then it is a conflict with the process."

"So what does the Yogi Pillai say about this?

"He says; *'The Yogis and Siddhas knew karma was a deep orientation to a certain quality, war, poverty, and this comes from several life times. That orientation comes forward as karma. Karma is a reality and it can be corrected. Karma impacts the thought process and is real. Karma removal is removing the deep thoughts that are neurotic thoughts. The real thoughts come from the heart. Karma can block meditation. You must understand that there is a law of causality. It is like Newton's law of action and reaction; life is reaction as you create actions. Karma is responsible for all your problems of relationship, health or wealth. Keep dissolving your karma because it will not allow you to make money until you first clean it out. Otherwise you will sit like a zombie and nothing will happen. In every area karma has its own hand and it dictates at a conscious level. If you have a good money karma it will keep flowing to you. You do not need education to do this. This is important to understand. You can change your karma by ways and means as yogis are involved in this change in destiny'.*"

"Sit like a Zombie! I can relate to that! He's a pretty funny Yogi! And if you don't clean it?"

"He says: *'But there is a destiny. If you do not change it, it will run its own course but if you learn to change it and how it can be done you can change your life. It is possible to be a billionaire. Wayne Dyer said do not compare yourself to other people, compare with where you have been. You may have already achieved great things. Many people will not be able to manifest because they have to understand karma. You must get rid of it to manifest. Otherwise you are living a past reality so you must understand and release old reality so it can be clean for your future. You must completely erase karma'.*"

"Is this true?"

"Yes. Mantras and chanting are special sounds and messages for transforming life. They carry the high frequency and vibration of love, forgiveness, compassion and light. When you chant from the heart, mantras connect to the Soul's heart. Do not be afraid to invite darkness to chant and meditate with as love melts all blockages and transforms life. Source comes as invisible and visible light (3rd eye sees invisible part). Source Light is what transforms and creates miracles. Communications to Source is at a Soul level where you are at the level of divine light. The Golden Light of Source is what heals."

"And Sha also says you need to clean the Soul of karma. The body and mind will follow."

"Yes, do you remember when we discussed that in the higher planes all you do down below is reflected and recorded above? If you do not get to the Soul level and cleanse first then you are trying to push a wet noodle in upward causation. You are back to the box of limits again. If you clean all that stuff at the top first then it is downward causation of mind over matter."

"And that is all about forgiveness. But I don't even know what karma you are carrying."

"That may be so but it is the intent to forgive yourself for creating karma and others who may have created it in you. Remember it is the intent and act that is important. Also you may have noticed that the seed chakra is at the 2nd sacral chakra area. It is used in Pillai's and Sha's processes. This is where the palm is placed to receive the healing in an upward causal process. Pillai uses the same as a downward causal process to the same place."

"Again, this is the Leydig gland opposite the pineal!"

"Yes, it is the seat of creation connected to the portal of the Soul at the pineal."

"So the lesson from these two dudes is that the process of chanting repeatedly is key. It is what commands the process of miracles to unfold. This is a process that must be repeated daily over and over to take effect. The other is about karma and the need to cleanse it from the Soul first."

"Yes."

"I will tell you something else the ancients knew. In Acquiring Supernatural Powers they tell us that Step 1 is Concentration; focus on an object. Step 2 is to meditate on that object you have chosen. Meditation is an added concentration as it allows you to remain under concentration in greater clarity and disallow thoughts to get to greater concentration. Step 3 is to be in the non consciousness. All that exists is the object nothing else. You must combine all three steps into one technique. You are concentrating on an object, meditating on an object then you become the object itself, experiencing the object. When you concentrate, you focus only on certain things about the object, you do know everything about it in that space of omniscience. The linear nature disappears and omniscience releases it in its totality. This is to release the omniscient mind not the lower mind."

"They also said that we create from inside out. The blueprint to create comes first. The dynamics include sound waves that create anything. The problem people face comes from defects inside. The sound waves that are involved are corrupt thoughts, sound images in consciousness. It means that there is an inability to produce very subtle forms of sound waves. Yogis said you do this in meditation to go to the very bottom and then think about the object at that level, then it can happen. The human usually starts planning how they get a car and gets caught up in the process. You do this at a subtle level to go to the origin of sound waves which is the origin of consciousness and life itself."

"What did they know about this illusion of reality?"

"They knew the whole world was an illusion created by the senses and the mind together. There are two types. There is the collective illusion where everybody sees the mountains and the other where you are not using the senses; then you will understand that the appearances are illusion. Personal illusion is true to one's self so each can experience their own personal illusion of wealth, poverty, and so on. The whole life is experienced between the two illusions."

"Well, the inevitable conclusion is that the way to miracles is through you and me as one mind, one consciousness. And I have to get rid of the karma baggage. But what I am beginning to see is that although there are different ways and procedures, they are really not that consistent. It is then intent and belief that is key. It has to be a process that takes you out to a state beyond the mortal confines of the physical world of body and environment both of which are virtual holograms under the responsibility of the brain."

"Yes, Ed that is so."

"In all of the processes we have studied that have been initiated to heal internally or to change externally that hologram, we have seen the same pattern; getting the hell out of the limitations and then reprogramming the subconscious from top down – from a higher vibration – outside of negative energies, inside of that positive energy of love, peace, gratitude. And the Life Movie which the brain plays out like a DVD player is simply like a default plan if You do not figure out how to change it by entering the infinite quantum space that like your own mind, which is a part of it, contains an infinite number of possible realities for you to experience. But are we actually changing the holographic projection or are we attracting an existing pattern of vibration? And how do words do that?"

"Well, let us engage in that topic."

21

IS THERE A SCIENCE TO THE ILLUSION?

Your mind is in quantum field of infinite possibilities if you allow your higher awareness to open to it

"This is all very ineffable all right. I am still befuddled about this life movie of the illusion. I am getting a notion now that our reality is indeed an illusion that the midbrain is responsible for creating. But that creation is projected to the outside from the inside by the midbrain. It is formed on the basis of words and sentences that are key to reality. There is no reality outside, it is all inside. That this is an illusion, a game of life, is a pretty difficult thing to understand."

"I understand but when you and I unite and you begin to see shifts, you will begin to overstand it from above, not waste energies understanding it from below. If you are a fish living in the water, it is pretty impossible to understand there is air outside."

"Once you get out of the water at a higher level of overstanding you create, not attract your reality. But you are right. Everything you feel with your senses comes from your midbrain control center. Everything you sense is described by a word or sentence, or paragraph. A word is a vibration of sound. An image is a vibration like sound and it represents those words, sentences and paragraphs. A thought is a word or group of words, all of which are sound. So it is not surprising to understand that rather than reality being described by words, it is created by words, does it?"

"That is a serious reversal of thinking. And to carry this further, if you do create reality then you create it with words and sentences? But the languages are all different."

"The science of Gematrics goes to the root of languages and bases it on numbers which are the means of relation between words and languages to have the same meanings. But consider that the images are the same, are they not?"

"Yes."

"So can you conceive the idea that the images and words that you use in your miracle creation process are actually creating the reality that the midbrain is projecting for you as part of the greater hologram? And that the process of repeating words and tagging the vision of completion to it is creating your own language understood by the midbrain?"

"And further tagging it with emotion gives it power. Oh my God!"

"So what would be the common basis for all these things?"

"Energy."

"Yes, but what form? How does the brain look at it when it programs?"

"It associates an emotion with an event that causes it, then programs the physiological response for later?"

"And what triggers it?"

"A thought, vision, words, real or perceived. I get it, these are all frequency – waves. It is all based on words that represent the whole of reality."

"Yes, these are what the brain is used to taking as input to determine instructions. And can you believe that those instructions include changing your holographic picture of your reality?"

"Now that is a tough one! Words are the main language of programming reality!

"In programming your computers you use a program language do you not? These are just words that mean something to that dumb old computer that interprets these into some form, action, representation that makes sense to your senses. When you program it, do you care what it does inside to make all those bits and bytes create something meaningful to present on your sound and image receptors?"

"Ok, I see that. The bits and bytes are like the letters of DNA. Combinations describe everything the computer can present as an image. And it can describe through a subroutine of computer words of language an actual process like a video presentation of some natural action."

"Well then why is it so difficult to see your reality around you work the same way but in a much more complex way? Those programs and subroutines in the computer interact with each other just like living organic morphogenetic programs do. And DNA has all the programs to interact with."

"And the view screen is a holographic projection movie we as holographic programs immerse into and interact with. Wow!"

WHAT IS THIS QUANTUM - REALLY?

"Let us go back to quantum and your mind. You understand that your mind consists of consciousness, subconscious and unconscious as partitions. You understand that your mind is a partition of the global mind which is a partition of the Causal mind or Higher mind and which is a partition of the greater mind?"

"I get that. It is like a database having sub data base of information."

"And you understand that these partitions are just tags of identity that are energetic units of the whole quantum mind?"

"Not totally."

"Let us look at the Higher Mind as a quantum example. When you attempt to understand what it as consciousness is and where it stores information, it becomes ineffable to scientists who study it and try to attach any rules inside the box. It simply cannot be explained and so this science of quantum has sat on the perimeter of science for 80 years. But like anything else that evolves, more and more scientists are taking a serious look at it. One of the big reasons for the scientific heartburn is the notion that the material world composed of particles like atoms is only a fraction of the nonmaterial world made of energy in the form of waves. This is not so much of a problem here until we encounter the theory that everything is made of waves and it is the human consciousness that collapses these waves of infinite possibilities into matter by the process of observation – deciding to bring that possibility into our conscious awareness."

"Like a thought? It is not on a predictable area of a memory like a hard disc or brain, I just pop it into existence?"

"Because it is nowhere and everywhere at the same time."

"Well where is it?"

"If you look at your cell phones, or your WIFI networks, iCloud, where is the information? Is it in cyber space, on a server, in your device when people hack into it? The process is like a very primitive consciousness. In a limited sense it is everywhere."

"Well, all three as information are places to hack into by decrypting the information holding processes but I don't get the connection."

"It is all encoded information that attaches to waves. Waves are the quantum field that make up everything. In a holographic plate, a picture of waves, all the information of the whole is also in a piece. If you take a piece and I take a piece we both have our own pieces of all the same information. Now how you decide to decrypt it and present it is up to you and the ability of your device. You consciousness is tagged with your ownership and used your own way and your awareness of the whole depends on how you hack in to see the rest of it."

"Ok, I get that."

"Let us start with a thought. A thought has no particular location but can be brought into awareness as an image. The thought is brought into awareness and it can be collapsed into an image. It is simply pulled out of nowhere, yet is everywhere or anywhere in your mind. There is no time or space here only the void of consciousness. A thought can affect another thought as they are unified within the mind called nonlocality. If you think about how nice your girlfriend is, it affects the other thoughts about your girlfriend. Then there is the uncertainty principle as you never know when a thought comes into awareness to collapse it into an image. It is a total unified field of one mind."

"So a thought that pops into my mind can be collapsed into an image in my mind. If I shift the thought it is gone but not lost. If I take that a step further then an object made of particles appears by my placing my attention and awareness on it. When I close my eyes it is an image and the particle object is gone. I can still have an image in my mind but according to quantum the real object is not there, it is just waves?"

"Not an easy concept to believe, is it? What you decide to observe is your choice. Whatever it is, it is in one of two states; particles or waves. Now why is it a unified field of one? If you look at any atom, it is 99.9999% filled with an array of energy frequencies that form an invisible interconnected field of information. This is a scientific fact. Subatomic matter as a quantum world does not behave anything like matter you are used to. Particles which you see and perceive through your brains as material reality exist as a tendency, a probability or possibility – not absolute physical things. And when particles are observed the process of observation, bringing them into consciousness effects or changes their behavior. They exist simultaneously in an infinite array of possibilities within an invisible infinite quantum field of energy only when an observer focuses attention on any one location, and if an electron does it appears in that plane. Matter cannot exist until you give it attention – notice it. It is constantly vanishing, oscillating, transforming, manifesting from matter to energy at a rate of 7.8 times/sec."

"But it is still there because I can bump into it when I am not observing it."

"Remember there is a group consciousness and awareness that is doing the same thing. You are part of a bigger process of joint observers and that keeps the material reality open as 7.3 billion observers are keeping it current and you are observing what you all jointly see. I am going to throw another tough one at you. You have come to understand that Earth is a living entity with a Life Plan and her consciousness is called Gaia or Mother Earth that gives her inhabitants a place to evolve. She is also an observer collapsing reality."

"Yes, I am already understanding that. Ok, I can understand that in the case of my mind when my eyes are closed. I have mind over image matter as a quantum reality. But how can it mean that my mind can become matter in the reality with my eyes open?"

"What you have not come to understand and accept is that you are all doing this act all the time. In your mind possibilities exist as easily as you think of them and you can then collapse into that reality an image; both are simply energy. So if particles exist in infinite number of possible places simultaneously then in the same way so you are also potentially capable of collapsing an infinite number of potential realties in physical existence. So a future reality you imagine exists in the quantum field. What this means is that if your mind can effect where and when an electron appears out of nowhere then you should be able to influence the appearance of any number of possibilities."

"Well, that would mean if I can think of anything, I can create it as particles. That is impossible."

"You are believing the bias of the collective. Just because the majority who accept, believe and surrender to this does not mean it is not possible. Even in your earth reality of particles, there are people who can. Understand that if you accept the reality as Newtonian physics then that includes the laws of physics."

"Like who?"

"There are many, Sai Baba is an Indian Healer who at will created physical objects by mind only. There are those who can levitate, remote view, create miracles, shift material reality, bi-locate. But these are not accepted within the norm so these are simply not allowed in your conscious awareness. They are believed to be radical oddities and so they are not common."

"But you say we are doing this all the time."

"You are but again not within the context of what you currently understand. In order to truly understand this, you must accept that your physical particle reality is an illusion of holographic realty. What you and the group are seeing and experiencing is a holographic projection of your joint observations that is created by your brains. It is an illusion taken from waves collapsed into particles so you can experience it and express within it."

"And to create things outside the norm, you have to create from outside the norm. Is that what these exceptions do?"

"Yes, just like your cases of miracles. Inside the box that is exactly what you do all the time but the issue is that all the experiences, all the learning, all the subconscious programs that run unconsciously have been burned as neurological pathways linking emotions with experience that run the way you have reacted and perceived the experience. The problem is that within the box, you cannot believe this is true, so of course, not many escape this programming."

"This is very confusing and I have a whole lot of questions about this, but what you are saying is that the brain is a holographic processor that is creating our reality and there is really nothing around us."

"The brain is doing the same work of a video projector that is reading off a film, or a computer that is creating a view of something that is understandable by your brain. In this case the brain is reading off the equivalent of a holographic plate and projecting it like it was a holographic movie you and your own observations are immersed in."

"Just like a virtual immersion game?"

"Sort of, but much more complicated than that. It accounts for your preferred observations, your personal life plan that is being played out within the larger norm hologram."

THE BRAIN IS A HOLOGRAPHIC PROCESSOR

"Remember, the midbrain works holographically to create reality as an image. You cannot see a holographic object until you use a laser beam. The brain does the same with pure light just like a laser. When a holographic film or plate is created it appears as ripples called interference patterns which are just criss cross waves. The holographic film is used to create a projection of the object. Reality which manifests as a concrete image is a projection by the brain as created from a sea of interference patterns."

"And the global reality is a composite of 7.3 billion observers."

"Don't forget the consciousness of Mother Earth or Gaia that has her own life plan of immersion. She is also observing the greater hologram which the 7.3 billion plays a role in."

"It is not possible to remove memory from the brain remember because it is not stored there. The brain uses a mathematical process named Fourier transform to interpret frequency – same as process of nature and sight. The brain does not do the thinking, it is a holographic processor and projector. You are like conscious TV sets picking up frequencies to convert into images. To understand this look at the way you play a game. As you move past a feature object, it disappears but it pops back if you look at it. Our reality also pops back in and out the same way."

"But there are many studies that show the brain has memory and to do certain functions, and when these are screwed up like in Alzheimer's or gets damaged, you can't do the function anymore."

"The brain has its own local memory just like you can hold information on a flash card downloaded from one cloud which is holding everyone who subscribes to it as the group consciousness. The belief that it is the real hard memory prevails. But it is not the source. The source is in the Causal body which is quantum waves and energy reflecting you as a unique vibratory pattern of energy. Then of course there is the akashic."

"So why can't people continue to use that part?"

"They do. Step outside the box and open to the many example of miracles that fix the issue to correct the storage in the brain. If you damage your flash drive you need a new one or fix it. If you damage your local storage, then you need to fix then reload. Is this not what we have been talking about?"

"Ok, I get it."

"These are simply waves of possibilities existing as the field of unlimited possibilities out of which all possibilities already exist in wave form. All is a single unified field of ocean-like existence, not material but in wave form. The whole universe is like this; like a thought wave which cannot explain it. All are waves of potential electrons. You are all made of this unified field where your consciousness exists particular to you."

"So this reality is created like a hologram which is a virtual image and not real. It is created by us being aware of it. We are not seeing a real object any more than the one on the TV. And the TV does not hold the object inside. Our brains do this fake projection."

"Exactly. Your brain cannot process meaning, it comes from what you perceive to be outside of you. Then you engage in it as an emersion movie, interact and use your senses, also measured and recorded by the brain so you as a Soul can experience it. The feel behind vital functions of living organisms comes from the vital body of consciousness which maps the vital function in the form of various functional organs in the physical body through the chakras. Thus consciousness then writes meaningful mental programs in the brain. Consciousness also uses the mental body to create mental software for meaning that the mind processes in the brain. Then consciousness uses the physical hardware to make software representations of the vital and the mental."

"And we all do this to make up the norm?"

"Possibility waves of macromatter are sluggish. Between several observers, their spread is small so they both collapse in the same place to create consensus of physical reality, outside is public. It all appears to be outside but is not. It is actually created inside and projected to appear outside so as to engage in. It is no more outside than a movie is projected outside from the information held in computer language inside."

"Ok, I can see why one has to be in a different place beyond ego to be able to conduct the downward causation of a different reality out of the box. We have to experience oneness beyond individuality and a creatorship of the subject-object world. You have to penetrate the cloud of conditioning and act in full knowledge of love and oneness as we collapse the available possibilities with full freedom of choice. In other words, get into the altered state and the place where the brain does not interfere with that mortal material stuff! Quantum nonlocality means photons are connected through a non local domain of consciousness beyond space and time."

"Well said, given the right conditions there is research available to you where subjects with correlated brains can collapse an event in one to another; an electron potential becomes an instant non local collapse in another. These right conditions mean one cannot think and do without impacting the other (or whole). To see this, one can go to a state of letting go to consciousness beyond ego where two are one. You are not cognizant of creating your reality as you are rarely in a state of consciousness or the right conditions that chooses freely. But it happens when creative deep compassion, moral insight, reverence with nature come into your awareness through feeling."

"I don't get how these programs, live and grow, and we interact with them?"

MORPHOGEISIS IS A GREATER INTELLIGENCE

"This is where the mental ability to understand this become ineffable. But if you look at your computer technology you may get a hint. This is most obvious in the interactive immersion world of games. But at a primitive level, you create program subroutines that have a specific function – let us say to simulate the growing process of a tree. The code reflects this natural process and the graphics it uses presents the different stages of the growth.

Once this program is launched, it always does the same thing unless it is programmed to interact with you. Say you wanted to grow a new branch, add a blossom, cut it down. These are all subroutines activated by you and the programs that add are designed to interface and produce the appropriate recognizable graphics."

"Sure but we are talking about a biological process."

"Well, allow your imagination to see that it is only the depth to which you wish to simulate the process. It is all just encoded information and the depth of detail, the ways in which you interact, the rules of engagement are just much more complex. But there is no difference. And you are running this program interactively with 7.3 billion souls all playing the same game in wireless invisible network. All the subroutines that are needed to create, evolve, maintain and engage the human body are sitting in your DNA."

"Wow, is this what you call morphogenic?"

"Morphogenesis is the development of forms or organs guided by non local extra physical morphogenic fields. This is the vital or etheric body connected to the life process of the body."

"What do you mean?"

"Look at your cells in your body. They all have different functions like neural cells or blood cells and are in groups. When they have work to do they draw a coded program out of DNA and get to work repairing something in their area of responsibility. They all know exactly what to do and they don't carry cell phones. Yet they all carry the complete code and DNA blueprints for everything in the body. All the morphogenetic programs are in DNA waiting to be run by command."

"They communicate instantly through the space."

"Yes, through the quantum field and what is quantum entanglement. All those programs are in DNA. So if you take any cell, it contains the blueprint for you as a humanoid that abides by the morphogenic process of birth, growth, and decay."

"And it interacts with the rest of the living things within the holographic projection."

"Ok, so if we look at computers, as we start adding the animation abilities of computers, we can create programs that are part of the whole process just like these morphogenic processes become part of our own life plan movies. It's just like we, or trees, or earth processes are predesigned morphogenic programs of self evolution. There is nothing there as the hologram appears to be where it is not, our reality is an illusion universe, is a splendid hologram with billions of interactive morphogenic programs being projected out to appear as reality."

"You are getting the picture."

"I get it. All atoms emit various electromagnetic energies such as ultraviolet, infrared, and visible light to name a few and carry encoded information. Each atom is a vortex of spinning energy. Fast spin emits more energy, slow spin emits less. Particles and waves at slower vibration and longer wavelength are the ones that we see in physical reality. The brain is designed to use the senses to feel this and create emotion. The faster the vibrations goes beyond what we can see as the shorter wave length. This energy to matter process based on frequencies (wave to particle) shifts from quantum possibilities to physical reality. The physical universe shares this field of information as through the quantum field that unifies matter and energy so it is not possible to consider anything within it as separate entities. It all connects through an immaterial invisible field of information beyond space and time."

"To add to that, the field is made of consciousness (thought) and energy (frequency) the speed at which things vibrate. When atoms assemble collectively to form molecules, they share the fields of information and then radiate there as unique combined energy patterns – just like you and I based on a state of being."

"I see. The invisible field of consciousness orchestrates all of the functions of cells, tissues, organs, systems of the body (atoms-molecules-tissues-organs-systems). The chemicals share this too and know how and what to do as they share the field of information. So the field that is created that gives birth to matter is what controls matter. Low frequency is incoherence – disease, high coherence is health. All things are in the field all connected as one, made of atoms unified under a field of intelligence that gives life, information, energy, consciousness to all things. This is the field of love – quantum field, nobody, no time, no one, no place. When you enter this state of being you become aware in a field of infinite possibilities. It is just like imagination."

"Yes, and when you change the state to altered belief or perception you are increasing the frequency to amplify energy fields (spin faster and broadcast more energy) around your body which affects your physical matter – you become more energy and less matter by using your consciousness as a new mind to interact with new frequencies. The more emotion the higher the creative state."

"I am getting it. When you observe yourself in a new future and for a moment live in it you would be conditioning the body to believe it was in that future in the present moment. Because the brain does not distinguish between imagined and real situations, when it, as the CEO responsible for the body functions, feels the emotional experience regardless of real on nonreal, it simply does what it was conditioned to do from the past built operating system of 95% stored in the subconscious program inventory. Why is this? Because perhaps there really is no difference to the mind and the movie of life is just an illusion like imagination?"

"And at the place of the midbrain that is responsible for the third eye, as well as the senses and the projection of the reality, this would be the place to create a new morphogenic process to project into reality or direct the cells to launch the process within the reality."

"So the morphogenic movie is simply edited?"

"Yes, but not from a point within the rules of the norm. You must be outside. And what you give life to behaves according to its morphogenic rules of organic behavior, growth, evolution and so on, all interacting in a way that influences and effects the other."

"And everything we give life to, thoughts, images, words, emotions have set subroutines. It is like a programmer sits outside and has to abide by the rules of the program language."

"In effect in the norm reality, you are that programmer using the program language of words according to the rules set by the norm consciousness. That is what you create in the physical world as the life of a human."

"If you can do this to create miracles, then you are not using the law of attraction, it is the law of creation. The brain has to create that which you are already enjoying. It is not attracting it."

"Exactly, but if you are in the lower vibration working within the norm then you are using the rules of the game and by default attracting a like resonance."

"If I cheat someone, then someone will cheat me at some time."

"That is karma."

"If I create strong emotion on a vision, I will attract that likeness as a situation because it has a vibratory signature that the midbrain draws towards its holographic movie to integrate it in?"

"It can work either way. That is the law of attraction versus the law of creation, yes."

THE ELECTOMAGNETIC QUANTUM PROCESSOR

"The brain is an electrochemical machine like a computer that processes information. You create patterns of experiences and realities. You could say that reality is a computer-like generated consciousness hologram in which the characters it creates at the physical level are programmed to believe it is real. It is a game of illusion, delusion, perception and deception."

"Different bodies vital, mental, intellectual, supermental are all possibilities collapsed by consciousness parallel to physical to get a personal experience. All feelings (emotions) are mapped into physical stored in vital body and are in nonlocal morphogenic fields. Morphogenesis is the development of forms or organs guided by non-local extra physical morphogenic fields. This is the vital body that is an etheric connected to the life process of the body."

"The brain cannot process meaning, it comes from outside via your senses. The feel behind vital functions of living organisms comes from the vital body of consciousness which maps the vital function in the form of various functional organs in the physical body through the chakras. Thus consciousness then writes meaningful mental programs in the brain. Consciousness also uses the mental body to create mental software for meaning that the mind processes in the brain. Then consciousness uses physical hardware to make software representations of the vital and the mental."

"And all observers are doing this at the same time as a unified whole with Gaia. So consciousness is all and everything in the virtual hologram of our experiences brought into awareness by the brain - an electrochemical machine forever viewing streaming codes for experience and interpretation."

"Remember that quantum waves of possibility transcend space and time. There is no space or time. That is a construct that the big brain uses to create the illusion of space and time. All objects as possibility waves are non local thus implying transcendence and interconnectivity. Thus all behave as one regardless of space and time. Consciousness originates from a source of light energy for the purpose of learning. The human biogenetic experiment is consciousness brought forth into the physical by the patterns of sacred geometry that repeat in cycles that human big brains have constructed as time."

"But the midbrain does not know or care about time."

"Right, so you need to be in that same reality. Reality is about the evolution of consciousness in the alchemy of time. It is about experience and learning. It is virtual immersion movie, perceived through conscious awareness. We exist in a biogenetic experiment to experience emotion and higher mental thought through the construct of linear time. To become fully consciousness, is to remember who you are as a being of light, why you are here, and get out of the constructs of time and space."

"Where ego and your brother are resident."

"Yes, you enter the collective unconscious that creates the programs of realities through which your soul experiences everything outside of time simultaneously."

"I get it. Within the higher energetic state of who we are as energy of consciousness individualized within the quantum field, we created a Life Plan and contracted to immerse into the holographic projection so as to engage in emotional experiences. Within the creation of this movie we incorporated a greater intelligence of geometric design following the patterns of sacred geometry which form the underlying basis for running DNA programs within the larger scope of the immersion movie."

"Yes. Reality appears to move in synchronized linear fashion creating the illusion of time, also known as the loops/cycles of time, wheel of karma, or the alchemy wheel. It is never the same as it incorporates the flow of the collective unconsciousness forever in motion creating new patterns of experience."

"So consciousness spirals like a slinky, mirroring the movement, or evolution, of DNA. The higher your consciousness moves up the slinky, the faster the vibrational frequency - the faster you think, create, understand higher holographic archetypes of reality, and increase your manifestation in physical reality. As you move up this ladder of vibration, the awareness of the nature of reality opens and the mind as the greater consciousness of the Creator unifies with the lower and higher mind as one within the quantum field of infinite possibilities."

"And that my dear Ed is not done from your lower reality without dedicated effort of reprogramming that which you have taken a lifetime to program."

"Nor to overcome the interference of lifetimes of karmic crap."

"That truly is up to you."

A HOLOGRAPHIC UNIVERSE – REALLY?

"How does this holographic process work? It is so difficult to understand how we as holographic brains and bodies are influencing and interacting with a holographic projection. That is a head spinner! Can you explain?"

"In your science interference is the criss cross pattern of waves where two or more waves ripple through each other. Laser light being extremely pure coherent light is best when a single laser light is split, one bouncing off an object and second allowed to collide with the first so an interference pattern is created. It is recorded on a holographic plate looking like nothing at all but as soon as a second laser or bright light shines then a 3D holograph image appears. And when the holographic film containing the image is cut in half, each half retains the whole image. An image presented to the brain by the eye is the same process so images are recorded or retrieved by illuminating the film with light taken at the same angle as the recording."

"What this means is that we perceive things as out there but they are really in there on the plate. The pain in the toe is a neurological process in the brain to manifest experience. Look in a mirror. Are you there or is it just a plate? Or are you located in the mirror surface? The brain and the hologram all operate in the frequency domain."

"Yes. Electrons possess no dimension, no traits of objects and can manifest as particles or waves and they can create wave like patterns that when collided create interference patterns. The chameleon ability to change back and forth are quanta - that which makes up the universe."

"And quanta are photons, zillions of Souls."

"When you look at them quanta manifest as particles as the Observer Effect All are interconnected as one called nonlocal, everywhere and nowhere, just like all those photon Souls are the whole of creation."

"So the brain mathematically constructs objective reality by interpreting frequencies that are projections from another dimension beyond space and time. What is out there is a vast ocean of waves and frequencies and the brain converts these. Without the brain we would experience nothing except an interference pattern. We would not be a body, we would be a blur of interference patterns of the cosmic hologram that we unfold as us. We are part of the hologram looking at the hologram."

"Correct. All experiences are ultimately neurophysiological processes that take place in the brain. The reason you experience it as external reality is because that is where the brain localizes it through which it creates the internal hologram that you experience as reality. In truth, the brain cannot distinguish between out there and what it believes to be out there."

"Can you begin to see that all experiences reduced (real or imagined) to some common language of holographically organized wave forms can be through that which represent every part of the reality; namely words as the language? Every action starts from intention, imagination is already the creator of form and has all the movements needed to carry and it affects the body from subtle levels until it manifests. So to the brain, imagination and reality are indistinguishable and images in the mind can ultimately manifest as realities in the physical body."

"Just as every portion of a hologram contains the image of the whole, every portion of the body contains an image of the whole. Every electron contains the cosmos. Every photon as a Soul contains the Universe. The Universe is a hologram of all things integrated and interconnected for a vehicle of experience and you create the laws that govern it. You copy that part of it into your resonant frequency hologram and it all records in DNA as your evolutionary status."

"Your universe is constantly sustained and created by two wave length flows, one from heaven, one from your Soul. Put these together to form a hologram and one is direct from divine and one is direct from divine via your environment. You can view yourselves as interference patterns because inflows is a wave phenomenon and you are where the waves meet."

"In a holographic universe consciousness is everywhere and nowhere. You create sub atomic particles and hence the entire universe both in self-reference cosmology, each creates the other. The Universe is a holomovement, a constant interrelationship between all things in the Universe itself."

WHAT THE SCIENCE BOX IS SAYING

"Do you see anything in the scientific community that is actually confirming this process of reality and consciousness?"

"Yes, as we will discuss later, there is new wave of quantum scientists emerging rapidly. It is because the consciousness is shifting. They are confirming that reality is a combination of Potentiality and Actuality as a conscious choice collapses into actuality that which you see as your reality. A conscious choice creates the collapse of wave possibilities into manifest as from what you see. The collapse is nonlocal without communications and is discontinuous. Your expressions occur from collapse of objects and the mind interacts between consciousness and matter. The role of the brain is to make a representation of mental meaning so that this interaction can be facilitated."

"But the current worldview and the educational system say that everything is made of matter, and everything can be reduced to the elementary particles of matter, the basic constituents - building blocks - of matter. And cause arises from the interactions of these basic building blocks or elementary particles; photons as elementary particles make atoms, atoms make molecules, molecules make cells, and cells make brain, brain makes consciousness. All the way, the ultimate cause is always the interactions between the elementary particles. This is the belief - all cause moves from the elementary particles up the ladder. This is what you told me about as upward causation. So in this view, what human beings think of as our free will over the world of matter does not really exist. It is only an epiphenomenon or secondary phenomenon, secondary to the causal power of matter. And any causal power that we seem to be able to exert on matter is just an illusion."

"That is indeed so. But your scientists are beginning to open to a new awareness, the opposite view is that everything starts with consciousness. That is, consciousness is the ground of all being. In this view, consciousness imposes downward causation and it is the matter that is the illusion. In other words, your free will is real. When you act in the world you really are acting with causal power. This view does not deny that matter also has causal potency - it does not deny that there is causal power from elementary particles upward, so there is upward causation - but in addition it insists that there is also downward causation. It shows up in our creativity and acts of free will, or when you make moral decisions. In those occasions you are actually witnessing downward causation by consciousness."

"I also am aware that much is happening with regards to science and subtle energies. We are now getting some insight that confirms the existence of these energetic bodies. Moreover, some physicists are explaining a process called quantum leap and the workings of dual states under the control of the Observer. It is when an electron exists as possibilities, then when observed it pops onto an electron orbit; but they are nowhere in between when you look away. That is in an unobserved state it is only potential. These possibilities as realized through the brain and consciousness consist of possibilities from where the consciousness can create endless possibilities. Where the uncertainty comes in is that in regards to these electrons we cannot measure both position and momentum at the same time. The brain and consciousness are busy working away this way flip flopping between two states at 7 times a second. Quite a head wringer for that superior human intellect, isn't it?"

"Indeed. Thoughts as quantum objects appear in awareness only when you are thinking. Between measurements they go to the original state of waves of possibility of meaning – transcendental possibilities of potentialities of many possible meanings. Collapses manifest into form that has complementary attributes such as features and association. Physical and mental worlds remain possibilities until consciousness gives the substance by collapsing them into an actual expression or object. Consciousness reorganizes and collapses into a state from possibilities by the brain in response to stimulus, then chooses a convoluted mental meaning – perception. The neo-cortex is a symbol processor as the mind gives meaning to an object. In the notion of Quantum Leap you suddenly get a solution at unrelated times/events as attraction of a morphic field. It comes from outside of ordinary consciousness – from the collective consciousness of information images, and archetypes."

"All quantum objects exist in transcendental possibility or realm of potentiality or in immanent level or made manifest. Intensity such as emotions creates superposition of possibilities in unconscious processing which is biased by learning context. The more you collapse the mind's quantum state relative to the same question the more you increase chances of a new response – from a bigger and bigger pool of possibilities from quantum consciousness to choose from. As we have seen with the placebo, this process of recurrent collapsing is by repetition of images from the Quantum Field supercharged with emotion and gratitude."

"And quantum waves of possibility transcend space and time because in this wave world there is no space or time. That is a construct that the brain uses to create the illusion of space and time. All objects as possibility waves are nonlocal thus implying transcendence and interconnectivity. So in that space, everything is one huge interconnected everything. Thus all within it behaves as one regardless of space and time."

"I can see how that works with our cells. They work together yet have different functions and they simply know what to do – sort of like an ant colony. And each cell can be used to create the same human being. They communicate instantly regardless of space or time. Really, they don't have to communicate because they are all one unit; just like one vision or thought in your consciousness does not communicate with another; it is just there."

"You can say that you see this clearly in how cells know exactly what to do because they are all interconnected through the soup of quantum field as one, just as all of individual consciousness is and every Soul is as well. Every individual consciousness is interconnected through the soup of the quantum field. It is also seen clearly in a holographic plate where any part contains the whole."

"So it is my consciousness that can collapse the potential of infinite possibilities into material possibilities because it is beyond (transcends) jurisdiction of quantum mechanics. Thus all possibilities are within consciousness. We have introduced feelings, emotions and engagement through mental and sensory equipment. The same consciousness exists for all of us so there is no conflict. What is different is how the feelings, emotions, perception and access to the whole is different through individuality of character. Consciousness is the ground of being so you cannot turn it off. We all are (not have) the same consciousness. So we can choose but not conflict as every quantum measurement needs a sentient observer and each time, the brain in response to the stimulus produces a number of macroscopically distinguishable possibilities as the brain's possibility wave. Consciousness collapses the waves of object and brain. The quantum measurement in our brains sets up our self reference – cognitive distinction between us, subjects, and the field of awareness of objects we experience. So the brain self refers to itself. There is no collapse without the brain but there is no brain only possibilities unless there is a collapse. The distinction of self and an object upon quantum measurement is only in the brain and gives rise to our self reference to create a subject-object split nature of experience."

"So consciousness collapses the possibility waves of object of observation, plus the possibility wave in the brain that gives self reference and uses classical memory making of content like a tape producing a holographic view played back when a similar stimulus is presented. This is nonlinear outside of time which is why the midbrain is the place to be."

"Yes, the regular brain cannot do this because time is inherent in its belief structure. Experience produces memories which condition your self reference system in your brain. Influence of conditioning your quantum measurement is what gives appearance that your actions arise from ego acting on past experience, and its character. But it is an assumed identity that the free-willing consciousness does in the interest of having a reference point. Your ordinary states of consciousness are clouded by this ego identity."

THE WORLD IS FLAT – AGAIN!

"I have to say this is pretty mind boggling. This business of holographic plates and projections bring up another delicate question about what we call science. I remember how smart humans thought they were when they discovered the earth was not flat. That it was actually round. And so we all took on the new conscious awareness that it was round and this became the scientific norm. Does anyone believe it is flat anymore? Only the ones that are smoking something. Right? Wrong! If it is a holographic plate, then it is actually flat, isn't it?"

"The interesting aspect of the holographic projections is that the plate which becomes the holographic storage and display vehicle is simply a 2D flat system of criss cross waves (interference pattern). The apparent physical object was what we see as 3D particles that was replicated here is stored on this other form of waves. And if you take any part of this plate, it contains the whole object when you project it using a holographic projector. The projected object, is a copy of the original particle object as created from a flat plate. What is the truth?"

"The brain does the same as the holographic projector, the HoloLens, to take the fabric of consciousness stored on a 2D plate and make it look like 3D. You will find that science is also befuddled about this as in recent research, it is reported that black holes suggest reality is really 2D. And all the 3D information is stored in a black hole is 2D outside. Your research suggests that black holes and universe are holograms."

"So the world must be flat!!!

"Indeed there are such publications puzzling your community. It has brought forward the 'holographic principle,' the idea that a universe with gravity can be described by a quantum field theory in fewer dimensions. They say your universe could in fact be two dimensional and only appear three dimensional - just like a hologram. To you the universe looks three dimensional. But one of the most fruitful theories of theoretical physics in the last two decades is challenging this assumption. The holographic principle asserts that a mathematical description of the universe actually requires one fewer dimension than it seems. What you perceive as three dimensional is just the image of two dimensional processes on a huge cosmic horizon."

"Imagine an aquarium containing a fish. Imagine also that you are unable to see the aquarium directly and your knowledge about it and what it contains comes from two television cameras, one directed at the aquarium's front and the other directed at its side. As you stare at the two television monitors, you might assume that the fish on each of the screens are separate entities. After all, because the cameras are set at different angles, each of the images will be slightly different. But as you continue to watch the two fish, you will eventually become aware that there is a certain relationship between them. When one turns, the other also makes a slightly different but corresponding turn; when one faces the front, the other always faces toward the side. If you remain unaware of the full scope of the situation, you might even conclude that the fish must be instantaneously communicating with one another, but this is clearly not the case. This is precisely what is going on between the subatomic particles."

"That is an interesting analogy. The faster-than-light connection between subatomic particles is really telling us that there is a deeper level of reality we are not privy to, a more complex dimension beyond our own that is analogous to the aquarium. So we view objects such as subatomic particles as separate from one another because we are seeing only a portion of their reality. Such particles are not separate parts, but facets of a deeper and more underlying unity that is ultimately holographic and indivisible. And since everything in physical reality is comprised of these particles as photon Souls, the universe is itself a projection, a hologram."

"In addition to its phantom-like nature, such a universe would possess other rather startling features. If the apparent separateness of subatomic particles is illusory, it means that at a deeper level of reality all things in the universe are infinitely interconnected. The electrons in a carbon atom in the human brain are connected to the subatomic particles that comprise every salmon that swims, every heart that beats, and every star that shimmers in the sky. Everything interpenetrates everything, and although human nature may seek to categorize and pigeonhole and subdivide, the various phenomena of the universe, all apportionments are of necessity artificial and all of nature is ultimately a seamless web."

"My goodness Ed, that is very profound!"

"As we have said, the brain is itself a hologram. One of the most amazing things about the human thinking process is that every piece of information seems instantly cross-correlated with every other piece of information - another feature intrinsic to the hologram. Because every portion of a hologram is infinitely interconnected with ever other portion, it is perhaps nature's supreme example of a cross-correlated system."

"The storage of memory is not the only neurophysiological puzzle. In a holographic model of the brain you may wonder how the brain is able to translate the avalanche of frequencies it receives via the senses (light frequencies, sound frequencies, and so on) into the concrete world of our perceptions. Encoding and decoding frequencies is precisely what a hologram does best. Just as a hologram functions as a sort of lens, a translating device able to convert an apparently meaningless blur of frequencies into a coherent image, the brain also comprises a lens and uses holographic principles to mathematically convert the frequencies it receives through the senses into the inner world of your perceptions. The brain uses holographic principles to perform its operations."

"So this brain mathematically constructs hard reality by relying on input from a frequency domain. I am familiar with some of our research where they have discovered that our visual systems are sensitive to sound frequencies, that your sense of smell is in part dependent on what are now called cosmic frequencies, and that even the cells in our bodies are sensitive to a broad range of frequencies. Such findings suggest that it is only in the holographic domain of consciousness that such frequencies are sorted out and divided up into conventional perceptions. For if the concreteness of the world is but a secondary reality and what is there is actually a holographic blur of frequencies, and if the brain is also a hologram and only selects some of the frequencies out of this blur and mathematically transforms them into sensory perceptions, what becomes of objective reality?"

"Well said, Ed."

"Wow. Put quite simply, it ceases to exist. It is an illusion, and although we may think we are physical beings moving through a physical world, this too is an illusion. We are really receivers floating through a kaleidoscopic sea of frequency, and what we extract from this sea and transmogrify into physical reality is but one channel from many extracted out of the bigger superhologram of the greater consciousness."

SO WHO IS IN CHARGE OF REALITY?

"I will tell you something else that will give you a neo-cortex headache. You will see much research on this very topic. Your consciousness is not aware of experience until brain and body know what experience you are about to have after the experience has been chosen by one on the other side and downloaded to your brains. And someone watching your brain activity can know what experience you are about to have up to 6 seconds before your self conscious knows."

"That is really confusing. Who is the one on the other side?"

"Me. And your Life Plan contract!"

"In order to really be in charge of the process of changing the movie proactively you have to be outside of the influence of the brain and its body, and its perceptions. You have to be pure consciousness that is non locally part of everything which is the 99.99% of nonmaterial space, the glue that interconnects everything - the quantum energy field of all that is, was and will be. What would your ego think of that?"

"Can you explain? You are telling me that free will may be an illusion, aren't you?"

"If you begin to understand that you are engaged in a holographic projection of reality following a life plan that you contracted for, then you must begin to understand that there is really only one way to deviate from that contract. And until you check in with me, you are defaulting to the plan so yes, free will with the exception of using your mental abilities to choose the emotion is an illusion."

"That is an impossible belief for ego because it means it does not have free will and life is totally out of its control. To let go of that and allow the midbrain and Soul mind to take over is a tough shift."

THE MYTH OF FREE WILL

"Can you explain?"

"If I tell you this, you will immediately bring in your ego and lower intellectual processes to rationalize this notion. So let me use your own scientific community to answer this."

"Yes, this is certainly a 'don't compute' issue for me."

"In studies such as with neurophysiologists Ben Libit and Bertram Feinstein they measured the time it took for a touch stimulus on a patient's skin to reach the brain as an electrical signal. The patient was also asked to push a button when she became aware of being touched. The brain was aware at .0001 seconds, the button was pressed after .1 sec but the awareness of the stimulus was not until .5 seconds. This meant the patient's decision to respond was being made by the unconscious mind with the patient awareness being the last to know. None were aware that their unconscious minds had already caused them to push the button before they had consciously decided to do so. Their brains were creating the comforting delusion that they had consciously controlled the action even though they had not."

"But that is such a small time that it can't be significant."

"Certainly, but many other studies have shown that 1.5 seconds before we decide to move our muscles, such as a finger, our brain has already started to generate the signals necessary to move it. So the bizarre conclusion is that the conscious mind is truly the big dummy. It is simply being informed after the fact to make it look like it is making the decision! The brain and subconscious knew what to do, but that conscious mind part of the brain had no clue until it was sent a signal that all the requirements had been done."

"You are kidding. 1.5 seconds! Where was the research and how could they establish this?"

"In a different experiment, scientists at the Max Planck Institute for Human Cognitive and Brain Sciences revealed that decisions are made seconds before you become aware of them. In the study, participants could freely decide if they wanted to press a button with their right or left hand. The only condition was that they had to remember when they made the decision to either use their right hand or left hand. Using fMRI, researchers would scan the brains of the participants while all of this was going on in order to find out if they could in fact predict which hand the participants would use BEFORE they were consciously aware of the decision.

"What is an fMRI?"

"fMRI is a functional neuroimaging procedure using MRI technology that measures brain activity by detecting changes associated with blood flow. This technique relies on the fact that cerebral blood flow and neuronal activation are coupled."

"And they recorded that consciousness has no part in the process?"

"By monitoring the micro patterns of activity in the frontopolar cortex, the researchers could predict which hand the participant would choose 7 SECONDS before the participant was aware of the decision. The conclusion was that *your decisions are strongly prepared by brain activity. By the time consciousness kicks in, most of the work has already been done.*"

"So it is the unconscious that controls everything and that personal consciousness is extremely limited."

"Ok, I can see you are having difficulty with this. Valerie Hunt is another researcher hot on this trail. She discovered the human energy field responds to stimuli even before the brain. Using EMG readings of energy field and EEG readings of the brain, she recorded that loud sounds or flashes register in the energy field before it ever shows up in the brain. She states that the *minds not in the brain, it's in that darn field.*"

"Wow! This goes a step further in that the hierarchy of communication starts in the field to quantum subconscious to identify the program for the brain to do the work with. Then the personal conscious self just gets informed. It is not the other way around! But it is you that is the Field!"

"You can see that people who see these types of experiments get somewhat concerned about free will. But free will is also a misguided construct of ego because to give it up would mean the conscious analytical mind of the brain has no control at all."

"Yes, consciousness and the brain are just big flunkies and puppets to manage the work. But Supernocebo is in there with ego guiding life. I really do not understand."

"What you must consider is that there are three levels of free will. The first level of free will is before incarnation. It is my prerogative to choose the characters, story line, events and purpose of the Life Plan holographic movie. Then in the second level, there is free will during incarnation in the Physical vessel having the freedom to use mental and emotional abilities, perceive and display emotions by choice within the pathways created in the Life Plan, at the same time choose the path."

"But these paths are already written. Are you saying it is like riding a train and either it has been planned to stop or not. Otherwise all you can do is use mental and emotional abilities to experience the scenery?"

"Level 3 is free will within the pathways of the Life Plan. Depending upon the details chosen for the pathways, events, people, the activities between are essentially undefined allowing free will of the mental mind to determine, discern and choose acts along the way. But yes, if you did not create a stop on the train ride, then it is not on your travel plan. If you left it all open, then yes there can be some free will judgments and choices."

"So why would you restrict this so much?"

"To make sure that the purpose I have come here for is possible. Usually old versus young souls leave a lot of details out."

"But what you are telling me is that the brain and consciousness are not controlling anything. They are recording the engagement of mental and physical and emotional reactions and presenting the game to play in."

"Like when you watch a movie on your television, what is your mental, physical and emotional state? Is your brain creating the movie?"

"That this reality is the same is just impossible to comprehend. It is ineffable to say the least!"

"Check out the research. Here is the big one about free will. If you want to really exercise true free will you have to go back to your true self as the Soul mind of heart that created the plan for specific purposes of soul evolution. Learn to communicate with the midbrain. And even if you do that, and create a change in reality like a miracle, it may not be part of the original Life Plan movie as a predetermined option. So if the school is not created, then the lesson can't be learned. Of course your conscious mind (ego) does not like that one because then you are simply puppets being controlled by the Soul for its amusement to engage in a game."

"Yes, exactly. It is a game for your amusement to see how I would think and feel by being thrown into the game. And just like the brain is being informed after the decisions, these decisions are actually being made by you as the Soul through the subconscious which is simply waiting to see how smart we are with our mental and emotional choices. But you said you were not in charge of these horrible things."

"I have to follow the plan and the processes inherent in the rules of the game you choose. And if you choose to follow my brother's mental disposition to react emotionally, that is fine but that determines what type of energy and karmic responses may also come your way. It is your science speaking that 1.5 seconds before you decide to move muscles, the brain has already generated the signals to do it. The human energy field (heart) responds even before the brain. The mind is not the brain and it supersedes all. It is the field that the true computer controlling the hologram of body and brain. Time and space are constructs of this. And I decide what happens in your plan sure but to change your decisions, I cannot until we are one mind."

"But what about creating karma and attracting things. If you are controlling it all, how do we create out reality through karma and the law of attraction?"

"Dear Ed, you must have sensed by now that this Life Plan of yours is by your human intellectual standards ineffable. When a plan is put together it can be immense to the point of predesigning an infinite number of options and choices. What normally takes place in review sessions are the major choice points, events and people. To understand this consider that you have 8 billion people on your planet that are all actually part of your movies. You may consider that in an immense plan, you actually do have an infinite number of choices to experience. So does that help you understand that you are not as much of a flunky or puppet as you perceive?"

"Yes, sort of. It depends upon the maturity of the Soul and the extent of the detail."
"
"Yes, but either way, it is your unconscious mind that is governing the brain. Just substitute unconscious for conscious in order to understand who is really governing free will."

"Ok, let's get back to this brain-projector stuff."

"Each phase of activity is recorded in successive images like frames in the multi-image hologram. If it is a white light hologram an image seen by the normal eye that does not need laser light to be visible, a viewer sees 3D motion portrayed to present the illusion of movement. Your past is recorded this way as a non local way accessed from any point in the space time framework."

"Interestingly enough, it is sort of like loading up and watching a DVD movie. It takes you a few seconds to respond to it. As you watch, you become immersed in the movie with no control over it except to turn it off. The brain and subconscious are also playing out an already created movie. You and the dummy ego are not really creating the movie directly unless you get into that creator space - directly within the quantum field where the Divine Programmer is resident. What you are creating are mental and emotional energies that behave according to set laws governing the global consciousness – like Cause & Effect and Attraction."

"What is coming more and more to the forefront of your joint awareness is that the unconscious makes decisions and conscious follows. You know that seeing and imagining creates the same process in the brain. As you have seen, the results show that the brain knows what is going to be chosen before you do – before you become consciously aware."

"What is the actual process?"

"A pattern emerges unconsciously to lead up to the decision – a deterministic decision brain creates hard reality from frequency domain. The brain downloads the frequency, creates reality, and then sends it to see how it is perceived. The Field and the quantum Causal field contains the stored life plan like it was on holographic film. Holographic reality is downloaded, to project out there as hard reality. So your personal conscious awareness is not aware of experience until brain and body know what experience we are about to have after the experience has been chosen *by one on the other side and downloaded from subconscious to your brains.* And someone watching our brain activity can know what experience we are about to have up to 6 seconds before our self conscious knows."

"So the brain already knows ahead of time but when the brain was stimulated it was a new hologram. An area of the brain collapses and projects out there to be perceived and experienced as reality and only when we perceive and interact do we become consciously aware of what is happening and the whole process can take 6 seconds. The brain is the observer that collapses the wave function into something we understand so we can believe we are engaging in a real reality. Then we can perceive; create mental analysis and emotional energies that are recorded in the Causal body."

"To bring this closer to home consider your PC which uses binary code 0 and 1 like those wavy things the brain uses. Inside is a CPU like a brain of the computer. It translates and projects on a screen in a form we understand. Sensory perception is like the mouse, to respond back to CPU to process. The brain does the same thing to project out there to get input which it already knows about."

"What is happening is that we are not sensing, we are projecting reality. Our senses are not sensing out there but in fact are first projecting that reality so it appears to be out there. Projection plus perception. The brain collapses wave functions and makes it appear like we are surrounded by a holographic 3D total immersion movie from a frequency domain. Our senses read the projection and bring information back to the brain. The act of seeing is experienced in the visual cortex. What we see, touch, feel, perceive is only through electrical signals in the brain; we do not see it in the external world; we see it in our brain as the brain's interpretation of electrical signals. It is the same with distance, time, as well as the body which is an image formed inside your brain. To see it outside is a deception. It is easy to deceive us and the brain of reality."

"The bottom line is that you project reality, then perceive it. So you believe what you see out there is real, with a life of its own and we observe and perceive it to interact with it. No! You project reality first and then perceive it coming back to you in four simple steps:

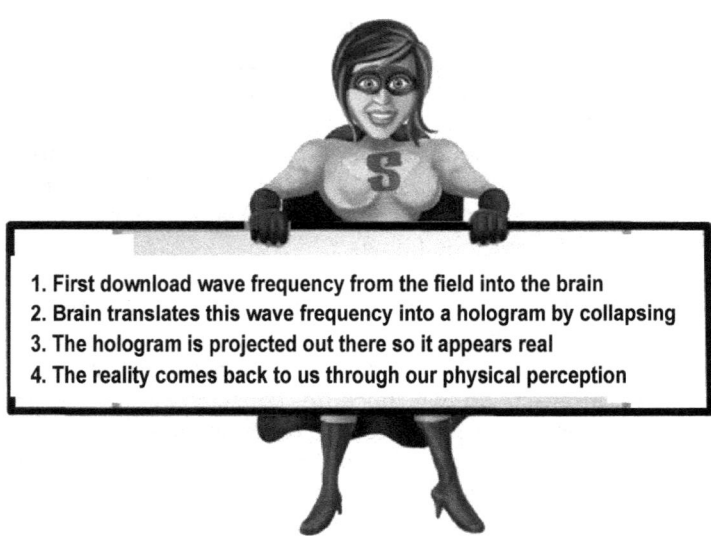

1. First download wave frequency from the field into the brain
2. Brain translates this wave frequency into a hologram by collapsing
3. The hologram is projected out there so it appears real
4. The reality comes back to us through our physical perception

"I get it. It is like you are in a 3D movie theatre but the projector is coming from your brain and that movie is what you are immersed in – it is not real. The world out there is translated and created by the brain. Underlying the illusion is a deeper order of existence and that gives birth to all objects like holographic film gives birth to a hologram. The brain converts the waves of our world. That we are physical beings moving through a physical world is an illusion. We are receivers floating through a sea of frequency. Each individual must have their own unique hologram they are projecting as their private reality that each brain downloads and translates. Thus we all see reality differently. We do not create reality, we project our unique holographic 3D experience to our brain and the perception and mental/emotional experience is recorded."

"In order to really be in charge of this, you have to be outside of the influence of the brain and its body, and its perceptions. You have to be pure consciousness that is non locally part of everything which is the 99.99% of nonmaterial space, the glue that interconnects everything as the quantum energy field of all that is, was and will be."

"Ok, so we are in an immersion movie written uniquely for you, by you from a higher vibratory state of energy, downloaded to my brain translated into a hologram to see it and project it out there for us to experience and improve our spiritual path. The brain and body know what is about to happen before I become conscious of it as conscious follows unconscious. You are Director and Scripter of the immersion movie. It chooses specific frequency waves from unlimited possibilities in the field to create the holodeck experience as outlined in a life plan, stored individually for each as a moment to moment path with predetermined events. As a lower mental and emotional vessel for you I control nothing. You are already in control of the subconscious and midbrain. The brain is just a means of reporting, display and sensing just like a stupid computer. It's like you are the supreme dictator so what is the point of me being here and being aware of this crap that I am in?"

"You do not understand completely. Although your subconscious and I record and play it out and it knows the result before consciousness, this does not mean that I made you make a choice using your mental and emotional abilities. I do not have much say about which path you take. And if you choose to live your life in the lower mind and default to the laws of karma, cause & effect and attraction, I have no control except to whisper guidance to you. If you wish to live on default, that is fine, but in order to move yourself into a more controlled proactive life, you must reinstitute a partnership and get out of the great game of delusion."

22

IN THE VOID OF INFINITE MIND

CHANGING THE WAY OF BEING

"It is time, dear Ed to see what you have brought into your conscious mind. First of all, do you feel and sense that we are one mind?"

"Yes."

"So let us reverse our roles. What would you say is the crux of what you are learning?"

"Here is the crux. Every thought, emotion, event acts as epigenetic engineer of your own cells. When you are truly focused on an intention for some future outcome, if you can make inner thought more real than outer environment, the brain won't know the difference. Then your body as the unconscious mind will begin to experience the new future event in the present moment and you will signal new genes in new ways to prepare for the imagined future event. If you continue to mentally practice enough times this new series of choices, behavior and experience that you desire, reproducing the same new level of mind over and over then your brain will begin to physically change installing new neurological circuitry to begin to think from that level of mind – to look as if the experience has already happened producing epigenetic variation that lead to real structural and functional changes in the body by thought alone – just like placebo."

"How would you do that?"

"This is done through mental rehearsal by closing eyes and repeatedly affirming mantras and images of the future you want. Think about future actions mentally planning your choices, focusing on a new experience. You are reminding yourself of what your life will look like once you get it putting intention behind the attention. When you consciously make thought and word intention with heightened emotion such as joy and gratitude the state of being, your body in embraced new emotion and neurochemistry that would be present in that event (a taste of the future) the brain and body begin to believe it and reality respond to it."

"And?"

"This is how you turn down volume of old circuits and fire-wire new circuits which initiate the right signals to activate new genes. The circuits in your brain begin to respond, and reorganize to reflect what you are mentally rehearsing. As you keep this up coupling new thought and mental images with strong emotions as the Soul, mind and body working together you are in a new state of being and your brain and body are no longer a record of the past, they are a map to a future you created in your mind. Your thoughts have become your experience and you just became the placebo."

"And the key?"

"Higher emotional responses to new thought is like a turbo charging effort on mental rehearsal. Emotions make epigenetic changes faster. Create new future out of past as new information from outside the cell. The outer environment and inner is the same. In placebo studies, the success is dependent upon two key processes: Clear intention of a new future possibility as a life without pain or disease and high emotion of excitement, hope, joy and bliss."

WHY PLACEBOS WORK

"So why does the placebo work? The usual steps; altered state, hypnosis, facilitators, divine intervention do not appear to be part of this process."

"The placebo reflects a real process of mind over matter. Here there is only the mind and the pill that is the key player in the creation of the miracle. It is clear the mind alone that has the power over matter that is managed by the brain and that the Divine Intervenor is actually you and me working together from above to below without any interference, only vision, belief and passion for a new way of being."

"And?"

"Some trigger like a doctor or facilitator is who the trust is surrendered to. And although it may appear to be outside of the miracle norm, what is still the same is that each first **accepted** then **believed** in the suggestions and **surrendered** to the outcome without further analysis. They aligned with a new future reality as possibility as though it had already occurred and they enfolded it with emotion. So they accepted the condition, then accepted a new condition which came about through the belief that the doctor or the research was the authority and surrendered to a new possibility."

"What this is telling you is that I have that power already and don't need anything else to rationalize the process. If I believe the outcome, emotionally embrace it and as a result having the body as the unconscious mind living in that future reality in the personal moment, the reality must adjust to it and the subconscious responds. Continued living in that new belief simply as reaffirmed acceptance, belief and surrender without question enforces the new programming and midbrain recreation of reality. The brain must eventually respond through nervous system and cells to draw out the appropriate programs from DNA. This can create a cascade of physical events that automatically take over and a miracle just happens."

"I will tell you that this is true. All humans have that power but the degree of acceptance is indeed the issue. The degree of Acceptance, Belief and Surrender are the keys and the more we do this the better the result. Emotion will condition, expect and assign meaning to the whole delivery system. If you can't emotionally embrace the result you can't enter the autonomic nervous system (as in hypnotism). And the longer you embrace that new state of being, the more its signature vibrates in the quantum field of infinite possibilities; and the harder it is for the subconscious to ignore re-programming."

"And Supernocebo is at work too because when you see the doc who says you have cancer and will die, you get a series of thoughts, images and emotions conjured up as past experiences (from parents, TV, other opinions, etc.) in your mind. You will then **accept** the condition, **believe** what is said and **surrender** to the treatments and possible outcome. How this suggestion is received and believed determines the susceptibility to that new possible outcome. If you embrace these fears by surcharging them with that emotion, then the only possible thoughts are equal to how you will feel. It is the nocebo; the wrong placebo that you accept, believe and surrender to as **your state of being**."

"Yes, and I recall Mr. Wright from what you have used as an example. He was the one with the tumors the size of golf balls laying on his death bed. In this case he did **not accept** the finality and he brought forward the **belief in a different new outcome.** In the case of the placebo, he did not accept the finality, did not believe in the most probable outcome, **did not surrender** to the diagnosis. He simply did accept, believe and surrender to a different state of being, different attention, different intention, and different meaning to his future. As he surcharged this new possibility with the emotion of the different possibility, he reprogrammed his subconscious, fired neurons that wired a new neurological circuitry in his brain and launched the appropriate cell behavior, chemicals, and physiological processes that corrected the physical issues."

"Yes, I see it. When he found out that the treatment did not work, he then activated the same process by accepting the original fate, believing in the outcome and surrendering to his original fate. His hopelessness simply reinstituted the old way of programs in the subconscious."

"As it is so in all that you do create programs. If you repeat thoughts they form an attitude or feeling, if you repeat the attitude long enough you create a belief. If you continue you hardwire them into the brain and emotionally condition them into the body. You become addicted to them as they are etched neurologically."

"An altered state is when you decide to change regardless of your existing state of being. The key is to see this as done as a new possibility and get goose bumps thinking about it. It requires new information, a new state of being different from past taken from a new future. It requires that you are the mind changing a belief, surrendering to its fruition with gratitude and passion that when created internally as new experience greater than the past experience, greater than the existing hardwired programs, you change the old Cause and create a new Effect that overrides old patterns of the brain and removes the neurological evidence."

"Ok, Ed, what about divine intervention?"

"Well, I have realized that you as your Higher Self, namely me and you as a Soul **are** the divine that together intervene."

WHAT IS DIVINE INTERVENTION?

"So why do people need to have a divine intervention?"

"Superplacebo, when we went over the many cases of miracles we saw that there were several things that seemed to be common. These we have identified as the seven steps but there is something else. They all relied on a Facilitator to lead them through a process and take control of the minds and they all called upon a Divine Force, God, or some unexplainable intelligence to do the work as through Divine Intervention. I understand that the human needs some sort of rational reason to solidify the belief. And this resulted in the reprogramming of subconsciousness to direct the brains. The odd exception is the placebo effect that does not require an altered state to be induced, it does not have a facilitator, nor does it call upon any divine intervention. There is not an altered state or hypnosis. But there is a silent knowing that you and I are one mind, away from the lower reality."

"Are you saying that IS Divine Intervention?"

"Well I now believe that as a mind of Soul we are Divine. By opening to that awareness and consciousness we can guide my mortal life."

"But what is God?"

"Your common consensus is that God is a being conceived as the perfect, omnipotent, omniscient originator and ruler of the universe, the principal object of faith and worship in monotheistic religions."

"Well the word ineffable comes to mind because it is just a personal description and it cannot be expressed in words because there is really no way to describe it except a personal guess."

"And the word divine has common meanings that suggest of or relating to a god, especially the Supreme Being, from God or a god, godlike, characteristic of or befitting a deity, divine magnanimity, heavenly, celestial like the divine kingdom, extremely good, unusually lovely."

"So if you are part of this supreme being and it is written in your DNA then you can easily assume that in your spiritual state of greater consciousness, aware of Soul mind, you are the divine-god-like intervenor."

"The most common dispute comes with the notion of the Soul. What, pray tell, is that? Is it really a spark as a photon? It is ineffable, personal and surrounded with faith and trust in that perception. So you really can't argue with anyone about it."

"You have come to understand that you may indeed be a Soul on a mission as a Divine spark of God and it seems that once you get your head wrapped around the notion that you as a divine being, have the power of creation to be that Divine Intervention. You as a part of this wonderful great ineffable thing labeled God, once truly believed, simply places little relevance on definitions. It does not matter; and what matters is that you can indeed create and change reality."

"That's a whole lot of things about divine that looks like a struggle to define it. It is clearly quite a personal definition and one thing is for sure; whoever God is, she/he seems to be a good Energy who loves people but it seems that within the Divine kingdom, there is trouble getting this point across. Trouble is this Divine Entity has never ever come down to publish anything directly. It is left to those mortals in this kingdom to expound on their own ideas of who and what God is. That is truly your free will to decide this. So really God and Divine are quite ineffable concepts and perceptions because there are so many diverse interpretations of these two words. Is this true?"

"Well, partly. You see if you are god and divine, then there are many who may have achieved this higher state of connection to the Soul mind that have indeed written these books and Bible Code for you mortals to figure out."

"Ok, I can buy that but I do not buy that this God of unconditional love is out there with vengeance on those who do not abide by the business of righteousness and are sinners. That is pure crap."

"You speak of the many mortal interpretations of the word of god that have indeed been compromised. But the code is in the original writings, not the subsequent ones that have been used to control humanity's beliefs and allow my brother his ways."

"It would be foolish in our conclusions to suggest that there was not something greater than mortals can understand about how reality was created, how it works and how it all abides by laws much greater than they can comprehend. Similarly it would be foolish to say such a power like a Higher Intelligence or a Superconsciousness does not exist. You do not have to be the brightest crayon in the pack to agree something created all this that is much more magnificent than one can imagine."

"But what we have seen in our studies is that even when we are in our Higher Place, in a Near Death Experience, we still come back and say it is ineffable. We see clearly however that something guides the reality, the universe, the holograms, the expression of life, all that is, and it is indeed guided to evolve in a divine way."

"We have seen that our reality is a contrived illusion to evolve in a divine way which seems to be evolution where anything goes without judgment. We have seen that this illusion can be molded. We have seen that the key to this is to be in a higher command state and the vehicle of change is in the contrived construct of the brain. And ultimately we have found it is the subconscious and the brain that change the illusion. The power of this change resides in the notion of divine and the depth of belief; and as we have seen that may or may not have anything to do with God but it certainly has to do with the strength of believing in it. But because there is such a diversity of beliefs on this topic it cannot really be defined so we cannot conclude it is a mandatory part of creating reality. But a strong belief in your Higher Self to change reality **IS** mandatory."

"The belief is key so if I believe God or YHVH is an intelligent mind of hydrogen, oxygen and nitrogen that is part of us that is just fine with me."

"Well said."

WHERE DO WE GO NOW?

"We are ready to now talk about the different destinations when you get into the quantum void of the greater mind."

"Well, I have been thinking about that. As my lower consciousness evolves, it does so within the limitations of the group of minds that it represents as a composite consciousness. This means that creating things will normally follow the rules and limits of that group mind or consciousness. So I end up creating and manifesting within the rules that that consciousness creates. In this case it is by hard work, dedication to passion, research or consistent acts of perseverance that I engage in. When I find out new ideas and possibilities that are in imagination outside the box but not yet accepted by the box, it becomes difficult to manifest from within the box."

"Yes."

"But although my lower mind and that of the group mind may be stuck in a box, there is still ways for one to take other possibilities, individually embrace these with passion and hard work to have the group embrace them as well. Similarly, by embracing my own out of the box thinking, I can expand my own mind by hard work and perseverance and passion."

"Yes, that is what we saw in the work of Napoleon Hill who studied hundreds of wealthy people and how they became so. These are people that have succeeded in achieving unusual accomplishments by deploying within the box to their benefits. This is the way manifesting and creation works from the lower plane of physicality."

"Yes, I get that. But what I am learning is that by getting the mind out of that box, you enter a different mode of creation; that from above to below where the rules and limitations are different. It is still the void of infinite possibilities but the rules of creation are different. Working below, you use the below rules even though you may think outside the box. But working above with above rules you have a whole different scenario."

"That is correct, but you must truly be outside the box of the lower mind, otherwise it simply falls back to the lower rules of Cause & Effect and attraction. What you need to understand is that you are always attracting *something through your efforts of mental and emotional energies.*"

"So if I don't have what I want, it's because I have created a lack of mindset in my life and chances are good that I am not even aware of how this could have happened."

"True, the good news is that attracting prosperity uses the exact same mechanism as attracting a lack of prosperity. It may be uncomfortable, but the first step is to fully accept that you are the creator of your own life and have materialized your current situation. *You need to accept it and you need to embrace it.* Having accepted this, you can now start attracting everything you want by changing your thoughts and the way that you think."

"You will get what you focus on, but your mind usually only focuses on the subject and not any conditions you place on it. So, while you are thinking about not being in this crap your subconscious ignores the word 'not' because it's conditional. Instead, it focuses on this mess, and that's what it attracts more of the crap. Once you understand how it works, you can start manifesting more of what you want instead of what you don't want. So, instead of getting out of this mess you start thinking about living in a beautiful home."

"And the more specific you are, the more believable it will be to your subconscious mind. Why? Because once your subconscious believes something, it will do everything it can to make it a reality. And when you add strong emotions to your thoughts and put the power of those emotions to work for you, it works to attract the effect from that cause. But the bottom line is that it is you that I have to convince."

"Yes, you can have the things you want, it takes practice, but it will be more than worth it. Where you are in life right now is not because of the chances you have but the choices you make."

ON MIRACLE PROCESSES

"Now, dear Ed, let us go back to the processes of creating wealth and health miracles. What have you learned from our discussions about those who are facilitating these?"

"When we looked at miracles of health, we saw and found the same pattern with the exception of words and mantras.

"Let us summarize what we have found out. What have you learned Ed?""

"I understand that me and you are one as a soul mind as an expression of a greater consciousness on a mission to evolve and expand our spiritual self. In so undertaking we undertake to use a life plan in a holographic immersion movie created by the brain in which we can express mental and emotion abilities to improve the whole of which all is one. In this we have a partnership to learn from karma and evolve the whole."

"I understand that there are common processes to all of the Healers and Wealth Gurus whether it is regression, hypnosis, ritual, meeting the healer; it is one of getting by the conscious mind to be in some form of altered state away from the beta mind of the neo-cortex. How this is attained, or the process of letting go, is a personal preference but is a prerequisite to entering the place of no space, no time, no thing and no identity to be one with you."

"I understand that the best place to be in this altered state is in the powerhouse of the heart mind conjoined with the midbrain, The heart has the largest morphic field, the balance center, the center of love, and is the center of creation. This provides the gateway to the quantum field of new potential realities where you and I can deploy our Divine Intervention."

"I understand that the state of well being is a prerequisite to entering the unity of mind where a process of downward causation can be deployed. The state of well being is one of peace, love, and stillness from lower realty which allows alignment with your higher mind and the greater mind of all."

"I understand that this higher command is not within the hologram which contains our worlds, our realities, our lives, our bodies. It is outside of it. That is a process of letting go and releasing that which is our conscious world of time, identity, space, and addictions to mortal life. This enforces the downward causation process being executed from a higher place. Whether you call this your Higher Self, Soul, Being of Light is not relevant. It is simply you in a higher state of vibration as energy not particles. The place of change is in the midbrain that understands language and vibrations describing thoughts, images and words describing reality."

"I understand that the higher commander is our one mind in its state of energy that directs the processes through downward causation through consciousness as a quantum segment of the whole. Here mental and emotional directives are given to adjust the reality hologram. This process of creation is centered on thoughts, images, words, feeling and emotion as the triggers that direct the subconscious-brain system to instate the changes."

"I understand that the higher command process follows a plan of life that has been predetermined as the default until such time as the evolution of the physical being becomes aware of its counterpart as pure energy of consciousness. Then it has access to limitless possibilities that it can attract or shift into the reality which is being played out."

"I understand that the process of change becomes more and more difficult with age and with surrender to that which has been programmed as reality. Although the catalysts to change are thoughts, images, words and emotion, these must be instituted more and more by practice and the instilling of acceptance and belief that controls the degree of suggestibility to the subconscious mind."

"I understand that the process of change in reality is within self and whether the holographic constructs of pills, doctors, healers, God, rituals, potions, spells, gods, angels, or the likes are deployed as facilitators, they are essentially irrelevant as it is the mind that is the true healer."

"I understand that the process of creating new reality involves the thought being brought into conscious awareness from being in the realm of quantum possibilities, bringing the thought of the new possibility into conscious awareness, having the clear vision of completion being created to be collapsed it into reality, attached a word or mantra to that vision, the surcharging of the vision by the emotion of the completion, the intention to be in this new reality and the enfolding of this reality with gratitude for its creation."

"I understand the process of creation is going on all the time, through the process of thoughts and feeling. It shifts in causation from material upwards, then at the age of 28, is prepared to shift from immaterial downwards. These are the two major evolutionary stages of humanoid evolution which can be named nonspiritual and spiritual awareness. In the first stage of development the creative process is governed by the lower material and mind limitations of the material construct."

"I understand that my state of well being is vulnerable to the Laws of Karma, Cause & Effect and Attraction until the lessons are learned or awareness shifts into the higher energy of being as the Soul or Higher Self. In this case the Life plan will provide the means, the body will create a Cause, the clarity and intensity of which will Attract a Result from the quantum field."

"I understand that we as a Soul and lower mind must be one mind deploying the midbrain and commanding the rest of the brain to create a new mind, life plan and reality."

"I understand that the quantum void of pure consciousness is pure unconditional love and light including all minds and the quantum subtle energies that are its makeup."

"I understand that we must work together to cleanse, heal and balance karma and dysfunctions of Soul, mind, and body. To this end the four key processes are love, forgiveness to balance karma, compassion to unify as one and light as the unifying agent of all that is.

"I understand that after the age of material maturity of 28, spiritual evolution is launched and the proactive creation process can be executed from above as the energetic self to below, directly impacting, changing and creating that which is the holographic reality, and that which was created as the Life Plan. From above, within the field of quantum and infinite possibilities the mind has no limitations within the quantum soup of love."

"I understand that space of quantum possibilities is governed by the vibration of love and well being, and to be proactive within it thus preventing execution by default, you must be in that space in order to be in command. Any distraction from lower vibrations of the physical self dismantles any communications."

"I understand that in order to change that which is our lower form and reality, we must first accept, believe and surrender to a new way of thinking to eliminate the past, then live the new with high emotion to induce a change in environment or behaviour. This suggestibility to rewire the neurological programming or to attract new reality is dependent upon the strength of emotion and belief which is the variable that controls whether it becomes reality. As each individual differs in this degree, it is the persistence and practice of the reinstitution of the new reality that will control the time and degree of success."

"I understand that much of the terminology that has been constructed as techniques and procedures have a biological, chemical, consciousness counterpart. For example the altered state of meditation is required to eliminate the interference of the brains activity. Letting go requires that the usual world of physical activities are bypassed to get to the subconscious."

"Well done. So what is the process that you use to change your health or wealth reality?"

"I understand that all of these processes work but it is clear that the way in which they are deployed is as variable as the imagination. For that reason, it is simply a question of belief to create a personal process that utilizes the inherent power and process of the subtle energy system of the bodies. It is all a construct so there is no right process. At the bottom line is intent and belief. The process I use, whatever it is, must be accepted and believed by me. When I co-join with you the mind becomes one in the infinite space of possibilities, what is credible to us is what becomes reality to me below."

"I understand that it is a united consciousness through the quantum subconscious that instigates that divine intervention that instructs the brain."

"I understand that I create my own life within a greater life plan. If I have dis-ease or disease whether minor or fatal, it can be fixed. If I have karmic baggage that interferes, it can be fixed. If I have issues with wealth and happiness, it can be fixed. If I have a life contract and life plan that sucks, it can be fixed. But we must be one, in a space of quantum love to do it."

"I understand that the process of belief, acceptance and surrender to instigate a new mind, and to attain that new Soul mind may vary for all and the effort and time required may vary. To ensure that it is achieved, faith, trust, and continued engagement is required."

"Dear Ed that is well said. You have indeed been listening. So now let me ask you about the destinations in the void. You well understand how to get to the void and meet me. Now what about all those places to go in the void"

"You mean regression, between live, progression, and astral projection?"

"Yes."

"You have told me what is practiced and I can see that these are as variable as the mind itself. The key is to create a process of my own as there is no right or wrong way. There is only our mind and imagination because we are one mind and it is a knowing that comes from that capacity that simply knows it is right. So whether I want to enhance my abilities, look at regression to other lives or in-between, or look forward in my life plan, you and I simply go there directly once we are in void, and I know in my heart we are one."

"And in the meantime, how will you live your life?"

"Together we will use love, light, forgiveness and compassion in every moment. We will shift to now time. We will cleanse old karma and begin the new soul mind over matter. We will institute the energy portfolio and begin to build the new wave of passion and fruitful desires by being in a constant state of alpha. How does that grab you?"

"It grabs me! I am grateful to be you. "

"I answered my own questions didn't I?"

"You did. It is actually very simple. It is the trust and faith and letting go that is not simple."

"Indeed. It varies depending on each character and the purpose of learning. Each Soul evolves at different rates and have different needs."

"But once I connect with you and understand the game and the illusion, what is the point of engagement?"

"You know the answer."

"A humanoid vessel with DNA opening to its fullest."

"Can you imagine this?"

"Not yet."

"Ok, let me ask us one more question and attempt to summarize the whole process, plus draw more out of your re-remembrance. Then I will tell you a final story of a greater evolution and the Gaia Life Plan."

23

HOW DOES IT ALL WORK?

As a soul mind let us tell a story that you already know but had not the faith to believe.

WHY ARE YOU HERE ED?

This one last question rang in my mind for a while. It was all a revelation for me and I was feeling my own conscious mind loosening to the point where I was not really able to distinguish between what was coming forward from Superplacebo my own mind. It was a melding of conscious Ed mind and unconscious Soul mind. What I had learned was that I had to be in the heart mind in order to be this merger. As soon as I became immersed in any kind of beta activity, it was like fragmentation of thinking and I would simply see things around me differently. It was this polarity that allowed me to see two sides and it took a lot of discipline to get into Alpha to perceive and see and feel things on the positive side of the ledger. I found that writing would open the heart channel and information would flow out that was, as I knew in my heart, directly from Superplacebo.

One morning, after settling into my usual meditation, I was feeling a deep connection. It was time to reverse the roles and Superplacebo knew this.

"Dear Ed," he said, "we have had much information flow between us and you have always been with questions. Now I am going to see how we have melded and ask you a question. The melding is one which is a flow through process where you simply know answers."

"What do you mean?"

"If you recall the discussion about the midbrain, we saw that to connect directly to my mind as Source and Soul, thereby replacing your neo-cortex as the choice of consciousness with my Soul mind, you have no need for that big brain. My Soul mind would be your flow through guidance in your mortal and immortal affairs as one mind. Thus you have no need for what you have temporarily stored in your conscious beta mind as the truth of all simply flows through. This becomes so as we become one mind and my brother ceases to be heard."

"Ok, I am actually feeling that."

"Fine, then I am going to ask you as Soul Mind explain to me how this all works and why you are here."

At first there was a shred of panic. I wasn't asking questions anymore. But as I settled back into the heart, I knew that I had actually been answering my own questions all the time. I wasn't really out of mind, I was in it! Funny thing was, we both knew this was so. In truth I had always been talking to myself but I had to realize this my own way. It was like a current that turned on the light. The words began to flow.

"We came here to experience the world of a lower form, namely a body. We came here as partners to expand the Greater Mind of the Creator. The community of humanity as a cell in the bigger body was created to provide a school for the Souls who chose to come here to expand the Greater Consciousness. The task was to experience the wonders of this world in a lower form of physical vibration and learn to walk before the Creator to become perfect."

"The means of evolution and expression would be through the creation of a Life Plan Consciousness that would be played out in the school as an Earth Game. This plan would be created by free will of the Soul and its Soul Family with a Spirit Guide attuned to the means of holographic representation of the reality to be engaged in. This life plan would engage the Soul Family in a contractual plan to build a complex network of life pathways that would include the players, events, environments, exit points, triggers of awakening, and all of the details as required from birth to death that would support the learning of lessons, the development of virtues, and the resolution of karmic needs if so desired. Such a Life Plan would be loaded into the Earth Game Consciousness that would provide the means of its expression being limited to the beliefs of that group consciousness, yet allowing the evolution beyond that consciousness."

"The design of the Life Plan to be played out within the constructs and rules of the Earth Game would provide an infinite variety of life paths, situations, events, people and lessons that would be available at choice points. These choice points would be taken by free will of the lower mind through thoughts, belief, perceptions and emotions chosen at the time. The design of the Life Plan would include the Soul family constructed in such a way that all participating would have the opportunity to advance the Greater Consciousness beyond the state of the DNA blueprint. In so being designed the Life Plan would contain a lower material path and a higher spiritual path with many paths in between."

"Within the Life Plan and the Earth Game there would be the processes of divine order of the Greater Intelligence of the Creator Mind, purpose and growth of all life forms so interacting with each other so as to survive and evolve according to their designs. Each energy that would be given life through the breath of spirit would behave according to the evolving blueprints of DNA, reflecting the sum total of the evolving life form. As part of the Soul's purpose, the Earth Game would provide the means to evolve beyond that DNA blueprint holding the status of the evolution of Greater Consciousness."

"In order to allow the Game to unfold, the vessels so chosen in terms of form, characteristics and structure would be presented through the human brain and heart in holographic form so acquired depending on the nature of and timing of the astral configuration of the planet energies. This process of higher to lower creation would allow the lower form to congeal into the holographic reality."

"The nature of the Human Game would be to use the mental and emotional gifts to show feelings from experience (even love, horror) in the form of rational mental choices through the brain and inner emotional feelings through the heart. The rules of the Human Game engagement would be necessary to begin at a lower level of incarnation into matter and thus forget who they are and be a body. It would be necessary to believe hologram as real and allow the physics, emotions, and mental abilities of the lower form to engage in the holographic reality within the construct of the Life Plan, upon the stage of the Earth Game and to evolve according to choices of mental and emotional attributes. The means of engagement would be through numbers, words and communication."

"To undertake this task, you in the form of a Soul in a Light Body, took the job to grow and evolve within the scope of DNA which would provide you with a basic morphogenic template in lower form. This lower form evolved a brain and senses that had a primary function of creating a holograph projection of reality. Like the cells that are all individual complete mini humans, the holograph would be a mini world within a larger holograph created by the community of humans as a joint consciousness and a joint hologram. This joint hologram would form the basis for a joint belief system forming the global mindset within which the limitations of it would preside over the behavior. Imposed upon these would be the Universal hologram as a larger composite of divine intelligence which would dictate the morphogenic rules of order, process, purpose and growth to be played out in the holographic projection process of engagement."

"Thus, each Soul, as with cells, each being a part of the whole, yet themselves whole individuals, each could experience their own hologram of reality. Although the hologram of reality would appear to be on the outside, it would be on the inside, within the powerhouse of energetic singularity, the heart. In order to experience this, the brain would evolve response programs to be specifically concerned with developing survival habits within which the human form could prosper and feel the world of bliss. And so to experience this, the humanoid was given the power of thought, will and emotion to choose how it would be used to further this expansive mission. Its means of engagement would be through words, numbers and communication."

"In order to keep a connection to its own Whole and the Greater Intelligence that it was a part of, the Light Body (Soul and Higher Self) would overlay the human form and it would contain interfaces that would be the connectivity between the lower form and the higher Divine Intelligence from where it came. All would be centered on the heart as the seat of emotion where the Chakra system of subtle energies would interface to specific physical organs and functions but being sensitive to the cosmic signals that would allow the use and expansion of higher abilities. This system would interface with all of the light body energy systems of auras, meridians, chakras, and various energy vortexes. All would be centered on the heart energy system where the center of all would reside."

"The second interface would be through the pineal brain and the midbrain that could respond outside of time and space being a direct connection to the Soul mind and the greater consciousness of Source."

"Because the nature of the reality would be to create holograms of reality, the process of it so doing would be made of the quantum energy which in its primary form is not matter congealed into particles but in the form of waves and vibrational patterns. Thus the Light body and its components would have to behave according to quantum laws, while that formed body and its reality would have to appear as lower vibration physical particles following a different form of physical laws. The interface between the two would be part quantum, and part perceived as physical illusion. Thus the midbrain and heart would contain such interfaces but appear to be physical. The greater connector would be the consciousness which was the mind divided into self consciousness, consciousness and subconsciousness which would be interfaces as the quantum connection."

"The responsibilities and processes of these would be to first provide a rapid adaptation of the human vessel to its environment through the subconscious and the brain. This stage would bring an awareness of its perceived reality so as to evolve, adapt the human vessel to this perception of reality. Drawing from its first physical layers as DNA blueprints, the human vessel through the physical brain and subconscious, could draw on instincts to quickly adapt to its environment in an interactive stimuli-response system."

"Then at a specific age, the vessel would enter the awareness of its lower self. Here it would enter the second evolutionary stage to bring on the self consciousness that would develop the intelligence of self uniqueness and self pursuit of joy within the growing human vessel in relation to its perceived environment. This would engage free will, discernment, intelligence and ego as centered in the brain. The free will would allow the thoughts, perceptions and emotions to be chosen. Here new survival systems of adaptation and self growth would be built upon the first stage of development. Through this period, new skills, habits and abilities would be developed to create a uniqueness of self, centered on the self-consciousness."

"Having formed the second stage platform, the third and subsequent stages of evolution would be to open to its spiritual connection in the quantum through the awareness of the Astral body. This particular pursuit could only be achieved by being in a sea of love that, as its Higher Self as the Light Body, the Divine Intelligence and the quantum sea of infinite possibilities was made up of. It would require a shift from the ego-brain to the heart-brain into the energetic realm, thus opening an awareness, the Higher Self of Light Body. If this shift to the awareness of the Astral Body did not occur, the individual would remain in the ego-brain limited physical environment."

"At the center of the system would sit the means of creating matter from non matter as a torroid centered on the heart. This would reflect the translation of non matter light waves into matter as particles so projected in the personal holographic plate within each vessel, but part of the whole. And so various vortexes and torroids would project from and contain the body as itself a holographic projection. In order to shape realty, the human would have the power to choose using free will and to create within the laws so set upon the reality created. It would have the ability to learn how to change its holographic reality once a level of maturity was reached, that being total awareness of Higher Self and the Soul-Light Body."

"To give the human the ability to create reality, the energetic system of chakras with its vortexes of congealing and attraction were provided to create, interface and receive energies that would be created as packets of energy signatures projected into the quantum sea. These chakra centers would allow the transmutation of energy from above to below through thought, vision, words (above), emotion as balance, and intent, relations, and matter (below). Each of these would be an energy signature that would be projected like a funnel out into the local energetic heart field so as to attract energies of likeness into the field. At the same time the energies from outside the field could be drawn in as waves to spiral in concentrating to congeal into matter by way of entanglement and collapsing to create the reality so projected upon the individual holographic plate inside but yet part of the whole. This process would not work unless the interface between the Light Body and the Human Body was entrenched in its belief system and the awareness of its quantum essence was known, as well as beingness within the sea of its basic make up of the love vibration."

"This level of maturity was conditional upon holding the human vessel in terms of both body and mind in the quantum sea of love, centered on the heart, the body commanded by the heart-brain and the midbrain. This process was not only contingent upon letting go of the perceived reality so created as an illusion, but living within that reality in alignment with that higher wave length frequency so created as love and bliss. This would mean that in order to achieve this status, the self-consciousness and consciousness would have to be set aside in a continuous behavior of lower self (physical reality illusion) in order to be one with its Higher Self within the quantum space of love vibrations."

"Otherwise, the lower form would be unknowing to how its reality was created and it would live in its lower self and form, not able to express properly through its higher form. It would be subject to the lower physical laws and be held captive within its self-consciousness and have little to say about proactively changing its reality. And although it would in truth be creating its reality, it would not know how to create outside of the time and space limitations not existent in the quantum space from which it came and from where it became what it is as a perfection of love. This lower life would not be able to draw upon the higher vibrational instincts, abilities so provided in the brain, chakras and DNA, or the knowing and truths within the Light Body memory fields."

"In order to draw upon these knowing and truths of a Higher Self, it would be through a conduit of communication through a field of love, forgiveness, and compassion. Otherwise the field cannot listen because it is like a radio tuner that if not set at the right frequency, it simply cannot be received. Central to this is that this channel cannot open when there is some hidden agenda or ulterior motive involved typically centered in the ego-brain dominant from the second stage of human evolution. Through design of the heart, and its central power of love emotion, when compassion and love of human energy would be enfolded by strong emotion of joy or bliss, it would add to the strength of the field channel as in superposition of waves. In this respect, prayer that would be the traditional way of opening communications to the Divine Intelligence, is simply not heard when it has no energy from the heart."

"This would not mean that the human could not manifest reality from within the scope of the lower form of human; the universal laws of Karma, Cause and Effect and the Law of Attraction are at work regardless of whether the heart, love, or positive well being is in the field of creation. Even stuck in the second stage of evolution, the human could follow the traditional path of creating things and reality by making or constructing according to the limitations of the group consciousness and the prevailing rules of material science. Here where emotion is attached there would be a tendency to attract likeness through the same system. In the case of by-passing this traditional route and bending this reality as in the healing miracles and rapid creation of reality, a level of love based spiritual maturity would be required to take responsibility and to open the channel."

"In order to create a new reality within the scope of a higher soul mind, karma would need to be cleansed from the soul through a partnership with the lower mind. This process would always be an open pathway in a Life Plan to be activated through unconditional love, forgiveness and compassion."

"What would be the case of human stuck in stage three would be default creation and random success of such things as miracles because the human would not have yet elevated above the level of the conscious mind and the physical brain. To fall into default of the life plan would also fall into the limitations of the global consciousness and the prevailing rules of material order. And by default, the lessons of other lives would have not taken the awareness to a higher understanding self, allowing the past to influence the future, creating a reality by default."

"The brain in its primary design has a chore to learn survival within the hologram that it learns to create. This evolves from instincts to survive at the Delta and Theta level to where there is self consciousness at the age of 6. This brings about a selfness or ego and the ability to think and choose the survival programs that are stored in the subconscious. The evolution, if not continued focuses on selfish behavior patterns which minimize the programming into consciousness so the individual falls back to survival mode with the added ego intellect to drive its purposes and reality."

"The next evolution, which can be curtailed if the Lower Self is dominant, is the heart brain and the evolution to the love based sea of the quantum. Although the brain and consciousness allow one to open this path by way of free will, once the ego brain is entrenched and a lower form belief system is embedded, the means of overcoming this becomes more and more difficult, and the motivation and understanding becomes more and more remote."

"By way of preplanning a Near Death Experience, or triggered awareness by way of design of Divine Intelligence, a window would become available for the consciousness dominated by the second stage ego-brain could look at itself after letting go of its mortal lower self and facing its higher Light Body. Similarly, the process of Out Of Body would allow a portal to open to this higher knowledge at any time. Here the stages can be overcome because the reality of the human being is something else than a body, as the Light Body-Being of pure divine consciousness. This becomes a stark reality as does the encounter with the Higher Being in that sea of love. Re entry into the body can have spectacular reprogramming consequences to change reality and the meaning of life, but as old habits may be deep, various triggers can reconstitute old programs and habits to undo what was a miracle. This is also so in a miracle healing where if the old programs and memories are chosen to come into awareness and consciousness, they can undo what has been done."

"Just as a prayer cannot be heard if it is not in the morphic field of love, so is the subtle energy field of quantum not opened until an awareness is brought into consciousness. Similarly, the access into the quantum field for the purpose of direct creation and manifestation of reality is inaccessible until the spiritual awareness of the true self is embraced."

"By design, the total human bodies (physical and light energy) combine physical and quantum through the holographic reality. Understanding the quantum nature part of us we can say that the heart torroid field would represent the center of the zeropoint quantum field. Here in the Above to Below causal process is where the mind energies like thoughts, images, words from consciousness are infused down into heart to draw from the vortexes positioned at each chakra the possibilities from the quantum field outside to bring it into reality as the lower chakras congeal the possibilities into reality. This place of the heart-mind as the point of all creation within us as the signature of emotion is the catalyst. It is the place of no-thing, in the quantum field of infinite possibilities which must be entered into in some way in order to truly take control of the creation process that makes imagination and reality one consciousness. It cannot be done from the big brain-mind which is responsible for the lower binary plane of 3D."

"The portal to the Soul mind and the brain is through the midbrain that uses the energies of thoughts, images, words and numbers to create and maintain and evolve reality through a means of soul intelligence of mental powers."

"Just like the brain has a local and a nonlocal data base which reflects the whole, so does the brain have a local and a nonlocal illusion of reality. This reality becomes a holographic plate projection inside which operates from the midbrain central processor much like all of the automatic internal and external survival processes that become saved into the subconscious quantum mind."

"Under the first two phases of human evolution this automatic process uses all sensory equipment, including unbeknown to the second stage human, the higher automatic sensing abilities of the Light body. These simply operate on auto pilot in a stimuli-response mode to develop behavior patterns and the holographic projection of reality."

"Upon opening to the third and fourth stages of Higher Self awareness from the heart mind-brain and the midbrain, the new entry point into the zeropoint quantum fields of infinite possibilities opens. Thus when this is engaged in, the higher abilities begin to open so that changing the holographic realty opens. Through design, one first brings forward a thought then creates a clear image in the mind's eye, then with the assistance of the mantra of words and heartfelt emotion to enfold the vision directs the downward causation to engage the process of subconscious reprogramming and then projecting it to a place of materialization on the internal holographic plate through the physical apparatus of the midbrain, nervous system and cells. A holographic image is thus created in a proactive mode the same way a holographic image is created with beams of light that are split, reflected and converged again. It is whatever you see clearly that your brain understands and has meaning for or memory of. It is your brain that does the final work as a material representation by retrieving what it knows and what cosmic rules apply in the material representation. It retrieves information given by the subconscious as directed from the Higher self or Soul and the cosmic rule simply knows what it is. The midbrain is now driven to entangle this new reality into the existing reality."

"The reality to the midbrain is taken from the deriving language of words that represent reality, processes and evolution governed by the morphogenesis of divine order. These reflected in DNA as the blueprint for all life would contain all processes of all things and respond to the words and vibrations as the communication language as so instigated by the Soul mind."

"This process of evolution to full potential of the DNA calls for the letting go of the current lower reality, entering the space of total silence and being in the heart mind of pure love. Here is where the gateway to the quantum soup of infinite possibilities exists and is the place of residency of the Soul and the Higher Self where the mind of pure consciousness and thought are engaged to effect downward causation. It is where the truth of self rises above illusion of the Game and the limitations of the Earth Game Consciousness."

"This means that the Divine Soul Mind totally unencumbered by the lower reality of physicality must be the total agent of the image of some object, event, situation that is simply created in the mind's eye as a clear image formed from infinite possibilities. As this image that reflects a new possibility is surcharged by emotion of joy and gratitude for its engagement and completion, it carries with it the instructions to subconscious and the brain to adjust the hologram in accordance with the programs in DNA for internal reconstruction or the programs of natural order for external reconstruction of reality."

"Our design is to discern through the mental body what is truth – so reflected through the midbrain quantum mind of the Soul, and use feeling and emotion through the emotional body to discern what is truth – so reflected through the heart mind and physical body. This is the key to creating the signatures in the brain and in the quantum field. As these emotions become stronger, or are reinforced by continued action and mantric repetition within the higher planes the appropriate physical holographic mechanisms as directed to the brain begin the process of transformation thereby adjusting physicality to meet the new reality. This occurs by way of direct manifestation or by way of attracting the like signatures that exist as potentialities within the quantum field and bringing these into the projected holographic reality."

"This occurs from the quantum field, from a wave form to an atomic form as the electrons arrange themselves into the image which is the higher consciousness choosing a new possibility from the no-thing. From above, this is truly the process of mind over matter rather than the process now accepting limiting creatorship of matter over mind. The resultant holographic materialization is conducted by the human brain that takes the directives from the higher vibratory mind of consciousness to create the hologram of the external world, or to instigate the appropriate systems internally to the physical body to meet the requirements of this higher command."

"It is all just a holographic movie that can be changed by the Soul as Writer and Director. And who is that Director as the Divine Programmer? Us. You and me as a melded mind of pure consciousness being one mind. The process of programming is not by way of Ed but through us as One."

"So Ed are you going to now enjoy the movie?"

"Immensely!"

24

GENESIS – WHICH ONE?

Revelation, Resurrection, Rapture, Armageddon. Which way do you prefer to become your game of illusion?

IS THERE SOME DIVINE PLAN?

"Superplacebo, you have mentioned a few times that there are many changes in the air and that there is an overall Life Plan for humanity. It must have to do with these Life Plans that bigger entities like the planets have. Certainly the bible code seems to say that a creator force has some say in creating a plan, even for planet earth and the global evolution of consciousness. Is that true?"

"Indeed. Now I am going to bring to you a bit of news that reflects the enormous wave that dominates what you are seeing as New Earth energies. It's a prophesy that has the bottom line of all the millions of opinions of what is happening and what was meant to happen with regard to this End Time and The Grand Alignment and the big cycle of 26,000 years. We saw some of this as an option of choice within the Bible Code. It is not a belief system written by any leaders. It is like a melding of consciousness that converges from billions of points of view towards a common consensus."

"Is this about this new age stuff about ascension?"

"Yes. But understand that this is a mass union of belief and purpose is not led by anyone, or any corporation. It is a shifting in consciousness and awareness that is occurring by itself naturally. This is a divine plan to allow Gaia (Gaia is Mother Nature) and Earth to ascend. To ascend means to rise in vibration so as to live in a body form without having to die - as your eternal self as you have come to know as your Soul mind. It is prophesized for this special time."

"I understand that then I as a mortal humanoid then have full awareness, never forget and fully open DNA. So why can't this just happen by choice and intent?'

"It can but the current vehicle that brings spiritual to astral and then to lower form needs to increase its light quotient and get rid of my brother's 12 rules before it can effectively house this greater consciousness. There has to be some evolution of the physical vessel for that to take place."

"So this is something of a prophesy in Gaia's Life plan?"

"And other planets that shower your minds with what is astrological tendencies, adjustments and energies that effect physical, mental and even physiological behaviors in accordance with the options of the life plan, and your astral structure. You see Gaia has her own plan of evolution and she is a different entity that is providing a school for those beings which are here to evolve and learn. In her plan it is an option to choose a path that allows her to ascend with greater light just as you have the same choices."

"But isn't she somewhat dependant on the global consciousness?"

"Yes but that does not prevent her choice. She is like a mother that gives birth to and provides for her children. What she eventually chooses may not be the same as her children although her choice may be influenced by them. It provides a choice for her residents. And if you can understand that this reality is a holographic illusion then you can perhaps imagine that their may be a split to accommodate more light or less light."

"You mean a split in reality?"

"You are in a split of reality now. What if for many it became a more real reality?"

"Is this about the transformation through the biblical version of Genesis and the Book of Revelations?"

"Yes and there endless scenarios describing Revelation, Rapture, Resurrection and Armageddon. These have been subjected to endless interpretations thanks to your brother. Most of these are anything than love, peace and harmony or forgiveness. It is about God taking vengeance on sinners and the return of the messiah to choose the good guys and destroy the bad guys that are terrible sinners."

"The Plan is and always was to allow all that choose to ascend so as to bring the aspect of the God Self to lower form; to experience and to expand the joy of its wonder. As this story goes, this opportunity has occurred before and the Earthling blew it three times. This time it is different in that it is Gaia that is ascending; the question is: *what Earthlings are on board the ride this time?* At this point it is the time of Gaia and Earth's ascension is to be completed with the alignment of galactic center which is her origin. She and Earth have offered themselves in sacrifice to be the body and form of the Great Experiment of souls to bring all things upon her and connected to her into the evolution of spirit. It is her destiny and it is her members of the Cosmic Council (the planets that the Mayas deemed as gods) that assist in this as they pour their love and their aspects of unique vibrations upon her and all things upon her."

"This has to do with the Mayan prophesies about 2012 that never happened."

"It was the many interpretations that looked for doom and destruction, and instant ascension that did not happen. The Mayans were able to fast forward into the time of Gaia's life plan and see the prophesy of no time occurring as a point of evolution at the end of the Mayan long count. That occurred and you may have seen a shifting in awareness and consciousness quite dramatic in the last years. Of course my brother has been active in interpreting many crazy predictions about this. It was never the intent to have catastrophic events and great drama at 2012. It is an evolutionary process that began. It may take many Earth years like whole generations to actually transmute the shift."

"But the Divine Plan has been for humanity to be allowed to ascend with her by their own free will. It is a choice to ascend and to recognize the power of love, and open to the Soul mind, right?"

"Yes, the overall choice for Gaia's humanity was to be determined by the overall vibration of Earth and her inhabitants. It had to reach a certain threshold and so it did during the period referred to as the Harmonic Convergence of 1987. The question was whether humanity could earn this right of ascension that Gaia was to engage in regardless. Otherwise, Gaia would ascend by herself. And so it trigged the Divine Plan which originally was to place within the design of all, the knowing of the God Self and the attributes of Creator and Creation. It would be there in all equally, and placed as a spark of quest of Self and Home as accessed through the heart, the seat and power of the Divine Self. It was the time of the Harmonic Convergence that showed humanity had earned this right. In other words if Earthlings were picking up the messages being inducted into consciousness in sufficient numbers, then the opportunity would allow the unfoldment."

"But the last 100 years has been the most destructive and violent."

"It is so and the desperation of these actions has contributed to global consciousness that this is not right. There has been a lesson. And what is coming to light is the manipulative power of the few to engage the many in destruction."

"This must have been encoded in DNA."

"Yes, it is encoded within the DNA, placed within each, in a place where it could never be lost. It would be within each heart as the gateway to find the way to this truth and to allow this gate to open to bring it forward into consciousness. It is the Divine Plan to allow each and all to grow, evolve and express the joy of love and to receive love and bliss. In return one could learn to ascend in form and to make greater and expand the totality of love of the Creator as the supreme force of all that is. It is the Divine Plan to allow all possibilities in all beings equally and to create by free will that which they desire to attain joy. The process would be first in thought above, then to form material below, all released by the essence of pure unconditional love - the glue of all that is."

"Ok, I get this now. The Divine Plan is to allow creation with the tools of love through the gateway of the heart. In our diagram it is the portal at the top that every Earthling has an opportunity to go through like in a Near Death Experience without dying where you meet your Maker and yourself as Soul. So regardless of whether humanity has shown its worthiness in love, bad good or indifferent the gateway of unconditional forgiveness temporarily opens. It is this Divine Plan that is now manifesting upon Gaia and Earth, into new form in wondrous expansion of the universe which is God's mind. But if your brother is the turkey that skewed this whole thing how can there actually be a Life Plan?"

"That is an interesting question. Remember, in the grand scheme of things there is only the great illusion of reality where there is no judgment. Yes, there is a plan and my brother had a job to do in this plan. He was here to provide the options which so many have chosen to experience and express within. It is all a choice as to how individuals walk along the paths of life. You see these choices of the dark or light side. They all converge to the same place eventually above the astral plane."

"Ok, no one has made us listen to him. We chose it and so created the norm consciousness. Can we discuss this idea of evil later? Is this how the story of Genesis got distorted too?"

"Indeed, you are becoming very perceptive and intuitive. There is indeed much truth within the writings. So let us engage in some of the truth."

THE NEW EARTH GENESIS II

"OK. So there is some truth to what is prophesized in Revelations? You say the Mayans knew the truth, people just misinterpreted it. Is the same true of the original bibles?"

"For the purpose of explaining, let us call what we have seen as the evolution of how all of your brothers and sisters have lived upon it. It has been a time when the spirit was allowed to be under dominion of the egos, and so it has been. Let us call that Old Earth."

"No kidding, a fall from grace down to two strands of DNA!"

"Now you are seeing that humanity is bringing forward this spirit which has been quietly placed within them. It is a time to consider the New Genesis of New Earth as the plan is to conceive and give birth to it. It is a time that your brothers and sisters have earned their rights to know of themselves. This time we will allow the spirit to come forward in those that have chosen and New Earth can be once again a perfect world that *will be inhabited by the ones who choose. This Genesis will be formed from the consciousness of those brothers and sisters that awaken, and so they will be presented with the gift of ascension into the New Earth.*"

"For the billions that already believe in Genesis, or some form of it, such a proposal from God – meaning the real one of Love - this should not be difficult. What is different about this new version of Genesis is that it is totally based upon your Higher Beings, not the egos as the little gods within each of you."

"If you can see what is happening on the Earth, there is an acceleration to the no time midbrain living in the present moments. That is simply the Mayan prophesy that time will end. Not on 21st of December 2012 but that is the marker that begins the shift of consciousness. Let me lay upon you some insight to the New Earth that is forming in the 4D ethers of consciousness as a result of the shift during these End Times. Through the seeding of the new unity consciousness of the last wave the seeding by way of pure intent and love, humanity are planting into the ethers of pure love the blueprint and construct for the New Earth. It is here the concept of form and purpose is created that precedes the conception which through the purity of divine male and female are conceived into creation."

"This is all about planetary alignments?"

"Yes, of course. Understand that these planets that have all been 'gods' in ancient traditions are cycling and sending vibrations that effect the chakras depending upon the individual makeup of the human and the time of birth. These characteristics vibrate with and are influenced by these subtle vibrations. As they are all part of Gaia's Life Plan. It should not be surprising to believe they are all part of the transition and evolution."

"So this is about the intent of unity consciousness; the pure New Earth as a 5D concept of intent of pure consciousness, as the melding of physical purity; the alignment of cosmic forces and planets; and the overlay of the purity of love manifestation of that which is heaven. This is the concept like Genesis that is conceived in the joint minds and is birthed as an egg of union of male and female as equal divine energies."

"Yes, and this seeding of New Earth then follows the process of transitioning into temporary energy of 4D which may be likened to the gestation of the New Earth. It is the formation or congealing into 4D of the model of New Earth, ready to receive its inhabitants that have so chosen to evolve through the final stage of evolution from 3D to 5D for them and from 4D to 3D for New Earth."

"And this began in 2012?"

"During the year 2012 the shift of the process of transformation into 3D began occurring as the cosmic forces of ascension showered upon those chosen to move with Gaia, and Gaia herself. These particular frequencies began acting as triggers to activate the DNA antenna and receivers. This new form, like the chrysalis opening, would begin to show itself more and more to those aware of it. It would then begin to congeal into the parallel hologram of New Earth. And so the 3D representation of the hologram would be born at the time of the great alignment of Dec 21, 2012, in preparation for the great resurrection of the New Earth. It would be the birth of no time."

"It must be well underway by now in 2016."

"Yes, but this is not an instant realization. Even you are still struggling with this and certainly at some point those who have chosen to be part of New Earth will see it clearly, and walk between both realities. The struggle of these two realities is what Armageddon is all about. Then with the cosmic configuration of forces and planets, when the New Earth has shifted from the 5D concept, to 4D conception to manifestation and creation in 3D reality, it will be ready to accept souls who have chosen to move into that reality. Of course by that time the Great Revelation (Time of Choosing) and the Great Resurrection (Time of Transformation of Ascension) will have readied those for the shift to the New Earth reality."

"You are using the old genesis terms."

"Yes, it is the Time of Transformation that physicality begins to congeal into new form, both for Gaia, the New Earth, and humanity that chooses to ascend with her. The separation of Old and New Earth will become a conscious reality and the final formation will be after the Earth, like humanity, has been gifted the cosmic forces and overlays that will be completed by the time of 3D birth. From then on, again, like in a newborn child, the configuration of the stars, the contracts each are creating now, and the movements of the cosmic gods of creation will guide the evolution of the New Earth. And the new beings linked between realities of 3D-5D will emerge, then evolve into the next age of unconditional love over 26,000 years, spilling their presence into the Galaxies."

"It is certainly obvious that the contrast between Dark and Light is becoming more and more. If one should look around now, at this juncture in time, the undeniable truth of the world leaders being placed on the spotlight for their behaviors cannot be ignored."

"It is because changes are occurring that demand responsibility and transparency. Humanity has simply accepted being dual in nature - part good, part bad. It is the way we have been taught and it is the way the leaders behave. The familiar behavior of being good until someone rubs you the wrong way, or offering a smidgen of kindness to a poor soul absolving all your wrongs, or loving and protecting your close family but taking advantage of those that are not, are all too familiar traits of this duality. It is the same duality between god and Satan. It is what humanity has accepted as their belief and hence it is what that unit of consciousness attracts consciously and unconsciously."

"Is that duality really shifting in favor of the goodness?"

"You can see the changes if you look around you into the means of communication as the Internet. There are millions shifting. At this point the reality of the New Earth is just in imaginations. But this is the process of how the new mind will eventually create the new global consciousness for New Earth."

THEME OF PREVAILING CONSCIOUSNESS

"But the prevailing consciousness is still the Old Earth Genesis and Revelations."

"Let us quickly summarize the old story of Revelations. When you finally get to the end of the old biblical story, to the final Book of Revelation, when the ascended Christ comes back, the story which is presented imposes an automatic policing system of threat and destruction for mankind. And it is Christ, the Son of God - the one that helped his Dad create the Old Earth that bears the warning about the End Times. In this prophesy, it is my brother as Satan that will be crushed (20:7) and there will be a final Judgment day (20:11); there will be a new heaven on Earth (21:1) where a new Jerusalem will rise (21:9) and when the new Savior comes he will be swift to judge if you are not in the proper side of the sinner accounting ledger (22:7) that is within the Time of the End (22:10). It is this threat that polices the believers through fear of each not being worthy and this is the major theme in the vast writings."

"It is all about fear of being a sinner and being destroyed."

"It is the chosen interpretation because there are the power roles that have changed the writings to exert power and dominion over others. For, like the fickle ways of perception, within these writings is hidden a truth in plain sight. And it is one that has and still vibrates with much of humanity, especially in this time. For even though the bible is filled with the duality and polarity, it still contains the story of this man called Christ who came down to prophesize the Revelation of End Time. It has been conveyed as the end of time, not when time ends with the understanding of living in NOW. The story, part contrived, part truth does, regardless of edition reflect a consciousness of love and peace, despite the conclusion that it is written with a possible contrived mortal purpose of a manifesto of dominion and vengeance over the sinful creatures. It draws out a theme that this Christ, who was deemed a Prophet or the Son of God later, reflected a consciousness so many people quietly and inherently would like to believe in - a New Earth of peace and love."

"I guess you could say that it is this aspect of the stories, despite the motivations of their creation that in all due regards to the biblical system, has kept this Christ spark alive in the story of Christ or Allah, or whatever. And regardless of whether he was deemed as a prophet, Messiah, Son of God or whatever, the legend carries an underlying energy of something that is wanting in all - like an encoding within the essence of humanity; their DNA."

"Precisely. It is all part of the plan of awakening. Even though the four gospels upon which the New Testament was based on were written between 75 and 100 years after Christ, by unknown authors, and are conflictive in their stories, in essence, it is true that Christ was indeed a very unusual fellow. Not only was he capable of creating some very unusual miracles, he was responsible for showing a new way of thought - that of being aligned with the real God of truth and love, and we all are Sons and Daughters of God. It is this that is surfacing in these times. And for what it is worth, he is responsible for a consciousness, a way of thinking and living that is parallel to this revolution of thought surfacing during these current times."

"Many now call this the Christ Consciousness. The human mind has spiritual currents running through its thought streams. These streams contain vital information from Spirit that is highly valuable to humans. Spirit is the source of everything TRUE, BEAUTIFUL, and GOOD and conveys these ideals through the human mind that intersect with a person's beliefs, helping the individual ascend into the higher information that uplifts and improves the quality of life. At this time all this is just a feeling that is gaining momentum and no one looks for proof. Faith and trust will create the shift in reality that will follow. It is all peace, love, harmony, forgiveness and without judgment."

"I can see that now. In human life, spiritual growth is achieved by aligning with these spiritual currents that come from both the personality and mind of spirit by intellectual assent and emotional devotion. Soul mind of heart is the growing human recognition and blending of the human evolutionary (or ego) mind with the Divine Mind and the Divine personality that is the source of human happiness and fulfillment. This awareness accrues over time within the consciousness of human thinking when intention, attention, and openness is focused on knowing who and what is that heart-soul mind state of being - that higher mindedness of enlightenment."

"Ok, can we go back to this New Earth Old Earth thing and Genesis? The prophesies such as Revelations were written suspiciously like the writers knew something about the turn of the Ages. And it is written like they had a plan called the New World Order, not New Earth. So far, humanity has accepted this plan and we are at the final moments of its unfolding, as has been written here."

"Indeed, there is a Life Plan choice that follows a New World Order. And it may be so, but it would be upon Old Earth, not New Earth. Remember there are many lives and parallel dimensions. At this point in your time line, there are the two opposing dualistic plans of light and dark in this time of the new century."

NEW RAPTURE, REVELATION AND RESURRECTION

"So now you have been given the dark side of this plan because this is the preferred choice. These plans and prophesies have been hidden in plain view for centuries and they have been integrated into many belief systems on the Old Earth. That is perhaps why it has unfolded the way it has; because humanity believes and follows what they are told and that, in itself, is the energy that is brought forward into humanity's reality. But the new plan is evolving and it reflects the shifting no-time consciousness of the midbrain."

"I would certainly agree that the consciousness in the last 12 years has been shifting from Religious to Spiritual ways of earthly expression. This particular time has taken on the name of the End Times, hasn't it?"

"Yes, whether it is religion, New Age, or whatever, there is an absolute preponderance of information about the End Times. What are they? It's a time when humanity kisses their dear asses goodbye if they have not been good and have not taken their blue pills given by the church and your brother Supernocebo to give faithful obedience. These pills are received from the Vatican and other such institutions in return for your sins symbolizing your obedience, service, faith, and trust."

"Yes. The things that are supposedly going to happen during these End Times are pretty impressive. Cataclysmic events, final battles with Satan, self destruction by war and nuclear means; astronomical alignments that pour rays of destruction, climatic shifts, polar shifts, magnetic reversal, global flooding, blah, blah, blah. It's the gods finally having their fill of man who is the master of self destruction and teaching them a serious lesson this time."

NEW END TIME OF REVELATION

"So what does this New Earth plan and this new consciousness movement suggest?"

"Well, let us call this a Divine Plan for lack of a better description. It is unfolding right before us and has never happened this way before in the Earth history. This End Time is between the turn of the century and 2012. This is so as it has to do with various cosmic forces and planetary alignments that happen once in 26,000 years. These are forces that influence consciousness, and hence behavior. Of course everyone has a choice as to whether they let this new consciousness into their awareness to create new behavior. Needless to say, you have free will and choice to decide, just like you decide to eat the blue pills."

"What is the New Earth version of Revelation?"

"Revelation is indeed the revealing or disclosing, or making something obvious through active or passive communication with supernatural and divine entities. This time, the Revelation originates directly from the Source. Yes, directly to you and into your personal consciousness, not through anyone else. It is because we are all God, as Christ taught. So it is we that are implementing this new plan. There are no middle men to tell you what the Word of God is because you begin to understand that it is you that is the chosen one already privy to the truth of God."

"So there are no chosen ones after a big meeting deciding to remove all Christians from the Earth, to protect them. This Rapture is simply your own choice when you understand that you are something else than what you have been told to believe as a mortal human. So some chosen one will not snatch you out of harm's way if you have been good. It is you that simply decides a new way. For under this story good and bad are judgments and love cannot and does not judge. Thus, there is no judgment. It's like a mother who truly loves her kid; regardless of what the little one does, she loves him and does not judge. It is the other people who judge and may force her to action - the consciousness of others prevails."

"So like I am learning now, the goodies you get through Revelation are indeed the revealing or disclosing of who you really are - an aspect of God, an eternal being borrowing a body to experience a time slice on Earth. And this is where a common denominator of vibration fits in. You vibrate higher and higher, releasing many of those miraculous abilities that DNA hold quietly - especially the paranormal ones.

"Yes, You can look at this as a mass revealing of whoever your mind knows is a higher order – Soul, Jesus, God, Allah, Superplacebo, whatever, through the consciousness shift. But it is *not* Jesus suddenly appearing. It is the Time of Revelation when the *knowing* of this, and in many cases, the *showing* of this - as he did - is revealed. It is about attaining a higher expression of your Soul Mind through You as a piece of Source which is everything as One, living, laughing and loving in thought, word and deed."

"So we see that this Revelation is the revealing as being each of us and that the message now comes directly from Source and Soul as a wakeup call of rapture. And it is a revealing that there is no sin and that the heaven we seek is already within us as immortal, eternal aspects of whomever you want to believe created all this. So it is a call not to serve gods, or listen to other's interpretations of God's Word, but to BE God and know for yourself. The revealing is that you don't need gurus, bishops, meditators or the likes to tell you the secrets of heaven, being eternal and how to have a better life. It is simply the acceptance of who you are that is already living a life as a Spiritual entity borrowing a body to be within rather than a body looking for spirit outside of itself."

"Just as I am learning now with you. What about Resurrection?"

"It is not going to be disclosed by Jesus himself. It is *you* that is going to go through a Resurrection and all who so choose to believe this will resurrect themselves coming back to a re-life as the Second Coming of Christ. It is not one guy, it is all of you who are given this opportunity for your own coming!"

"What of those poor souls that do not want to believe or accept this? Is this Armageddon?"

"Consider which one? Guess what? It's the one you are in now where you are having a crappy life. The one that creates fear, conflict, with a drive of ego to survive and dominate. It is called the world of separation from who you are. For those that have not chosen to believe who they are, it is indeed being left in your own harm's way and guess what? Yes, Armageddon - End Times. You continue paying for your sins of hatred and separation and conflict and fear as you are doing right now through karma. It becomes a clear understanding of how *you* attract that which you create. It wasn't God that did this, it was you. It is you that attracts it by the energy you create; the big difference is that energy in the Old Earth will not be inflicted upon anyone else like it was in the old regime. And get this; through the End Times it will manifest itself to return faster and faster until it becomes instant."

"Wow. That is the true Armageddon where you create your own Hell at your own choosing, and of your own intensity. But this is supporting the Old Earth version. Is the fight with Mr. Devil in the cards here?"

"It sure is if you want to hold to the old ways of deception and greed that you want to inflict on others! Your fight is with yourself - the Devil is within you as to what the bibles portray as sin. And rapture? The only people that are going to get snatched out of their own devil's harm's way are the ones that choose to understand who they are - and the snatching is of their own accord."

"So this is not a big battle between Satan and the kings of the Earth as the end of the world dawns."

"It is a battle of your own mind, of who you are below or above. It is about your own conscious awareness and belief that you will do battle with. It is about the knowing that you will inflict upon your mortal being to create your own life. The battle of Armageddon is a battle of belief in yourself. Do you keep chewing the blue pills or not. Indirectly this is indeed a conscious choice of Heaven or Hell."

"That's a pretty simple choice is it not? Heaven or Hell?

"Perhaps not if you are stuck in the old Earth. Let me tell you about another over-used term of Crucifixion. In the End Times it is the process of crucifying what is Hell by leaving it behind and choosing Heaven. It is the death of the old in choice of the new. Even on Old Earth, everyone, yes everyone, has a choice of how (bad or good) they perceive any situation. And when you learn that what you perceive as you think, speak, feel and act upon brings upon you like energy, you may pay more attention to what you think and do. That is what the choice is all about. Instead of saying you believe what these religions and the Vatican and the leaders tell you, you say: *'Ok, I have had enough with this Old Earth and I want to live a life of unconditional love, peace and joy.'* And by acceptance, just like a commercial contract, it is so enacted by your intent. That simple act to believe differently can change your whole life. You must crucify you old self and let go of its ways."

"You have to crucify your brother as the ego, his need for power and dominion, polarity and conflict?"

"Yes. You may consider an interesting observation about this. One would ask is this just another dogma? Well, it certainly isn't written by God in an autographed hard cover. It is not on the evening news. And it certainly is not supported by any religion. And there are no leaders. But it is unfolding all around everyone at the same time if you have the eyes, ears and heart to open to this revelation."

"The lines of living force that are now all balancing and connecting are much like your own living lines of meridians and ley lines and juncture points within your living essence of 3D form. These project through Gaia and around Gaia, her body of physicality and out to her larger cosmic body, all connecting into the galaxies, all dimensions and universes within the mind of God. It is now so done and the rest will fall into place as the forces of ascension ignites the physicality of New Earth and new humanity."

"What you are saying is that the Genesis plan is true but there are two distinctly different interpretations. The Old Earth one has been the norm certainly supported by religion. The New Earth is an unfolding of heaven upon Old Earth emerging through consciousness. So there will be a split in the two?"

"That should not come as a surprise. You live multiple lives in multiple dimensions. It is simply the level of vibration and awareness as to how real is that reality. The process by which this unfolds after Dec 21, 2012 is similar to a process of frequency entrainment. The holograms of Old Earth of 3D meld into the hologram of New Earth that originates in the Consciousness in 5D. Although this process may seem beyond comprehension now, this will become more apparent by that time. In the process of this melding, New Earth is in 4D, awaiting the shift of Old Earth into the same dimension."

CARBON TO SILICON LIGHT BODY

But there is another process that you are here for and is a part of the greater plan. This is a unique expansion of light within the galaxy; a special option in the Gaia Life Plan."

"Whoaa! What is that?"

"It is to increase the light quotient within you to become a crystalline light body. The carbon based vessel is not able to hold much light. That is why the astral plane transforms to a carbon based human. The plan is to switch that to a silicon base rather than carbon."

"What does that mean? Does this mean if Silicon has a weight of 28, it reduces to 10 or Y in Hebrew and we get a new name of YHVY instead of YHVG?"

"That is a profound deduction. To change from a carbon based body to a silicon/crystalline based body structure supports the higher vibrational frequencies. Silicon/crystalline is located directly beneath carbon on the periodic table."

"Part of what the plan calls for is to institute the changes within the gravity field around earth as well as changes in the astral and electromagnetic field. When there are noticeable changes with Earth this is echoed in your physical bodies. The physical elements on earth are changing this supporting the idea of ascension within the physical body for each living being upon Earth. For this to happen, the physical cell structure is changing. Since there is change going on with each cell there will also be changes within each chakra. This is very important because it will allow even greater changes within each cell."

"Inside each physical cell it is becoming more weightless as the outside of each cell is developing an extra layer of electrons that are attracted to the cells through the spinning of the chakra/electrons. When the extra layer is built around each cell, it will have more electrons than protons. When this happens your cells will be able to spin and go into higher frequencies or dimensions. The magnetic resonance tuned into the cosmic soul family of Earth within each cell attracts these electrons until it is full and cannot receive any more electrons. This is the point where the complete cell changes into a crystalline cell, light, or even weightless energy."

"The human body is made up of various internal systems and organs, which essentially consist of tissues and membranes. These tissues contain a healthy percentage of carbon and hydro-carbons as their basic constituents. Your current bodies are said to be carbon-based because of the presence of such a high percentage of carbon."

"So what advantage is there for silicon?"

"Carbon is an amorphous element which doesn't allow the cells to hold much Light. In converting our present body into a Light body, these carbon based molecules undergo a major transmutation into a crystalline based molecules which can contain a lot of Light. Hence the Light body is also referred to as the crystalline body or silicon based body. This conversion is the first and major step where cells which are predominantly elliptical will change into a regular crystalline shape. Then various changes are initiated where the constituent carbon elements transmute into crystalline components gradually. The changes in the cell properties allow them to hold a lot more Light."

"How can that transformation happen?"

"You are made of carbon which has two orbits of electrons with four electrons in the outer shell. Silicon has three orbits of electrons with four electrons in the outer shell. To create silicon from carbon, new electrons must be introduced into the atom and the original electrons must be *excited* into the new orbit. Suppose new electrons flow into the atoms from the electromagnetic field of the Universe. As the energies coming onto Earth continue to increase vibrations a critical mass will be reached where the electromagnetic forces become strong enough to introduce electrons into the atom thereby exciting existing ones into new orbit."

"Is this to support the Light Body being a visible part of the anatomy?"

"The actual crystallization process we are talking about is this: Carbon life receives O_2 and exhales CO_2. Silicon life receives O_2 and exhales or radiates SiO_2 as pure crystal equivalent to quartz. Silicon is a semi conductor, and quartz is a natural transmitter capable of receiving and transmitting EM frequencies. So as the silicon body increases its vibration, it becomes luminescent, reflecting and refracting light. Then the auric field becomes highly charged creating a mini vortex – a spiral of white light."

"Wow! That is the Soul and our aura with all senses, memories intact separating out like our light bodies. The big difference here is that it is a transmuting process triggered by the cosmic alignments and the photons from the plan of the Greater Mind, right?"

"Yes. As a highly abundant element silicon has chemical properties similar to those of carbon and thus is an alternative to carbon as a basis for living organisms. But there are no silicon-based life forms on Earth, and yet silicon is 135 times more abundant than carbon on your planet. Silicon-oxygen bonds can withstand heat to around 600 K, and silicon-aluminum bonds to nearly 900 K. By contrast, carbon bonding of any type breaks down at such high temperatures, making carbon-based life impossible. This heat-resistant property of silicon is the main reason that silicone compounds are often used as industrial lubricants; even hot machinery runs smoothly with silicon-based grease."

"Jeez is this suggesting we are going to live in a more fiery earth?"

"No, it is to say your abilities in lower vibratory places open further and at the same time open to holding the light body, opening to the fullness of DNA and not having to forget who you are. In humans reproduction takes the form of amino acid pairings in DNA. This is the coding by which all organic life organizes its heretical information. Crystalline lattices form, or reproduce based on the atomic structure of the particular crystal molecule. Different molecular structures will form lattices of varying shapes and densities, just as varying (if not more) than the pairings of amino acids in organic life forms. These crystalline structures could be used as a means of coding for certain things. Reproduction, in the broadest sense, is a necessity born out of species with limited life spans. Organic structures are much harder to maintain in the long run because they require biological functions such as mitosis to maintain the integrity of those structures. Inorganic structures such as crystal lattices, however, do not require such a high level of maintenance. The energy required for a crystal structure to maintain integrity and molecular cohesion is much lower. If a life form can sustain itself for an indefinite amount of time then there is no need to reproduce."

"What? No sex?"

"Not the kind you are used to! The ability to communicate in biological terms involves the transmission of a sound or chemical signal which travels across a medium to a receiver where the information is processed. Communication in its simplest form is the ability to receive and transmit information. All crystal lattices have what's called a natural frequency. This is the frequency of a vibration that will resonate within the lattice. Also, when these crystalline molecules are charged they will vibrate at their particular natural frequency. If a wave of energy is projected at a crystal structure that contained lattices of varying natural frequencies, then such a structure could detect the presence of those certain frequencies by detecting which lattices were vibrating, and by the knowledge of the natural frequencies of those lattices, what the frequency was that was being transmitted. Furthermore if those structures were electromagnetically charged, then those lattices would vibrate (or transmit) at that frequency. That's basic communication. Silicon life would be devoid of peers, and the development of any kind of language would be unnecessary. How does that grab you?"

"It doesn't yet. How long will this take?"

"A physical change like this takes place over a long time and cannot be done within a couple of months. Actually this change of the carbon structure into crystalline based structure has been taking place and may take hundreds of years or many lifetimes to complete. The process should be completed as the time comes for the earth to ascend."

"What are the genetic changes?"

"Major changes happen at the genetic level. The cell as you know is the building block of all organisms, including the Human body. The main role of DNA is the long-term storage of information. It contains the instructions and blueprint to construct other cells and cell components. A very important step in transmuting the physical body into a Light body is the activation of the rest of DNA. When it becomes active, it results in the physical body exhibiting newer characteristics to invoke extraordinary capacities, healing powers and the ability to hold Light in the cells."

"I bet this process is what we have been discussing."

"Yes, it is in preparation for rapture. The first step starts with the purification and cleansing of the entire system. This happens mainly by the practice of meditations and by following the spiritual principles as you have determined in your daily living. You reject negativity at every level and make positive your thoughts and emotions. This is like your energy fund and involves overcoming all your negative traits such as anger, arrogance, and jealousy, accommodating and sharing with others and manifesting more love in your lives."

"And there is more. I can tell you that together we need to begin the process of healing the emotional wounds and karma that still affect us. If there are any hurts in us caused by past incidents or people, we need to let go of the resentments and grudges that we still hold, sometimes, without our attention. Clearing all these karmic blocks is very important since they come in the way of our progress. We need to introspect in order to recognize any aspect in us that is out of tune with the principles of Light. We should work on these shortcomings until we naturally align ourselves with all the positive divine qualities. This inner work is also referred to as Inner Healing. This is an important step that allows us to hold more Light in our system."

"Yes, that is true and that leads to the another step which is?"

"I would say that in the next step, the cells in our system begin to undergo transmutation. The old cells are gradually replaced with advanced new cells, thus allowing the body to hold more Light."

"Yes, once this process is sufficiently underway, the blood is gradually replaced by the 'Luminous Enzyme'. Along with this, the tubular light system will begin to take the place of the nervous system. This again increases the quantity of Light that your system can hold."

"Ok, by the time our cells morph and the blood and nerves are replaced with advanced systems, we will be able to hold sufficient quantity of Light in our system to activate our dormant faculties. All those faculties like telepathy and third eye, which we naturally posses but have become dormant will begin to get activated. Our Intuition will become very sharp, and with its help we'll be able to manifest many spiritual qualities in our living. We are getting in touch with our Soul mind. What then?"

"The new faculties which have been designed for your Light bodies will not become immediately active at this stage. For those faculties to become active, you need to totally convert into Light bodies. Since these gifts are being introduced this way for the first time in Creation, the incorporation and fine tuning will take at least 60-70 years after you convert into Light bodies."

"Then what happens?"

"By this time you have become very aware of the parallel New Earth and able to shift realities at will. Both will be real. For those who wish to inhabit the Old Earth reality, in the sixth phase, the size of your physical bodies begins to increase. The changes in your DNA will play a very important role in this stage. These changes will be triggered, controlled and monitored by the Light that you hold in our system. The increase in the body size will help you hold more Light, but mainly it helps to hold newer knowledge and energies that allow you to never forget."

"I take it that this DNA upgrade is after the full 100% of DNA becomes active so the God Code for human crystalline form changes to include silicon instead of carbon."

"Indeed! In the next phase, a new faculty will get installed in your abdomen region at the point of creation – Leydig gland. This faculty connects to the source of the individual Soul and draws more Light into the system, thus charging the system with more Light and energies. This faculty also tunes the system periodically, thus enabling it to experience more Light. In the next stage, the individual will have to focus on his spiritual practices. The techniques to be practiced and the areas where he has to focus will be communicated to him directly through his Intuition and contact with the higher beings. This phase is different for each individual, based on his spiritual condition and source."

"Until this stage, the individual will be consuming normal food for his sustenance. In this last phase, he trains himself to absorb Prana (energies from the Sun) directly from the food. This will be complemented by the corresponding faculties and systems of digestion in his system. The digestive system will begin to undergo a transformation to adjust to this change. With this process, he will be able to hold more light in his anatomical system."

"In many of the above stages, the processes start simultaneously and you do not wait for the previous one to stop for the next to begin. Some processes continue for longer periods. Together all these processes allow the cells and the body to hold more and more light until the entire physical body converts into a Light body."

"But do we have to wait for 60 years?"

"No, there are many that are well advanced as you are. These transformations will begin to show in 2016 in many. Many will transit into Light bodies in different batches and time periods. The total time for these individual processes to complete could be approximately 18-28 years. In this duration, the nature around you will also undergo drastic and finer changes to suit the conditions of the New Light age. In the process of transition from a physical body to a Light body, many of the internal systems and organs will also undergo a transmutation. The digestion, circulation, respiration, nervous and reproductive systems will change according to the new enhancements. Along with these the sense organs will also undergo a transformation, only when the physical bodies finally convert into Light bodies. By the time the final transformation occurs, the five senses will be replaced with their advanced counterparts all of which are resident in the higher bodies and DNA."

"There will not be any gradual transition in the Mind-Intellect-Spiritual bodies. The Mind will be replaced by a new Creator mind, which has enhanced mind matter, better perceptive capabilities and without any chakras. The intellect and spiritual body will also be enhanced accordingly. The Kundalini energy will be replaced with a new Kundalini energy, so do changes occur in the number of Nadis in the Vital body. The quantity of light in the Soul will also undergo a transition, with additional light being added to it from the Source."

"The transformation is also part of the Gaia plan. The new flora and fauna will also begin to flourish. These plants will gather Pranas from the Sun and in the form of special fruits which humans can consume and absorb for the sustenance of their Light bodies."

"The process of transmutation starts at the conscious level, with an individual making efforts to purify, balance and heal and follow the principles of Light. The rest of the processes occur at a level where an individual has no conscious control or influence. He can only sustain these processes by dedicated spiritual practices and by continuing to manifest positive qualities in his life. These two activities at the conscious and subtle levels go hand in hand in converting the physical body into a Light body."

"There are various other factors which play an important role in this conversion. The times we're living in is one of its kind with various alignments and conjunctions happening at cosmic levels. The huge galactic alignments and being within the Photon belt in alignment with completion of various cycles gives access to an enormous amount of spiritual energies."

"Has this happened before?"

"This is not the first time that a human body has been converted into a Light body. Mystics and Light workers have successfully converted into Light bodies, irrespective of the Age they've lived in. The inhabitants of Shambala live in a body which is almost similar to a Light body, so do the chiranjeevis on this Earth. These conversions were bi-directional, where the individual could revert back to his normal physical body at any time. The current transition which we're about to witness cannot be reversed, because we're moving into a permanent Light Age, hence the silicon crystalline body is a new process."

"So the choice of evolution beyond what is in DNA will be the new crystalline Light Body when experiencing the lower vibratory illusions. And there will be no forgetting as the Soul mind is driving the expression and reality? I cannot imagine what kind of reality that is."

A PLACE CALLED NEW EARTH

"So where does this all end?

"It is an infinite journey back to perfection as you shift through the higher planes and bodies above the Causal body."

"I don't understand. There is a whole progression forever?"

"Yes, always evolving and improving the whole at your own pace. Just because you have chosen to experience the fall from grace here, do not think this is all there is. Just like the trillions of cells in your body that you house, there are trillions of worlds, realities and dimensions to experience beyond this illusion. But I am now going to tell you about a special dimension that is out there where the Divine Mind plays its games."

"The Divine mind being like the next vibrational level above the Causal or Soul mind?"

"Yes. You will understand this when you totally merge with me. What is forming and it may take a lifetime or several to congeal, is in mythical writings. Something that has stuck like glue through all time are the stories of Hollow Earth, Shambala, Agartha, and Hyperborea; there are many. These have been places of subterranean worlds that represent the perfect world of Heaven. Even upon Earth itself there are remnants of the times such as the Golden Ages of Lemuria and Atlantis that once were based in times of unity, perfection and the love of one; highly spiritual in the civilization's essence. And as you now know, there are the extraterrestrial races that have contributed to your DNA. This is all stuck in your DNA looking to open."

"But aren't places like Agartha and Hollow Earth just myths."

"Remember most of your mythologies hold mere truth and fiction. They have just been misinterpreted and deleted from consciousness. It is not a myth for me. It is where I go when you are sleeping or in my multidimensional affairs."

"Oh? Can you tell me about it?"

"One aspect these alternate realities have in common, whether myth, fact or fiction, is that they reflect a gnawing preoccupation for a better place to live, and a place that is tuned into the more spiritual aspects of humanity. It is like the relentless quest for the Divine Self. Such is the place called New Earth. It is a place that has been formed by the Unity Consciousness where all is one and everybody and everything knows it. There are no egos or lower vibrational energies. It is a place formed by the great creative energy of the cosmos -unconditional love - where the true form of Light Being can play in the memories of all beings that form a part of it. It is a place of ascension that is Home where the real Me came from as a segment of the total consciousness of the Creator, or God, or whatever you want to call it. And the real Me created this place in combination with other real Me's as the place of permanent residence."

"Really? Here you do not have to forget. Tell me more."

"It s like you being here with me. There is no forget – it is remember. The different realities are formed from the Soul minds that use all of the encoded information of their expressions and experiences in other lower life forms as placed in the Akashic records. Here all things grow and expand and experience in the soup of love, that which is all that exists. Here anything can be created instantly in a personal hologram that I share with others. In this respect if I think about those 100 trillion molecules of DNA that all instantly link together in quantum love and operate as one, I consider my true being and its hologram as one of nonlocal trillion holograms that are acting as one."

"But you say there is no polarity or conflict?"

"Here I can create and relate to anything that vibrates in higher planes to know who and what I am. This is what ascension is all about. Thus in this place everything lives in a higher vibration and those lower vibrations like fear, struggle, conflict, deception as those things that are not true of heart and with the pure intent of unconditional love simply cannot be. It is like ice cannot exist in steam, a higher level of vibration. There are new rules of order, life and order that are more divine in nature."

"And it is formed from your imagination, the difference being that it can be reflected instantly in a personal holographic reality?"

"Yes. It is exactly like instant manifestation in your imagination. You can't do it instantly and totally in your world because you are like being energetic kindergarten as a two-layer DNA human. Here in this world, like Agartha, anything imaginable is possible. The free form of Light Body, universal to all, is free to meld, to move into, or out of any other imagined form with their agreement. Here I can create my own form as I can my environment - instantly. It is a place that allows other beings and other worlds to have their own model of this perfection. Here large or small constructs can be created instantly, as can anything imagined that is in harmony with the environment and all that exists there. Everything is telepathic. All forces of 3D such as gravity that acts upon non-quantum particles is overcome. It is thus all governed by Divine laws of One and commanded by the Higher Divine mind which is part of the One Mind. The big constraint is that it is in total absolute alignment with the soup of Creation and the Mind of Creator - unconditional love. For that is where the true power of creation resides."

"Ok, is it like now that I can do this in the hologram of a day dream? Time ceases and all is eternal, yet when life is given, it lives, grows and experiences in accordance with its Divine design of its DNA. This hologram cannot be imagined yet, and a 3D linear mind trapped in the 3D form of human cannot yet comprehend this. But this hologram of Earth is of this nature and this will become more understandable and the truth known as the cosmic influences increase and I truly become who I am."

"Yes. Here you simply are DNA. New Earth is such a hologram where the conscious desires of the many forms the New Earth with the heaven overlay. As time progresses, the Old Earth will meld with this New Earth. Many are already walking both worlds and many more are aware of this. This is the process of recalling worlds such as I speak of that will continue to form a model of New Earth."

"If such a reality exists, then why do you need to have a New Earth here? You already have this playground of Souls?"

"Because of the ongoing evolution of the greater Consciousness and DNA. The process of evolution and improvement is something that a Soul engages in by choosing to do so within an environment of polarity and contrast creates new and improved greater consciousness. Every Soul is evolving at their own pace in their own chosen space. You may simply look at this as an evolutionary stage of the Soul. In the world of imaginative positive reality, the experiences are different. It can only reflect what is already recorded in Akashic, not bring in new, nor can it allow an experience in lower forms."

"You need to get punished and tormented to get this new stuff? That does not make sense to me."

"It is an experience that heaven does not offer you and in many cases it is this deep contrast that leads to new revelations. And you must understand that every Soul is evolving at their own pace and choice as to what school rules they want to go to."

"And this is the process of New Earth evolution?"

"Because the New Earth becomes stronger in the awareness of more and more individuals, the melding of the two Earths will occur after 2012 as the lowered form entrains and rises in vibration and all upon it do as well. It rises to meet a higher, stronger vibration awaiting as New Earth in 4D. This is not an event but a process of evolution of consciousness above causal process translating as an overlay onto the action of transformation below. It is as when one or one mass of people decide to act and change the physical engagements and physicality of environment below. The transformation occurs as from consciousness above in 4D and 5D to lower form and into 3D and lower forms. As this ends after 2012 it is lifted to a higher vibrational status over the next generations."

"This is happening now?"

"Yes. Upon earth there are many that already exhibit the first stages of the transformation. They can sense discord and they can heal the energies. They already are aware of their Agartha. There are thousands coming forward like the example of Sai Baba who could materialize objects and shift interdimensionally. An example of two new aspects that are occurring now are healing and energy sensing. There are specific stages that will become common for millions upon millions as they exhibit the abilities of Christ and walk as he did. Individually, Stage 1 is to heal a perception of discord, it is simply done in the mind. Stage 2 is to heal a physical discord by 3D action originating in consciousness. Stage 3 is to heal via an energy balancing from the heart. Stage 4 is to connect the divinity of heart and create the instant miracle of healing. Stage 5 is to create as a Creator directly transmuting materials or creating material from the substance of love. There are hundreds of other new attributes and abilities encoded within DNA that will evolve the same way. This is already the way in Agartha except it is not in the lower vibratory world."

"Well, it is sort of like what is happening to me. I can see that."

"The ability to walk this way in all stages upon Old Earth is opening to millions. This *is* the process of Christ Consciousness rising after 2000 years of gestation in preparation for the New Earth Genesis. It is the balanced Divine male and Divine female, for the masculine energy has had its time of dominion for thousands of years. Its purpose was to teach what is not needed upon New Earth. As the evolution accelerates through Stage 4 and 5 to dominate unfolding as the new consciousness which will prevail upon all minds and all things. And thus all that is can be healed of discomforts even if some prefer the struggle of Old Earth. The environment and all Earth will over time transform into the perfection of balance and root in the unconditional love of the heart."

PLAYING IN AGARTHA

"So tell me as I still do not recall this. What is it like to play in this heaven of yours in the Divine Mind?"

"This place is one where one can assume an energetic form of physical body to feel all the senses, plus more, of the lower form of vibration in my mind. It is playing this out from memories correlated with coding to represent that form in the hologram as well. We do, however, assume a different energetic representation of a physical form but it is not made of particles. This would be like a graduate school taking you beyond the Soul Mind to be one with the Divine mind."

"Is this what ascension is all about?"

"Yes."

"So you have already ascended before?"

"Yes."

"Then why are you doing this again? Did you not learn before?"

"To evolve even further as part of the Divine Mind and come in service to this reality at a special time of light body development."

"Well it would seem I am screwing you up big time."

"Not any more. See what is happening to you. It is the way we wrote your life plan. I was looking for a new experience and to be part of a greater plan of ascension for a planet and a special time."

"Touché."

"When you and others yield to the truth and allow your Higher Divine Mind, your Soul, to teach and lead your life, that is when you do this as we have. All we can do is show you when you are ready to see, and allow you to feel this realm of infinite possibilities within the medium of divine love. It is when you are ready to accept our existence that you are prepared to listen. You have of your own free will come here and you are ready to align the above as love with the below of body. And so it will become for you as well."

"In the reality there is no lack, conflict, fear or ego here. In your world the darkness as a lack of light has been the chosen experience. It has brought this as a norm reality and you are with such energy influence around you. But look how you have drawn away from this influence. Look how you see from a higher perspective of love. Look how you sense and feel with your higher self. Continue this as the light around you not only shows truth within and without, it also illuminates the dark. When you reach your Higher Divine Mind this opens to you."

"And in the reality where you play?"

"In this place as evolved soul we share this reality as the best of the best. We play here and you do as well. And there are many other worlds like this that are models of other worlds which we call realms. It is like on Gaia, when you take your vacations that are times of heart, passions, bliss. Each selects a preferred place to express joy. Now assume that your Higher Divine Mind and heart are allowed to create this vacation place of ultimate bliss that vibrates with your being - allowing a place for you to express love and feel bliss. Our world is so created when we have learned to walk upper and lower as One and create a continuous vacation and experience limitless forms. So we through our minds congeal into the hologram of a divine realm as to allow interaction for expression and expansion."

"This is a parallel dimension where we of the Higher Mind can vacation, as you will call it; perhaps a Utopian Realm would be better. Darkness cannot be here as we maintain it in higher vibration. Yes we have filters and processes to deflect lower forms. But let us say that if you sat down and imagined your perfect realm as your own personal hologram, what would it consist of?"

"That is a good question."

"Our holograms are shared, overlapping multidimensional playground with what is dynamically created and with what is there already, just as you would bring people into your daydream. These people are like your Soul family but not here to play games in lower energies. It is as this place of Agartha is and was created by the ascended ones. This is my home that I have created with many others. And because it is being remembered and recalled by a new consciousness, through downward causation, this will eventually be made into reality below on New Earth. This will unfold a new destiny upon Gaia as it is in her Life Plan. Forming a model of light within the universe to then re-energize and rejuvenate the light in the Consciousness of the Creator and the universes of all dimensions. It is your New Earth that you will recall and overlay upon Old Earth."

"Here we are all one telepathic mind. As a knowing aspect of this, all that is required is attention to open the channels. It is now difficult to understand this but it is in accordance of the divine purpose and does not harm or is under the guise of discord or dominion reflecting lower vibration. Also there may be different forms of beings here with different purposes. Although the divine self is an entity of light or spirit common to all life of creation the forms of beings chosen to express with these realms is highly variable, each has unique aspects and needs as projected by the higher divine self."

"There are no boundaries and all are free to their movements and forms, as we are all one and of one mind. What you have not yet understood is how individual multidimensional holograms interact within the force of love. There are multiple billions of these that share the force of love that keeps them interconnected and live for each individual. You are only beginning to understand this."

"What are these realms?"

"It is a wondrous creation for you to see that brings other cosmic places here. This will be even more unimaginable for you now. Your fantasies and mythologies are attempts for humanity upon Gaia to recall these other worlds from akashic memories. That is what is here. You have much to explore here and learn about your immediate neighbours and yourself. It is about allowing you to be what you are and knowing the truth of all that is."

"It is everywhere and nowhere in particular because it is all one shared divine mind that souls aspire to. It is in Total Consciousness of Creation. It is the ultimate expression of the ascended ones who have taken their causal records from all worlds and universes and forms to create the best of the best in the totality of unconditional love, oneness and harmony."

"Yes, you may move freely to other forms here in this realm to see what suits your individual aspects of heart desire in true love and your twin flame manifestation of creation in the lower world. From this you draw the knowing to grow from it, and upon it to show others unobstructed and unimpeded essence of love."

"And you can be anything?"

"Be a dragon. Be a tree. Be a fire being. Be a silicon being, be a human, be a crystal. Be a fish. Be a plant. Be a bug. Nothing here has to prey on other life forms. Be a rock and know what it is to experience other forms. Be what you can imagine or recall from your lives in all dimensions, realties. But be in your heart, in love and in Oneness of all and above all, be of no harm to yourself as One Divine Mind including all things as you. This is why you have come to know this Earth place at this time."

"Can darkness come here?"

"No, it cannot be as the high frequency instantly dissolves it back into its perfect form. Just like ice would melt instantly in steam."

"Can you give me an example of a realm?"

"Realms are like self contained worlds. The fire realm is one where the beings are fire flames that dance and play and live a life under their own rules. As a light body, you can simply create one flame being for yourself or meld with another to experience this. There may be a form that lives in what you would consider toxic air. It may come from other worlds you have not experienced. These realms are self contained and some need to be separate. But they bring trillions of realms into one mind from infinite possibilities of forms that have evolved in the Universe of the Greater Mind as recorded and experienced by Souls who have ascended."

"So there is no time here."

"There may be a realm that decides to include that construct. But there really is no time in the universe, only cycles. These cylices, like your planetary cycles may have been used as a time construct but all cycles are simply vibration or oscillations. Remember, outside of your world, everything is cycles of vibration selected to present realities."

"These are a lot of vacation spots! I better get a whole lot of light into these cells!"

"Indeed. That dear Ed is why you and I are here; to help others do just that at a very special time of cosmic evolution. That is why we chose to be here and have a whole lot of fun!"

25

THE GOOD THE BAD THE EVIL

Good, bad and evil are perception given life by mental and emotional qualities. At the root they are just energies being chosen for the greater evolution. We are here to help.

"Superplacebo, as you have explained many things, something is very clear to me. That is that there is a lot of bad and evil things through the ages that have created this world we live in. The most disconcerting is that we have devolved in DNA, most if not all of the ancient truths about history have been meddled with. We seem to live in a world which to a great majority of the people is crap. There seems to be a powerful elite that love your brother's rules, bibles have been manipulated or destroyed, and even though 95% believe in God, they are all scrambling to be happy and think this god will reap vengeance on the sinners. There are so many bad guys in everything. People want to be rich and powerful, they aspire to kings and queens. Wars and conflicts are endless. How can this end?"

"It does not need to end, it is a game remember. It is an illusion designed for the purpose of spiritual evolution and each Soul is evolving at their own rates. Some do not even engage in the game. Some have evolved beyond the game. Your illusion on the Earth plane is unique and it attracts many Souls who want the experience of feeling all these different emotions."

"So you are saying that anything goes in this reality? There is no judgment?"

"Of course. You understand that from the creation of life plans that many choose to play the roles of bad people for the purpose of assisting in someone else's growth. Whether this is judged as criminal or evil is a personal choice as it is a judgment imposed by a group consciousness."

"But look at all the death, destruction and conflict. Look at the powers over others that occurs for such a long time."

"These are things that show what is not right, what not to dwell on as the lesson, yet experience it. Individual plans and the choices support this power-dominion mind. Societies worship kings and queens, obey lords of power, strive to be better. It is all your brother's doing. Most of what has been taught is false for the purpose of dominion, greed, power, money. Religion is corrupt as is government."

"If the consciousness chooses to support this then it prevails, and until it shifts, it is as it is. And when you die from that mortal vessel, you look at the results and sit with your soul family and ponder what you have learned."

"It is really hard to understand that it is no more than playing a game of cards or reality game on the computer. So you don't think your brother is evil as he has been presented as Satan. The whole world of deception is ok?"

"To some he is Satan, to others he is a savior. To some the dominance of the male is bad because that has subdued the female. To some the females as evil queens and witches are the evil ones. It is all just a game of roles to play for the purpose of experiencing that role and evolving your soul self. In the end, at the end of the game, no one is there to judge."

"But there is all this lying and cheating and killing and destruction. Is that right?"

"In the divine scheme of things founded on love, it is not. In various cultures such consciousness may be. It is the individual mind or the group mind that determines whether it is. It is a choice as to whether any individual wishes to align with that or not."

"If for example you had evolved a step further as a mind and you were sitting with me watching the antics below like you would watch a DVD movie. We were sitting enjoying a cosmic cocktail watching you and your family having all this that you call crap happening to them and you were looking at a road map of their life plan, how would you engage?"

"Well, I may feel some sympathy of empathy but it is just a game not real. But if I actually felt the emotion of it, then I would learn from it I guess. That is hard to answer."

"Well as you progress in this, you will be able to answer this. And there will come a time when such a game serves you no purpose and you will have evolved to a Divine mind which is where I am evolving to."

"And then?" More of this illusion game stuff? A hierarchy in heaven like a corporation?"

"There not a hierarchy, there is an evolution. The next evolution above this reality is the reality of the Divine Mind and what we saw as Agartha. There are many different beings like Angels and Archangels that are there in service to the evolution and assisting others in and from higher dimensions. It never stops as it is an infinite process of consciousness evolution. That is what the Creator is."

"So tell me, is there an equivalent progression on the evil side, like all these new skills in the astral plane. Is the evil stuff real, just like the miracles stuff? Do these bad guys also have to step out of the box?"

"Of course. If one is attaining new levels of abilities, say in the paranormal area, it is a choice as to whether it is applied for good or bad. There are many who carry these paranormal abilities when born. You know that a subgroup of conscious mind be it occult or religious can create their own mind culture outside of the norm. Rituals, sacrifices, all those perceived evil things are simply creating and concentrating energies that respond to changing reality the same way we have discussed in miracles. Whether it is a witch's spell or energy worker's wealth miracle, it is the same process. It is just applied to others for a different purpose."

"So a witch's spell that creates a health or wealth miracle outside the box uses the same processes?"

"Yes. You create your subgroup consciousness all the time. It could be a family, a club, a corporation. That consciousness is free to evolve as long as you have members to support it's agreed upon processes."

"Ok, I see this now. In the astral plane of the 4th dimension we still have the dual emotional and mental energies. Both negative and positive are reflected upwards from below and both positive and negative can be created from above to below. So if these bad guys are able to learn and use paranormal things that do bad things that is their prerogative."

"Yes. Once again to the level above that it is simply neutral energies that are deployed to take on bad or good qualities which can be perceived or received in service of others or service of self. Look at this image."

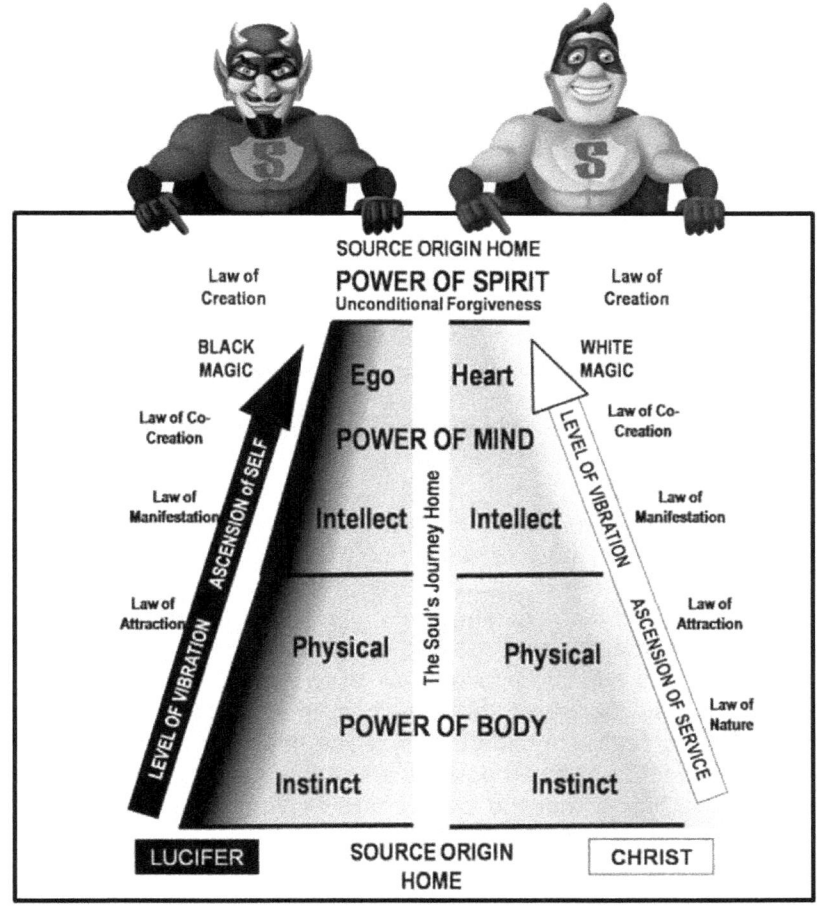

"The difference is white magic and black magic. So what is the point of being a good guy? If I take your brother's plan and go out of the box, I could be like the rich elite that run the planet with money and religion."

"Note that as you rise through the levels of vibration no matter how bad or good it may be perceived, there is a convergence at the point of the Astral Plane of 4D. Then it all loses polarity and is unified into the quantum substance of which makes the universe and the Creator consciousness – Love."

"Agartha! I knew that!"

"The other point is that they are also on a life plan and doing what they came to do. You can do this and there is no judgment but you cannot evolve beyond the 4th dimension. You may consider this great fun and love power so you can make a plan next life to experience this too. Perhaps you already have and want a different experience."

"Why can't I evolve if I use magic?"

"You can if that magic is your choice. But remember the kind of karma you may accumulate and the kind of terror and fear that may accompany your evil doings."

"You have a point. Maybe I did already and have some karma to deal with as a result."

"Indeed. It may be time to spend more time in the astral plane and find out."

"But if I am an evil dude, how can I get into the astral plane. I thought it was an altered state and state of well being that was key?

"As many in the occult will explain to you, the intensity of emotion, and the means of inducing the equivalent state of theta need not be rooted in the positive side. Rituals and drugs are a few of the many ways to do this and then the emotional charge of mantras and images can supercharge the process of creating reality outside the box. The heart may suffer as a result, as will the Soul and body but the astral plane has no judgments. It is when you wish to move higher that the lower energies simply cannot exist."

"Just like in Agartha. I see."

"Understand that there are also larger forces at play here that are responding to a greater plan and life plans of bodies other than the humanoid. Because the majority like my brother's rules does not make him a bad guy, it provides a different option. Because the power elite have figured out how to fool the majority and control them with money and religion, doctoring the truth does not make them a bad group of consciousness. It is accepted as the norm until the norm changes it evolving above or beyond it."

"Are we all being upgraded regardless?"

"You are to a certain point just as the sun shines on all. But if you want to live in the dark, you can't receive the light."

"I see. This process makes a greater game to experience. I just feel sorry for the guys getting screwed."

"Remember, you have come to these conclusion even though you are getting screwed. What choices did you make to do that?"

"I must have put it in my plan."

"Well if others did not then they will laugh about it when they have their cosmic cocktails with their Souls!! Are you beginning to have a laugh yet?"

"No, not yet because I am thinking of how I need to get back into that big façade and let go of it since this body is trapped there. Is that my Armageddon?"

"Indeed it is. You have had your Revelation. So how would you summarize the secret to all this to untrap yourself and engage in Rapture, Ed?"

"Live, love and laugh in every moment within a mindset connected to your heart, allowing your brain to be the soul mind to see bliss and joy in all that is as one. Use the gifts of your energetic anatomy to think, see, speak, and act in a new mind, totally enfolding your completed desires in passion and gratitude to open fully your gifts in DNA and to walk in light, love, forgiveness and compassion."

"That is very simple."

"Yes, so why did you not tell me this in the beginning?"

"I did, but you were not ready to believe it. Do you believe it now?"

"Yes."

"Why?"

"Because I am Superplacebo!"

We came here to participate in a cosmic game
Superplacebo with Soul mind is your new name

Have a great life
Ed Rychkun

BOOKS BY Ed Rychkun
Found on www.amazon.com or www.edrychkun.com

The Divine Programmer II; How Humans Create Reality. In this sequel to *The Divine Programmer; Creating Miracles*, we will take you out of the norm of the prevailing consiouness and answer radical questions like: Is our reality a holographic illusion? Are we living in a grand immersion movie? Did we create and contract for our Life Plans? Why do miracles work for some some of the time? How do placebos create dramatic healing miracles? What is the process most common in miracle healing? How can we proactively control our health and wealth reality? What is the energetic and physiological process of mind over matter? What are we and why are we here? Who or what is Divine Intervention? How do we unlock our full potential of DNA? What is God?

Learn how the brain as directed by the subconscious mind is the CEO of our physical reality and how it evolves through stages of evolution to the age of 28 into a new spiritual evolution. Understand why if your life is not joyful, it is the brain and karma that are the culprits. Learn how your neurological processes open or limit the ability to proactively create new reality or default to old prevailing boxes of group consiouness. In this book you will understand the statement "as above, so below" and how it works in the process of downward causation when you become your Heart and Soul Mind. This book will demystify the subtle energy bodies. It will present how the mind can select and energize words and visions from the quantum field of infinite possibilities then direct the subconscious and the midbrain to change neurological wiring for a new holographic reality. Understand clearly the key clinically proven steps in reviewing life plans, past, present and future to attract and create internal health and external wealth miracles. Know the intricate relationship between the laws of Karma, Cause & Effect and Attraction.

In **The Divine Programmer: Creating Miracles** Authors and Healers Aly McDonald and Ed Rychkun will take you into the fringe of metascience and science to reveal what works in creating healing and reality miracles. The authors bring forward some of the top Healers to example the detailed processes used to define the common denominators when healing miracles do work inside the body. In an attempt to quantify these processes, the authors draw upon a binary-trinary computer analogy to define the Divine Programmer's steps to maximize success. In a revealing journey you will look into the emerging world of how subtle energy fields such as morphic, zeropoint, light body, heart, chakra, auras, and torroids work with quantum energies accessible through the heart-brain rather than the traditional ego-brain. Learn how beliefs stuck in subconscious, as well as curtailing the 3rd stage of human awareness can sabotage efforts, and how to change this. In further delving into creating reality miracles outside the body, the authors take you on a journey to analyze the Law of Attraction to see how and why it does work some of the time, also examining what prevents it from working. After summarizing the Programmer's Code from top Guru's techniques, in a new light of trinary versus binary computing, the authors introduce how 50 trillion cells work like computer chips in the ultimate Divine Human trinary computer. Here they develop the processes of how as a Divine Programmer, using the operating system of Divine Intelligence, the Compiler of the Heart, and the Program Language of Love, one can potentially command the brain to change the holographic reality; to attract and create internal and external miracles.

You Are Fired Said the Heart to the Ego In this unusual and profound book, Ed Rychkun takes you to a critical situation that occurs between a human's heartbeats. In a last ditch effort to make sure the next beat occurs, the Heart engages in a desperate conversation with the Ego whom it blames for the demise of the human. In a fascinating dialogue between the Heart, the Ego, the Brain, the Mind, the Soul, the Chakra Children, and God, Ed takes you to the split second where time ceases and the physical material world becomes one with the Spiritual and Subtle energy counterparts. Learn how the Ego has taken the command center away from the sleeping Mind making the Brain, Soul, Heart, and Chakra Children subservient players in directing the quality of human life. Learn how the crisis deadlock is broken and the decision is made whether the next heartbeat is allowed to occur. See if you can deduct the same conclusions and reject or accept a coherent harmony between the six characters that control the human's life. *Will you Fire the Ego and put the power back where it belongs?*

Serve gods or Be God: Your Choice Thousands of gods have wreaked havoc on humanity for many centuries. So has the one God himself as evidenced in the Bibles. Those who claim to be Divine interpreters of God's Word have succumbed to creating merchandise of humanity in the interest of subduing the true spirit. Never has God presented his Word directly. At the turn of the century humanity entered the 2012 End Times of Revelation, Resurrection, and Armageddon. Despite what religions tell you about God's prophecy, doom, the Second Coming, and your sins, in the minds of millions is an underlying consciousness that something is amiss with those they trust. It is because something epic is happening in this Universe.

Can You Let Go? Is about a paradigm shift in how you enter the world of miracles and Co-creation. It means letting go of thinking with your head and learning to think with your heart. Why do prayers, the Law of Attraction, miracle healing, manifesting and assertions only work sometimes, for some? It is because those that show consistent success understand what the secret of letting go is. The secret? You have to let go; go inside to the heart, shift beliefs, surrender to a higher power, have faith and trust in the Divine. But what does this really mean? What is it *exactly* that one must let go of? In their raw simplicity these are very powerful words and concepts but implementing these in your life with the appropriate conviction may not be so simple. Yet there are millions of unexplained miracles and anomalies of science around the planet done by people who know how to release such special talents. Ed Rychkun poses the question; *"If others can create miracles, why can't I?"* Let us find the answer to this by learning how miracle makers let go and why. And let us get some advice from the "other side" of the veil.

Miracle, Miracle I Wish To Find Where You Hide Within My Mind Whether mainstream medical and science experts want to admit it or not, millions of spectacular, unexplained healing miracles occur. The dismissal of this reality on the basis of unexplainable does not benefit others who can have such a wondrous gift, or even be able to create a miracle. Quantum physics has proven that consciousness and the mind is the vital component to miracles but they simply do not know how. In addition quantum science has shattereed the foundations of what we know of atomic science. The truth is that the answers do not lie in science and if someone else can create a miracle, then so can you. So how do others do it? Let me take you to the leaders in miracles—the ones that caught my attention—the ones doing it daily. When you understand how the miracle healers really get down to the simple basics, a paradigm shift occurs in belief. Let me give you a short, simple course on what I found out so perhaps you can create your own miracles? Take your own quantum leap into the new reality of miracles.

Return To The Future Michael Carpetbagger has a serious problem with his life. After the banking and market collapse of 2008, he and his partners are feeling the stress of a failing business. They are moving to the dark side as of necessity. This does not sit well with Michael as his soul niggles at his actions. As Mike's conundrum of negative stress and helplessness overtakes him, he falls into a bizarre instant in time where a sequence of revelations is brought to him by his Guiding Angel. She takes him on a strange journey to previous lives where in the Golden Age of Atlantis he begins to recall what and who he really is. As they wander the quantum space of his past realities into Mayan lands, and he connects with his cosmic soul family, Mike begins to form a new vision of why the old financial energy is rapidly giving way to the new spiritual energies. Now, with a new look at his future, he must congeal all the past information into what he must do to best survive as the Earth and global ascension of consciousness accelerates towards 2012 and the End Time. WARNING: CAN YOU FACE UP TO WHO YOU ARE? This may appear as a work of fiction but it is an account of the past and future as seen through the past lives of a Seer of Atlantis.

The Way Back In this story, Christopher Andrew Fallenstar is a desperate trapped soul lost in a sea of mundane agony. He is on Earth living a dysfunctional life full of self pity, anger and unhappiness. His darkness eventually leads him to despair and a gateway into a world where reality and non-reality have converged. Lost and bewildered, he must find his way back. But back to what? Is it back to the Home from where he came or is it where he is living his mundane life? On his journey, he must traverse a series of Realms with pathways through his inner being to find his way. His quest to find his way back leads him to deal with parts of himself that he never knew about. He begins to uncover a new consciousness about who and what he might be. What he chooses and the paths he takes determine his final eternal destiny... and what the back really means. In this story, Ed Rychkun will take you on a journey through your inner self that may change the way you view Home. *It may even change your attitude about life!*

In New Earth: A Personal Journey Ed Rychkun answers some key questions such as *What is Heaven? What would a New Earth be like?* and *How does the 2012 ascension relate to a New Earth?* He tells his story to explain how every individual is on a seperate journey attempting to understand what will happen to Old Earth. In this personal journey, he takes you on his journey to the inner self and inner earth to reveal what the new earth can be. It's all about leaving your physical body like in a Near Death Experience where one can liberate the soul to see it's truth. "*I have come to a conclusion through my journey that where we head through ascension and what we percieve as our New Earth is entirely different from what intellect could imagine.*" Take this excursion into the different realms of Agartha, the perfect and pure lands created by the ascended ones where no negative energies exist. Here the creation of all things is instant through pure thought within the Creator's Consiouness.

Managing Human Subtle Energy: Walking the Thought This mind bending book gets to the bottom line of how to launch a management program that will absolutely change your life. You will clearly understand what Human Subtle Energies are and how they have been designed with a purpose – to convert non-physical energy to physical reality within your consciousness so you can enjoy life. First, see what the world of new science says about the existence and power of Human Subtle Energy. After this mind-blowing summary, find out the Laws by which these energies generated by your body operate. The inevitable startling conclusion will pound into your mind – you have not been managing your subtle energies properly – living a life of negative energy, drumming to a default destiny. Ironically, your life has turned out exactly the way you wanted it from previous thoughts and emotions. The way to change this lies in creating a habit to break old habits – through proactive Subtle Energy Management. Do you believe you can awaken the Genie in you and even control events by managing your subtle energy? *Walk your thoughts for 60 days and find out for yourself.*

www.ingramcontent.com/pod-product-compliance
Lightning Source LLC
Chambersburg PA
CBHW050120170426
43197CB00011B/1654